JAVASCRIPT & JQUERY

Interactive Front-End Web Development

JON DUCKETT

Design by:
EMME STONE

Additional material by:
GILLES RUPPERT & JACK MOORE

WILEY

TABLE OF CONTENTS

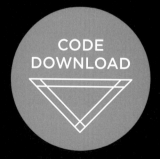

CODE
DOWNLOAD

Try out & download the code in this book

www.javascriptbook.com

CREDITS

For John Wiley & Sons, Inc.

Executive Editor
Carol Long

Project Editor
Kevin Kent

Production Editor
Daniel Scribner

Editorial Manager
Mary Beth Wakefield

Associate Director of Marketing
David Mayhew

Marketing Manager
Lorna Mein

Business Manager
Amy Knies

**Vice President and Executive
Group Publisher**
Richard Swadley

Associate Publisher
Jim Minatel

Project Coordinator, Cover
Todd Klemme

For Wagon Ltd.

Author
Jon Duckett

Co-Authors
Jack Moore
(Chapters 11 & 12)

Gilles Ruppert
(Chapter 13)

Technical Review
Mathias Bynens

Review Team
Chris Ullman
David Lean
Harrison Thrift
Jay Bursky
Richard Eskins
Scott Robin
Stachu Korick

Thank you
Annette Loudon
Michael Tomko
Michael Vella Zarb
Pam Coca
Rishabh Pugalia

Cover Design
Emme Stone

Design
Emme Stone
Jon Duckett

Photography
John Stewardson
johnstewardson.com

Illustration
Matthew Cencich
(Hotel in Chapter 3)

Emme Stone
(Teacher in Chapter 4)

Additional Photography

Electronics in Chapters 8 & 9:
Aaron Nielsen
Arkadiusz Jan Sikorski
Matt Mets
Mirsad Dedović
Steve Lodefink

javascriptbook.com/credits

INTRODUCTION

This book explains how JavaScript can be used in browsers to make websites more interactive, interesting, and user-friendly. You will also learn about jQuery because it makes writing JavaScript a lot easier.

To get the most out of this book, you will need to know how to build web pages using HTML and CSS. Beyond that, no prior experience with programming is necessary. Learning to program with JavaScript involves:

1

Understanding some **basic programming concepts** and the terms that JavaScript programmers use to describe them.

2

Learning **the language** itself, and, like all languages, you need to know its vocabulary and how to structure your sentences.

3

Becoming familiar with **how it is applied** by looking at examples of how JavaScript is commonly used in websites today.

The only equipment you need to use this book are a computer with a modern web browser installed, and your favorite code editor, (e.g., Notepad, TextEdit, Sublime Text, or Coda).

Introduction pages come at the beginning of each chapter. They introduce the key topics you will learn about.

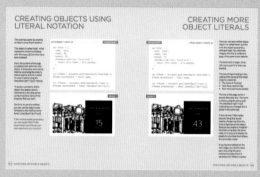

Reference pages introduce key pieces of JavaScript. HTML code is shown in blue, CSS code in pink, and JavaScript in green.

Background pages appear on white. They explain the context of the topics covered that are discussed in each chapter.

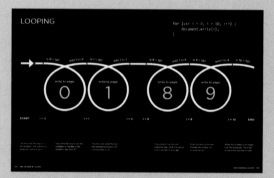

Diagram and infographics pages are shown on a dark background. They provide a simple, visual reference to topics discussed.

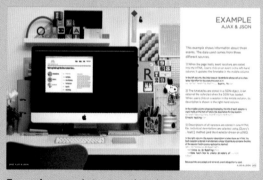

Example pages bring together the topics you have learned in that chapter and demonstrate how they can be applied.

Summary pages come at the end of each chapter. They remind you of the key topics that were covered in each chapter.

HOW JAVASCRIPT MAKES WEB PAGES MORE INTERACTIVE

JavaScript allows you to make web pages more interactive by accessing and modifying the content and markup used in a web page while it is being viewed in the browser.

1

ACCESS CONTENT

You can use JavaScript to select any element, attribute, or text from an HTML page. For example:

- Select the text inside all of the <h1> elements on a page
- Select any elements that have a `class` attribute with a value of `note`
- Find out what was entered into a text input whose `id` attribute has a value of `email`

2

MODIFY CONTENT

You can use JavaScript to add elements, attributes, and text to the page, or remove them. For example:

- Add a paragraph of text after the first <h1> element
- Change the value of `class` attributes to trigger new CSS rules for those elements
- Change the size or position of an <img> element

3
PROGRAM RULES

You can specify a set of steps for the browser to follow (like a recipe), which allows it to access or change the content of a page. For example:

- A gallery script could check which image a user clicked on and display a larger version of that image.
- A mortgage calculator could collect values from a form, perform a calculation, and display repayments.
- An animation could check the dimensions of the browser window and move an image to the bottom of the viewable area (also known as the viewport).

JavaScript encompasses many of the traditional rules of programming.

It can make the web page feel interactive by responding to what the user does.

4
REACT TO EVENTS

You can specify that a script should run when a specific event has occurred. For example, it could be run when:

- A button is pressed
- A link is clicked (or tapped) on
- A cursor hovers over an element
- Information is added to a form
- An interval of time has passed
- A web page has finished loading

EXAMPLES OF JAVASCRIPT IN THE BROWSER

Being able to change the content of an HTML page while it is loaded in the browser is very powerful. The examples below rely on the ability to:

Access the content of the page
Modify the content of the page
Program rules or instructions the browser can follow
React to events triggered by the user or browser

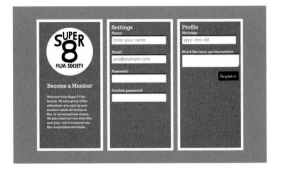

SLIDESHOWS
Shown in Chapter 11

Slideshows can display a number of different images (or other HTML content) within the same space on a given page. They can play automatically as a sequence, or users can click through the slides manually. They allow more content to be displayed within a limited amount of space.

React: Script triggered when the page loads
Access: Get each slide from the slideshow
Modify: Only show the first slide (hide others)
Program: Set a timer: when to show next slide
Modify: Change which slide is shown
React: When user clicks button for different slide
Program: Determine which slide to show
Modify: Show the requested slide

FORMS
Shown in Chapter 13

Validating forms (checking whether they have been filled in correctly) is important when information is supplied by users. JavaScript lets you alert the user if mistakes have been made. It can also perform sophisticated calculations based on any data entered and reveal the results to the user.

React: User presses the submit button when they have entered their name
Access: Get value from form field
Program: Check that the name is long enough
Modify: Show a warning message if the name is not long enough

The examples on these two pages give you a taste of what JavaScript can do within a web page, and of the techniques you will be learning throughout this book.

In the coming chapters, you will learn how and when to access or modify content, add programming rules, and react to events.

RELOAD PART OF PAGE
Shown in Chapter 8

You might not want to force visitors to reload the content of an entire web page, particularly if you only need to refresh a small portion of a page. Just reloading a section of the page can make a site feel like it is faster to load and more like an application.

React: Script triggered when user clicks on link
Access: The link that they clicked on
Program: Load the new content that was requested from that link
Access: Find the element to replace in the page
Modify: Replace that content with the new content

FILTERING DATA
Shown in Chapter 12

If you have a lot of information to display on a page, you can help users find information they need by providing filters. Here, buttons are generated using data in the attributes of the HTML <img> elements. When the user clicks on one of the buttons, they are only shown the images with that keyword.

React: Script triggered when page loads
Program: Collect keywords from images
Program: Turn the keywords into buttons the user can click on
React: User clicks on one of the buttons
Program: Find the relevant subset of images that should be shown
Modify: Show the subset of images that use that tag

THE STRUCTURE OF THIS BOOK

In order to teach you JavaScript, this book is divided into two sections:

CORE CONCEPTS

The first nine chapters introduce you to the basics of programming and the JavaScript language. Along the way you will learn how it is used to create more engaging, interactive, and usable websites.

Chapter 1 looks at some key concepts in computer programming, showing you how computers create models of the world using data, and how JavaScript is used to change the contents of an HTML page.

Chapters 2-4 cover the basics of the JavaScript language.

Chapter 5 explains how the Document Object Model (DOM) lets you access and change a document's contents while it is loaded into the browser.

Chapter 6 discusses how events can be used to trigger code.

Chapter 7 shows you how jQuery can make the process of writing scripts faster and easier.

Chapter 8 introduces you to Ajax, a set of techniques that allow you to just change part of a web page without reloading the entire page.

Chapter 9 covers Application Programming Interfaces (APIs), including new APIs that are part of HTML5 and those of sites like Google Maps.

PRACTICAL APPLICATIONS

By this point you will already have seen many examples of how JavaScript is used on popular websites. This section brings together all of the techniques you have learned so far, to give you practical demonstrations of how JavaScript is used by professional developers. Not only will you see a selection of in-depth examples, you will also learn more about the process of designing and writing scripts from scratch.

Chapter 10 deals with error-handling and debugging, and explains more about how JavaScript is processed.

Chapter 11 shows you techniques for creating content panels such as sliders, modal windows, tabbed panels, and accordions.

Chapter 12 demonstrates several techniques for filtering and sorting data. This includes filtering a gallery of images, and re-ordering the rows of a table by clicking on the column headings.

Chapter 13 deals with form enhancements and how to validate form entries.

Unless you are already a confident programmer, you will probably find it helpful to read the book from start to finish the first time. However, once you have grasped the basics, we hope it will continue to be a helpful reference as you create your own scripts.

HTML & CSS:
A QUICK REFRESHER

Before looking at JavaScript, let's clarify some HTML & CSS terms.
Note how HTML attributes and CSS properties use name/value pairs.

HTML ELEMENTS

HTML elements are added to the content of a page to describe its structure. An element consists of the opening and closing tags, plus its content.

Tags usually come in pairs with an opening tag and a closing tag. There are a few empty elements with no content, (e.g., **<img>**). They have one self-closing tag.

Opening tags can carry attributes, which tell us more about that element. Attributes have a name and a value. The value is usually given in quotes.

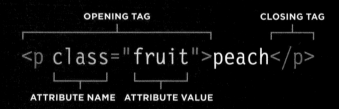

OPENING TAG   CLOSING TAG

`<p class="fruit">peach</p>`

ATTRIBUTE NAME   ATTRIBUTE VALUE

CSS RULES

CSS uses rules to indicate how the contents of one or more elements should be displayed in the browser. Each rule has a selector and a declaration block.

The CSS selector indicates which element(s) the rule applies to. The declaration block contains rules that indicate how those elements should appear.

Each declaration in the declaration block has a property (the aspect you want to control), and a value, which is the setting for that property.

SELECTOR   DECLARATION BLOCK

`.fruit {color: pink;}`

PROPERTY NAME   PROPERTY VALUE

BROWSER SUPPORT

Some early examples in this book do not work with Internet Explorer 8 and earlier (but alternative code samples that work in IE8 are available to download from `http://javascriptbook.com`). We explain techniques for dealing with older browsers in later chapters.

Each version of a web browser adds new features. Often these new features make tasks easier, or are considered better, than using older techniques.

But, website visitors do not always keep up with the latest browser releases, so website developers cannot always rely upon the latest technologies.

As you will see, there are many inconsistencies between browsers that affect JavaScript developers. jQuery will help you deal with cross-browser inconsistencies (it is one of the major reasons why jQuery rapidly gained popularity amongst web developers). But, before you learn jQuery, it helps to know what it is helping you to achieve.

To make JavaScript easier to learn, the first few chapters use some features of JavaScript that are not supported in IE8. But:

- You **will** learn how to deal with IE8 and older browsers in later chapters (because we know that many clients expect sites to work in IE8). It just requires knowledge of some extra code or requires you to be aware of some additional issues.
- Online, you will find alternatives available for each example that does not work in IE8. But please check the comments in those code samples to make sure you know about the about issues involved in using them.

1

THE ABC OF PROGRAMMING

Before you learn how to read and write the JavaScript language itself, you need to become familiar with some key concepts in computer programming. They will be covered in three sections:

A	B	C
What is a script and how do I create one?	How do computers fit in with the world around them?	How do I write a script for a web page?

Once you have learned the basics, the following chapters will show how the JavaScript language can be used to tell browsers what you want them to do.

1/a

WHAT IS A SCRIPT AND HOW DO I CREATE ONE?

A SCRIPT IS A SERIES OF INSTRUCTIONS

A script is a series of instructions that a computer can follow to achieve a goal.
You could compare scripts to any of the following:

RECIPES

By following the instructions in a recipe, one-by-one in the order set out, cooks can create a dish they have never made before.

Some scripts are simple and only deal with one individual scenario, like a simple recipe for a basic dish. Other scripts can perform many tasks, like a recipe for a complicated three-course meal.

Another similarity is that, if you are new to cooking or programming, there is a lot of new terminology to learn.

HANDBOOKS

Large companies often provide handbooks for new employees that contain procedures to follow in certain situations.

For example, hotel handbooks may contain steps to follow in different scenarios such as when a guest checks in, when a room needs to be tidied, when a fire alarm goes off, and so forth.

In any of these scenarios, the employees need to follow only the steps for that one type of event. (You would not want someone going through every single step in the entire handbook while you were waiting to check in.) Similarly, in a complex script, the browser might use only a subset of the code available at any given time.

MANUALS

Mechanics often refer to car repair manuals when servicing models they are not familiar with. These manuals contain a series of tests to check the key functions of the car, along with details of how to fix.

For example, there might be details about how to test the brakes. If they pass this test, the mechanic can then go on to the next test without needing to fix the brakes. But, if they fail, the mechanic will need to follow the instructions to repair them.

The mechanic can then go back and test the brakes again to see if the problem is fixed. If the brakes now pass the test, the mechanic knows they are fixed and can move onto the next test.

Similarly, scripts can allow the browser to check the current situation and only perform a set of steps if that action is appropriate.

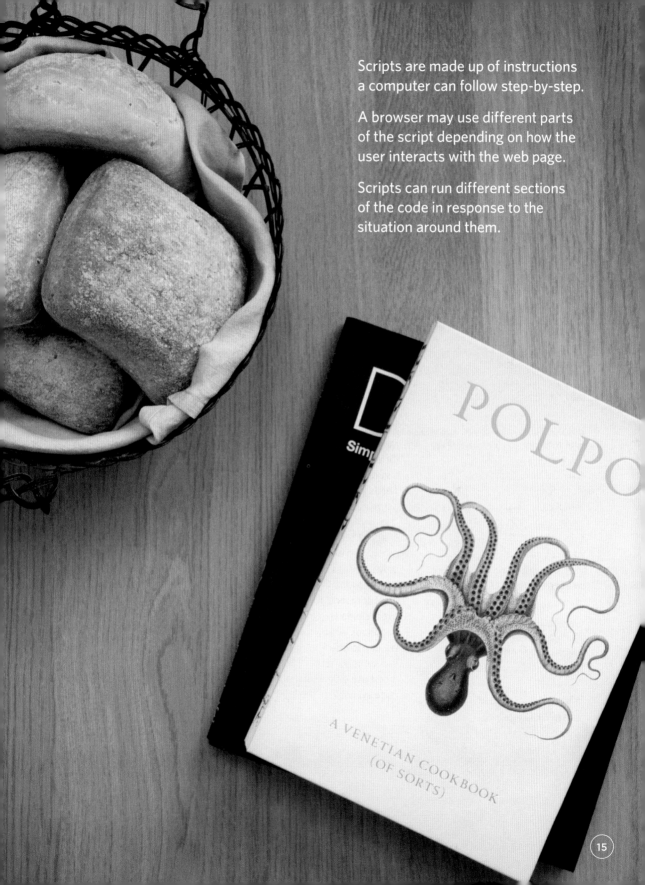

Scripts are made up of instructions a computer can follow step-by-step.

A browser may use different parts of the script depending on how the user interacts with the web page.

Scripts can run different sections of the code in response to the situation around them.

WRITING A SCRIPT

To write a script, you need to first state your goal and then list the tasks that need to be completed in order to achieve it.

Humans can achieve complex goals without thinking about them too much, for example you might be able to drive a car, cook breakfast, or send an email without a set of detailed instructions. But the first time we do these things they can seem daunting. Therefore, when learning a new skill, we often break it down into smaller tasks, and learn one of these at a time. With experience these individual tasks grow familiar and seem simpler.

Some of the scripts you will be reading or writing when you have finished this book will be quite complicated and might look intimidating at first. However, a script is just a series of short instructions, each of which is performed in order to solve the problem in hand. This is why creating a script is like writing a recipe or manual that allows a computer to solve a puzzle one step at a time.

It is worth noting, however, that a computer doesn't learn how to perform tasks like you or I might; it needs to follow instructions every time it performs the task. So a program must give the computer enough detail to perform the task as if every time were its first time.

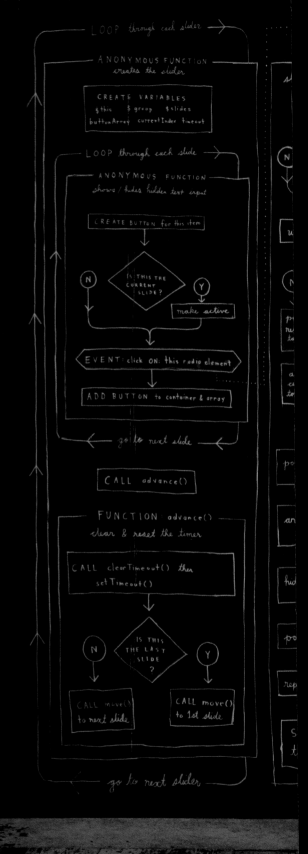

Start with the big picture of what you want to achieve, and break that down into smaller steps.

1: DEFINE THE GOAL

First, you need to define the task you want to achieve. You can think of this as a puzzle for the computer to solve.

2: DESIGN THE SCRIPT

To design a script you split the goal out into a series of tasks that are going to be involved in solving this puzzle. This can be represented using a flowchart.

You can then write down individual steps that the computer needs to perform in order to complete each individual task (and any information it needs to perform the task), rather like writing a recipe that it can follow.

3: CODE EACH STEP

Each of the steps needs to be written in a programming language that the computer understands. In our case, this is JavaScript.

As tempting as it can be to start coding straight away, it pays to spend time designing your script before you start writing it.

DESIGNING A SCRIPT: TASKS

Once you know the **goal** of your script, you
can work out the individual tasks needed to
achieve it. This high-level view of the tasks
can be represented using a flowchart.

FLOWCHART: TASKS OF A HOTEL CLEANER

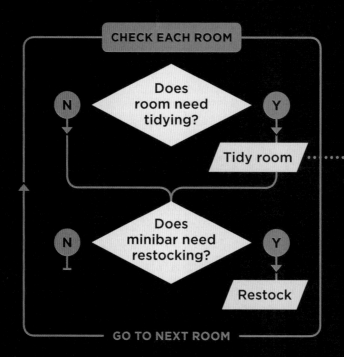

CHECK EACH ROOM

Does room need tidying?

N

Y

Tidy room

Does minibar need restocking?

N

Y

Restock

GO TO NEXT ROOM

DESIGNING A SCRIPT: STEPS

Each individual task may be broken down into a sequence of steps. When you are ready to code the script, these steps can then be translated into individual lines of code.

LIST: STEPS REQUIRED TO TIDY A ROOM

STEP 1	Remove used bedding
STEP 2	Wipe all surfaces
STEP 3	Vacuum floors
STEP 4	Fit new bedding
STEP 5	Remove used towels and soaps
STEP 6	Clean toilet, bath, sink, surfaces
STEP 7	Place new towels and soaps
STEP 8	Wipe bathroom floor

As you will see on the next page, the steps that a computer needs to follow in order to perform a task are often very different from those that you or I might take.

FROM STEPS TO CODE

Every step for every task shown in a flowchart needs to be written in a language the computer can understand and follow.

In this book, we are focussing on the JavaScript language and how it is used in web browsers.

Just like learning any new language, you need to get to grips with the:

- **Vocabulary:** The words that computers understand
- **Syntax:** How you put those words together to create instructions computers can follow

Along with learning the language itself, if you are new to programming, you will also need to learn how a computer achieves different types of goals using a **programmatic** approach to problem-solving.

Computers are very logical and obedient. They need to be told every detail of what they are expected to do, and they will do it without question. Because they need different types of instructions compared to you or I, everyone who learns to program makes lots of mistakes at the start. Don't be disheartened; in Chapter 10 you will see several ways to discover what might have gone wrong – programmers call this **debugging**.

You need to learn to "think" like a computer because they solve tasks in different ways than you or I might approach them.

Computers solve problems **programmatically**; they follow series of instructions, one after another. The type of instructions they need are often different to the type of instructions you might give to another human. Therefore, throughout the book you will not only learn the vocabulary and syntax that JavaScript uses, but you will also learn how to write instructions that computers can follow.

For example, when you look at the picture on the left how do you tell which person is the tallest? A computer would need explicit, step-by-step instructions, such as:

1. Find the height of the first person
2. Assume he or she is the "tallest person"
3. Look at the height of the remaining people one-by-one and compare their height to the "tallest person" you have found so far
4. At each step, if you find someone whose height is greater than the current "tallest person", he or she becomes the new "tallest person"
5. Once you have checked all the people, tell me which one is the tallest

So the computer needs to look at each person in turn, and for each one it performs a test ("Are they taller than the current tallest person?"). Once it has done this for each person it can give its answer.

DEFINING A GOAL & DESIGNING THE SCRIPT

Consider how you might approach a different type of script.
This example calculates the cost of a name plaque.
Customers are charged by the letter.

The first thing you should do is detail your goals for the script (what you want it to achieve):

Customers can have a name added to a plaque; each letter costs $5. When a user enters a name, show them how much it will cost.

Next, break it into a series of tasks that have to be performed in order to achieve the goals:

1. The script is triggered when the button is clicked.
2. It collects the name entered into the form field.
3. It checks that the user has entered a value.
4. If the user has not entered anything, a message will appear telling them to enter a name.
5. If a name has been entered, calculate the cost of the sign by multiplying the number of letters by the cost per letter.
6. Show how much the plaque costs.

(These numbers correspond with the flowchart on the right-hand page.)

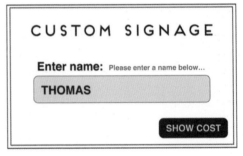

SKETCHING OUT THE TASKS IN A FLOWCHART

Often scripts will need to perform different tasks in different situations.
You can use flowcharts to work out how the tasks fit together.
The flowcharts show the paths between each step.

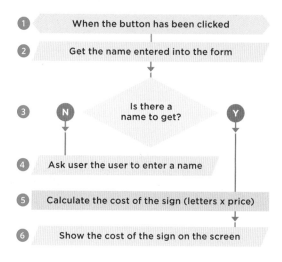

Arrows show how the script moves from one task to the next. The different shapes represent different types of tasks. In some places there are decisions which cause the code to follow different paths.

You will learn how to turn this example into code in Chapter 2. You will also see many more examples of different flowcharts throughout the book, and you will meet code that helps you deal with each of these types of situations.

Some experienced programmers use more complex diagram styles that are specifically designed to represent code – however, they have a steeper learning curve. These informal flowcharts will help you understand how scripts work while you are in the process of learning the language.

FLOWCHART KEY

Generic step	Event
Input or output	Decision

SUMMARY
THE ABC OF PROGRAMMING

A: What is a script and how do I create one?

▶ A script is a series of instructions that the computer can follow in order to achieve a goal.

▶ Each time the script runs, it might only use a subset of all the instructions.

▶ Computers approach tasks in a different way than humans, so your instructions must let the computer solve the task programmatically.

▶ To approach writing a script, break down your goal into a series of tasks and then work out each step needed to complete that task (a flowchart can help).

1/b

HOW DO COMPUTERS FIT IN WITH THE WORLD AROUND THEM?

COMPUTERS CREATE MODELS OF THE WORLD USING DATA

Here is a model of a hotel, along with some model trees, model people, and model cars. To a human, it is clear what kind of real-world object each one represents.

QUAY
HOTEL

A computer has no predefined concept of what a hotel or car is. It does not know what they are used for. Your laptop or phone will not have a favorite brand of car, nor will it know what star rating your hotel is.

So how do we use computers to create hotel booking apps, or video games where players can race a car? The answer is that programmers create a very different kind of model, especially for computers.

Programmers make these models using data. That is not as strange or as scary as it sounds because the data is all the computer needs in order to follow the instructions you give it to carry out its tasks.

OBJECT TYPE: HOTEL

OBJECT TYPE: CAR

OBJECT TYPE: CAR

OBJECTS & PROPERTIES

If you could not see the picture of the hotel and cars, the data in the information boxes alone would still tell you a lot about this scene.

OBJECTS (THINGS)

In computer programming, each physical thing in the world can be represented as an **object**. There are two different **types** of objects here: a hotel and a car.

Programmers might say that there is one **instance** of the hotel object, and two **instances** of the car object.

Each object can have its own:

- Properties
- Events
- Methods

Together they create a working model of that object.

PROPERTIES (CHARACTERISTICS)

Both of the cars share common characteristics. In fact, all cars have a make, a color, and engine size. You could even determine their current speed. Programmers call these characteristics the **properties** of an object.

Each property has a **name** and a **value**, and each of these name/value pairs tells you something about each individual instance of the object.

The most obvious property of this hotel is its name. The value for that property is Quay. You can tell the number of rooms the hotel has by looking at the value next to the rooms property.

The idea of name/value pairs is used in both HTML and CSS. In HTML, an attribute is like a property; different attributes have different names, and each attribute can have a value. Similarly, in CSS you can change the color of a heading by creating a rule that gives the color property a specific value, or you can change the typeface it is written in by giving the font-family property a specific value. Name/value pairs are used a lot in programming.

HOTEL OBJECT

The hotel object uses property names and values to tell you about this particular hotel, such as the hotel's name, its rating, the number of rooms it has, and how many of these are booked. You can also tell whether or not this hotel has certain facilities.

CAR OBJECTS

The car objects both share the same properties, but each one has different values for those properties. They tell you the make of car, what speed each car is currently traveling at, what color it is, and what type of fuel it requires.

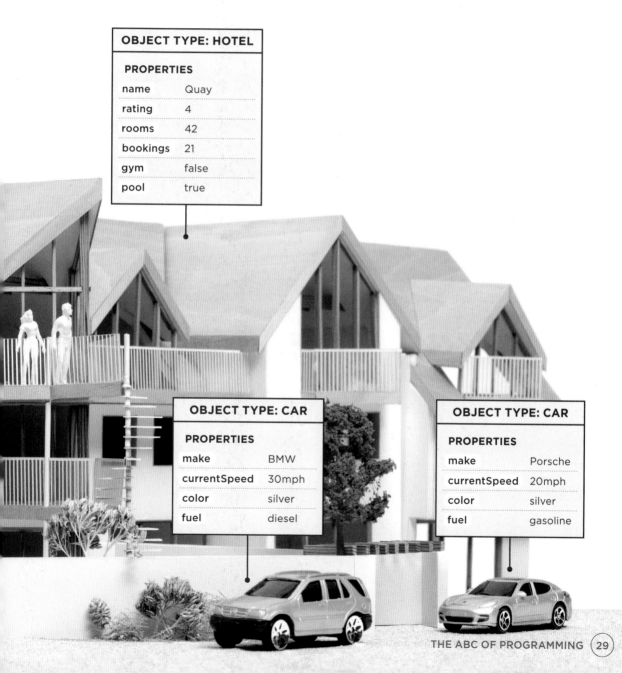

OBJECT TYPE: HOTEL

PROPERTIES

name	Quay
rating	4
rooms	42
bookings	21
gym	false
pool	true

OBJECT TYPE: CAR

PROPERTIES

make	BMW
currentSpeed	30mph
color	silver
fuel	diesel

OBJECT TYPE: CAR

PROPERTIES

make	Porsche
currentSpeed	20mph
color	silver
fuel	gasoline

EVENTS

In the real world, people interact with objects. These interactions can change the values of the properties in these objects.

WHAT IS AN EVENT?

There are common ways in which people interact with each type of object. For example, in a car a driver will typically use at least two pedals. The car has been designed to respond differently when the driver interacts with each of the different pedals:

- The accelerator makes the car go faster
- The brake slows it down

Similarly, programs are designed to do different things when users interact with the computer in different ways. For example, clicking on a contact link on a web page could bring up a contact form, and entering text into a search box may automatically trigger the search functionality.

An **event** is the computer's way of sticking up its hand to say, "Hey, this just happened!"

WHAT DOES AN EVENT DO?

Programmers choose which events they respond to. When a specific event happens, that event can be used to trigger a specific section of the code.

Scripts often use different events to trigger different types of functionality.

So a script will state which events the programmer wants to respond to, and what part of the script should be run when each of those events occur.

HOTEL OBJECT

A hotel will regularly have bookings for rooms. Each time a room is reserved, an event called **book** can be used to trigger code that will increase the value of the **bookings** property. Likewise, a **cancel** event can trigger code that decreases the value of the **bookings** property.

CAR OBJECTS

A driver will accelerate and brake throughout any car journey. An **accelerate** event can trigger code to increase the value of the **currentSpeed** property and a **brake** event can trigger code to decrease it. You will learn about the code that responds to the events and changes these properties on the next page.

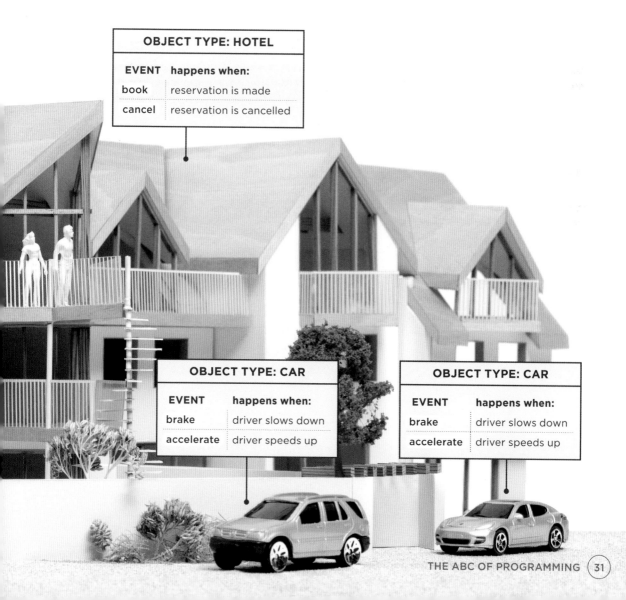

OBJECT TYPE: HOTEL

EVENT	happens when:
book	reservation is made
cancel	reservation is cancelled

OBJECT TYPE: CAR

EVENT	happens when:
brake	driver slows down
accelerate	driver speeds up

OBJECT TYPE: CAR

EVENT	happens when:
brake	driver slows down
accelerate	driver speeds up

METHODS

Methods represent things people need to do with objects. They can
retrieve or update the values of an object's properties.

WHAT IS A METHOD?

Methods typically represent how people (or other
things) interact with an object in the real world.

They are like questions and instructions that:

- Tell you something about that object (using
  information stored in its properties)
- Change the value of one or more of that object's
  properties

WHAT DOES A METHOD DO?

The code for a method can contain lots of
instructions that together represent one task.

When you use a method, you do not always need to
know *how* it achieves its task; you just need to know
how to ask the question and how to interpret any
answers it gives you.

HOTEL OBJECT

Hotels will commonly be asked if any rooms are free. To answer this question, a method can be written that subtracts the number of bookings from the total number of rooms. Methods can also be used to increase and decrease the value of the `bookings` property when rooms are booked or cancelled.

CAR OBJECTS

The value of the `currentSpeed` property needs to go up and down as the driver accelerates and brakes. The code to increase or decrease the value of the `currentSpeed` property could be written in a method, and that method could be called `changeSpeed()`.

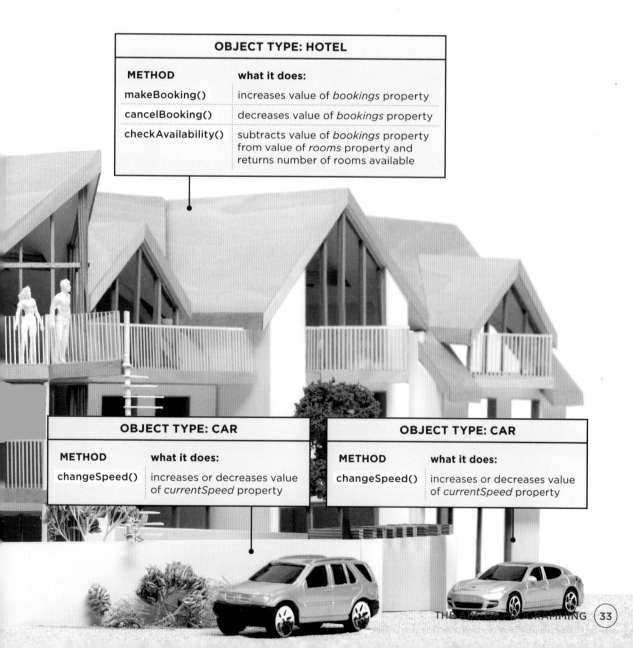

OBJECT TYPE: HOTEL

METHOD	what it does:
makeBooking()	increases value of *bookings* property
cancelBooking()	decreases value of *bookings* property
checkAvailability()	subtracts value of *bookings* property from value of *rooms* property and returns number of rooms available

OBJECT TYPE: CAR

METHOD	what it does:
changeSpeed()	increases or decreases value of *currentSpeed* property

OBJECT TYPE: CAR

METHOD	what it does:
changeSpeed()	increases or decreases value of *currentSpeed* property

PUTTING IT ALL TOGETHER

Computers use data to create models of things in the real world. The events, methods, and properties of an object all relate to each other: Events can trigger methods, and methods can retrieve or update an object's properties.

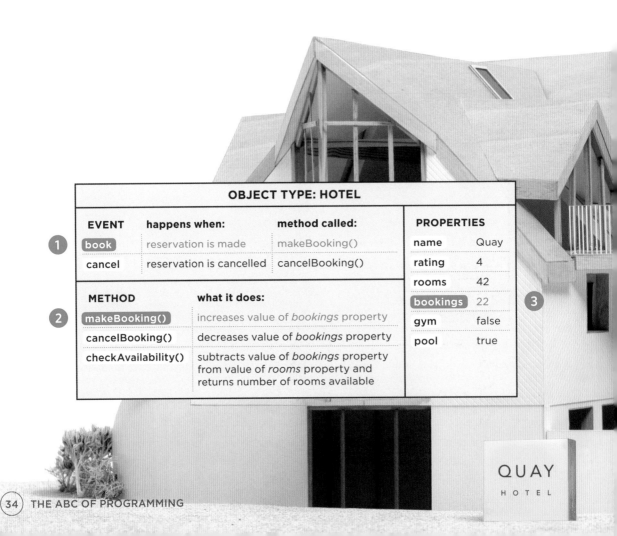

OBJECT TYPE: HOTEL

EVENT	happens when:	method called:
book	reservation is made	makeBooking()
cancel	reservation is cancelled	cancelBooking()

METHOD	what it does:
makeBooking()	increases value of *bookings* property
cancelBooking()	decreases value of *bookings* property
checkAvailability()	subtracts value of *bookings* property from value of *rooms* property and returns number of rooms available

PROPERTIES	
name	Quay
rating	4
rooms	42
bookings	22
gym	false
pool	true

QUAY
HOTEL

HOTEL OBJECT

1. When a reservation is made, the book event fires.
2. The book event triggers the makeBooking() method, which increases the value of the bookings property.
3. The value of the bookings property is changed to reflect how many rooms the hotel has available.

CAR OBJECTS

1. As a driver speeds up, the accelerate event fires.
2. The accelerate event calls the changeSpeed() method, which in turn increases the value of the currentSpeed property.
3. The value of the currentSpeed property reflects how fast the car is traveling.

OBJECT TYPE: CAR

EVENT	happens when:	method called:
brake	driver slows down	changeSpeed()
accelerate	driver speeds up	changeSpeed()

METHOD	what it does:
changeSpeed()	increases or decreases value of *currentSpeed* property

PROPERTIES	
make	BMW
currentSpeed	45mph
color	silver
fuel	diesel

WEB BROWSERS ARE PROGRAMS BUILT USING OBJECTS

You have seen how data can be used to create a model of a hotel or a car. Web browsers create similar models of the web page they are showing and of the browser window that the page is being shown in.

WINDOW OBJECT

On the right-hand page you can see a model of a computer with a browser open on the screen.

The browser represents each window or tab using a window object. The location property of the window object will tell you the URL of the current page.

DOCUMENT OBJECT

The current web page loaded into each window is modelled using a document object.

The title property of the document object tells you what is between the opening <title> and closing </title> tag for that web page, and the lastModified property of the document object tells you the date this page was last updated.

OBJECT TYPE: WINDOW

PROPERTIES

location   http://www.javascriptbook.com/

OBJECT TYPE: DOCUMENT

PROPERTIES

URL   http://www.javascriptbook.com/

lastModified   09/04/2014 15:33:37

title   Learn JavaScript & jQuery -
               A book that teaches you
               in a nicer way

THE DOCUMENT OBJECT REPRESENTS AN HTML PAGE

Using the document object, you can access and change what content users see on the page and respond to how they interact with it.

Like other objects that represent real-world things, the document object has:

PROPERTIES

Properties describe characteristics of the current web page (such as the title of the page).

METHODS

Methods perform tasks associated with the document currently loaded in the browser (such as getting information from a specified element or adding new content).

EVENTS

You can respond to events, such as a user clicking or tapping on an element.

Because all major web browsers implement the document object in the same way, the people who create the browsers have already:

- Implemented properties that you can access to find out about the current page in the browser
- Written methods that achieve some common tasks that you are likely to want to do with an HTML page

So you will be learning how to work with this object. In fact, the document object is just one of a set of objects that all major browsers support. When the browser creates a model of a web page, it not only creates a document object, but it also creates a new object for each element on the page. Together these objects are described in the **Document Object Model**, which you will meet in Chapter 5.

OBJECT TYPE: DOCUMENT

PROPERTIES

URL	http://www.javascriptbook.com/
lastModified	09/04/2014 15:33:37
title	Learn JavaScript & jQuery - A book that teaches you in a nicer way

EVENT	happens when:
load	page and assets have finished loading
click	user clicks the mouse over the page
keypress	user presses down on a key

METHOD	what it does:
write()	adds new content to the document
getElementById()	accesses an element when you state its id attribute

JAVASCRIPT
& JQUERY
interactive front-end
web development

HOW A BROWSER
SEES A WEB PAGE

In order to understand how you can change the content of an HTML page using JavaScript, you need to know how a browser interprets the HTML code and applies styling to it.

1: RECEIVE A PAGE AS HTML CODE

Each page on a website can be seen as a separate **document**. So, the web consists of many sites, each made up of one or more documents.

2: CREATE A MODEL OF THE PAGE AND STORE IT IN MEMORY

The model shown on the right hand page is a representation of one very basic page. Its structure is reminiscent of a family tree. At the top of the model is a **document object**, which represents the whole document.

Beneath the **document** object each box is called a **node**. Each of these nodes is another object. This example features three types of nodes representing elements, text within the elements, and attribute.

3: USE A RENDERING ENGINE TO SHOW THE PAGE ON SCREEN

If there is no CSS, the rendering engine will apply default styles to HTML elements. However, the HTML code for this example links to a CSS style sheet, so the browser requests that file and displays the page accordingly.

When the browser receives CSS rules, the rendering engine processes them and applies each rule to its corresponding elements. This is how the browser positions the elements in the correct place, with the right colors, fonts, and so on.

All major browsers use a JavaScript interpreter to translate your instructions (in JavaScript) into instructions the computer can follow.

When you use JavaScript in the browser, there is a part of the browser that is called an **interpreter** (or scripting engine).

The interpreter takes your instructions (in JavaScript) and translates them into instructions the browser can use to achieve the tasks you want it to perform.

In an **interpreted programming language**, like JavaScript, each line of code is translated one-by-one as the script is run.

```
<!DOCTYPE html>
<html>
  <head>
    <title>Constructive &amp; Co.</title>
    <link rel="stylesheet" href="css/c01.css" />
  </head>
  <body>
    <h1>Constructive &amp; Co.</h1>
    <p>For all orders and inquiries please call
      <em>555-3344</em></p>
  </body>
</html>
```

1

The browser receives an HTML page.

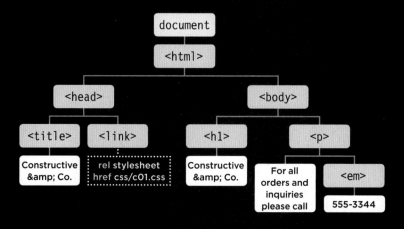

2

It creates a model of the page and stores it in memory.

● OBJECT
● ELEMENT
● TEXT
⋮⋮⋮ ATTRIBUTES

3

It shows the page on screen using a rendering engine.

SUMMARY
THE ABC OF PROGRAMMING

B: How do computers fit in with the world around them?

▶ Computers create models of the world using data.

▶ The models use objects to represent physical things. Objects can have: properties that tell us about the object; methods that perform tasks using the properties of that object; events which are triggered when a user interacts with the computer.

▶ Programmers can write code to say "When this event occurs, run that code."

▶ Web browsers use HTML markup to create a model of the web page. Each element creates its own node (which is a kind of object).

▶ To make web pages interactive, you write code that uses the browser's model of the web page.

1/c

HOW DO I WRITE A SCRIPT FOR A WEB PAGE?

HOW HTML, CSS, & JAVASCRIPT FIT TOGETHER

Before diving into the JavaScript language, you need to know how it will fit together with the HTML and CSS in your web pages.

Web developers usually talk about three languages that are used to create web pages: HTML, CSS, and JavaScript.

Where possible, aim to keep the three languages in separate files, with the HTML page linking to CSS and JavaScript files.

Each language forms a separate **layer** with a different purpose. Each layer, from left to right, builds on the previous one.

`<html>`

`{css}`

`javascript()`

CONTENT LAYER

.html files

This is where the content of the page lives. The HTML gives the page structure and adds semantics.

PRESENTATION LAYER

.css files

The CSS enhances the HTML page with rules that state how the HTML content is presented (backgrounds, borders, box dimensions, colors, fonts, etc.).

BEHAVIOR LAYER

.js files

This is where we can change how the page behaves, adding interactivity. We will aim to keep as much of our JavaScript as possible in separate files.

Programmers often refer to this as a **separation of concerns**.

PROGRESSIVE ENHANCEMENT

These three layers form the basis of a popular approach to building web pages called progressive enhancement.

As more and more web-enabled devices come onto the market, this concept is becoming more widely adopted.

It's not just screen sizes that are varied - connection speeds and capabilities of each device can also differ.

Also, some people browse with JavaScript turned off, so you need to make sure that the page still works for them.

Constructive & Co.

For all orders and inquiries please call *555-3344*

HTML ONLY

Starting with the HTML layer allows you to focus on the most important thing about your site: its content.

Being plain HTML, this layer should work on all kinds of devices, be accessible to all users, and load quite quickly on slow connections.

HTML+CSS

Adding the CSS rules in a separate file keeps rules regarding how the page looks away from the content itself.

You can use the same style sheet with all of your site, making your sites faster to load and easier to maintain. Or you can use different style sheets with the same content to create different views of the same data.

HTML+CSS+JAVASCRIPT

The JavaScript is added last and enhances the usability of the page or the experience of interacting with the site.

Keeping it separate means that the page still works if the user cannot load or run the JavaScript. You can also reuse the code on several pages (making the site faster to load and easier to maintain).

CREATING A BASIC JAVASCRIPT

JavaScript is written in plain text, just like HTML and CSS, so you do not need any new tools to write a script. This example adds a greeting into an HTML page. The greeting changes depending on the time of day.

1 Create a folder to put the example in called c01, then start up your favorite code editor, and enter the text to the right.

A JavaScript file is just a text file (like HTML and CSS files are) but it has a .js file extension, so save this file with the name add-content.js

Don't worry about what the code means yet, for now we will focus on how the script is created and how it fits with an HTML page.

```javascript
var today = new Date();
var hourNow = today.getHours();
var greeting;

if (hourNow > 18) {
    greeting = 'Good evening!';
} else if (hourNow > 12) {
    greeting = 'Good afternoon!';
} else if (hourNow > 0) {
    greeting = 'Good morning!';
} else {
    greeting = 'Welcome!';
}

document.write('<h3>' + greeting  + '</h3>');
```

2 Get the CSS and images for this example from the website that accompanies the book: www.javascriptbook.com

To keep the files organized, in the same way that CSS files often live in a folder called styles or css, your JavaScript files can live in a folder called scripts, javascript, or js. In this case, save your file in a folder called js

Here you can see the file structure that you will end up with when you finish the example. Always treat file names as being case-sensitive.

LINKING TO A JAVASCRIPT FILE FROM AN HTML PAGE

When you want to use JavaScript with a web page, you use the HTML `<script>` element to tell the browser it is coming across a script. Its `src` attribute tells people where the JavaScript file is stored.

```
<!DOCTYPE html>
<html>
  <head>
    <title>Constructive &amp; Co.</title>
    <link rel="stylesheet" href="css/c01.css" />
  </head>
  <body>
    <h1>Constructive &amp; Co.</h1>
    <script src="js/add-content.js"></script>
    <p>For all orders and inquiries please call
      <em>555-3344</em></p>
  </body>
</html>
```

③ In your code editor, enter the HTML shown on the left. Save this file with the name `add-content.html`

The HTML `<script>` element is used to load the JavaScript file into the page. It has an attribute called `src`, whose value is the path to the script you created.

This tells the browser to find and load the script file (just like the `src` attribute on an `<img>` tag).

④ Open the HTML file in your browser. You should see that the JavaScript has added a greeting (in this case, *Good Afternoon!*) to the page. (These greetings are coming from the JavaScript file; they are not in the HTML file.)

Please note: Internet Explorer sometimes prevents JavaScript running when you open a page stored on your hard drive. If this affects you, please try Chrome, Firefox, Opera, or Safari instead.

THE SOURCE CODE
IS NOT AMENDED

If you look at the source code for the example you just created, you will see that the HTML is still exactly the same.

5 Once you have tried the example in your browser, view the source code for the page. (This option is usually under the *View*, *Tools* or *Develop* menu of the browser.)

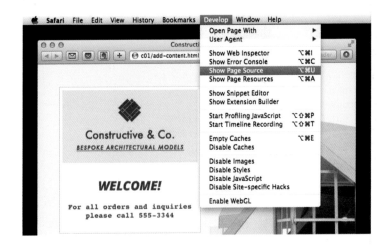

6 The source of the web page does not actually show the new element that has been added into the page; it just shows the link to the JavaScript file.

As you move through the book, you will see most of the scripts are added just before the closing </body> tag (this is often considered a better place to put your scripts).

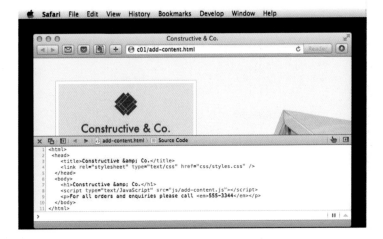

PLACING THE SCRIPT IN THE PAGE

You may see JavaScript in the HTML between opening `<script>` and closing `</script>` tags (but it is better to put scripts in their own files).

```
<!DOCTYPE html>
<html>
  <head>
    <title>Constructive &amp; Co.</title>
    <link rel="stylesheet" href="css/c01.css" />
  </head>
  <body>
    <h1>Constructive &amp; Co.</h1>
    <script>document.write('<h3>Welcome!</h3>');
    </script>
    <p>For all orders and inquiries please call
      <em>555-3344</em></p>
  </body>
</html>
```

7 Finally, try opening the HTML file, removing the `src` attribute from the opening `<script>` tag, and adding the new code shown on the left between the opening `<script>` tag and the closing `</script>` tag. The `src` attribute is no longer needed because the JavaScript is in the HTML page.

As noted on p44, it is better not to mix JavaScript in your HTML pages like this, but it is mentioned here as you may come across this technique.

8 Open the HTML file in your web browser and the welcome greeting is written into the page.

As you may have guessed, `document.write()` *writes* content into the *document* (the web page). It is a simple way to add content to a page, but not always the best. Chapter 5 discusses various ways to update the content of a page.

HOW TO USE OBJECTS & METHODS

This one line of JavaScript shows how to use objects and methods. Programmers refer to this as **calling** a method of an object.

The **document** object represents the entire web page. All web browsers implement this object, and you can use it just by giving its name.

The **write()** method of the **document** object allows new content to be written into the page where the **<script>** element sits.

OBJECT

METHOD

```
document.write('Good afternoon!');
```

MEMBER OPERATOR

The **document** object has several methods and properties. They are known as **members** of that object.

You can access the members of an object using a dot between the object name and the member you want to access. It is called a **member operator**.

PARAMETERS

Whenever a method requires some information in order to work, the data is given inside the parentheses.

Each piece of information is called a **parameter** of the method. In this case, the **write()** method needs to know what to write into the page.

Behind the scenes, the browser uses a lot more code to make the words appear on the screen, but you don't need to know how the browser does this.

You only need to know how to call the object and method, and how to tell it the information it needs to do the job you want it to. It will do the rest.

There are lots of objects like the **document** object, and lots of methods like the **write()** method that will help you write your own scripts.

JAVASCRIPT RUNS WHERE IT IS FOUND IN THE HTML

When the browser comes across a `<script>` element, it stops to load the script and then checks to see if it needs to do anything.

```html
<!DOCTYPE html>
<html>
  <head>
    <title>Constructive &amp; Co.</title>
    <link rel="stylesheet" href="css/c01.css" />
  </head>
  <body>
    <h1>Constructive &amp; Co.</h1>
    <p>For all orders and inquiries please call <em>555-3344</em></p>
    <script src="js/add-content.js"></script>
  </body>
</html>
```

Note how the **<script>** element can be moved below the first paragraph, and this affects where the new greeting is written into the page.

This has implications for where **<script>** elements should be placed, and can affect the loading time of pages (see p356).

SUMMARY
THE ABC OF PROGRAMMING

C: How do I write a script for a web page?

▶ It is best to keep JavaScript code in its own JavaScript file. JavaScript files are text files (like HTML pages and CSS style sheets), but they have the `.js` extension.

▶ The HTML `<script>` element is used in HTML pages to tell the browser to load the JavaScript file (rather like the `<link>` element can be used to load a CSS file).

▶ If you view the source code of the page in the browser, the JavaScript will not have changed the HTML, because the script works with the model of the web page that the browser has created.

2

BASIC
JAVASCRIPT
INSTRUCTIONS

In this chapter, you will start learning to read and write JavaScript. You will also learn how to give a web browser instructions you want it to follow.

THE LANGUAGE: SYNTAX AND GRAMMAR

Like any new language, there are new words to learn (the vocabulary) and rules for how these can be put together (the grammar and syntax of the language).

GIVING INSTRUCTIONS: FOR A BROWSER TO FOLLOW

Web browsers (and computers in general) approach tasks in a very different way than a human might. Your instructions need to reflect how computers get things done.

We will start with a few of the key building blocks of the language and look at how they can be used to write some very basic scripts (consisting of a few simple steps) before going on to look at some more complex concepts in subsequent chapters.

STATEMENTS

A script is a series of instructions that a computer can follow one-by-one. Each individual instruction or step is known as a **statement**. Statements should end with a semicolon.

We will look at what the code on the right does shortly, but for the moment note that:

- Each of the lines of code in green is a **statement**.
- The pink curly braces indicate the start and end of a **code block**. (Each code block could contain many more statements.)
- The code in purple determines which code should run (as you will see on p149).

JAVASCRIPT IS CASE SENSITIVE

JavaScript is case sensitive so hourNow means something different than HourNow or HOURNOW.

```
var today = new Date();
var hourNow = today.getHours();
var greeting;

if (hourNow > 18) {
  greeting = 'Good evening';
} else if (hourNow > 12) {
  greeting = 'Good afternoon';
} else if (hourNow > 0) {
  greeting = 'Good morning';
} else {
  greeting = 'Welcome';
}
document.write(greeting);
```

STATEMENTS ARE INSTRUCTIONS AND EACH ONE STARTS ON A NEW LINE

A statement is an individual instruction that the computer should follow. Each one should start on a new line and end with a semicolon. This makes your code easier to read and follow.

The semicolon also tells the JavaScript interpreter when a step is over, indicating that it should move to the next step.

STATEMENTS CAN BE ORGANIZED INTO CODE BLOCKS

Some statements are surrounded by curly braces; these are known as **code blocks**. The closing curly brace is not followed by a semicolon.

Above, each code block contains one statement related to what the current time is. Code blocks will often be used to group together many more statements. This helps programmers organize their code and makes it more readable.

COMMENTS

You should write **comments** to explain what your code does.
They help make your code easier to read and understand.
This can help you and others who read your code.

```
/* This script displays a greeting to the user based upon the current time.
   It is an example from JavaScript & jQuery book */

var today = new Date();              // Create a new date object
var hourNow = today.getHours();      // Find the current hour
var greeting;

// Display the appropriate greeting based on the current time
if (hourNow > 18) {
  greeting = 'Good evening';
} else if (hourNow > 12) {
  greeting = 'Good afternoon';
} else if (hourNow > 0) {
  greeting = 'Good morning';
} else {
  greeting = 'Welcome';
}
document.write(greeting);
```

JavaScript code is **green**
Multi-line comments are **pink**
Single-line comments are **gray**

MULTI-LINE COMMENTS

To write a comment that stretches over more than one line, you use a **multi-line** comment, starting with the /* characters and ending with the */ characters. Anything between these characters is not processed by the JavaScript interpreter.

Multi-line comments are often used for descriptions of how the script works, or to prevent a section of the script from running when testing it.

SINGLE-LINE COMMENTS

In a **single-line** comment, anything that follows the two forward slash characters // on that line will not be processed by the JavaScript interpreter. Single-line comments are often used for short descriptions of what the code is doing.

Good use of comments will help you if you come back to your code after several days or months. They also help those who are new to your code.

WHAT IS A VARIABLE?

A script will have to temporarily store the bits of information it needs to do its job. It can store this data in **variables**.

When you write JavaScript, you have to tell the interpreter every individual step that you want it to perform. This sometimes involves more detail than you might expect.

Think about calculating the area of a wall; in math the area of a rectangle is obtained by multiplying two numbers:

   width × height = area

You may be able to do calculations like this in your head, but when writing a script to do this calculation, you need to give the computer very detailed instructions. You might tell it to perform the following four steps in order:

1. Remember the value for *width*
2. Remember the value for *height*
3. Multiply *width* by *height* to get the *area*
4. Return the result to the user

In this case, you would use variables to "remember" the values for *width* and *height*. (This also illustrates how a script contains very explicit instructions about exactly what you want the computer to do.)
You can compare variables to short-term memory, because once you leave the page, the browser will forget any information it holds.

A variable is a good name for this concept because the data stored in a variable can change (or vary) each time a script runs.

No matter what the dimensions of any individual wall are, you know that you can find its *area* by multiplying the *width* of that wall by its *height*. Similarly, scripts often need to achieve the same goal even when they are run with different data, so variables can be used to represent values in your scripts that are likely to change. The result is said to be **calculated** or **computed** using the data stored in the variables.

The use of variables to represent numbers or other kinds of data is very similar to the concept of algebra (where letters are used to represent numbers). There is one key difference, however. The equals sign does something very different in programming (as you will see on the next two pages).

VARIABLES: HOW TO DECLARE THEM

Before you can use a variable, you need to announce that you want
to use it. This involves creating the variable and giving it a name.
Programmers say that you **declare** the variable.

VARIABLE KEYWORD   **VARIABLE NAME**

var is an example of what
programmers call a **keyword**.
The JavaScript interpreter
knows that this keyword is
used to create a variable.

In order to use the variable, you
must give it a name. (This is
sometimes called an identifier.)
In this case, the variable is called
`quantity`.

If a variable name is more than
one word, it is usually written in
camelCase. This means the first
word is all lowercase and any
subsequent words have their
first letter capitalized.

VARIABLES: HOW TO ASSIGN THEM A VALUE

Once you have created a variable, you can tell it what information you would like it to store for you. Programmers say that you **assign a value** to the variable.

ASSIGNMENT OPERATOR

quantity = 3;

VARIABLE NAME   **VARIABLE VALUE**

You can now use the variable by its name. Here we set a value for the variable called **quantity**. Where possible, a variable's name should describe the kind of data the variable holds.

The equals sign (=) is an **assignment operator**. It says that you are going to assign a value to the variable. It is also used to update the value given to a variable (see p68).

Until you have assigned a value to a variable, programmers say the value is **undefined**.

Where a variable is declared can have an effect upon whether the rest of the script can use it. Programmers call this the **scope** of a variable and it is covered on p98.

DATA TYPES

JavaScript distinguishes between numbers, strings, and `true` or `false` values known as Booleans.

NUMERIC DATA TYPE

The numeric data type handles numbers.

0.75

For tasks that involve counting or calculating sums, you will use numbers 0-9. For example, five thousand, two hundred and seventy-two would be written 5272 (note there is no comma between the thousands and the hundreds). You can also have negative numbers (such as -23678) and decimals (three quarters is written as 0.75).

STRING DATA TYPE

The string data type consists of letters and other characters.

'Hi, Ivy!'

Note how the string data type is enclosed within a pair of quotes. These can be single or double quotes, but the opening quote must match the closing quote.

Strings can be used when working with any kind of text. They are frequently used to add new content into a page and they can contain HTML markup.

BOOLEAN DATA TYPE

Boolean data types can have one of two values: `true` or `false`.

true

It might seem a little abstract at first, but the Boolean data type is actually very helpful.

You can think of it a little like a light switch – it is either on or off. As you will see in Chapter 4, Booleans are helpful when determining which part of a script should run.

Numbers are not only used for things like calculators; they are also used for tasks such as determining the size of the screen, moving the position of an element on a page, or setting the amount of time an element should take to fade in.

In addition to these three data types, JavaScript also has others (arrays, objects, undefined, and null) that you will meet in later chapters.

Unlike some other programming languages, when declaring a variable in JavaScript, you do not need to specify what type of data it will hold.

USING A VARIABLE TO STORE A NUMBER

JAVASCRIPT c02/js/numeric-variable.js

```javascript
var price;
var quantity;
var total;

price = 5;
quantity = 14;
total = price * quantity;

var el = document.getElementById('cost');
el.textContent = '$' + total;
```

HTML c02/numeric-variable.html

```html
<h1>Elderflower</h1>
<div id="content">
  <h2>Custom Signage</h2>
  <div id="cost">Cost: $5 per tile</div>
  <img src="images/preview.jpg" alt="Sign" />
</div>
<script src="js/numeric-variable.js"></script>
```

RESULT

Here, three variables are created and values are assigned to them.

- **price** holds the price of an individual tile
- **quantity** holds the number of tiles a customer wants
- **total** holds the total cost of the tiles

Note that the numbers are not written inside quotation marks. Once a value has been assigned to a variable, you can use the variable name to represent that value (much like you might have done in algebra). Here, the total cost is calculated by multiplying the price of a single tile by the number of tiles the customer wants.

The result is then written into the page on the final two lines. You see this technique in more detail on p194 and p216. The first of these two lines finds the element whose **id** attribute has a value of **cost**, and the final line replaces the content of that element with new content.

Note: There are many ways to write content into a page, and several places you can place your script. The advantages and disadvantages of each technique are discussed on p226. This technique will not work in IE8.

USING A VARIABLE TO STORE A STRING

For the moment, concentrate on the first four lines of JavaScript. Two variables are declared (username and message), and they are used to hold strings (the user's name and a message for that user).

The code to update the page (shown in the last four lines) is discussed fully in Chapter 5. This code selects two elements using the values of their id attributes. The text in those elements is updated using the values stored in these variables.

Note how the string is placed inside quote marks. The quotes can be single or double quotes, but they must match. If you start with a single quote, you must end with a single quote, and if you start with a double quote, you must end with a double quote:

✓ "hello" ✗ "hello'
✓ 'hello' ✗ 'hello"

Quotes should be straight (not curly) quotes:

✓ " " ✗ " "
✓ ' ' ✗ ' '

Strings must always be written on one line:

✓ 'See our upcoming range'
✗ 'See our
   upcoming range'

---

c02/js/string-variable.js **`JAVASCRIPT`**

```javascript
var username;
var message;
username = 'Molly';
message = 'See our upcoming range';

var elName = document.getElementById('name');
elName.textContent = username;
var elNote = document.getElementById('note');
elNote.textContent = message;
```

c02/string-variable.html **`HTML`**

```html
<h1>Elderflower</h1>
<div id="content">
  <div id="title">Howdy
    <span id="name">friend</span>!</div>
  <div id="note">Take a look around...</div>
</div>
<script src="js/string-variable.js"></script>
```

`RESULT`

USING QUOTES INSIDE A STRING

```javascript
var title;
var message;
title = "Molly's Special Offers";
message = '<a href=\"sale.html\">25% off!</a>';

var elTitle = document.getElementById('title');
elTitle.innerHTML = title;
var elNote = document.getElementById('note');
elNote.innerHTML = message;
```

HTML   c02/string-with-quotes.html

```html
<h1>Elderflower</h1>
<div id="content">
  <div id="title">Special Offers</div>
  <div id="note">Sign-up to receive personalized
    offers!</div>
</div>
<script src="js/string-with-quotes.js"></script>
```

RESULT

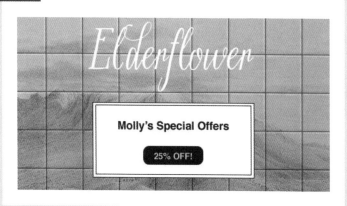

Sometimes you will want to use a double or single quote mark *within* a string.

Because strings can live in single or double quotes, if you just want to use double quotes in the string, you could surround the entire string in single quotes.

If you just want to use single quotes in the string, you could surround the string in double quotes (as shown in the third line of this code example).

You can also use a technique called **escaping** the quotation characters. This is done by using a **backwards slash** (or "backslash") *before* any type of quote mark that appears within a string (as shown on the fourth line of this code sample). The backwards slash tells the interpreter that the following character is part of the string, rather than the end of it.

Techniques for adding content to a page are covered in Chapter 5. This example uses a property called innerHTML to add HTML to the page. In certain cases, this property *can* pose a security risk (discussed on p228 – p231).

USING A VARIABLE TO STORE A BOOLEAN

A Boolean variable can only have a value of true or false, but this data type is very helpful.

In the example on the right, the values true or false are used in the class attributes of HTML elements. These values trigger different CSS class rules: true shows a check, false shows a cross. (You learn how the class attribute is set in Chapter 5.)

It is rare that you would want to write the words true or false into the page for the user to read, but this data type does have two very popular uses:

First, Booleans are used when the value can only be true/false. You could also think of these values as on/off or 0/1: true is equivalent to on or 1, false is equivalent to off or 0

Second, Booleans are used when your code can take more than one path. Remember, different code may run in different circumstances (as shown in the flowcharts throughout the book).

The path the code takes depends on a test or condition.

c02/js/boolean-variable.js — JAVASCRIPT

```javascript
var inStock;
var shipping;
inStock = true;
shipping = false;

var elStock = document.getElementById('stock');
elStock.className = inStock;

var elShip = document.getElementById('shipping');
elShip.className = shipping;
```

c02/boolean-variable.html — HTML

```html
<h1>Elderflower</h1>
<div id="content">
  <div class="message">Available:
    <span id="stock"></span></div>
  <div class="message">Shipping:
    <span id="shipping"></span></div>
</div>
<script src="js/boolean-variable.js"></script>
```

RESULT

SHORTHAND FOR CREATING VARIABLES

JAVASCRIPT `c02/js/shorthand-variable.js`

```javascript
① var price = 5;
   var quantity = 14;
   var total = price * quantity;


② var price, quantity, total;
   price = 5;
   quantity = 14;
   total = price * quantity;


③ var price = 5, quantity = 14;
   var total = price * quantity;


④ // Write total into the element with id of cost
   var el = document.getElementById('cost');
   el.textContent = '$' + total;
```

RESULT

Programmers sometimes use shorthand to create variables. Here are three variations of how to declare variables and assign them values:

1. Variables are declared and values assigned in the same statement.

2. Three variables are declared on the same line, then values assigned to each.

3. Two variables are declared and assigned values on the same line. Then one is declared and assigned a value on the next line.

(The third example shows two numbers, but you can declare variables that hold different types of data on the same line, e.g., a string and a number.)

4. Here, a variable is used to hold a reference to an element in the HTML page. This allows you to work directly with the element stored in that variable. (See more about this on p190.)

While the shorthand might save you a little bit of typing, it can make your code a little harder to follow. So, when you are starting off, you will find it easier to spread your code over a few more lines to make it easier to read and understand.

CHANGING THE VALUE OF A VARIABLE

Once you have assigned a value to a variable, you can then change what is stored in the variable later in the same script.

Once the variable has been created, you do not need to use the var keyword to assign it a new value. You just use the variable name, the equals sign (also known as the assignment operator), and the new value for that attribute.

For example, the value of a shipping variable might start out as being false. Then something in the code might change the ability to ship the item and you could therefore change the value to true.

In this code example, the values of the two variables are both swapped from being true to false and vice versa.

c02/js/update-variable.js

JAVASCRIPT

```javascript
var inStock;
var shipping;

inStock = true;
shipping = false;

/* Some other processing might go here and, as
a result, the script might need to change these
values */

inStock = false;
shipping = true;

var elStock = document.getElementById('stock');
elStock.className = inStock;
var elShip = document.getElementById('shipping');
elShip.className = shipping;
```

RESULT

Available: ✖
Shipping: ✔

RULES FOR NAMING VARIABLES

Here are six rules you must always follow when giving a variable a name:

1

The name must begin with a letter, dollar sign ($), or an underscore (_). It must **not** start with a number.

2

The name can contain letters, numbers, dollar sign ($), or an underscore (_). Note that you must not use a dash (-) or a period (.) in a variable name.

3

You cannot use **keywords** or **reserved** words. Keywords are special words that tell the interpreter to do something. For example, var is a keyword used to declare a variable. Reserved words are ones that may be used in a *future* version of JavaScript.

ONLINE EXTRA

View a full list of keywords and reserved words in JavaScript.

4

All variables are case sensitive, so score and Score would be different variable names, but it is bad practice to create two variables that have the same name using different cases.

5

Use a name that describes the kind of information that the variable stores. For example, firstName might be used to store a person's first name, lastName for their last name, and age for their age.

6

If your variable name is made up of more than one word, use a capital letter for the first letter of every word *after* the first word. For example, firstName rather than firstname (this is referred to as camel case). You can also use an underscore between each word (you cannot use a dash).

ARRAYS

An array is a special type of variable. It doesn't just store one value; it stores a list of values.

You should consider using an array whenever you are working with a **list** or a set of values that are **related** to each other.

Arrays are especially helpful when you do not know how many items a list will contain because, when you create the array, you do not need to specify how many values it will hold.

If you don't know how many items a list will contain, rather than creating enough variables for a long list (when you might only use a small percentage of them), using an array is considered a better solution.

For example, an array can be suited to storing the individual items on a shopping list because it is a list of related items.

Additionally, each time you write a new shopping list, the number of items on it may differ.

As you will see on the next page, values in an array are separated by commas.

In Chapter 12, you will see that arrays can be very helpful when representing complex data.

SHOPPING LIST

cheese
pumpkin
baby spinach
bread
eggs
almonds

CREATING AN ARRAY

c02/js/array-literal.js

```javascript
var colors;
colors = ['white', 'black', 'custom'];

var el = document.getElementById('colors');
el.textContent = colors[0];
```

RESULT

Color: white

JAVASCRIPT c02/js/array-constructor.js

```javascript
var colors = new Array('white',
                       'black',
                       'custom');

var el = document.getElementById('colors');
el.textContent = colors[0];
```

The array literal (shown in the first code sample) is preferred over the array constructor when creating arrays.

You create an array and give it a name just like you would any other variable (using the var keyword followed by the name of the array).

The values are assigned to the array inside a pair of square brackets, and each value is separated by a comma. The values in the array do not need to be the same data type, so you can store a string, a number and a Boolean all in the same array.

This technique for creating an array is known as an **array literal**. It is usually the preferred method for creating an array. You can also write each value on a separate line:

```javascript
colors = ['white',
          'black',
          'custom'];
```

On the left, you can see an array created using a different technique called an **array constructor**. This uses the new keyword followed by Array(); The values are then specified in parentheses (not square brackets), and each value is separated by a comma.

VALUES IN ARRAYS

Values in an array are accessed as if they are in a numbered list. It is important to know that the numbering of this list starts at zero (not one).

NUMBERING ITEMS IN AN ARRAY

Each item in an array is automatically given a number called an **index**. This can be used to access specific items in the array. Consider the following array which holds three colors:

```
var colors;
colors = ['white',
          'black',
          'custom'];
```

Confusingly, index values start at 0 (not 1), so the following table shows items from the array and their corresponding index values:

INDEX	VALUE
0	'white'
1	'black'
2	'custom'

ACCESSING ITEMS IN AN ARRAY

To retrieve the third item on the list, the array name is specified along with the index number in square brackets.

Here you can see a variable called itemThree is declared. Its value is set to be the third color from the colors array.

```
var itemThree;
itemThree = colors[2];
```

NUMBER OF ITEMS IN AN ARRAY

Each array has a property called length, which holds the number of items in the array.

Below you can see that a variable called numColors is declared. Its value is set to be the number of the items in the array.

The name of the array is followed by a period symbol (or full stop) which is then followed by the length keyword.

```
var numColors;
numColors = colors.length;
```

Throughout the book (especially in Chapter 12) you meet more features of arrays, which are a very flexible and powerful feature of JavaScript.

ACCESSING & CHANGING VALUES IN AN ARRAY

`c02/js/update-array.js`

```javascript
// Create the array
var colors = ['white',
              'black',
              'custom'];

// Update the third item in the array
colors[2] = 'beige';

// Get the element with an id of colors
var el = document.getElementById('colors');

// Replace with third item from the array
el.textContent = colors[2];
```

RESULT

The first lines of code on the left create an array containing a list of three colors. (The values can be added on the same line or on separate lines as shown here.)

Having created the array, the third item on the list is changed from `'custom'` to `'beige'`.

To access a value from an array, after the array name you specify the index number for that value inside square brackets.

You can change the value of an item in an array by selecting it and assigning it a new value just as you would any other variable (using the equals sign and the new value for that item).

In the last two statements, the newly updated third item in the array is added to the page.

If you wanted to write out *all* of the items in an array, you would use a loop, which you will meet on p170.

EXPRESSIONS

An **expression** evaluates into (results in) a single value. Broadly speaking there are two types of expressions.

1

EXPRESSIONS THAT JUST ASSIGN A VALUE TO A VARIABLE

In order for a variable to be useful, it needs to be given a value. As you have seen, this is done using the assignment operator (the equals sign).

```
var color = 'beige';
```

The value of `color` is now `beige`.

When you first declare a variable using the `var` keyword, it is given a special value of `undefined`. This will change when you assign a value to it. Technically, undefined is a data type like a number, string, or Boolean.

2

EXPRESSIONS THAT USE TWO OR MORE VALUES TO RETURN A SINGLE VALUE

You can perform operations on any number of individual values (see next page) to determine a single value. For example:

```
var area = 3 * 2;
```

The value of `area` is now 6.

Here the expression 3 * 2 evaluates into 6. This example also uses the assignment operator, so the result of the expression 3 * 2 is stored in the variable called `area`.

Another example where an expression uses two values to yield a single value would be where two strings are joined to create a single string.

OPERATORS

Expressions rely on things called **operators**; they allow programmers to create a single value from one or more values.

Covered in this chapter:

ASSIGNMENT OPERATORS
Assign a value to a variable

```
color = 'beige';
```

The value of color is now beige.
(See p61)

ARITHMETIC OPERATORS
Perform basic math

```
area = 3 * 2;
```

The value of area is now 6.
(See p76)

STRING OPERATORS
Combine two strings

```
greeting = 'Hi ' + 'Molly';
```

The value of greeting is now Hi Molly.
(See p78)

Covered in Chapter 4:

COMPARISON OPERATORS
Compare two values and return true or false

```
buy = 3 > 5;
```

The value of buy is false.
(See p150)

LOGICAL OPERATORS
Combine expressions and return true or false

```
buy = (5 > 3) && (2 < 4);
```

The value of buy is now true.
(See p156)

ARITHMETIC OPERATORS

JavaScript contains the following mathematical operators, which you can use with numbers. You may remember some from math class.

NAME	OPERATOR	PURPOSE & NOTES	EXAMPLE	RESULT
ADDITION	+	Adds one value to another	10 + 5	15
SUBTRACTION	−	Subtracts one value from another	10 - 5	5
DIVISION	/	Divides two values	10 / 5	2
MULTIPLICATION	*	Multiplies two values using an asterisk (Note that this is not the letter x)	10 * 5	50
INCREMENT	++	Adds one to the current number	i = 10; i++;	11
DECREMENT	−−	Subtracts one from the current number	i = 10; i--;	9
MODULUS	%	Divides two values and returns the remainder	10 % 3	1

ORDER OF EXECUTION

Several arithmetic operations can be performed in one expression, but it is important to understand how the result will be calculated. Multiplication and division are performed *before* addition or subtraction. This can affect the number that you expect to see. To illustrate this effect, look at the following examples.

Here the numbers are calculated left to right, so the total is 16:
```
total = 2 + 4 + 10;
```

But in the following example the total is 42 (not 60):
```
total = 2 + 4 * 10;
```

This is because multiplication and division happen *before* addition and subtraction.

To change the order in which operations are performed, place the calculation you want done *first* inside parentheses. So for the following, the total is 60:
```
total = (2 + 4) * 10;
```

The parentheses indicate that the 2 is added to the 4, and *then* the resulting figure is multiplied by 10.

USING ARITHMETIC OPERATORS

JAVASCRIPT   c02/js/arithmetic-operator.js

```javascript
var subtotal = (13 + 1) * 5;      // Subtotal is 70
var shipping = 0.5 * (13 + 1);    // Shipping is 7

var total = subtotal + shipping; // Total is 77

var elSub = document.getElementById('subtotal');
elSub.textContent = subtotal;

var elShip = document.getElementById('shipping');
elShip.textContent = shipping;

var elTotal = document.getElementById('total');
elTotal.textContent = total;
```

RESULT

This example demonstrates how mathematical operators are used with numbers to calculate the combined values of two costs.

The first couple of lines create two variables: one to store the subtotal of the order, the other to hold the cost of shipping the order; so the variables are named accordingly: subtotal and shipping.

On the third line, the total is calculated by adding together these two values.

This demonstrates how the mathematical operators can use variables that represent numbers. (That is, the numbers do not need to be written explicitly into the code.)

The remaining six lines of code write the results to the screen.

STRING OPERATOR

There is just one string operator: the + symbol.
It is used to join the strings on either side of it.

There are many occasions where you may need to join two or more strings to create a single value. Programmers call the process of joining together two or more strings to create one new string **concatenation**.

For example, you might have a first and last name in two separate variables and want to join them to show a full name. In this example, the variable called `fullName` would hold the string `'Ivy Stone'`.

```
var firstName = 'Ivy ';
var lastName = 'Stone';
var fullName = firstName + lastName;
```

MIXING NUMBERS AND STRINGS TOGETHER

When you place quotes around a number, it is a string (not a numeric data type), and you cannot perform addition operations on strings.

```
var cost1 = '7';
var cost2 = '9';
var total = cost1 + cost2;
```

You would end up with a string saying `'79'`.

If you try to add a numeric data type to a string, then the number becomes part of the string, e.g., adding a house number to a street name:

```
var number = 12;
var street = 'Ivy Road';
var add = number + street;
```

You would end up with a string saying `'12Ivy Road'`.

If you try to use any of the other arithmetic operators on a string, then the value that results is usually a value called NaN. This means "not a number."

```
var score = 'seven';
var score2 = 'nine';
var total = score * score2;
```

You would end up with the value NaN.

USING STRING OPERATORS

c02/js/string-operator.js

```javascript
var greeting = 'Howdy ';
var name = 'Molly';

var welcomeMessage = greeting + name + '!';

var el = document.getElementById('greeting');
el.textContent = welcomeMessage;
```

HTML c02/string-operator.html

```html
<h1>Elderflower</h1>
<div id="content">
  <div id="greeting" class="message">Hello
    <span id="name">friend</span>!
  </div>
</div>
<script src="js/string-operator.js"></script>
```

RESULT

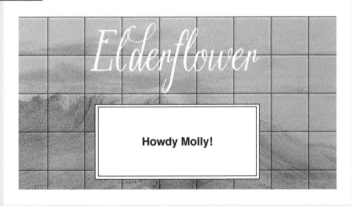

This example will display a personalized welcome message on the page.

The first line creates a variable called `greeting`, which stores the message for the user. Here the greeting is the word Howdy.

The second line creates a variable that stores the name of the user. The variable is called `name`, and the user in this case is Molly.

The personal welcome message is created by concatenating (or joining) these two variables, adding an exclamation mark, and storing them in a new variable called `welcomeMessage`.

Look back at the `greeting` variable on the first line, and note how there is a space after the word Howdy. If the space was omitted, the value of `welcomeMessage` would be "HowdyMolly!"

EXAMPLE
BASIC JAVASCRIPT
INSTRUCTIONS

This example combines several techniques that you have seen throughout this chapter.

You can see the code for this example on the next two pages. Single line comments are used to describe what each section of the code does.

To start, three variables are created that store information that is used in the welcome message. These variables are then concatenated (joined together) to create the full message the user sees.

The next part of the example demonstrates how basic math is performed on numbers to calculate the cost of a sign.

- A variable called sign holds the text the sign will show.
- A property called length is used to determine how many characters are in the string (you will meet this property on p128).
- The cost of the sign (the subtotal) is calculated by multiplying the number of tiles by the cost of each one.
- The grand total is created by adding $7 for shipping.

Finally, the information is written into the page by selecting elements and then replacing the content of that element (using a technique you meet fully in Chapter 5). It selects elements from the HTML page using the value of their id attributes and then updates the text inside those elements.

Once you have worked your way through this example, you should have a good basic understanding of how data is stored in variables and how to perform basic operations with the data in those variables.

EXAMPLE
BASIC JAVASCRIPT INSTRUCTIONS

```html
<!DOCTYPE html>
<html>
  <head>
    <title>JavaScript &amp; jQuery - Chapter 2: Basic JavaScript Instructions -
      Example</title>
    <link rel="stylesheet" href="css/c02.css" />
  </head>
  <body>
    <h1>Elderflower</h1>
    <div id="content">
      <div id="greeting" class="message">Hello!</div>
      <table>
        <tr>
          <td>Custom sign: </td>
          <td id="userSign"></td>
        </tr>
        <tr>
          <td>Total tiles: </td>
          <td id="tiles"></td>
        </tr>
        <tr>
          <td>Subtotal: </td>
          <td id="subTotal">$</td>
        </tr>
        <tr>
          <td>Shipping: </td>
          <td id="shipping">$</td>
        </tr>
        <tr>
          <td>Grand total: </td>
          <td id="grandTotal">$</td>
        </tr>
      </table>
      <a href="#" class="action">Pay Now</a>
    </div>
    <script src="js/example.js"></script>
  </body>
</html>
```

EXAMPLE
BASIC JAVASCRIPT INSTRUCTIONS

```javascript
// Create variables for the welcome message
var greeting = 'Howdy ';
var name = 'Molly';
var message = ', please check your order:';
// Concatenate the three variables above to create the welcome message
var welcome = greeting + name + message;

// Create variables to hold details about the sign
var sign = 'Montague House';
var tiles = sign.length;
var subTotal = tiles * 5;
var shipping = 7;
var grandTotal = subTotal + shipping;

// Get the element that has an id of greeting
var el = document.getElementById('greeting');
// Replace the content of that element with the personalized welcome message
el.textContent = welcome;

// Get the element that has an id of userSign then update its contents
var elSign = document.getElementById('userSign');
elSign.textContent = sign;

// Get the element that has an id of tiles then update its contents
var elTiles = document.getElementById('tiles');
elTiles.textContent = tiles;

// Get the element that has an id of subTotal then update its contents
var elSubTotal = document.getElementById('subTotal');
elSubTotal.textContent = '$' + subTotal;

// Get the element that has an id of shipping then update its contents
var elShipping = document.getElementById('shipping');
elShipping.textContent = '$' + shipping;

// Get the element that has an id of grandTotal then update its contents
var elGrandTotal = document.getElementById('grandTotal');
elGrandTotal.textContent = '$' + grandTotal;
```

SUMMARY
BASIC JAVASCRIPT INSTRUCTIONS

▶ A script is made up of a series of statements. Each statement is like a step in a recipe.

▶ Scripts contain very precise instructions. For example, you might specify that a value must be remembered before creating a calculation using that value.

▶ Variables are used to temporarily store pieces of information used in the script.

▶ Arrays are special types of variables that store more than one piece of related information.

▶ JavaScript distinguishes between numbers (0-9), strings (text), and Boolean values (true or false).

▶ Expressions evaluate into a single value.

▶ Expressions rely on operators to calculate a value.

3

FUNCTIONS, METHODS & OBJECTS

Browsers require very detailed instructions about what we want them to do. Therefore, complex scripts can run to hundreds (even thousands) of lines. Programmers use functions, methods, and objects to organize their code. This chapter is divided into three sections that introduce:

FUNCTIONS & METHODS

Functions consist of a series of statements that have been grouped together because they perform a specific task. A method is the same as a function, except methods are created inside (and are part of) an object.

OBJECTS

In Chapter 1 you saw that programmers use objects to create models of the world using data, and that objects are made up of properties and methods. In this section, you learn how to create your own objects using JavaScript.

BUILT-IN OBJECTS

The browser comes with a set of objects that act like a toolkit for creating interactive web pages. This section introduces you to a number of built-in objects, which you will then see used throughout the rest of the book.

杉本博司
時間の終わり
HIROSHI SUGIMOTO
End of Time
MORI ART MUSEUM
TravelWorthy
latest hotel offer
PARK
$204

WHAT IS A FUNCTION?

Functions let you group a series of statements together to perform a specific task. If different parts of a script repeat the same task, you can reuse the function (rather than repeating the same set of statements).

Grouping together the statements that are required to answer a question or perform a task helps organize your code.

Furthermore, the statements in a function are not always executed when a page loads, so functions also offer a way to *store* the steps needed to achieve a task. The script can then ask the function to perform all of those steps as and when they are required. For example, you might have a task that you only want to perform if the user clicks on a specific element in the page.

If you are going to ask the function to perform its task later, you need to give your function a name. That name should describe the task it is performing. When you ask it to perform its task, it is known as **calling** the function.

The steps that the function needs to perform in order to perform its task are packaged up in a code block. You may remember from the last chapter that a code block consists of one or more statements contained within curly braces. (And you do not write a semicolon after the closing curly brace – like you do after a statement.)

Some functions need to be provided with information in order to achieve a given task. For example, a function to calculate the area of a box would need to know its width and height. Pieces of information passed to a function are known as **parameters**.

When you write a function and you expect it to provide you with an answer, the response is known as a **return value**.

On the right, there is an example of a function in the JavaScript file. It is called updateMessage().

Don't worry if you do not understand the syntax of the example on the right; you will take a closer look at how to write and use functions in the pages that follow.

Remember that programming languages often rely upon on name/value pairs. The function has a name, updateMessage, and the value is the code block (which consists of statements). When you call the function by its name, those statements will run.

You can also have anonymous functions. They do not have a name, so they cannot be called. Instead, they are executed as soon as the interpreter comes across them.

A BASIC FUNCTION

In this example, the user is shown a message at the top of the page. The message is held in an HTML element whose id attribute has a value of message. The message is going to be changed using JavaScript.

Before the closing </body> tag, you can see the link to the JavaScript file. The JavaScript file starts with a variable used to hold a new message, and is followed by a function called updateMessage().

You do not need to worry about *how* this function works yet – you will learn about that over the next few pages. For the moment, it is just worth noting that inside the curly braces of the function are two statements.

c03/basic-function.html

HTML

```
<!DOCTYPE html>
<html>
  <head>
    <title>Basic Function</title>
    <link rel="stylesheet" href="css/c03.css" />
  </head>
  <body>
    <h1>TravelWorthy</h1>
    <div id="message">Welcome to our site!</div>
    <script src="js/basic-function.js"></script>
  </body>
</html>
```

c03/js/basic-function.js

JAVASCRIPT

```
var msg = 'Sign up to receive our newsletter for 10% off!';
function updateMessage() {
  var el = document.getElementById('message');
  el.textContent = msg;
}
updateMessage();
```

RESULT

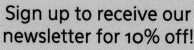
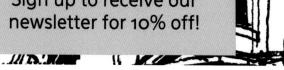

These statements update the message at the top of the page. The function acts like a store; it holds the statements that are contained in the curly braces until you are ready to use them. Those statements are not run until the function is **called**. The function is only called on the last line of this script.

DECLARING A FUNCTION

To create a function, you give it a name and then write the statements needed to achieve its task inside the curly braces.
This is known as a **function declaration**.

You declare a **function** using the `function` keyword.

You give the function a **name** (sometimes called an **identifier**) followed by parentheses.

The **statements** that perform the task sit in a code block. (They are inside curly braces.)

FUNCTION KEYWORD

FUNCTION NAME

```
function sayHello() {
    document.write('Hello!');
}
```

CODE BLOCK (IN CURLY BRACES)

This function is very basic (it only contains one statement), but it illustrates how to write a function. Most functions that you will see or write are likely to consist of more statements.

The point to remember is that functions store the code required to perform a specific task, and that the script can ask the function to perform that task whenever needed.

If different parts of a script need to perform the same task, you do not need to repeat the same statements multiple times – you use a function to do it (and reuse the same code).

CALLING A FUNCTION

Having declared the function, you can then execute all of the statements between its curly braces with just one line of code.
This is known as **calling the function**.

To run the code in the function, you use the function name followed by parentheses.

In programmer-speak, you would say that this code **calls** a function.

You can call the same function as many times as you want within the same JavaScript file.

FUNCTION NAME

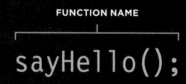

sayHello();

1. The function can store the instructions for a specific task.
2. When you need the script to perform that task, you call the function.
3. The function executes the code in that code block.
4. When it has finished, the code continues to run from the point where it was initially called.

```
① function sayHello() {
③   document.write('Hello!');
  }

    // Code before hello...
② sayHello();
④ // Code after hello...
```

Sometimes you will see a function called *before* it has been declared. This still works because the interpreter runs through a script before executing each statement, so it will know that a function declaration appears later in the script. But for the moment, we will declare the function before calling it.

DECLARING FUNCTIONS THAT NEED INFORMATION

Sometimes a function needs specific information to perform its task. In such cases, when you declare the function you give it **parameters**. Inside the function, the parameters act like variables.

If a function needs information to work, you indicate what it needs to know in parentheses after the function name.

The items that appear inside these parentheses are known as the **parameters** of the function. Inside the function those words act like variable names.

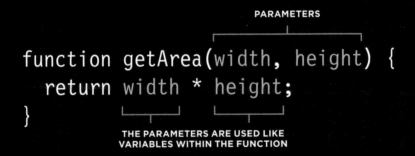

PARAMETERS

```
function getArea(width, height) {
    return width * height;
}
```

THE PARAMETERS ARE USED LIKE
VARIABLES WITHIN THE FUNCTION

This function will calculate and return the area of a rectangle. To do this, it needs the rectangle's width and height. Each time you call the function these values could be different.

This demonstrates how the code can perform a task without knowing the *exact* details in advance, as long as it has rules it can follow to achieve the task.

So, when you design a script, you need to note the information the function will require in order to perform its task.

If you look inside the function, the parameter names are used just as you would use variables. Here, the parameter names **width** and **height** represent the width and height of the wall.

CALLING FUNCTIONS THAT NEED INFORMATION

When you call a function that has parameters, you specify the values it should use in the parentheses that follow its name. The values are called **arguments**, and they can be provided as values or as variables.

ARGUMENTS AS VALUES

When the function below is called, the number 3 will be used for the width of the wall, and 5 will be used for its height.

```
getArea(3, 5);
```

ARGUMENTS AS VARIABLES

You do not have to specify actual values when calling a function – you can use variables in their place. So the following does the same thing.

```
wallWidth = 3;
wallHeight = 5;
getArea(wallWidth, wallHeight);
```

PARAMETERS VS ARGUMENTS

People often use the terms **parameter** and **argument** interchangeably, but there *is* a subtle difference.

On the left-hand page, when the function is declared, you can see the words **width** and **height** used (in parentheses on the first line). Inside the curly braces of the function, those words act like variables. These names are the parameters.

On this page, you can see that the **getArea()** function is being called and the code specifies real numbers that will be used to perform the calculation (or variables that hold real numbers).

These values that you pass into the code (the information it needs to calculate the size of this particular wall) are called arguments.

GETTING A SINGLE VALUE OUT OF A FUNCTION

Some functions return information to the code that called them.
For example, when they perform a calculation, they return the result.

This `calculateArea()` function returns the area of a rectangle to the code that called it.

Inside the function, a variable called **area** is created. It holds the calculated area of the box.

The **return** keyword is used to return a value to the code that called the function.

```
function calculateArea(width, height) {
  var area = width * height;
  return area;
}
var wallOne = calculateArea(3, 5);
var wallTwo = calculateArea(8, 5);
```

Note that the intrepreter leaves the function when **return** is used. It goes back to the statement that called it. If there had been any subsequent statements in this function, they would not be processed.

The `wallOne` variable holds the value **15**, which was calculated by the `calculateArea()` function.

The `wallTwo` variable holds the value **40**, which was calculated by the same `calculateArea()` function.

This also demonstrates how the same function can be used to perform the same steps with different values.

GETTING MULTIPLE VALUES
OUT OF A FUNCTION

Functions can return more than one value using an array.
For example, this function calculates the area and volume of a box.

First, a new function is created called **getSize()**. The area of the box is calculated and stored in a variable called **area**.

The volume is calculated and stored in a variable called **volume**. Both are then placed into an array called **sizes**.

This array is then returned to the code that called the **getSize()** function, allowing the values to be used.

```
function getSize(width, height, depth) {
  var area = width * height;
  var volume = width * height * depth;
  var sizes = [area, volume];
  return sizes;
}
var areaOne = getSize(3, 2, 3)[0];
var volumeOne = getSize(3, 2, 3)[1];
```

The **areaOne** variable holds the area of a box that is 3 x 2. The area is the *first* value in the **sizes** array.

The **volumeOne** variable holds the volume of a box that is 3 x 2 x 3. The volume is the *second* value in the **sizes** array.

ANONYMOUS FUNCTIONS & FUNCTION EXPRESSIONS

Expressions produce a value. They can be used where values are expected. If a function is placed where a browser expects to see an expression, (e.g., as an argument to a function), then it gets treated as an expression.

FUNCTION DECLARATION

A **function declaration** creates a function that you can call later in your code. It is the type of function you have seen so far in this book.

In order to call the function later in your code, you must give it a name, so these are known as **named functions**. Below, a function called `area()` is declared, which can then be called using its name.

```
function area(width, height) {
  return width * height;
};

var size = area(3, 4);
```

As you will see on p456, the interpreter always looks for variables and function declarations *before* going through each section of a script, line-by-line. This means that a function created with a function declaration can be called *before* it has even been declared.

For more information about how variables and functions are processed first, see the discussion about execution context and hoisting on p452 – p457.

FUNCTION EXPRESSION

If you put a function where the interpreter would expect to see an expression, then it is treated as an expression, and it is known as a **function expression**. In function expressions, the name is usually omitted. A function with no name is called an **anonymous function**. Below, the function is stored in a variable called `area`. It can be called like any function created with a function declaration.

```
var area = function(width, height) {
  return width * height;
};

var size = area(3, 4);
```

In a function expression, the function is not processed until the interpreter gets to that statement. This means you cannot call this function *before* the interpreter has discovered it. It also means that any code that appears up to that point could potentially alter what goes on inside this function.

IMMEDIATELY INVOKED FUNCTION EXPRESSIONS

This way of writing a function is used in several different situations. Often functions are used to ensure that the variable names do not conflict with each other (especially if the page uses more than one script).

IMMEDIATELY INVOKED FUNCTION EXPRESSIONS (IIFE)

Pronounced "iffy," these functions are not given a name. Instead, they are executed once as the interpreter comes across them.

Below, the variable called **area** will hold the value returned from the function (rather than storing the function itself so that it can be called later).

```
var area = ((function() {
  var width = 3;
  var height = 2;
  return width * height;
}()));
```

The **final parentheses** (shown on green) after the closing curly brace of the code block tell the interpreter to call the function immediately. The **grouping operators** (shown on pink) are parentheses there to ensure the interpreter treats this as an expression.

You may see the final parentheses in an IIFE placed *after* the closing grouping operator but it is commonly considered better practice to place the final parentheses *before* the closing grouping operator, as shown in the code above.

WHEN TO USE ANONYMOUS FUNCTIONS AND IIFES

You will see many ways in which anonymous function expressions and IIFEs are used throughout the book.

They are used for code that only needs to run once within a task, rather than repeatedly being called by other parts of the script. For example:

- As an argument when a function is called (to calculate a value for that function).

- To assign the value of a property to an object.

- In event handlers and listeners (see Chapter 6) to perform a task when an event occurs.

- To prevent conflicts between two scripts that might use the same variable names (see p99).

IIFEs are commonly used as a wrapper around a set of code. Any variables declared within that anonymous function are effectively protected from variables in other scripts that might have the same name. This is due to a concept called scope, which you meet on the next page. It is also a very popular technique with jQuery.

VARIABLE SCOPE

The location where you declare a variable will affect where it can be used within your code. If you declare it within a function, it can only be used within that function. This is known as the variable's **scope**.

LOCAL VARIABLES

When a variable is created *inside* a function using the var keyword, it can only be used in that function. It is called a **local** variable or **function-level** variable. It is said to have **local scope** or **function-level scope**. It cannot be accessed outside of the function in which it was declared. Below, **area** is a local variable.

The interpreter creates local variables when the function is run, and removes them as soon as the function has finished its task. This means that:

- If the function runs twice, the variable can have different values each time.
- Two different functions can use variables with the same name without any kind of naming conflict.

GLOBAL VARIABLES

If you create a variable *outside* of a function, then it can be used anywhere within the script. It is called a **global** variable and has **global scope**. In the example shown, wallSize is a global variable.

Global variables are stored in memory for as long as the web page is loaded into the web browser. This means they take up more memory than local variables, and it also increases the risk of naming conflicts (see next page). For these reasons, you should use local variables wherever possible.

If you forget to declare a variable using the var keyword, the variable will work, but it will be treated as a *global* variable (this is considered bad practice).

```
function getArea(width, height) {
  var area = width * height;
  return area;
}

var wallSize = getArea(3, 2);
document.write(wallSize);
```

● LOCAL (OR FUNCTION-LEVEL) SCOPE
● GLOBAL SCOPE

HOW MEMORY & VARIABLES WORK

Global variables use more memory. The browser has to remember them for as long as the web page using them is loaded. Local variables are only remembered during the period of time that a function is being executed.

CREATING THE VARIABLES IN CODE

Each variable that you declare takes up memory. The more variables a browser has to remember, the more memory your script requires to run. Scripts that require a lot of memory can perform slower, which in turn makes your web page take longer to respond to the user.

```
var width = 15;
var height = 30;
var isWall = true;
var canPaint = true;
```

A variable actually references a value that is stored in memory. The same value can be used with more than one variable:

```
var width = 15; ─────────────→ (15)

var height = 30; ────────────→ (30)

var isWall = true; ──────────→
var canPaint = true; ────────→ (true)
```

Here the values for the `width` and `height` of the wall are stored separately, but the same value of `true` can be used for both `isWall` and `canPaint`.

NAMING COLLISIONS

You might think you would avoid naming collisions; after all *you* know which variables you are using. But many sites use scripts written by several people. If an HTML page uses two JavaScript files, and both have a global variable with the same name, it can cause errors. Imagine a page using these two scripts:

```
// Show size of the building plot
function showPlotSize(){
  var width = 3;
  var height = 2;
  return 'Area: " + (width * height);
}
var msg = showArea()
```

```
// Show size of the garden
function showGardenSize() {
  var width = 12;
  var height = 25;
  return width * height;
}
var msg = showGardenSize();
```

● Variables in global scope: have naming conflicts.
● Variables in function scope: there is no conflict between them.

WHAT IS AN OBJECT?

Objects group together a set of variables and functions to create a model of something you would recognize from the real world. In an object, variables and functions take on new names.

IN AN OBJECT: VARIABLES BECOME KNOWN AS PROPERTIES

If a variable is part of an object, it is called a **property**. Properties tell us about the object, such as the name of a hotel or the number of rooms it has. Each individual hotel might have a different name and a different number of rooms.

IN AN OBJECT: FUNCTIONS BECOME KNOWN AS METHODS

If a function is part of an object, it is called a **method**. Methods represent tasks that are associated with the object. For example, you can check how many rooms are available by subtracting the number of booked rooms from the total number of rooms.

This object represents a hotel. It has five properties and one method. The object is in curly braces. It is stored in a variable called `hotel`.

Like variables and named functions, properties and methods have a name and a value. In an object, that name is called a **key**.

An object cannot have two keys with the same name. This is because keys are used to access their corresponding values.

The value of a property can be a string, number, Boolean, array, or even another object. The value of a method is always a function.

```
var hotel = {
    name: 'Quay',
    rooms: 40,
    booked: 25,
    gym: true,
    roomTypes: ['twin', 'double', 'suite'],

    checkAvailability: function() {
        return this.rooms - this.booked;
    }
};
```

● KEY
● VALUE

PROPERTIES
These are variables

METHOD
This is a function

Above you can see a `hotel` object. The object contains the following key/value pairs:

PROPERTIES:	KEY	VALUE
	name	string
	rooms	number
	booked	number
	gym	Boolean
	roomTypes	array
METHODS:	checkAvailability	function

As you will see over the next few pages, this is just one of the ways you can create an object.

Programmers use a lot of name/value pairs:
- HTML uses attribute names and values.
- CSS uses property names and values.

In JavaScript:
- Variables have a name and you can assign them a value of a string, number, or Boolean.
- Arrays have a name and a group of values. (Each item in an array is a name/value pair because it has an index number and a value.)
- Named functions have a name and value that is a set of statements to run if the function is called.
- Objects consist of a set of name/value pairs (but the names are referred to as keys).

CREATING AN OBJECT: LITERAL NOTATION

Literal notation is the easiest and most popular way to create objects.
(There are several ways to create objects.)

The object is the curly braces and their contents.
The object is stored in a variable called **hotel**,
so you would refer to it as the **hotel** object.

Separate each key from its value using a colon.
Separate each property and method with a comma
(but not after the last value).

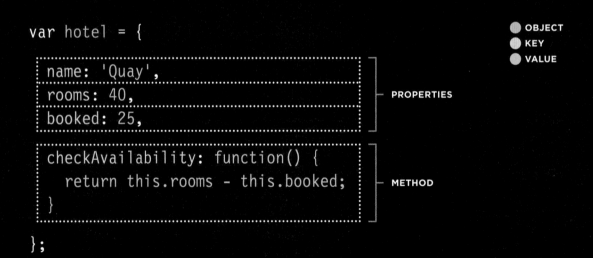

```
var hotel = {

    name: 'Quay',
    rooms: 40,                                          PROPERTIES
    booked: 25,

    checkAvailability: function() {
        return this.rooms - this.booked;                METHOD
    }

};
```

● OBJECT
● KEY
● VALUE

In the **checkAvailability()** method, the **this**
keyword is used to indicate that it is using the **rooms**
and **booked** properties of *this* object.

When setting properties, treat the values like you
would do for variables: strings live in quotes and
arrays live in square brackets.

ACCESSING AN OBJECT AND DOT NOTATION

You access the properties or methods of an object using dot notation.
You can also access properties using square brackets.

To access a property or method of an object you use the name of the object, followed by a period, then the name of the property or method you want to access. This is known as **dot notation**.

The period is known as the **member operator**. The property or method on its right is a member of the object on its left. Here, two variables are created to hold the hotel name and number of vacant rooms.

OBJECT   PROPERTY/METHOD NAME

```
var hotelName = hotel.name;
var roomsFree = hotel.checkAvailability();
```

MEMBER OPERATOR

You can also access the properties of an object (but not its methods) using square bracket syntax.

This time the object name is followed by square brackets, and the property name is inside them.

```
var hotelName = hotel['name'];
```

This notation is most commonly used when:
- The name of the property is a number (technically allowed, but should generally be avoided)
- A variable is being used in place of the property name (you will see this technique used in Chapter 12)

CREATING OBJECTS USING LITERAL NOTATION

This example starts by creating an object using literal notation.

This object is called `hotel` which represents a hotel called **Quay** with 40 rooms (25 of which have been booked).

Next, the content of the page is updated with data from this object. It shows the name of the hotel by accessing the object's `name` property and the number of vacant rooms using the `checkAvailability()` method.

To access a property of this object, the object name is followed by a dot (the period symbol) and the name of the property that you want.

Similarly, to use the method, you can use the object name followed by the method name. `hotel.checkAvailability()`

If the method needs parameters, you can supply them in the parentheses (just like you can pass arguments to a function).

c3/js/object-literal.js   `JAVASCRIPT`

```javascript
var hotel = {
  name: 'Quay',
  rooms: 40,
  booked: 25,
  checkAvailability: function() {
    return this.rooms - this.booked;
  }
};

var elName = document.getElementById('hotelName');
elName.textContent = hotel.name;

var elRooms = document.getElementById('rooms');
elRooms.textContent = hotel.checkAvailability();
```

`RESULT`

hotel availability

QUAY

15
rooms left

CREATING MORE OBJECT LITERALS

JAVASCRIPT c03/js/object-literal2.js

```javascript
var hotel = {
  name: 'Park',
  rooms: 120,
  booked: 77,
  checkAvailability: function() {
    return this.rooms - this.booked;
  }
};

var elName = document.getElementById('hotelName');
elName.textContent = hotel.name;

var elRooms = document.getElementById('rooms');
elRooms.textContent = hotel.checkAvailability();
```

RESULT

Here you can see another object. Again it is called hotel, but this time the model represents a different hotel. For a moment, imagine that this is a different page of the same travel website.

The Park hotel is larger. It has 120 rooms and 77 of them are booked.

The only things changing in the code are the values of the hotel object's properties:
● The name of the hotel
● How many rooms it has
● How many rooms are booked

The rest of the page works in exactly the same way. The name is shown using the same code. The checkAvailability() method has not changed and is called in the same way.

If this site had 1,000 hotels, the only thing that would need to change would be the three properties of this object. Because we created a model for the hotel using data, the same code can access and display the details for any hotel that follows the same data model.

If you had two objects on the same page, you would create each one using the same notation but store them in variables with different names.

CREATING AN OBJECT: CONSTRUCTOR NOTATION

The **new** keyword and the object constructor create a blank object. You can then add properties and methods to the object.

First, you create a new object using a combination of the **new** keyword and the **Object()** constructor function. (This function is part of the JavaScript language and is used to create objects.)

Next, having created the blank object, you can add properties and methods to it using dot notation. Each statement that adds a property or method should end with a semicolon.

```
var hotel = new Object();

hotel.name = 'Quay';
hotel.rooms = 40;
hotel.booked = 25;

hotel.checkAvailability = function() {
    return this.rooms - this.booked;
};
```

- OBJECT
- KEY
- VALUE

PROPERTIES

METHOD

You can use this syntax to add properties and methods to any object you have created (no matter which notation you used to create it).

To create an empty object using literal notation use:
`var hotel = {}`
The curly brackets create an empty object.

UPDATING AN OBJECT

To update the value of properties, use dot notation or square brackets.
They work on objects created using literal or constructor notation.
To delete a property, use the **delete** keyword.

To update a property, use the same technique that was shown on the left-hand page to add properties to the object, but give it a new value.

If the object does not have the property you are trying to update, it will be added to the object.

OBJECT   PROPERTY NAME   PROPERTY VALUE

```
hotel.name = 'Park';
```

MEMBER OPERATOR   ASSIGNMENT OPERATOR

You can also update the properties of an object (but not its methods) using square bracket syntax. The object name is followed by square brackets, and the property name is inside them.

A new value for the property is added after the assignment operator. Again, if the property you are attempting to update does not exist, it will be added to the object.

```
hotel['name'] = 'Park';
```

To delete a property, use the **delete** keyword followed by the object name and property name.

If you just want to clear the value of a property, you could set it to a blank string.

```
delete hotel.name;
```

```
hotel.name = '';
```

CREATING MANY OBJECTS: CONSTRUCTOR NOTATION

Sometimes you will want several objects to represent similar things.
Object constructors can use a function as a **template** for creating objects.
First, create the template with the object's properties and methods.

A function called **Hotel** will be used as a template for creating new objects that represent hotels. Like all functions, it contains statements. In this case, they add properties or methods to the object.

The function has three parameters. Each one sets the value of a property in the object. The methods will be the same for each object created using this function.

```
function Hotel(name, rooms, booked) {

    this.name = name;
    this.rooms = rooms;
    this.booked = booked;

    this.checkAvailability = function() {
        return this.rooms - this.booked;
    };

}
```

PROPERTIES

METHOD

● KEY
● VALUE

The **this** keyword is used instead of the object name to indicate that the property or method belongs to the object that *this* function creates.

Each statement that creates a new property or method for this object ends in a semicolon (not a comma, which is used in the literal syntax).

The name of a constructor function usually begins with a capital letter (unlike other functions, which tend to begin with a lowercase character).

The uppercase letter is supposed to help remind developers to use the **new** keyword when they create an object using that function (see next page).

You create **instances** of the object using the constructor function.
The **new** keyword followed by a call to the function creates a new object.
The properties of each object are given as arguments to the function.

Here, two objects are used to represent two hotels, so each object needs a different name. When the **new** keyword calls the constructor function (defined on the left-hand page), it creates a new object.

Each time it is called, the arguments are different because they are the values for the properties of each hotel. Both objects automatically get the same method defined in the constructor function.

OBJECT   CONSTRUCTOR FUNCTION

```
var quayHotel = new Hotel('Quay', 40, 25);
var parkHotel = new Hotel('Park', 120, 77);
```

ASSIGNMENT OPERATOR   NEW KEYWORD   VALUES USED IN PROPERTIES
                                            OF THIS OBJECT

The first object is called **quayHotel**. Its name is 'Quay' and it has 40 rooms, 25 of which are booked.

The second object is called **parkHotel**. Its name is 'Park' and it has 120 rooms, 77 of which are booked.

Even when many objects are created using the same constructor function, the methods stay the same because they access, update, or perform a calculation on the data stored in the properties.

You might use this technique if your script contains a very complex object that needs to be available but might not be used. The object is *defined* in the function, but it is only *created* if it is needed.

CREATING OBJECTS USING CONSTRUCTOR SYNTAX

On the right, an empty object called `hotel` is created using the constructor function.

Once it has been created, three properties and a method are then assigned to the object.

(If the object already had any of these properties, this would overwrite the values in those properties.)

To access a property of this object, you can use dot notation, just as you can with any object.

For example, to get the hotel's name you could use:
`hotel.name`

Similarly, to use the method, you can use the object name followed by the method name:
`hotel.checkAvailability()`

```
c3/js/object-constructor.js                          JAVASCRIPT

var hotel = new Object();

hotel.name = 'Park';
hotel.rooms = 120;
hotel.booked = 77;
hotel.checkAvailability = function() {
    return this.rooms - this.booked;
};

var elName = document.getElementById('hotelName');
elName.textContent = hotel.name;

var elRooms = document.getElementById('rooms');
elRooms.textContent = hotel.checkAvailability();
```

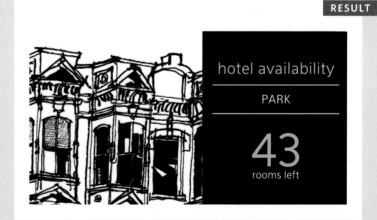

RESULT

hotel availability

PARK

43
rooms left

CREATE & ACCESS OBJECTS CONSTRUCTOR NOTATION

JAVASCRIPT c03/js/multiple-objects.js

```javascript
function Hotel(name, rooms, booked) {
  this.name = name;
  this.rooms = rooms;
  this.booked = booked;
  this.checkAvailability = function() {
    return this.rooms - this.booked;
  };
}

var quayHotel = new Hotel('Quay', 40, 25);
var parkHotel = new Hotel('Park', 120, 77);

var details1 = quayHotel.name + ' rooms: ';
    details1 += quayHotel.checkAvailability();
var elHotel1 = document.getElementById('hotel1');
elHotel1.textContent = details1;

var details2 = parkHotel.name + ' rooms: ';
    details2 += parkHotel.checkAvailability();
var elHotel2 = document.getElementById('hotel2');
elHotel2.textContent = details2;
```

To get a better idea of why you might want to create multiple objects on the same page, here is an example that shows room availability in two hotels.

First, a constructor function defines a template for the hotels. Next, two different instances of this type of hotel object are created. The first represents a hotel called Quay and the second a hotel called Park.

Having created instances of these objects, you can then access their properties and methods using the same dot notation that you use with all other objects.

In this example, data from both objects is accessed and written into the page. (The HTML for this example changes to accommodate the extra hotel.)

For each hotel, a variable is created to hold the hotel name, followed by space, and the word rooms.

The line after it adds to that variable with the number of available rooms in that hotel.

(The += operator is used to add content to an existing variable.)

RESULT

hotel availability

Quay rooms: 15
Park rooms: 43

ADDING AND REMOVING PROPERTIES

Once you have created an object (using literal or constructor notation), you can add new properties to it.

You do this using the dot notation that you saw for adding properties to objects on p103.

In this example, you can see that an instance of the **hotel** object is created using an object literal.

Immediately after this, the **hotel** object is given two extra properties that show the facilities (whether or not it has a gym and/or a pool). These properties are given values that are Booleans (**true** or **false**).

Having added these properties to the object, you can access them just like any of the objects other properties. Here, they update the value of the **class** attribute on their respective elements to show either a check mark or a cross mark.

To delete a property, you use the keyword **delete**, and then use dot notation to identify the property or method you want to remove from the object.

In this case, the **booked** property is removed from the object.

```
c3/js/adding-and-removing-properties.js                JAVASCRIPT

var hotel = {
  name : 'Park',
  rooms : 120,
  booked : 77
};

hotel.gym = true;
hotel.pool = false;
delete hotel.booked;

var elName = document.getElementById('hotelName');
elName.textContent = hotel.name;

var elPool = document.getElementById('pool');
elPool.className = 'Pool: ' + hotel.pool;

var elGym = document.getElementById('gym');
elGym.className = 'Gym: ' + hotel.gym;
```

If an object is created using a constructor function, this syntax only adds or removes the properties from the one instance of the object (not all objects created with that function).

RECAP: WAYS TO CREATE OBJECTS

CREATE THE OBJECT, THEN ADD PROPERTIES & METHODS

In both of these examples, the object is created on the first line of the code sample. The properties and methods are then added to it afterwards.

Once you have created an object, the syntax for adding or removing any properties and methods from that object is the same.

LITERAL NOTATION

```
var hotel = {}

hotel.name = 'Quay';
hotel.rooms = 40;
hotel.booked = 25;
hotel.checkAvailability = function() {
  return this.rooms - this.booked;
};
```

OBJECT CONSTRUCTOR NOTATION

```
var hotel = new Object();

hotel.name = 'Quay';
hotel.rooms = 40;
hotel.booked = 25;
hotel.checkAvailability = function() {
  return this.rooms - this.booked;
};
```

CREATING AN OBJECT WITH PROPERTIES & METHODS

LITERAL NOTATION

A colon separates the key/value pairs.
There is a comma between each key/value pair.

```
var hotel = {
  name: 'Quay',
  rooms: 40,
  booked: 25,
  checkAvailability: function() {
    return this.rooms - this.booked;
  }
};
```

OBJECT CONSTRUCTOR NOTATION

The function can be used to create multiple objects.
The this keyword is used instead of the object name.

```
function Hotel(name, rooms, booked) {
  this.name = name;
  this.rooms = rooms;
  this.booked = booked;
  this.checkAvailability = function() {
    return this.rooms - this.booked;
  };
}
var quayHotel = new Hotel('Quay', 40, 25);
var parkHotel = new Hotel('Park', 120, 77);
```

THIS (IT IS A KEYWORD)

The keyword this is commonly used inside functions and objects. Where the function is declared alters what this means. It always refers to one object, usually the object in which the function operates.

A FUNCTION IN GLOBAL SCOPE

When a function is created at the top level of a script (that is, not inside another object or function), then it is in the **global scope** or **global context**.

The default object in this context is the window object, so when this is used inside a function in the global context it refers to the window object.

Below, this is being used to return properties of the window object (you meet these properties on p124).

```
function windowSize() {
  var width = this.innerWidth;
  var height = this.innerHeight;
  return [height, width];
}
```

Under the hood, the this keyword is a reference to the object that the function is created inside.

GLOBAL VARIABLES

All global variables also become properties of the window object, so when a function is in the global context, you can access global variables using the window object, as well as its other properties.

Here, the showWidth() function is in global scope, and this.width refers to the width variable:

```
var width = 600;
var shape = {width: 300};

var showWidth = function() {
  document.write(this.width);
};

showWidth();
```

Here, the function would write a value of **600** into the page (using the **document** object's **write()** method).

As you can see, the value of this changes in different situations. But don't worry if you do not follow these two pages on your first read through. As you write more functions and objects, these concepts will become more familiar, and if this is not returning the value you expected, these pages will help you work out why.

Another scenario to mention is when one function is nested inside another function. It is only done in more complicated scripts, but the value of this can vary (depending on which browser you are using). You could work around this by storing the value of this in a variable in the first function and using the variable name in child functions instead of this.

A METHOD OF AN OBJECT

When a function is defined *inside* an object, it becomes a method. In a method, this refers to the containing object.

In the example below, the getArea() method appears inside the shape object, so this refers to the shape object it is contained in:

```
var shape = {
  width: 600,
  height: 400,
  getArea: function() {
    return this.width * this.height;
  }
};
```

Because the this keyword here refers to the shape object, it would be the same as writing:

```
return shape.width * shape.height;
```

If you were creating several objects using an object constructor (and each shape had different dimensions), this would refer to the individual instance of the new object you are creating. When you called getArea(), it would calculate the dimensions of that particular instance of the object.

FUNCTION EXPRESSION AS METHOD

If a named function has been defined in global scope, and it is then used as a method of an object, this refers to the object it is contained within.

The next example uses the same showWidth() function expression as the one on the left-hand page, but it is assigned as a method of an object.

```
var width = 600;
var shape = {width: 300};

var showWidth = function() {
  document.write(this.width) ;
};

shape.getWidth = showWidth;
shape.getWidth();
```

The last but one line indicates that the showWidth() function is used as a method of the shape object. The method is given a different name: getWidth().

When the getWidth() method is called, even though it uses the showWidth() function, this now refers to the shape object, not the global context (and this.width refers to the width property of the shape object). So it writes a value of 300 to the page.

RECAP: STORING DATA

In JavaScript, data is represented using name/value pairs.
To organize your data, you can use an array or object to group a set of related values. In arrays and objects the name is also known as a key.

VARIABLES

A variable has just one key (the variable name) and one value.

Variable names are separated from their value by an equals sign (the assignment operator):

```
var hotel = 'Quay';
```

To retrieve the value of a variable, use its name:

```
// This retrieves Quay:
hotel;
```

When a variable has been declared but has not yet been assigned a value, it is undefined.

If the var keyword is not used, the variable is declared in global scope (you should always use it).

ARRAYS

Arrays can store multiple pieces of information. Each piece of information is separated by a comma. The order of the values is important because items in an array are assigned a number (called an index).

Values in an array are put in square brackets, separated by commas:

```
var hotels = [
    'Quay',
    'Park',
    'Beach',
    'Bloomsbury'
]
```

You can think of each item in the array as another key/value pair, the key is the index number, and the values are shown in the comma-separated list.

To retrieve an item, use its index number:

```
// This retrieves Park:
hotels[1];
```

If a key is a number, to retrieve the value you must place the number in square brackets.

Generally speaking, arrays are the only times when the key would be a number.

If you want to access items via a property name or key, use an object (but note that each key in the object must be unique).
If the order of the items is important, use an array.

INDIVIDUAL OBJECTS

Objects store sets of name/value pairs. They can be properties (variables) or methods (functions).

The order of them is not important (unlike the array). You access each piece of data by its key.

In object literal notation, properties and methods of an object are given in curly braces:

```
var hotel = {
    name: 'Quay',
    rooms: 40
};
```

Objects created with literal notation are good:

- When you are storing / transmitting data between applications
- For global or configuration objects that set up information for the page

To access the properties or methods of the object, use dot notation:

```
// This retrieves Quay:
hotel.name;
```

MULTIPLE OBJECTS

When you need to create multiple objects within the same page, you should use an object constructor to provide a template for the objects.

```
function Hotel(name, rooms) {
    this.name = name;
    this.rooms = rooms;
}
```

You then create instances of the object using the **new** keyword and then a call to the constructor function.

```
var hotel1 = new Hotel('Quay', 40);
var hotel2 = new Hotel('Park', 120);
```

Objects created with constructors are good when:

- You have lots of objects used with similar functionality (e.g., multiple slideshows / media players / game characters) within a page
- A complex object might not be used in code

To access the properties or methods of the object, use dot notation:

```
// This retrieves Park:
hotel2.name;
```

ARRAYS ARE OBJECTS

Arrays are actually a special type of object. They hold a related set of key/value pairs (like all objects), but the key for each value is its index number.

As you saw (on p72), arrays have a **length** property telling you how many items are in the array. In Chapter 12, you will see that arrays also have several other helpful methods.

AN OBJECT

PROPERTY:		VALUE:
room1	⋮	420
room2	⋮	460
room3	⋮	230
room4	⋮	620

Here, hotel room costs are stored in an object. The example covers four rooms, and the cost for each room is a property of the object:

```
costs = {
    room1: 420,
    room2: 460,
    room3: 230,
    room4: 620
};
```

AN ARRAY

INDEX NUMBER:		VALUE:
0	⋮	420
1	⋮	460
2	⋮	230
3	⋮	620

Here is the the same data in an array. Instead of property names, it has index numbers:

```
costs = [420, 460, 230, 620];
```

ARRAYS OF OBJECTS
& OBJECTS IN ARRAYS

You can combine arrays and objects to create complex data structures:
Arrays can store a series of objects (and remember their order).
Objects can also hold arrays (as values of their properties).

In an object, the order in which the properties appear is not important. In an array, the index numbers dictate the order of the properties. You will see more examples of these data structures in Chapter 12.

ARRAYS IN AN OBJECT

The property of any object can hold an array. On the left, each item on a hotel bill is stored separately in an array. To access the first charge for **room1** you would use:

```
costs.room1.items[0];
```

PROPERTY:	VALUE:
room1	items[420, 40, 10]
room2	items[460, 20, 20]
room3	items[230, 0, 0]
room4	items[620, 150, 60]

OBJECTS IN AN ARRAY

The value of any element in an array can be an object (written using the object literal syntax). Here, to access the phone charge for room three, you would use:

```
costs[2].phone;
```

INDEX NUMBER:	VALUE:
0	{accom: 420, food: 40, phone: 10}
1	{accom: 460, food: 20, phone: 20}
2	{accom: 230, food: 0, phone: 0}
3	{accom: 620, food: 150, phone: 60}

WHAT ARE BUILT-IN OBJECTS?

Browsers come with a set of built-in objects that represent things like the browser window and the current web page shown in that window. These built-in objects act like a toolkit for creating interactive web pages.

The objects *you* create will usually be specifically written to suit *your* needs. They model the data used within, or contain functionality needed by, your script. Whereas, the built-in objects contain functionality commonly needed by many scripts.

As soon as a web page has loaded into the browser, these objects are available to use in your scripts.

These built-in objects help you get a wide range of information such as the width of the browser window, the content of the main heading in the page, or the length of text a user entered into a form field.

You access their properties or methods using dot notation, just like you would access the properties or methods of an object you had written yourself.

The first thing you need to do is get to know what tools are available. You can imagine that your new toolkit has three compartments:

1
BROWSER OBJECT MODEL

The Browser Object Model contains objects that represent the current browser window or tab. It contains objects that model things like browser history and the device's screen.

2
DOCUMENT OBJECT MODEL

The Document Object Model uses objects to create a representation of the current page. It creates a new object for each element (and each individual section of text) within the page.

3
GLOBAL JAVASCRIPT OBJECTS

The global JavaScript objects represent things that the JavaScript language needs to create a model of. For example, there is an object that deals only with dates and times.

WHAT DOES THIS SECTION COVER?

You have already seen how to access the properties and methods of an object, so the purpose of this section is to let you know:

- What built-in objects are available to you
- What their main properties and methods do

There will be a few examples in the remaining part of this chapter to ensure you know how to use them. Then, throughout the rest of the entire book, you will see many practical examples of how they are used in a range of situations.

WHAT IS AN OBJECT MODEL?

You have seen that an object can be used to create a model of something from the real world using data.

An **object model** is a group of objects, each of which represent related things from the real world. Together they form a model of something larger.

Two pages back, it was noted that an array can hold a set of objects, or that the property of an object could be an array. It is also possible for the property of an object to be another object. When an object is nested inside another object, you may hear it referred to as a child object.

THREE GROUPS OF BUILT-IN OBJECTS

USING BUILT-IN OBJECTS:

The three sets of built-in objects each offer a different range of tools that help you write scripts for web pages.

Chapter 5 is dedicated to the Document Object Model because it is needed to access and update the contents of a web page.

The other two sets of objects will be introduced in this chapter, and then you will see them used throughout the rest of the book.

This book will teach you how to use these built-in objects and what type of information you can get from each one. You will also see examples that use many of their most popular features.

We do not have space to exhaustively document every object in each of these models in this book, so you can find a list of links to online resources at: http://javascriptbook.com/resources

BROWSER OBJECT MODEL

The Browser Object Model creates a model of the browser tab or window.

The topmost object is the `window` object, which represents current browser window or tab. Its child objects represent other browser features.

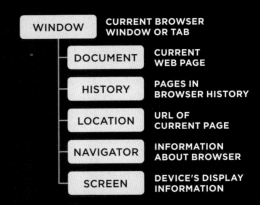

WINDOW	CURRENT BROWSER WINDOW OR TAB
DOCUMENT	CURRENT WEB PAGE
HISTORY	PAGES IN BROWSER HISTORY
LOCATION	URL OF CURRENT PAGE
NAVIGATOR	INFORMATION ABOUT BROWSER
SCREEN	DEVICE'S DISPLAY INFORMATION

EXAMPLES

The `window` object's `print()` method will cause the browser's print dialog box to be shown:
`window.print();`

The `screen` object's `width` property will let you find the width of the device's screen in pixels:
`window.screen.width;`

You meet the `window` object on p124 along with some properties of the `screen` and `history` objects.

DOCUMENT OBJECT MODEL

The Document Object Model (DOM) creates a model of the current web page.

The topmost object is the **document** object, which represents the page as a whole. Its child objects represent other items on the page.

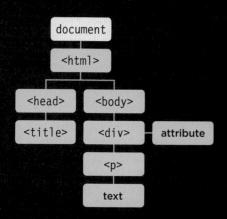

GLOBAL JAVASCRIPT OBJECTS

The global objects do not form a single model. They are a group of individual objects that relate to different parts of the JavaScript language.

The names of the global objects usually start with a capital letter, e.g., the **String** and **Date** objects.

These objects represent basic data types:

STRING	FOR WORKING WITH STRING VALUES
NUMBER	FOR WORKING WITH NUMERIC VALUES
BOOLEAN	FOR WORKING WITH BOOLEAN VALUES

These objects help deal with real-world concepts:

DATE	TO REPRESENT AND HANDLE DATES
MATH	FOR WORKING WITH NUMBERS AND CALCULATIONS
REGEX	FOR MATCHING PATTERNS WITHIN STRINGS OF TEXT

EXAMPLES

The **document** object's **getElementById()** method gets an element by the value of its **id** attribute:
`document.getElementById('one');`

The **document** object's **lastModified** property will tell you the date that the page was last updated:
`document.lastModified;`

You meet the **document** object on p126.
Chapter 5 goes into this object model in depth.

EXAMPLES

The **String** object's **toUpperCase()** method makes all letters in the following variable uppercase:
`hotel.toUpperCase();`

The **Math** object's **PI** property will return the value of pi:
`Math.PI();`

You meet the **String**, **Number**, **Date**, and **Math** objects later in this chapter.

THE BROWSER OBJECT MODEL: THE WINDOW OBJECT

The **window** object represents the current browser window or tab. It is the topmost object in the Browser Object Model, and it contains other objects that tell you about the browser.

Here are a selection of the **window** object's properties and methods. You can also see some properties of the **screen** and **history** objects (which are children of the **window** object).

PROPERTY	DESCRIPTION
window.innerHeight	Height of window (excluding browser chrome/user interface) (in pixels)
window.innerWidth	Width of window (excluding browser chrome/user interface) (in pixels)
window.pageXOffset	Distance document has been scrolled horizontally (in pixels)
window.pageYOffset	Distance document has been scrolled vertically (in pixels)
window.screenX	X-coordinate of pointer, relative to top left corner of screen (in pixels)
window.screenY	Y-coordinate of pointer, relative to top left corner of screen (in pixels)
window.location	Current URL of **window** object (or local file path)
window.document	Reference to **document** object, which is used to represent the current page contained in window
window.history	Reference to **history** object for browser window or tab, which contains details of the pages that have been viewed in that window or tab
window.history.length	Number of items in **history** object for browser window or tab
window.screen	Reference to **screen** object
window.screen.width	Accesses **screen** object and finds value of its **width** property (in pixels)
window.screen.height	Accesses **screen** object and finds value of its **height** property (in pixels)

METHOD	DESCRIPTION
window.alert()	Creates dialog box with message (user must click OK button to close it)
window.open()	Opens new browser window with URL specified as parameter (if browser has pop-up blocking software installed, this method may not work)
window.print()	Tells browser that user wants to print contents of current page (acts like user has clicked a print option in the browser's user interface)

USING THE BROWSER OBJECT MODEL

Here, data about the browser is collected from the `window` object and its children, stored in the `msg` variable, and shown in the page. The `+=` operator adds data onto the end of the `msg` variable.

1. Two of the `window` object's properties, `innerWidth` and `innerHeight`, show width and height of the browser window.

2. Child objects are stored as properties of their parent object. So dot notation is used to access them, just like you would access any other property of that object.

In turn, to access the properties of the child object, another dot is used between the child object's name and its properties, e.g., `window.history.length`

3. The element whose `id` attribute has a value of `info` is selected, and the message that has been built up to this point is written into the page.

See p228 for notes on using `innerHTML` because it can be a security risk if it is not used correctly.

See p228 for notes on using

```javascript
var msg = '<h2>browser window</h2><p>width: ' + window.innerWidth + '</p>';
msg += '<p>height: ' + window.innerHeight + '</p>';
msg += '<h2>history</h2><p>items: ' + window.history.length + '</p>';
msg += '<h2>screen</h2><p>width: ' + window.screen.width + '</p>';
msg += '<p>height: ' + window.screen.height + '</p>';
var el = document.getElementById('info');
el.innerHTML = msg;
alert('Current page: ' + window.location);
```

RESULT

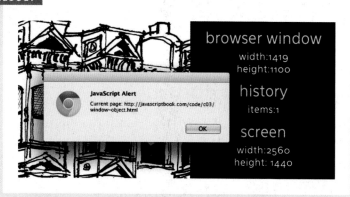

4. The `window` object's `alert()` method is used to create a dialog box shown on top of the page. It is known as an **alert box**. Although this is a method of the `window` object, you may see it used on its own (as shown here) because the `window` object is treated as the default object if none is specified. (Historically, the `alert()` method was used to display warnings to users. These days there are better ways to provide feedback.)

THE DOCUMENT OBJECT MODEL: THE DOCUMENT OBJECT

The topmost object in the Document Object Model (or DOM) is the document object. It represents the web page loaded into the current browser window or tab. You meet its child objects in Chapter 5.

Here are some properties of the document object, which tell you about the current page.

As you will see in Chapter 5, the DOM also creates an object for each element on the page.

PROPERTY	DESCRIPTION
document.title	Title of current document
document.lastModified	Date on which document was last modified
document.URL	Returns string containing URL of current document
document.domain	Returns domain of current document

The DOM is vital to accessing and amending the contents of the current web page.

The following are a few of the methods that select content or update the content of a page.

METHOD	DESCRIPTION
document.write()	Writes text to document (see restrictions on p226)
document.getElementById()	Returns element, if there is an element with the value of the id attribute that matches (full description see p195)
document.querySelectorAll()	Returns list of elements that match a CSS selector, which is specified as a parameter (see p202)
document.createElement()	Creates new element (see p222)
document.createTextNode()	Creates new text node (see p222)

USING THE DOCUMENT OBJECT

This example gets information about the page, and then adds that information to the footer.

1. The details about the page are collected from properties of the `document` object.

These details are stored inside a variable called `msg`, along with HTML markup to display the information. Again, the `+=` operator adds the new value onto the existing content of the `msg` variable.

2. You have seen the `document` object's `getElementById()` method in several examples so far. It selects an element from the page using the value of its `id` attribute. You will see this method in more depth on p195.

JAVASCRIPT   c03/js/document-object.js

```
var msg = '<p><b>page title: </b>' + document.title + '<br />';
msg += '<b>page address: </b>' + document.URL + '<br />';
msg += '<b>last modified: </b>' + document.lastModified + '</p>';

var el = document.getElementById('footer');
el.innerHTML = msg;
```

RESULT

page title: TravelWorthy
page address: http://javascriptbook.com/code/c03/document-object.html
last modified: 03/10/2014 14:46:23

See p228 for notes on using `innerHTML` because it can be a security risk if it is not used correctly.

The URL will look very different if you run this page locally rather than on a web server. It will likely begin with `file:///` rather than with `http://`.

GLOBAL OBJECTS: STRING OBJECT

Whenever you have a value that is a string, you can use the properties and methods of the `String` object on that value. This example stores the phrase "Home sweet home " in a variable.

```
var saying = 'Home sweet home ';
```

These properties and methods are often used to work with text stored in variables or objects.

On the right-hand page, note how the variable name (`saying`) is followed by a dot, then the property or method that is being demonstrated (like the name of an object is followed by a dot and its properties or methods).

This is why the `String` object is known as both a **global object**, because it works anywhere within your script, and a **wrapper object** because it acts like a wrapper around any value that is a string – you can use this object's properties and methods on any value that is a string.

The `length` property counts the number of "code units" in a string. In the majority of cases, one character uses one code unit, and most programmers use it like this. But some of the rarely used characters take up two code units.

PROPERTY	DESCRIPTION
`length`	Returns number of characters in the string in most cases (see note bottom-left)

METHOD	DESCRIPTION
`toUpperCase()`	Changes string to uppercase characters
`toLowerCase()`	Changes string to lowercase characters
`charAt()`	Takes an index number as a parameter, and returns the character found at that position
`indexOf()`	Returns index number of the first time a character or set of characters is found within the string
`lastIndexOf()`	Returns index number of the last time a character or set of characters is found within the string
`substring()`	Returns characters found between two index numbers where the character for the first index number is included and the character for the last index number is not included
`split()`	When a character is specified, it splits the string each time it is found, then stores each individual part in an array
`trim()`	Removes whitespace from start and end of string
`replace()`	Like find and replace, it takes one value that should be found, and another to replace it (by default, it only replaces the first match it finds)

Each character in a string is automatically given a number, called an **index number**. Index numbers always start at zero and not one (just like for items in an array).

EXAMPLE		RESULT
saying.length;	Home sweet home	16

EXAMPLE		RESULT
saying.toUpperCase();	Home sweet home	'HOME SWEET HOME '
saying.toLowerCase();	Home sweet home	'home sweet home '
saying.charAt(12);	Home sweet home	'o'
saying.indexOf('ee');	Home sweet home	7
saying.lastIndexOf('e');	Home sweet home	14
saying.substring(8,14);	Home sweet home	'et hom'
saying.split(' ');	Home sweet home	['Home', 'sweet', 'home', '']
saying.trim();	Home sweet home	'Home sweet home'
saying.replace('me','w');	Home sweet home	'How sweet home '

WORKING WITH STRINGS

This example demonstrates the `length` property and many of the `string` object's methods shown on the previous page.

1. This example starts by storing the phrase `"Home sweet home "` in a variable called `saying`.

2. The next line tells you how many characters are in the string using the `length` property of the `String` object and stores the result in a variable called `msg`.
3. This is followed by examples showing several of the `String` object's methods.

The name of the variable (`saying`) is followed by a dot, then the property or method that is being demonstrated (in the same way that the other objects in this chapter used the dot notation to indicate a property or method of an object).

```
JAVASCRIPT                                            c03/js/string-object.js

(1) var saying = 'Home sweet home ';
(2) var msg = '<h2>length</h2><p>' + saying.length + '</p>';
    msg += '<h2>uppercase</h2><p>' + saying.toUpperCase() + '</p>';
    msg += '<h2>lowercase</h2><p>' + saying.toLowerCase() + '</p>';
    msg += '<h2>character index: 12</h2><p>' + saying.charAt(12) + '</p>';
(3) msg += '<h2>first ee</h2><p>' + saying.indexOf('ee') + '</p>';
    msg += '<h2>last e</h2><p>' + saying.lastIndexOf('e') + '</p>';
    msg += '<h2>character index: 8-14</h2><p>' + saying.substring(8, 14) + '</p>';
    msg += '<h2>replace</h2><p>' + saying.replace('me', 'w') + '</p>';

(4) var el = document.getElementById('info');
    el.innerHTML = msg;
```

RESULT

4. The final two lines select the element with an `id` attribute whose value is `info` and then add the value of the `msg` variable inside that element.

(Remember, security issues with using the `innerHTML` property are discussed on p228.)

DATA TYPES REVISITED

In JavaScript there are six data types:
Five of them are described as simple (or primitive) data types.
The sixth is the object (and is referred to as a complex data type).

SIMPLE OR PRIMITIVE DATA TYPES

JavaScript has five **simple** (or **primitive**) data types:

1. **String**
2. **Number**
3. **Boolean**
4. **Undefined** (a variable that has been declared, but no value has been assigned to it yet)
5. **Null** (a variable with no value – it may have had one at some point, but no longer has a value)

As you have seen, both the web browser and the current document can be modeled using objects (and objects can have methods and properties).

But it can be confusing to discover that a simple value (like a string, a number, or a Boolean) can have methods and properties. Under the hood, JavaScript treats every variable as an object in its own right.

String: If a variable, or the property of an object, contains a string, you can use the properties and methods of the String object on it.

Number: If a variable, or property of an object stores a number, you can use the properties and methods of the Number object on it (see next page).

Boolean: There is a Boolean object. It is rarely used.

(Undefined and null values do not have objects.)

COMPLEX DATA TYPE

JavaScript also defines a complex data type:

6. **Object**

Under the hood, arrays and functions are considered types of objects.

ARRAYS ARE OBJECTS

As you saw on p118, an array is a set of key/value pairs (just like any other object). But you do not specify the name in the key/value pair of an array – it is an index number.

Like other objects, arrays have properties and methods. On p72 you saw that arrays have a property called length, which tells you how many items are in that array. There is also a set of methods you can use with any array to add items to it, remove items from it, or reorder its contents. You will meet those methods in Chapter 12.

FUNCTIONS ARE OBJECTS

Technically, functions are also objects. But they have an additional feature: they are callable, which means you can tell the interpreter when you want to execute the statements that it contains.

GLOBAL OBJECTS: NUMBER OBJECT

Whenever you have a value that is a number, you can use the methods and properties of the **Number** object on it.

These methods are helpful when dealing with a range of applications from financial calculations to animations.

Many calculations involving currency (such as tax rates) will need to be rounded to a specific number of decimal places.

Or, in an animation, you might want to specify that certain elements should be evenly spaced out across the page.

METHOD	DESCRIPTION
isNaN()	Checks if the value is not a number
toFixed()	Rounds to specified number of decimal places (returns a string)
toPrecision()	Rounds to total number of places (returns a string)
toExponential()	Returns a string representing the number in exponential notation

COMMONLY USED TERMS:

- An **integer** is a whole number (not a fraction).
- A **real number** is a number that can contain a fractional part.
- A **floating point number** is a real number that uses decimals to represent a fraction. The term *floating point* refers to the decimal point.
- **Scientific notation** is a way of writing numbers that are too big or too small to be conveniently written in decimal form. For example: 3,750,000,000 can be represented as 3.75×10^9 or 3.75e+12.

WORKING WITH DECIMAL NUMBERS

As with the String object, the properties and methods of the Number object can be used with with any value that is a number.

1. In this example, a number is stored in a variable called **originalNumber**, and it is then rounded up or down using two different techniques.

In both cases, you need to indicate how many digits you want to round to. This is provided as a parameter in the parentheses for that method.

c03/js/number-object.js

```
① var originalNumber = 10.23456;

   var msg = '<h2>original number</h2><p>' + originalNumber + '</p>';
② msg += '<h2>3 decimal places</h2><p>' + originalNumber.toFixed(3); + '</p>';
③ msg += '<h2>3 digits</h2><p>' + originalNumber.toPrecision(3) + '</p>';
   var el = document.getElementById('info');
   el.innerHTML = msg;
```

RESULT

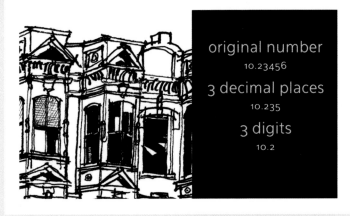

original number
10.23456

3 decimal places
10.235

3 digits
10.2

2. **originalNumber.toFixed(3)** will round the number stored in the variable **originalNumber** to three decimal places. (The number of decimal places is specified in the parentheses.) It will return the number as a string. It returns a string because fractions cannot always be accurately represented using floating point numbers.

2. **toPrecision(3)** uses the number in parentheses to indicate the total number of digits the number should have. It will also return the number as a string. (It may return a scientific notation if there are more digits than the specified number of positions.)

GLOBAL OBJECTS: MATH OBJECT

The `Math` object has properties and methods for mathematical constants and functions.

PROPERTY	DESCRIPTION
`Math.PI`	Returns pi (approximately 3.14159265359)

METHOD	DESCRIPTION
`Math.round()`	Rounds number to the nearest integer
`Math.sqrt(n)`	Returns square root of positive number, e.g., `Math.sqrt(9)` returns 3
`Math.ceil()`	Rounds number up to the nearest integer
`Math.floor()`	Rounds number down to the nearest integer
`Math.random()`	Generates a random number between 0 (inclusive) and 1 (not inclusive)

Because it is known as a **global object**, you can just use the name of the `Math` object followed by the property or method you want to access.

Typically you will then store the resulting number in a variable. This object also has many trigonometric functions such as `sin()`, `cos()`, and `tan()`.

The trigonometric functions return angles in radians which can then be converted into degrees if you divide the number by (pi/ 180).

MATH OBJECT TO CREATE RANDOM NUMBERS

This example is designed to generate a random whole number between 1 and 10.

The Math object's random() method generates a random number between 0 and 1 (with many decimal places).

To get a random whole number between 1 and 10, you need to multiply the randomly generated number by 10.

This number will still have many decimal places, so you can round it down to the nearest integer.

The floor() method is used to specifically round a number down (rather than up or down).

This will give you a value between 0 and 9. You then add 1 to make it a number between 1 and 10.

c03/js/math-object.js

```javascript
var randomNum = Math.floor((Math.random() * 10) + 1);

var el = document.getElementById('info');
el.innerHTML = '<h2>random number</h2><p>' + randomNum + '</p>';
```

RESULT

random number
7

If you used the round() method instead of the floor() method, the numbers 1 and 10 would be chosen around half of the number of times that 2-9 would be chosen.

Anything between 1.5 and 1.999 would get rounded up to 2, and anything between 9 and 9.5 would be rounded down to 9.

Using the floor() method ensures that the number is always rounded down to the nearest integer, and you can then add 1 to ensure the number is between 1 and 10.

CREATING AN INSTANCE OF THE DATE OBJECT

In order to work with dates, you create an instance of the **Date** object. You can then specify the time and date that you want it to represent.

To create a **Date** object, use the **Date()** object constructor. The syntax is the same for creating any object with a constructor function (see p108). You can use it to create more than one **Date** object.

By default, when you create a **Date** object it will hold today's date and the current time. If you want it to store another date, you must explicitly specify the date and time you want it to hold.

VARIABLE NAME   NEW KEYWORD

```
var today = new Date();
```

VARIABLE DECLARATION   ASSIGNMENT OPERATOR   DATE OBJECT CONSTRUCTOR

You can think of the above as creating a variable called **today** that holds a number. This is because in JavaScript, dates are stored as a number: specifically the number of milliseconds since midnight on January 1, 1970.

Note that the current date / time is determined by the computer's clock. If the user is in a different time zone than you, their day may start earlier or later than yours. Also, if the internal clock on their computer has the wrong date or time, the **Date** object could reflect this by holding the wrong date.

The **Date()** object constructor tells the JavaScript interpreter that this variable is a date, and this in turn allows you to use the **Date** object's methods to set and retrieve dates and times from this **Date** object (see right-hand page for a list of methods).

You can set the date and/or time using any of the following formats (or methods shown on the right):

```
var dob = new Date(1996, 11, 26, 15, 45, 55);
var dob = new Date('Dec 26, 1996 15:45:55');
var dob = new Date(1996, 11, 26);
```

GLOBAL OBJECTS: DATE OBJECT (AND TIME)

Once you have created a `Date` object, the following methods let you set and retrieve the time and date that it represents.

METHOD		DESCRIPTION
`getDate()`	`setDate()`	Returns / sets the day of the month (1-31)
`getDay()`		Returns the day of the week (0-6)
`getFullYear()`	`setFullYear()`	Returns / sets the year (4 digits)
`getHours()`	`setHours()`	Returns / sets the hour (0-23)
`getMilliseconds()`	`setMilliseconds()`	Returns / sets the milliseconds (0-999)
`getMinutes()`	`setMinutes()`	Returns / sets the minutes (0-59)
`getMonth()`	`setMonth()`	Returns / sets the month (0-11)
`getSeconds()`	`setSeconds()`	Returns / sets the seconds (0-59)
`getTime()`	`setTime()`	Number of milliseconds since January 1, 1970, 00:00:00 UTC (Coordinated Universal Time) and a negative number for any time before
`getTimezoneOffset()`		Returns time zone offset in mins for locale
`toDateString()`		Returns "date" as a human-readable string
`toTimeString()`		Returns "time" as a human-readable string
`toString()`		Returns a string representing the specified date

The `toDateString()` method will display the date in the following format: `Wed Apr 16 1975`.

If you want to display the date in another way, you can construct a different date format using the individual methods listed above to represent the individual parts: day, date, month, year.

`toTimeString()` shows the time. Several programming languages specify dates in milliseconds since midnight on Jan 1, 1970. This is known as Unix time.

A visitor's location may affect time zones and language spoken. Programmers use the term **locale** to refer to this kind of location-based information.

The `Date` object does not store the names of days or months as they vary between languages.

Instead, it uses a number from 0 to 6 for the days of the week and 0 to 11 for the months.

To show their names, you need to create an array to hold them (see p143).

CREATING A DATE OBJECT

1. In this example, a new **Date** object is created using the **Date()** object constructor It is called **today**.

If you do not specify a date when creating a **Date** object, it will contain the date and time when the JavaScript interpreter encounters that line of code.

Once you have an instance of the **Date** object (holding the current date and time), you can use any of its properties or methods.

c03/js/date-object.js

```
① var today = new Date();
② var year = today.getFullYear();

③ var el = document.getElementById('footer');
   el.innerHTML = '<p>Copyright &copy;' + year + '</p>';
```

RESULT

Copyright ©2014

2. In this example, you can see that **getFullYear()** is used to return the year of the date being stored in the **Date** object.

3. In this case, it is being used to write the current year in a copyright statement.

WORKING WITH DATES & TIMES

To specify a date and time, you can use this format:

```
YYYY, MM, DD, HH, MM, SS
1996, 03, 16, 15, 45, 55
```

This represents 3:45pm and 55 seconds on April 16, 1996.

The order and syntax for this is:

Year	four digits
Month	0-11 (Jan is 0)
Day	1-31
Hour	0-23
Minutes	0-59
Seconds	0-59
Milliseconds	0-999

Another way to format the date and time is like this:

```
MMM DD, YYYY HH:MM:SS
Apr 16, 1996 15:45:55
```

You can omit the time portion if you do not need it.

c03/js/date-object-difference.js

JAVASCRIPT

```javascript
 ⌈ var today = new Date();
①⟨ var year = today.getFullYear();
 ⌊ var est = new Date('Apr 16, 1996 15:45:55');
② var difference = today.getTime() - est.getTime();
③ difference = (difference / 31556900000);

   var elMsg = document.getElementById('message');
   elMsg.textContent = Math.floor(difference) + ' years of online travel advice';
```

RESULT

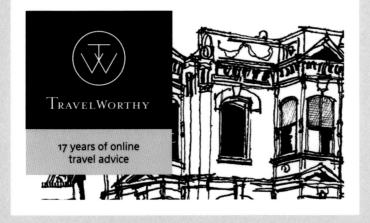

TRAVELWORTHY

17 years of online travel advice

1. In this example, you can see a date being set in the past.

2. If you try to find the difference between two dates, you will end up with a result in milliseconds.

3. To get the difference in days/weeks/years, you divide this number by the number of milliseconds in a day/week/year.

Here the number is divided by 31,556,900,000 – the number of milliseconds in a year (that is not a leap year).

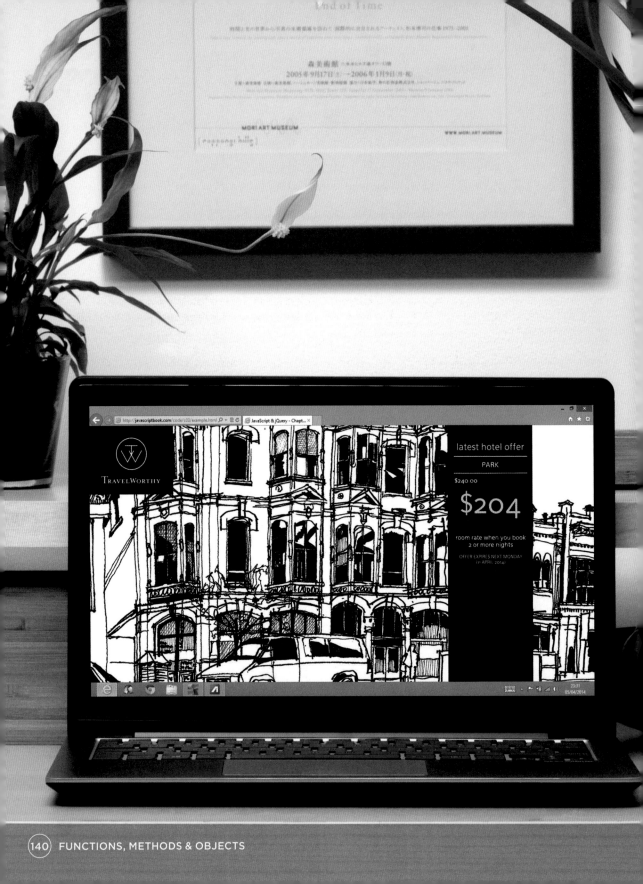

EXAMPLE
FUNCTIONS, METHODS & OBJECTS

This example is split into two parts. The first shows you the details about the hotel, room rate, and offer rate. The second part indicates when the offer expires.

All of the code is placed inside an immediately invoked function expression (IIFE) to ensure any variable names used in the script do not clash with variable names used in other scripts.

The first part of the script creates a `hotel` object; it has three properties (the hotel name, room rate, and percentage discount being offered), plus a method to calculate the offer price which is shown to the user.

The details of the discount are written into the page using information from this `hotel` object. To ensure that the discounted rate is shown with two decimal places (like most prices are shown) the `.toFixed()` method of the `Number` object is used.

The second part of the script shows that the offer will expire in seven days. It does this using a function called `offerExpires()`. The date currently set on the user's computer is passed as an argument to the `offerExpires()` function so that it can calculate when the offer ends.

Inside the function, a new `Date` object is created; and seven days is added to today's date. The `Date` object represents the days and months as numbers (starting at 0) so - to show the name of the day and month - two arrays are created storing all possible day and month names. When the message is written, it retrieves the appropriate day/month from those arrays.

The message to show the expiry date is built up inside a variable called `expiryMsg`. The code that calls the `offerExpires()` function and displays the message is at the end of the script. It selects the element where the message should appear and updates its content using the `innerHTML` property, which you will meet in Chapter 5.

EXAMPLE
FUNCTIONS, METHODS & OBJECTS

```javascript
/* The script is placed inside an immediately invoked function expression
   which helps protect the scope of variables */

(function() {

  // PART ONE: CREATE HOTEL OBJECT AND WRITE OUT THE OFFER DETAILS

  // Create a hotel object using object literal syntax
  var hotel = {
    name: 'Park',
    roomRate: 240, // Amount in dollars
    discount: 15,  // Percentage discount
    offerPrice: function() {
      var offerRate = this.roomRate * ((100 - this.discount) / 100);
      return offerRate;
    }
  }

  // Write out the hotel name, standard rate, and the special rate
  var hotelName, roomRate, specialRate;                // Declare variables

  hotelName = document.getElementById('hotelName');    // Get elements
  roomRate = document.getElementById('roomRate');
  specialRate = document.getElementById('specialRate');

  hotelName.textContent = hotel.name;                  // Write hotel name
  roomRate.textContent = '$' + hotel.roomRate.toFixed(2); // Write room rate
  specialRate.textContent = '$' + hotel.offerPrice();  // Write offer price
```

If you read the comments in the code, you can see how this example works.

EXAMPLE
FUNCTIONS, METHODS & OBJECTS

```javascript
// PART TWO: CALCULATE AND WRITE OUT THE EXPIRY DETAILS FOR THE OFFER
var expiryMsg; // Message displayed to users
var today;      // Today's date
var elEnds;     // The element that shows the message about the offer ending

function offerExpires(today) {
  // Declare variables within the function for local scope
  var weekFromToday, day, date, month, year, dayNames, monthNames;
  // Add 7 days time (added in milliseconds)
  weekFromToday = new Date(today.getTime() + 7 * 24 * 60 * 60 * 1000);
  // Create arrays to hold the names of days / months
  dayNames = ['Sunday', 'Monday', 'Tuesday', 'Wednesday', 'Thursday',
  'Friday', 'Saturday'];
  monthNames = ['January', 'February', 'March', 'April', 'May', 'June',
  'July', 'August', 'September', 'October', 'November', 'December'];
  // Collect the parts of the date to show on the page
  day = dayNames[weekFromToday.getDay()];
  date = weekFromToday.getDate();
  month = monthNames[weekFromToday.getMonth()];
  year = weekFromToday.getFullYear();
  // Create the message
  expiryMsg = 'Offer expires next ';
  expiryMsg += day + ' <br />(' + date + ' ' + month + ' ' + year + ')';
  return expiryMsg;
}

today = new Date();                              // Put today's date in variable
elEnds = document.getElementById('offerEnds');   // Get the offerEnds element
elEnds.innerHTML = offerExpires(today);          // Add the expiry message

// Finish the immediately invoked function expression
}());
```

This symbol indicates that the code is wrapping from the previous line and should not contain line breaks.

This is a good demonstration of several concepts relating to date, but if the user has the wrong date on their computer (perhaps their clock is set incorrectly), it will not show a date seven days from now – it will show a date seven days from the time the computer thinks it is.

SUMMARY
FUNCTIONS, METHODS & OBJECTS

▶ Functions allow you to group a set of related statements together that represent a single task.

▶ Functions can take parameters (information required to do their job) and may return a value.

▶ An object is a series of variables and functions that represent something from the world around you.

▶ In an object, variables are known as properties of the object; functions are known as methods of the object.

▶ Web browsers implement objects that represent both the browser window and the document loaded into the browser window.

▶ JavaScript also has several built-in objects such as `String`, `Number`, `Math`, and `Date`. Their properties and methods offer functionality that help you write scripts.

▶ Arrays and objects can be used to create complex data sets (and both can contain the other).

4

DECISIONS & LOOPS

Looking at a flowchart (for all but the most basic scripts), the code can take more than one path, which means the browser runs different code in different situations. In this chapter, you will learn how to create and control the flow of data in your scripts to handle different situations.

Scripts often need to behave differently depending upon how the user interacts with the web page and/or the browser window itself. To determine which path to take, programmers often rely upon the following three concepts:

EVALUATIONS
You can analyze values in your scripts to determine whether or note they match expected results.

DECISIONS
Using the results of evaluations, you can decide which path your script should go down.

LOOPS
There are also many occasions where you will want to perform the same set of steps repeatedly.

DECISION MAKING

There are often several places in a script where decisions are made that determine which lines of code should be run next. Flowcharts can help you plan for these occasions.

In a flowchart, the diamond shape represents a point where a decision must be made and the code can take one of two different paths. Each path is made up of a different set of tasks, which means you have to write different code for each situation.

In order to determine which path to take, you set a **condition**. For example, you can check that one value is equal to another, greater than another, or less than another. If the condition returns **true**, you take one path; if it is **false**, you take another path.

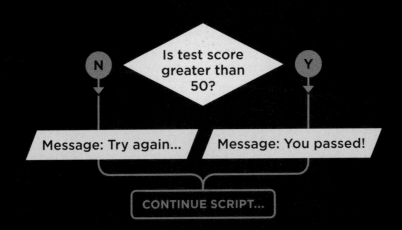

In the same way that there are operators to do basic math, or to join two strings, there are **comparison operators** that allow you to compare values and test whether a condition is met or not.

Examples of comparison operators include the greater than (**>**) and less than (**<**) symbols, and double equals sign (**==**) which checks whether two values are the same.

EVALUATING CONDITIONS & CONDITIONAL STATEMENTS

There are two components to a decision:
1: An expression is evaluated, which returns a value
2: A conditional statement says what to do in a given situation

EVALUATION OF A CONDITION

In order to make a decision, your code checks the current status of the script. This is commonly done by comparing two values using a comparison operator which returns a value of **true** or **false**.

CONDITIONAL STATEMENTS

A conditional statement is based on a concept of if/then/else; *if* a condition is met, *then* your code executes one or more statements, *else* your code does something different (or just skips the step).

CONDITION

```
if (score > 50) {
  document.write('You passed!');
} else {
  document.write('Try again...');
}
```

WHAT THIS IS SAYING:

if the condition returns **true**

execute the statements between the **first** set of curly brackets

otherwise

execute the statements between the **second** set of curly brackets

(You will also meet truthy and falsy values on p167. They are treated as if true or false.)

You can also have multiple conditions by combining two or more comparison operators. For example, you can check whether two conditions are both met, or if just one of several conditions is met.

Over the next few pages, you will meet several permutations of the **if...** statements, and also a statement called a **switch** statement. Collectively, these are known as **conditional** statements.

COMPARISON OPERATORS: EVALUATING CONDITIONS

You can evaluate a situation by comparing one value in the script to what you expect it might be. The result will be a Boolean: `true` or `false`.

IS EQUAL TO

This operator compares two values (numbers, strings, or Booleans) to see if they are the same.

`'Hello' == 'Goodbye'` returns `false`
because they are *not* the same string.
`'Hello' == 'Hello'` returns `true`
because they *are* the same string.

It is usually preferable to use the strict method:

IS NOT EQUAL TO

This operator compares two values (numbers, strings, or Booleans) to see if they are *not* the same.

`'Hello' != 'Goodbye'` returns `true`
because they are *not* the same string.
`'Hello' != 'Hello'` returns `false`
because they *are* the same string.

It is usually preferable to use the strict method:

STRICT EQUAL TO

This operator compares two values to check that both the data type and value are the same.

`'3' === 3` returns `false`
because they are *not* the same data type or value.
`'3' === '3'` returns `true`
because they *are* the same data type and value.

STRICT NOT EQUAL TO

This operator compares two values to check that both the data type and value are *not* the same.

`'3' !== 3` returns `true`
because they are *not* the same data type or value.
`'3' !== '3'` returns `false`
because they *are* the same data type and value.

Programmers refer to the testing or checking of a condition as **evaluating** the condition. Conditions can be much more complex than those shown here, but they usually result in a value of `true` or `false`.

There are a couple of notable exceptions:
i) Every value can be *treated* as true or false even if it is not a Boolean **true** or `false` value (see p167).
ii) In short-circuit evaluation, a condition might not need to run (see p169).

GREATER THAN

This operator checks if the number on the left is *greater than* the number on the right.

4 > 3 returns `true`
3 > 4 returns `false`

LESS THAN

This operator checks if the number on the left is *less than* the number on the right.

4 < 3 returns `false`
3 < 4 returns `true`

GREATER THAN OR EQUAL TO

This operator checks if the number on the left is *greater than or equal to* the number on the right.

4 >= 3 returns `true`
3 >= 4 returns `false`
3 >= 3 returns `true`

LESS THAN OR EQUAL TO

This operator checks if the number on the left is *less than or equal to* the number on the right.

4 <= 3 returns `false`
3 <= 4 returns `true`
3 <= 3 returns `true`

STRUCTURING COMPARISON OPERATORS

In any condition, there is usually one operator and two operands. The operands are placed on each side of the operator. They can be values or variables. You often see expressions enclosed in brackets.

ENCLOSING BRACKETS

$$(score >= pass)$$

OPERAND   COMPARISON   OPERAND
           OPERATOR

If you remember back to Chapter 2, this is an example of an **expression** because the condition resolves into a single value: in this case it will be either **true** or **false**.

The enclosing brackets are important when the expression is used as a condition in a comparison operator. But when you are assigning a value to a variable, they are not needed (see right-hand page).

USING COMPARISON OPERATORS

`c04/js/comparison-operator.js`

```javascript
var pass = 50;    // Pass mark
var score = 90;   // Score

// Check if the user has passed
var hasPassed = score >= pass;

// Write the message into the page
var el = document.getElementById('answer');
el.textContent = 'Level passed: ' + hasPassed;
```

RESULT

Level passed: true

At the most basic level, you can evaluate two variables using a comparison operator to return a true or false value.

In this example, a user is taking a test, and the script tells the user whether they have passed this round of the test.

The example starts by setting two variables:
1. pass to hold the pass mark
2. score to hold the users score

To see if the user has passed, a comparison operator checks whether score is greater than or equal to pass. The result will be true or false, and is stored in a variable called hasPassed. On the next line, the result is written to the screen.

The last two lines select the element whose id attribute has a value of answer, and then updates its contents. You will learn more about this technique in the next chapter.

USING EXPRESSIONS WITH COMPARISON OPERATORS

The operand does not have to be a single value or variable name.
An operand can be an *expression* (because each expression evaluates
into a single value).

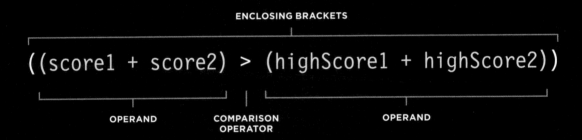

ENCLOSING BRACKETS

`((score1 + score2) > (highScore1 + highScore2))`

OPERAND   COMPARISON OPERATOR   OPERAND

COMPARING TWO EXPRESSIONS

In this example, there are two rounds to the test and the code will check if the user has achieved a new high score, beating the previous record.

The script starts by storing the user's scores for each round in variables. Then the highest scores for each round are stored in two more variables.

The comparison operator checks if the user's total score is greater than the highest score for the test and stores the result in a variable called comparison.

c04/js/comparison-operator-continued.js

JAVASCRIPT

```javascript
var score1 = 90;      // Round 1 score
var score2 = 95;      // Round 2 score
var highScore1 = 75; // Round 1 high score
var highScore2 = 95; // Round 2 high score

// Check if scores are higher than current high scores
var comparison = (score1 + score2) > (highScore1 + highScore2);

// Write the message into the page
var el = document.getElementById('answer');
el.textContent = 'New high score: ' + comparison;
```

RESULT

In the comparison operator, the operand on the left calculates the user's total score. The operand on the right adds together the highest scores for each round. The result is then added to the page.

When you assign the result of the comparison to a variable, you do not strictly need the containing parentheses (shown in white on the left-hand page).

Some programmers use them anyway to indicate that the code evaluates into a single value. Others only use containing parentheses when they form part of a condition.

LOGICAL OPERATORS

Comparison operators usually return single values of **true** or **false**. Logical operators allow you to compare the results of more than one comparison operator.

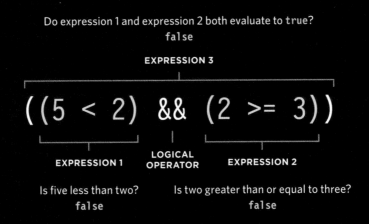

Do expression 1 and expression 2 both evaluate to **true**?
false

EXPRESSION 3

$$((5 < 2) \ \&\& \ (2 >= 3))$$

EXPRESSION 1

LOGICAL OPERATOR

EXPRESSION 2

Is five less than two?
false

Is two greater than or equal to three?
false

In this one line of code are three expressions, each of which will resolve to the value **true** or **false**.

The expressions on the left and the right both use comparison operators, and both return **false**.

The third expression uses a logical operator (rather than a comparison operator). The logical AND operator checks to see whether both expressions on either side of it return **true** (in this case they do not, so it evaluates to **false**).

LOGICAL AND

This operator tests more than one condition.

```
((2 < 5) && (3 >= 2))
returns true
```

If both expressions evaluate to true then the expression returns true. If just one of these returns false, then the expression will return false.

```
true  && true   returns true
true  && false  returns false
false && true   returns false
false && false  returns false
```

LOGICAL OR

This operator tests at least one condition.

```
((2 < 5) || (2 < 1))
returns true
```

If either expression evaluates to true, then the expression returns true. If both return false, then the expression will return false.

```
true  || true   returns true
true  || false  returns true
false || true   returns true
false || false  returns false
```

LOGICAL NOT

This operator takes a single Boolean value and inverts it.

```
!(2 < 1)
returns true
```

This reverses the state of an expression. If it was false (without the ! before it) it would return true. If the statement was true, it would return false.

```
!true   returns false
!false  returns true
```

SHORT-CIRCUIT EVALUATION

Logical expressions are evaluated **left** to **right**.
If the first condition can provide enough information to get the answer, then there is no need to evaluate the second condition.

```
false && anything
      ^
    it has found a false
```

There is no point continuing to determine the other result. They cannot both be true.

```
true || anything
   ^
    it has found a true
```

There is no point continuing because at least one of the values is true.

USING LOGICAL AND

In this example, a math test has two rounds. For each round there are two variables: one holds the user's score for that round; the other holds the pass mark for that round.

The logical AND is used to see if the user's score is greater than or equal to the pass mark in both of the rounds of the test. The result is stored in a variable called passBoth.

The example finishes off by letting the user know whether or not they have passed both rounds.

```
c04/js/logical-and.js                                          JAVASCRIPT

var score1 = 8;     // Round 1 score
var score2 = 8;     // Round 2 score
var pass1 = 6;      // Round 1 pass mark
var pass2 = 6;      // Round 2 pass mark

// Check whether user passed both rounds, store result in variable
var passBoth = (score1 >= pass1) && (score2 >= pass2);

// Create message
var msg = 'Both rounds passed: ' + passBoth;

// Write the message into the page
var el = document.getElementById('answer');
el.textContent = msg;
```

It is rare that you would ever write the Boolean result into the page (like we are doing here). As you will see later in the chapter, it is more likely that you would check a condition, and if it is true, run other statements.

RESULT

Both rounds passed:
true

USING LOGICAL OR & LOGICAL NOT

Here is the same test but this time using the logical OR operator to find out if the user has passed at least one of the two rounds. If they pass just one round, they do not need to retake the test.

Look at the numbers stored in the four variables at the start of the example. The user has passed both rounds, so the `minPass` variable will hold the Boolean value of `true`.

Next, the message is stored in a variable called `msg`. At the end of the message, the logical NOT will invert the result of the Boolean variable so it is `false`. It is then written into the page.

```javascript
var score1 = 8;    // Round 1 score
var score2 = 8;    // Round 2 score
var pass1 = 6;     // Round 1 pass mark
var pass2 = 6;     // Round 2 pass mark

// Check whether user passed one of the two rounds, store result in variable
var minPass = ((score1 >= pass1) || (score2 >= pass2));

// Create message
var msg = 'Resit required: ' + !(minPass);

// Write the message into the page
var el = document.getElementById('answer');
el.textContent = msg;
```

RESULT

Resit required: false

IF STATEMENTS

The **if** statement evaluates (or checks) a condition. If the condition evaluates to `true`, any statements in the subsequent code block are executed.

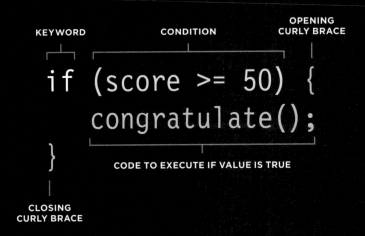

KEYWORD   CONDITION   OPENING CURLY BRACE

```
if (score >= 50) {
    congratulate();
}
```

CODE TO EXECUTE IF VALUE IS TRUE

CLOSING CURLY BRACE

If the condition evaluates to `true`, the following code block (the code in the next set of curly braces) is executed.

If the condition resolves to `false`, the statements in that code block are *not* run. (The script continues to run from the end of the next code block.)

USING IF STATEMENTS

```javascript
var score = 75;        // Score
var msg;               // Message

if (score >= 50) {  // If score is 50 or higher
  msg = 'Congratulations!';
  msg += ' Proceed to the next round.';
}
var el = document.getElementById('answer');
el.textContent = msg;
```

RESULT

Congratulations!
Proceed to the next
round.

```javascript
var score = 75;        // Score
var msg = '';          // Message

function congratulate() {
②    msg += 'Congratulations! ';
}

if (score >= 50) {  // If score is 50 or more
①  congratulate();
③  msg += 'Proceed to the next round.';
}
var el = document.getElementById('answer');
el.innerHTML = msg;
```

In this example, the if statement is checking if the value currently held in a variable called **score** is 50 or more.

In this case, the statement evaluates to **true** (because the score is 75, which is greater than 50). Therefore, the contents of the statements within the subsequent code block are run, creating a message that congratulates the user and tells them to proceed.

After the code block, the message is written to the page.

If the value of the **score** variable had been less than 50, the statements in the code block would not have run, and the code would have continued on to the next line after the code block.

On the left is an alternative version of the same example that demonstrates how lines of code do not always run in the order you expect them to. **If** the condition is met then:
1. The first statement in the code block calls the **congratulate()** function.
2. The code within the **congratulate()** function runs.
3. The second line within the **if** statement's code block runs.

IF...ELSE STATEMENTS

The **if...else** statement checks a condition.
If it resolves to `true` the first code block is executed.
If the condition resolves to `false` the second code block is run instead.

```
if (score >= 50) {
    congratulate();
}
else {
    encourage();
}
```

CODE TO EXECUTE IF VALUE IS TRUE

CODE TO EXECUTE IF VALUE IS FALSE

● CONDITIONAL STATEMENT ● CONDITION ● IF CODE BLOCK ● ELSE CODE BLOCK

USING IF...ELSE STATEMENTS

c04/js/if-else-statement.js

```javascript
var pass = 50;        // Pass mark
var score = 75;       // Current score
var msg;              // Message

// Select message to write based on score
if (score >= pass) {
  msg = 'Congratulations, you passed!';
} else {
  msg = 'Have another go!';
}

var el = document.getElementById('answer');
el.textContent = msg;
```

RESULT

Congratulations, you passed!

Here you can see that an `if...else` statement allows you to provide two sets of code:
1. one set if the condition evaluates to `true`
2. another set if the condition is `false`

In this test, there are two possible outcomes: a user can either get a score equal to or greater than the pass mark (which means they pass), or they can score less than the pass mark (which means they fail). One response is required for each eventuality. The response is then written to the page.

Note that the statements inside an `if` statement should be followed by a semicolon, but there is no need to place one after the closing curly brace of the code blocks.

An `if` statement only runs a set of statements if the condition is `true`:

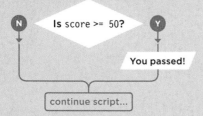

An `if...else` statement runs one set of code if the condition is `true` or a different set if it is `false`:

SWITCH STATEMENTS

A **switch** statement starts with a variable called the **switch value**. Each case indicates a possible value for this variable and the code that should run if the variable matches that value.

Here, the variable named `level` is the switch value. If the value of the `level` variable is the string One, then the code for the first case is executed. If it is Two, the second case is executed. If it is Three, the third case is executed. If it is none of these, the code for the `default` case is executed.

The entire statement lives in one code block (set of curly braces), and a colon separates the option from the statements that are to be run if the case matches the switch value.

At the end of each case is the **break** keyword. It tells the JavaScript interpreter that it has finished with this **switch** statement and to proceed to run any subsequent code that appears after it.

```
switch (level) {

    case 'One':
        title = 'Level 1';
        break;

    case 'Two':
        title = 'Level 2';
        break;

    case 'Three':
        title = 'Level 3';
        break;

    default:
        title = 'Test';
        break;

}
```

IF... ELSE

- There is no need to provide an `else` option. (You can just use an `if` statement.)
- With a series of `if` statements, they are all checked *even if* a match has been found (so it performs more slowly than `switch`).

VS.

SWITCH

- You have a **default** option that is run if none of the cases match.
- If a match is found, that code is run; then the **break** statement stops the rest of the `switch` statement running (providing better performance than multiple `if` statements).

USING SWITCH STATEMENTS

c04/js/switch-statement.js

```javascript
var msg;          // Message
var level = 2;    // Level

// Determine message based on level
switch (level) {
case 1:
    msg = 'Good luck on the first test';
    break;

case 2:
    msg = 'Second of three - keep going!';
    break;

case 3:
    msg = 'Final round, almost there!';
    break;

default:
    msg = 'Good luck!';
    break;
}

var el = document.getElementById('answer');
el.textContent = msg;
```

RESULT

Second of three -
keep going!

In this example, the purpose of the switch statement is to present the user with a different message depending on which level they are at. The message is stored in a variable called msg.

The variable called level contains a number indicating which level the user is on. This is then used as the switch value. (The switch value could also be an expression.)

In the following code block (inside the curly braces), there are three options for what the value of the level variable might be: the numbers 1, 2, or 3.

If the value of the level variable is the number 1, the value of the msg variable is set to 'Good luck on the first test'.

If the value is 2, it will read: 'Second of three - keep going!'

If the value is 3, the message will read: 'Final round, almost there!'

If no match is found, then the value of the msg variable is set to 'Good luck!'

Each case ends with the break keyword which will tell the JavaScript interpreter to skip the rest of this code block and continue onto the next.

TYPE COERCION & WEAK TYPING

If you use a data type JavaScript did not expect, it tries to make sense of the operation rather than report an error.

JavaScript can convert data types behind the scenes to complete an operation. This is known as **type coercion**. For example, a string `'1'` could be converted to a number 1 in the following expression: (`'1' > 0`). As a result, the above expression would evaluate to `true`.

JavaScript is said to use **weak typing** because the data type for a value can change. Some other languages require that you specify what data type each variable will be. They are said to use **strong typing**.

Type coercion can lead to unexpected values in your code (and also cause errors). Therefore, when checking if two values are equal, it is considered better to use strict equals operators `===` and `!==` rather than `==` and `!=` as these strict operators check that the value and data types match.

DATA TYPE	PURPOSE
string	Text
number	Number
Boolean	`true` or `false`
null	Empty value
undefined	Variable has been declared but not yet assigned a value

NaN is a value that is counted as a number. You may see it when a number is expected, but is not returned, e.g., (`'ten'/2`) results in NaN.

TRUTHY & FALSY VALUES

Due to type coercion, every value in JavaScript can be treated as if it were true or false; and this has some interesting side effects.

FALSY VALUES

VALUE	DESCRIPTION
var highScore = false;	The traditional Boolean false
var highScore = 0;	The number zero
var highScore = '';	Empty value
var highScore = 10/'score';	NaN (Not a Number)
var highScore;	A variable with no value assigned to it

Almost everything else evaluates to truthy...

TRUTHY VALUES

VALUE	DESCRIPTION
var highScore = true;	The traditional Boolean true
var highScore = 1;	Numbers other than zero
var highScore = 'carrot';	Strings with content
var highScore = 10/5;	Number calculations
var highScore = 'true';	true written as a string
var highScore = '0';	Zero written as a string
var highScore = 'false';	false written as a string

Falsy values are treated *as if* they are false. The table to the left shows a highScore variable with a series of values, all of which are falsy.

Falsy values can also be treated as the number 0.

Truthy values are treated *as if* they are true. Almost everything that is not in the falsy table can be treated as if it were true.

Truthy values can also be treated as the number 1.

In addition, the presence of an object or an array is usually considered truthy, too. This is commonly used when checking for the presence of an element in a page.

The next page will explain more about why these concepts are important.

CHECKING EQUALITY & EXISTENCE

Because the presence of an object or array can be considered truthy, it is often used to check for the existence of an element within a page.

A **unary operator** returns a result with just one operand. Here you can see an if statement checking for the presence of an element. If the element is found, the result is truthy, so the first set of code is run. If it is not found, the second set is run instead.

```
if (document.getElementById('header')) {
  // Found: do something
} else {
  // Not found: do something else
}
```

Those new to JavaScript often think the following would do the same:
`if (document.getElementById('header') == true)`
but `document.getElementById('header')` would return an object which is a truthy value but it is *not* equal to a Boolean value of true.

Because of type coercion, the strict equality operators === and !== result in fewer unexpected values than == and != do.

If you use == the following values can be considered equal: `false`, 0, and '' (empty string). However, they are not equivalent when using the strict operators.

EXPRESSION	RESULT
(false == 0)	true
(false === 0)	false
(false == '')	true
(false === '')	false
(0 == '')	true
(0 === '')	false

Although `null` and `undefined` are both falsy, they are not equal to anything other than themselves. Again, they are not equivalent when using strict operators.

EXPRESSION	RESULT
(undefined == null)	true
(null == false)	false
(undefined == false)	false
(null == 0)	false
(undefined == 0)	false
(undefined === null)	false

Although **NaN** is considered falsy, it is not equivalent to anything; it is not even equivalent to itself (since NaN is an undefinable number, two cannot be equal).

EXPRESSION	RESULT
(Nan == null)	false
(NaN == NaN)	false

SHORT CIRCUIT VALUES

Logical operators are processed left to right. They short-circuit (stop) as soon as they have a result – but they return the value that stopped the processing (not necessarily `true` or `false`).

On line 1, the variable `artist` is given a value of Rembrandt.
On line 2, if the variable `artist` has a value, then `artistA` will be given the same value as `artist` (because a non-empty string is truthy).

```
var artist = 'Rembrandt';
var artistA = (artist || 'Unknown');
```

If the string is empty (see below), `artistA` becomes a string `'Unknown'`.

```
var artist = '';
var artistA = (artist || 'Unknown');
```

You could even create an empty object if artist does not have a value:

```
var artist = '';
var artistA = (artist || {});
```

Logical operators will not always return `true` or `false`, because:

- They return the value that stopped processing.
- That value might have been treated as truthy or falsy although it was not a Boolean.

Programmers use this creatively (for example, to set values for variables or even create objects).

Here are three values. If any one of them is considered truthy, the code inside the `if` statement will execute. When the script encounters `valueB` in the logical operator, it will short circuit because the number 1 is considered truthy and the subsequent code block is executed.

```
valueA = 0;
valueB = 1;
valueC = 2;

if (valueA || valueB || valueC) {
  // Do something here
}
```

This technique could also be used to check for the existence of elements within a page, as shown on p168.

As soon as a truthy value is found, the remaining options are not checked. Therefore, experienced programmers often:

- Put the code most likely to return true *first* in OR operations, and false answers first in AND operations.
- Place the options requiring the most processing power last, just in case another value returns `true` and they do not need to be run.

Loops check a condition. If it returns **true**, a code block will run. Then the condition will be checked again and if it still returns **true**, the code block will run again. It repeats until the condition returns **false**. There are three common types of loops:

FOR

If you need to run code a specific number of times, use a **for** loop. (It is the most common loop.) In a **for** loop, the condition is usually a counter which is used to tell how many times the loop should run.

WHILE

If you do not know how many times the code should run, you can use a **while** loop. Here the condition can be something other than a counter, and the code will continue to loop for as long as the condition is **true**.

DO WHILE

The **do...while** loop is very similar to the **while** loop, but has one key difference: it will always run the statements inside the curly braces at least once, even if the condition evaluates to **false**.

KEYWORD
CONDITION (COUNTER)
OPENING CURLY BRACE

```
for (var i = 0; i < 10; i++) {
    document.write(i);
}
```

CODE TO EXECUTE DURING LOOP

CLOSING CURLY BRACE

This is a **for** loop. The condition is a counter that counts to ten. The result would write "0123456789" to the page

If the variable **i** is less than ten, the code inside the curly braces is executed. Then the counter is

The condition is checked again, if **i** is less than ten it runs again. The next three pages show how

LOOP COUNTERS

A **for** loop uses a counter as a condition.
This instructs the code to run a specified number of times.
Here you can see the condition is made up of three statements:

INITIALIZATION

Create a variable and set it to **0**. This variable is commonly called **i**, and it acts as the counter.

$$var\ i = 0;$$

The variable is only created the first time the loop is run.
(You may also see the variable called **index**, rather than just **i**.)

You will sometimes see this variable declared before the condition. The following is the same and it is mainly a preference of the coder.

```
var i;
for (i = 0; i < 10; i++) {
  // Code goes here
}
```

CONDITION

The loop should continue to run until the counter reaches a specified number.

$$i < 10;$$

The value of **i** was initially set to **0**, so in this case the loop will run 10 times before stopping.

The condition may also use a variable that holds a number. If a variable called **rounds** held the number of rounds in a test and the loop ran once for each round, the condition would be:

```
var rounds = 3;
i < (rounds);
```

UPDATE

Every time the loop has run the statements in the curly braces, it adds one to the counter.

$$i++$$

One is added to the counter using the increment (**++**) operator.

Another way of reading this is that it says, "Take the variable **i**, and add one using the **++** operator."

It is also possible for loops to count downwards using the decrement operator (**--**).

LOOPING

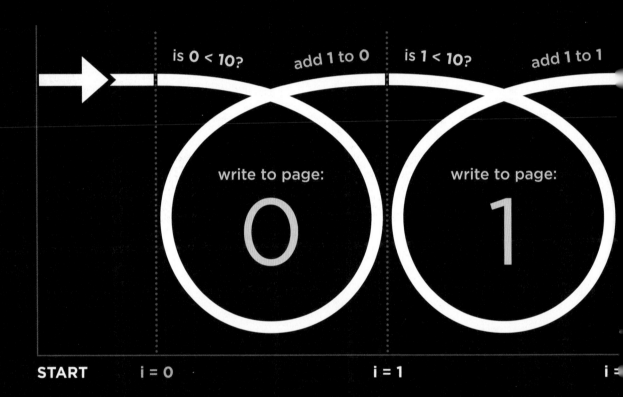

is **0 < 10?**   add 1 to 0   is **1 < 10?**   add 1 to 1

write to page:

0

write to page:

1

START   i = 0   i = 1   i =

The first time the loop is run, the variable **i** (the counter) is assigned a value of zero.

Every time the loop is run, the condition is checked. Is the variable **i** less than 10?

Then the code inside the loop (the statements between the curly brackets) is run.

```
for (var i = 0; i < 10; i++) {
    document.write(i);
}
```

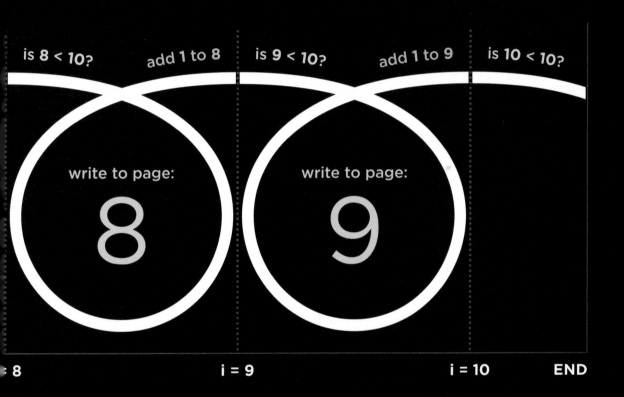

is 8 < 10?   add 1 to 8   is 9 < 10?   add 1 to 9   is 10 < 10?

write to page: write to page:

8   9

8   i = 9   i = 10   END

The variable **i** can be used inside the loop. Here it is used to write a number to the page.

When the statements have finished, the variable **i** is incremented by 1.

When the condition is no longer true, the loop ends. The script moves to the next line of code.

KEY LOOP CONCEPTS

Here are three points to consider when you are working with loops. Each is illustrated in examples on the following three pages.

KEYWORDS

You will commonly see these two keywords used with loops:

break

This keyword causes the termination of the loop and tells the interpreter to go onto the next statement of code outside of the loop. (You may also see it used in functions.)

continue

This keyword tells the interpreter to stop the current iteration, and then check the condition again. (If it is `true`, the code runs again.)

LOOPS & ARRAYS

Loops are very helpful when dealing with arrays if you want to run the same code for each item in the array.

For example, you might want to write the value of each item stored in an array into the page.

You may not know how many items will be in an array when writing a script, but, when the code runs, it can check the total number of items in a loop. That figure can then be used in the counter to control how many times a set of statements is run.

Once the loop has run the right number of times, the loop stops.

PERFORMANCE ISSUES

It is important to remember that when a browser comes across JavaScript, it will stop doing anything else until it has processed that script.

If your loop is dealing with only a small number of items, this will not be an issue. If, however, your loop contains a lot of items, it can make the page slower to load.

If the condition never returns `false`, you get what is commonly referred to as an **infinite loop**. The code will not stop running until your browser runs out of memory (breaking your script).

Any variable you can define outside of the loop and that does not change *within* the loop should be defined outside of it. If it were declared inside the loop, it would be recalculated every time the loop ran, needlessly using resources.

USING FOR LOOPS

c04/js/for-loop.js

JAVASCRIPT

```javascript
var scores = [24, 32, 17];      // Array of scores
var arrayLength = scores.length;// Items in array
var roundNumber = 0;            // Current round
var msg = '';                   // Message
var i;                          // Counter

// Loop through the items in the array
for (i = 0; i < arrayLength; i++) {

  // Arrays are zero based (so 0 is round 1)
  // Add 1 to the current round
  roundNumber = (i + 1);

  // Write the current round to message
  msg += 'Round ' + roundNumber + ': ';

  // Get the score from the scores array
  msg += scores[i] + '<br />';
}

document.getElementById('answer').innerHTML = msg;
```

RESULT

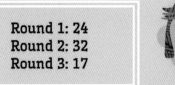

Round 1: 24
Round 2: 32
Round 3: 17

A **for** loop is often used to loop through the items in an array.

In this example, the scores for each round of a test are stored in an array called **scores**.

The total number of items in the array is stored in a variable called **arrayLength**. This number is obtained using the **length** property of the array.

There are three more variables: **roundNumber** holds the round of the test; **msg** holds the message to display; **i** is the counter (declared outside the loop).

The loop starts with the **for** keyword, then contains the condition inside the parentheses. As long as the counter is less than the total number of items in the array, the contents of the curly braces will continue to run. Each time the loop runs, the round number is increased by 1.

Inside the curly braces are rules that write the round number and the score to the **msg** variable. The variables declared outside of the loop are used within the loop.

The **msg** variable is then written into the page. It contains HTML so the **innerHTML** property is used to do this. Remember, p228 will talk about security issues relating to this property.

The counter and array both start from 0 (rather than 1). So, within the loop, to select the current item from the array, you use the counter variable **i** to specify the item from the array, e.g., **scores[i]**. But remember that it is a number lower then you might expect (e.g., first iteration is 0, second is 1).

USING WHILE LOOPS

Here is an example of a `while` loop. It writes out the 5 times table. Each time the loop is run, another calculation is written into the variable called `msg`.

This loop will continue to run for as long as the condition in the parentheses is true. That condition is a counter indicating that, as long as the variable `i` remains less than 10, the statements in the subsequent code block should run.

Inside the code block there are two statements:

The first statement uses the `+=` operator, which is used to add new content to the `msg` variable. Each time the loop runs, a new calculation and line break is added to the end of the message being stored in it. So `+=` works as a shorthand for writing:
`msg = msg + 'new msg'`
(See bottom of the next page for a breakdown of this statement.)

The second statement increments the counter variable by one. (This is done inside the loop rather than with the condition.)

When the loop has finished, the interpreter goes to the next line of code, which writes the `msg` variable to the page.

```
c04/js/while-loop.js                                    JAVASCRIPT

var i = 1;          // Set counter to 1
var msg = '';       // Message

// Store 5 times table in a variable
while (i < 10) {
  msg += i + ' x 5 = ' + (i * 5) + '<br />';
  i++;
}

document.getElementById('answer').innerHTML = msg;
```

RESULT

```
1 x 5 = 5
2 x 5 = 10
3 x 5 = 15
4 x 5 = 20
5 x 5 = 25
6 x 5 = 30
7 x 5 = 35
8 x 5 = 40
9 x 5 = 45
```

In this example, the condition specifies that the code should run nine times. A more typical use of a `while` loop would be when you *do not know* how many times you want the code to run. It should continue to run as long as a condition is met.

USING DO WHILE LOOPS

JAVASCRIPT   c04/js/do-while-loop.js

```
var i = 1;        // Set counter to 1
var msg = '';     // Message

// Store 5 times table in a variable
do {
  msg += i + ' x 5 = ' + (i * 5) + '<br />';
  i++;
} while (i < 1);
// Note how this is already 1 and it still runs

document.getElementById('answer').innerHTML = msg;
```

The key difference between a while loop and a do while loop is that the statements in the code block come *before* the condition. This means that those statements are run once whether or not the condition is met.

If you take a look at the condition, it is checking that the value of the variable called i is less than 1, but that variable has already been set to a value of 1.

Therefore, in this example the result is that the 5 times table is written out once, even though the counter is not less than 1.

Some people like to write while on a separate line from the closing curly brace before it.

RESULT

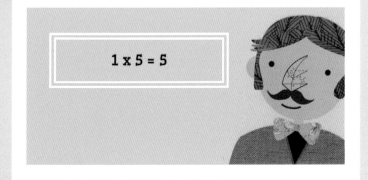

1 x 5 = 5

Breaking down the first statement in these examples:

① ② ③   ④   ⑤   ⑥

```
msg += i + ' x 5 = ' + (i * 5) + '<br />';
```

1. Take variable called msg
2. Add to the following to its value
3. The number in the counter

4. Write out the string **x 5 =**
5. The counter multiplied by **5**
6. Add a line break

EXAMPLE
DECISIONS & LOOPS

In this example, the user can either be shown addition or multiplication of a given number. The script demonstrates the use of both conditional logic and loops.

The example starts with two variables:

1. number holds the number that the calculations will be performed with (in this case it is the number 3)
2. operator indicates whether it should be addition or multiplication (in this case it is performing addition)

An if...else statement is used to decide whether to perform addition or multiplication with the number. If the variable called operator has the value addition, the numbers will be added together; otherwise they will be multiplied.

Inside the conditional statement, a while loop is used to calculate the results. It will run 10 times because the condition is checking whether the value of the counter is less than 11.

EXAMPLE
DECISIONS & LOOPS

```
c04/example.html                                              HTML

<!DOCTYPE html>
<html>
  <head>
    <title>Bullseye! Tutoring</title>
    <link rel="stylesheet" href="css/c04.css" />
  </head>
  <body>
    <section id="page2">
      <h1>Bullseye</h1>
      <img src="images/teacher.png" id="teacher2" alt="" />
      <section id="blackboard"></section>
    </section>
    <script src="js/example.js"></script>
  </body>
</html>
```

The HTML for this example is very slightly different than the other examples in this chapter because there is a blackboard which the table is written onto.

You can see the script is added to the page just before the closing </body> tag.

EXAMPLE
DECISIONS & LOOPS

JAVASCRIPT

c04/js/example.js

```javascript
var table = 3;                  // Unit of table
var operator = 'addition';      // Type of calculation (defaults to addition)
var i = 1;                      // Set counter to 1
var msg = '';                   // Message

if (operator === 'addition') {  // If the operator variable says addition
  while (i < 11) {              // While counter is less than 11
    msg += i + ' + ' + table + ' = ' + (i + table) + '<br />'; // Calculation
    i++;                        // Add 1 to the counter
  }
} else {                        // Otherwise
  while (i < 11) {              // While counter is less than 11
    msg += i + ' x ' + table + ' = ' + (i * table) + '<br />'; // Calculation
    i++;                        // Add 1 to the counter
  }
}

// Write the message into the page
var el = document.getElementById('blackboard');
el.innerHTML = msg;
```

If you read the comments in the code, you can see how this example works. The script starts by declaring four variables and setting values for them.

Then, an if statement checks whether the value of the variable called operator is addition. If it is, it uses a while loop to perform the calculations and store the results in a variable called msg.

If you change the value of the operator variable to anything other than addition, the conditional statement will select the second set of statements. These also contain a while loop, but this time it will perform multiplication (rather than addition).

When one of the loops has finished running, the last two lines of the script select the element whose id attribute has a value of blackboard, and updates the the page with the content of the msg variable.

SUMMARY
DECISIONS & LOOPS

▶ Conditional statements allow your code to make decisions about what to do next.

▶ Comparison operators (===, !==, ==, !=, <, >, <=, =>) are used to compare two operands.

▶ Logical operators allow you to combine more than one set of comparison operators.

▶ `if...else` statements allow you to run one set of code if a condition is true, and another if it is false.

▶ `switch` statements allow you to compare a value against possible outcomes (and also provides a default option if none match).

▶ Data types can be coerced from one type to another.

▶ All values evaluate to either truthy or falsy.

▶ There are three types of loop: `for`, `while`, and `do...while`. Each repeats a set of statements.

DOCUMENT OBJECT MODEL

The Document Object Model (DOM) specifies
how browsers should create a model of an HTML
page and how JavaScript can access and update the
contents of a web page while it is in the browser window.

The DOM is neither part of HTML, nor part of JavaScript; it is a separate set of rules.
It is implemented by all major browser makers, and covers two primary areas:

MAKING A MODEL OF THE HTML PAGE

When the browser loads a web page, it creates a model of the page in memory.

The DOM specifies the way in which the browser should structure this model using a **DOM tree**.

The DOM is called an object model because the model (the DOM tree) is made of objects.

Each object represents a different part of the page loaded in the browser window.

ACCESSING AND CHANGING THE HTML PAGE

The DOM also defines methods and properties to access and update each object in this model, which in turn updates what the user sees in the browser.

You will hear people call the DOM an **Application Programming Interface** (**API**). User interfaces let humans interact with programs; APIs let programs (and scripts) talk to each other. The DOM states what your script can ask the browser about the current page, and how to tell the browser to update what is being shown to the user.

In each example of this chapter, the JavaScript will amend the HTML list shown here. Colors are used to convey the priority and status of each list item:

HOT
COOL
NORMAL
COMPLETE

LISTKING

BUY GROCERIES

fresh figs
pine nuts
honey
balsamic vinegar

THE DOM TREE IS A MODEL OF A WEB PAGE

As a browser loads a web page, it creates a model of that page.
The model is called a DOM tree, and it is stored in the browsers' memory.
It consists of four main types of nodes.

BODY OF HTML PAGE

```
<html>
  <body>
    <div id="page">
      <h1 id="header">List</h1>
      <h2>Buy groceries</h2>
      <ul>
        <li id="one" class="hot"><em>fresh</em> figs</li>
        <li id="two" class="hot">pine nuts</li>
        <li id="three" class="hot">honey</li>
        <li id="four">balsamic vinegar</li>
      </ul>
      <script src="js/list.js"></script>
    </div>
  </body>
</html>
```

● THE DOCUMENT NODE

Above, you can see the HTML code for a shopping list, and on the right hand page is its **DOM tree**. Every element, attribute, and piece of text in the HTML is represented by its own **DOM node**. At the top of the tree a **document node** is added; it represents the entire page (and also corresponds to the document object, which you first met on p36).

When you access any element, attribute, or text node, you navigate to it via the document node. It is the starting point for all visits to the DOM tree.

● ELEMENT NODES

HTML elements describe the structure of an HTML page. (The <h1> - <h6> elements describe what parts are headings; the <p> tags indicate where paragraphs of text start and finish; and so on.)

To access the DOM tree, you start by looking for elements. Once you find the element you want, *then* you can access its text and attribute nodes if you want to. This is why you start by learning methods that allow you to access element nodes, before learning to access and alter text or attributes.

Note: We will continue to use this list example throughout this chapter and the next two chapters so that you can see how different techniques allow you to access and update the web page (which is represented by this DOM tree).

Relationships between the document and all of the element nodes are described using the same terms as a family tree: parents, children, siblings, ancestors, and descendants. (Every node is a descendant of the document node.)

Each node is an object with methods and properties.
Scripts access and update this DOM tree (not the source HTML file).
Any changes made to the DOM tree are reflected in the browser.

DOM TREE

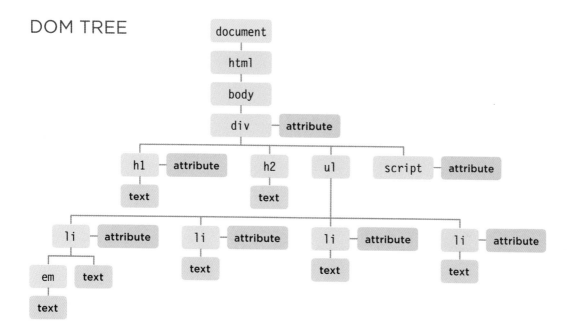

ATTRIBUTE NODES

The opening tags of HTML elements can carry attributes and these are represented by attribute nodes in the DOM tree.

Attribute nodes are not *children* of the element that carries them; they are *part of* that element. Once you access an element, there are specific JavaScript methods and properties to read or change that element's attributes. For example, it is common to change the values of class attributes to trigger new CSS rules that affect their presentation.

TEXT NODES

Once you have accessed an element node, you can then reach the text within that element. This is stored in its own text node.

Text nodes cannot have children. If an element contains text and another child element, the child element is *not* a child of the text node but rather a child of the *containing* element. (See the <em> element on the first <li> item.) This illustrates how the text node is always a new branch of the DOM tree, and no further branches come off of it.

WORKING WITH THE DOM TREE

Accessing and updating the DOM tree involves two steps:
1: Locate the node that represents the element you want to work with.
2: Use its text content, child elements, and attributes.

STEP 1: ACCESS THE ELEMENTS

Here is an overview of the methods and properties that access elements covered on p192 – p211.
The first two columns are known as DOM queries. The last column is known as traversing the DOM.

SELECT AN INDIVIDUAL ELEMENT NODE

Here are three common ways to select an individual element:

`getElementById()`
Uses the value of an element's id attribute (which should be unique within the page).
See p195

`querySelector()`
Uses a CSS selector, and returns the first matching element.
See p202

You can also select individual elements by traversing from one element to another within the DOM tree (see third column).

SELECT MULTIPLE ELEMENTS (NODELISTS)

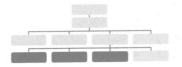

There are three common ways to select multiple elements.

`getElementsByClassName()`
Selects all elements that have a specific value for their class attribute.
See p200

`getElementsByTagName()`
Selects all elements that have the specified tag name.
See p201

`querySelectorAll()`
Uses a CSS selector to select all matching elements.
See p202

TRAVERSING BETWEEN ELEMENT NODES

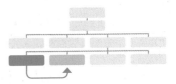

You can move from one element node to a related element node.

`parentNode`
Selects the parent of the current element node (which will return just one element).
See p208

`previousSibling / nextSibling`
Selects the previous or next sibling from the DOM tree.
See p210

`firstChild / lastChild`
Select the first or last child of the current element.
See p211

Throughout the chapter you will see notes where DOM methods only work in certain browsers or are buggy. Inconsistent browser support for the DOM was a key reason why jQuery became so popular.

The terms **elements** and **element nodes** are used interchangeably but when people say the DOM is working with an element, it is actually working with a node that *represents* that element.

STEP 2: WORK WITH THOSE ELEMENTS

Here is an overview of methods and properties that work with the elements introduced on p186.

ACCESS / UPDATE TEXT NODES

The text inside any element is stored inside a text node. To access the text node above:
1. Select the `<li>` element
2. Use the `firstChild` property to get the text node
3. Use the text node's only property (`nodeValue`) to get the text from the element

`nodeValue`
This property lets you access or update contents of a text node.
See p214

The text node does not include text inside any child elements.

WORK WITH HTML CONTENT

One property allows access to child elements and text content:
`innerHTML`
See p220

Another just the text content:
`textContent`
See p216

Several methods let you create new nodes, add nodes to a tree, and remove nodes from a tree:
`createElement()`
`createTextNode()`
`appendChild()` / `removeChild()`
This is called DOM manipulation.
See p222

ACCESS OR UPDATE ATTRIBUTE VALUES

Here are some of the properties and methods you can use to work with attributes:
`className / id`
Lets you get or update the value of the `class` and `id` attributes.
See p232

`hasAttribute()`
`getAttribute()`
`setAttribute()`
`removeAttribute()`
The first checks if an attribute exists. The second gets its value. The third updates the value. The fourth removes an attribute.
See p232

CACHING DOM QUERIES

Methods that find elements in the DOM tree are called DOM queries. When you need to work with an element more than once, you should use a variable to store the result of this query.

When a script selects an element to access or update, the interpreter must find the element(s) in the DOM tree.

Below, the interpreter is told to look through the DOM tree for an element whose **id** attribute has a value of **one**.

Once it has found the node that represents the element(s), you can work with that node, its parent, or any children.

```
getElementById('one');
```

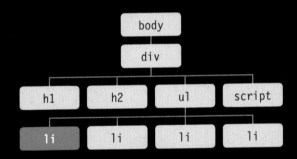

When people talk about storing elements in variables, they are really storing the location of the element(s) within the DOM tree in a variable. The properties and methods of that element node work on the variable.

If your script needs to use the the same element(s) more than once, you can store the location of the element(s) in a variable.

This saves the browser looking through the DOM tree to find the same element(s) again. It is known as **caching** the selection.

Programmers would say that the variable stores a **reference** to the object in the DOM tree. (It is storing the *location* of the node.)

```
var itemOne = getElementById('one');
```

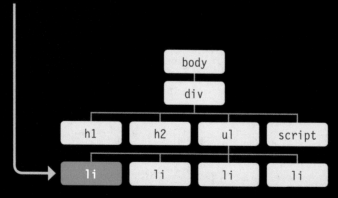

itemOne does not store the **<li>** element, it stores a *reference* to where that node is in the DOM tree. To access the text content of this element, you might use the variable name: **itemOne.textContent**

ACCESSING ELEMENTS

DOM queries may return one element, or they may return a NodeList, which is a collection of nodes.

Sometimes you will just want to access one individual element (or a fragment of the page that is stored within that one element). Other times you may want to select a group of elements, for example, every <h1> element in the page or every <li> element within a particular list.

Here, the DOM tree shows the body of the page of the list example. We focus on accessing elements first so it only shows element nodes. The diagrams in the coming pages highlight which elements a DOM query would return. (Remember, element *nodes* are the DOM representation of an element.)

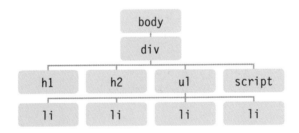

GROUPS OF ELEMENT NODES

If a method *can* return more than one node, it will always return a **NodeList**, which is a **collection** of nodes (even if it only finds one matching element). You then need to select the element you want from this list using an index number (which means the numbering starts at 0 like the items in an array).

For example, several elements can have the same tag name, so getElementsByTagName() will always return a NodeList.

FASTEST ROUTE

Finding the quickest way to access an element within your web page will make the page seem faster and/or more responsive. This usually means evaluating the minimum number of nodes on the way to the element you want to work with. For example, getElementById() will quickly return one element (because no two elements on the same page should have the same value for an id attribute), but it can only be used when the element you want to access has an id attribute.

METHODS THAT RETURN A SINGLE ELEMENT NODE:

getElementById('*id*')

Selects an individual element given the value of its id attribute.
The HTML must have an id attribute in order for it to be selectable.

First supported: IE5.5, Opera 7, all versions of Chrome, Firefox, Safari.

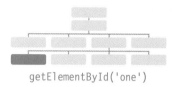

getElementById('one')

querySelector('*css selector*')

Uses CSS selector syntax that would select one or more elements.
This method returns only the first of the matching elements.

First supported: IE8, Firefox 3.5, Safari 4, Chrome 4, Opera 10

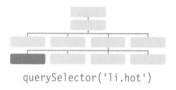

querySelector('li.hot')

METHODS THAT RETURN ONE OR MORE ELEMENTS (AS A NODELIST):

getElementsByClassName('*class*')

Selects one or more elements given the value of their class attribute.
The HTML must have a class attribute for it to be selectable.
This method is faster than querySelectorAll().

First supported: IE9, Firefox 3, Safari 4, Chrome 4, Opera 10
(Several browsers had partial / buggy support in earlier versions)

getElementsByClassName('hot')

getElementsByTagName('*tagName*')

Selects all elements on the page with the specified tag name.
This method is faster than querySelectorAll().

First supported: IE6+, Firefox 3, Safari 4, Chrome, Opera 10
(Several browsers had partial / buggy support in earlier versions)

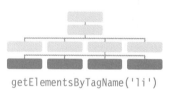

getElementsByTagName('li')

querySelectorAll('*css selector*')

Uses CSS selector syntax to select one or more elements and returns all
of those that match.

First supported: IE8, Firefox 3.5, Safari 4, Chrome 4, Opera 10

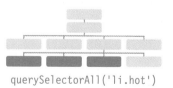

querySelectorAll('li.hot')

METHODS THAT SELECT INDIVIDUAL ELEMENTS

getElementById() and **querySelector()** can both search an entire document and return individual elements. Both use a similar syntax.

getElementById() is the quickest and most efficient way to access an element because no two elements can share the same value for their **id** attribute. The syntax for this method is shown below, and an example of its use is on the page to the right.

querySelector() is a more recent addition to the DOM, so it is not supported in older browsers. But it is very flexible because its parameter is a CSS selector, which means it can be used to accurately target many more elements.

document refers to the **document** object. You always have to access individual elements via the **document** object.

The **getElementById()** method indicates that you want to find an element based upon the value of its **id** attribute.

OBJECT

METHOD

```
document.getElementById('one')
```

MEMBER OPERATOR

The dot notation indicates that the method (on the right) is being applied to the node on the left of the period.

PARAMETER

The method needs to know the value of the **id** attribute on the element you want. It is the parameter of the method.

This code will return the element node for the element whose **id** attribute has a value of **one**. You often see element nodes stored in a variable for use later in the script (as you saw on p190).

Here the method is used on the **document** object so it looks for that element anywhere within the page. DOM methods can also be used on element nodes within the page to find descendants of that node.

SELECTING ELEMENTS USING ID ATTRIBUTES

```html
<h1 id="header">List King</h1>
<h2>Buy groceries</h2>
<ul>
  <li id="one" class="hot"><em>fresh</em>
    figs</li>
  <li id="two" class="hot">pine nuts</li>
  <li id="three" class="hot">honey</li>
  <li id="four">balsamic vinegar</li>
</ul>
```

```javascript
// Select the element and store it in a variable.
var el = document.getElementById('one');

// Change the value of the class attribute.
el.className = 'cool';
```

RESULT

This result window shows the example after the script has updated the first list item. The original state, before the script ran, is shown on p185.

getElementById() allows you to select a single element node by specifying the value of its id attribute.

This method has one parameter: the value of the id attribute on the element you want to select. This value is placed inside quote marks because it is a string. The quotes can be single or double quotes, but they must match.

In the example on the left , the first line of JavaScript code finds the element whose id attribute has a value of **one**, and stores a reference to that node in a variable called **el**.

The code then uses a property called **className** (which you meet on p232) to update the value of the **class** attribute of the element stored in this variable. Its value is **cool**, and this triggers a new rule in the CSS that sets the background color of the element to aqua.

Note how the **className** property is used on the variable that stores the reference to the element.

Browser Support: This is one of the oldest and best supported methods for accessing elements.

NODELISTS: DOM QUERIES THAT RETURN MORE THAN ONE ELEMENT

When a DOM method *can* return more than one element, it returns a NodeList (even if it only finds one matching element).

A NodeList is a collection of element nodes. Each node is given an index number (a number that starts at zero, just like an array).

The order in which the element nodes are stored in a NodeList is the same order that they appeared in the HTML page.

When a DOM query returns a NodeList, you may want to:
- Select one element from the NodeList.
- Loop through each item in the NodeList and perform the same statements on each of the element nodes.

NodeLists look like arrays and are numbered like arrays, but they are not actually arrays; they are a type of object called a **collection**.

Like any other object, a NodeList has properties and methods, notably:
- The `length` property tells you how many items are in the NodeList.
- The `item()` method returns a specific node from the NodeList when you tell it the index number of the item that you want (in the parentheses). However, it is more common to use array syntax (with square brackets) to retrieve an item from a NodeList (as you will see on p199).

LIVE & STATIC NODELISTS

There are times when you will want to work with the same selection of elements several times, so the NodeList can be stored in a variable and re-used (rather than collecting the same elements again).

In a **live NodeList**, when your script updates the page, the NodeList is updated at the same time. The methods beginning `getElementsBy…` return live NodeLists. They are also typically faster to generate than static NodeLists.

In a **static NodeList** when your script updates the page, the NodeList is not updated to reflect the changes made by the script.

The new methods that begin `querySelector…` (which use CSS selector syntax) return static NodeLists. They reflect the document when the query was made. If the script changes the content of the page, the NodeList is not updated to reflect those changes.

Here you can see four different DOM queries that all return a NodeList. For each query, you can see the elements and their index numbers in the NodeList that is returned.

getElementsByTagName('h1')

Even though this query only returns one element, the method still returns a NodeList because of the potential for returning more than one element.

INDEX NUMBER & ELEMENT

0	`<h1>`

getElementsByTagName('li')

This method returns four elements, one for each of the `<li>` elements on the page. They appear in the same order as they do in the HTML page.

INDEX NUMBER & ELEMENT

0	`<li id="one" class="hot">`
1	`<li id="two" class="hot">`
2	`<li id="three" class="hot">`
3	`<li id="four">`

getElementsByClassName('hot')

This NodeList contains only three of the `<li>` elements because we are searching for elements by the value of their `class` attribute, not tag name.

INDEX NUMBER & ELEMENT

0	`<li id="one" class="hot">`
1	`<li id="two" class="hot">`
2	`<li id="three" class="hot">`

querySelectorAll('li[id]')

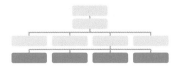

This method returns four elements, one for each of the `<li>` elements on the page that have an `id` attribute (regardless of the values of the `id` attributes).

INDEX NUMBER & ELEMENT

0	`<li id="one" class="hot">`
1	`<li id="two" class="hot">`
2	`<li id="three" class="hot">`
3	`<li id="four">`

SELECTING AN ELEMENT FROM A NODELIST

There are two ways to select an element from a NodeList:
The **item()** method and array syntax.
Both require the index number of the element you want.

THE **item()** METHOD

NodeLists have a method called **item()** which will return an individual node from the NodeList.

You specify the index number of the element you want as a parameter of the method (inside the parentheses).

Executing code when there are no elements to work with wastes resources. So programmers often check that there is at least one item in the NodeList before running any code. To do this, use the **length** property of the NodeList – it tells you how many items the NodeList contains.

Here you can see that an **if** statement is used. The condition for the **if** statement is whether the **length** property of the NodeList is greater than zero. If it is, then the statements inside the **if** statement are executed. If not, the code continues to run after the second curly brace.

```
var elements = document.getElementsByClassName('hot')
if (elements.length >= 1) {
    var firstItem = elements.item(0);
}
```

1

Select elements that have a **class** attribute whose value is **hot** and store the NodeList in a variable called **elements**.

2

Use the **length** property to check how many elements were found. If 1 or more are found, run the code in the **if** statement.

3

Store the first element from the NodeList in a variable called **firstItem**. (It says **0** because index numbers start at zero.)

Array syntax is preferred over the **item()** method because it is faster. Before selecting a node from a NodeList, check that it contains nodes. If you repeatedly use the NodeList, store it in a variable.

ARRAY SYNTAX

You can access individual nodes using a square bracket syntax similar to that used to access individual items from an array.

You specify the index number of the element you want inside square brackets that follow the NodeList.

As with all DOM queries, if you need to access the same NodeList several times, store the result of the DOM query in a variable.

In the examples on both of these pages, the NodeList is stored in a variable called **elements**.

If you create a variable to hold a NodeList (as shown below) but there are no matching elements, the variable will be an empty NodeList. When you check the **length** property of the variable, it will return the number **0** because it does not contain any elements.

```
var elements = document.getElementsByClassName('hot');
if (elements.length >= 1) {
    var firstItem = elements[0];
}
```

1
Create a NodeList containing elements that have a **class** attribute whose value is **hot**, and store it in the variable **elements**.

2
If that number is greater than or equal to one, run the code inside the **if** statement.

3
Get the first element from the NodeList (it says **0** because index numbers start at zero).

SELECTING ELEMENTS USING CLASS ATTRIBUTES

The `getElementsByClassName()` method allows you to select elements whose `class` attribute contains a specific value.

The method has one parameter: the `class` name which is given in quotes within the parentheses after the method name.

Because several elements can have the same value for their `class` attribute, this method always returns a NodeList.

```javascript
var elements = document.getElementsByClassName('hot'); // Find hot items

if (elements.length > 2) {                             // If 3 or more are found

    var el = elements[2];             // Select the third one from the NodeList
    el.className = 'cool';            // Change the value of its class attribute

}
```

This example starts by looking for elements whose `class` attribute *contains* hot. (The value of a `class` attribute can contain several class names, each separated by a space.) The result of this DOM query is stored in a variable called `elements` because it is used more than once in the example.

An `if` statement checks if the query found more than two elements. If so, the third one is selected and stored in a variable called `el`. The `class` attribute of that element is then updated to say `class`. (In turn, this triggers a new CSS style, changing the presentation of that element.)

Browser Support: IE9, Firefox 3, Chrome 4, Opera 9.5, Safari 3.1

RESULT

fresh figs

pine nuts

honey

balsamic vinegar

SELECTING ELEMENTS BY TAG NAME

The `getElementsByTagName()` method allows you to select elements using their tag name.

The element name is specified as a parameter, so it is placed inside the parentheses and is contained by quote marks.

Note that you do not include the angled brackets that surround the tag name in the HTML (just the letters inside the brackets).

`c05/js/get-elements-by-tag-name.js`

```javascript
var elements = document.getElementsByTagName('li');   // Find <li> elements

if (elements.length > 0) {                            // If 1 or more are found

    var el = elements[0];              // Select the first one using array syntax
    el.className = 'cool';             // Change the value of the class attribute

}
```

RESULT

This example looks for any `<li>` elements in the document. It stores the result in a variable called `elements` because the result is used more than once in this example.

An `if` statement checks if any `<li>` elements were found. As with any element that can return a `NodeList`, you check that there will be a suitable element before you try to work with it.

If matching elements were found, the first one is selected and its `class` attribute is updated. This changes the color of the list item to make it aqua.

Browser Support: Very good – it is safe to use in any scripts.

SELECTING ELEMENTS USING CSS SELECTORS

querySelector() returns the first element node that matches the CSS-style selector. querySelectorAll() returns a NodeList of all of the matches.

Both methods take a CSS selector as their only parameter. The CSS selector syntax offers more flexibility and accuracy when selecting an element than

just specifying a class name or a tag name, and should also be familiar to front-end web developers who are used to targeting elements using CSS.

c05/js/query-selector.js

JAVASCRIPT

```javascript
// querySelector() only returns the first match
var el = document.querySelector('li.hot');
el.className = 'cool';

// querySelectorAll returns a NodeList
// The second matching element (the third list item) is selected and changed
var els = document.querySelectorAll('li.hot');
els[1].className = 'cool';
```

These two methods were introduced by browser manufacturers because a lot of developers were including scripts like jQuery in their pages so that they could select elements using CSS selectors. (You meet jQuery in Chapter 7.)

If you look at the final line of code, array syntax is used to select the second item from the NodeList, even though that NodeList is stored in a variable.

RESULT

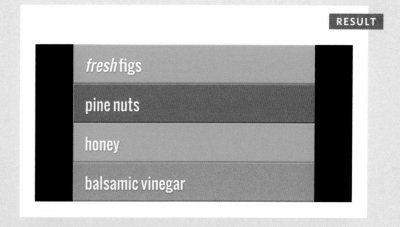

Browser Support: The drawback with these two methods is that they are only supported in more recent browsers.

IE8+ (released Mar 2009)
Firefox 3.5+ (released Jun 2009)
Chrome 1+ (released Sep 2008)
Opera 10+ (released Sep 2009)
Safari 3.2+ (released Nov 2008)

JavaScript code runs one line at a time, and statements affect the content of a page as the interpreter processes them.

If a DOM query runs when a page loads, the same query could return different elements if it is used again later in the page.

Below you can see how the example on the left-hand page (query-selector.js) changes the DOM tree as it runs.

1: WHEN THE PAGE FIRST LOADS

```
HTML                                          c05/query-selector.html

<ul>
  <li id="one" class="hot">
    <em>fresh</em> figs</li>
  <li id="two" class="hot">pine nuts</li>
  <li id="three" class="hot">honey</li>
  <li id="four">balsamic vinegar</li>
</ul>
```

1. This is how the page starts. There are three `<li>` elements that have a `class` attribute whose value is `hot`. The `querySelector()` method finds the first one, and updates the value of its `class` attribute from `hot` to `cool`. This also updates the DOM tree stored in memory so – after this line has run – only the second and third `<li>` elements have a `class` attribute with a value of `hot`.

2: AFTER THE FIRST SET OF STATEMENTS

```
HTML                                          c05/query-selector.html

<ul>
  <li id="one" class="cool">
    <em>fresh</em> figs</li>
  <li id="two" class="hot">pine nuts</li>
  <li id="three" class="hot">honey</li>
  <li id="four">balsamic vinegar</li>
</ul>
```

2. When the second selector runs, there are now only two `<li>` elements whose `class` attributes have a value of `hot` (see left), so it just selects these two. This time, array syntax is used to work with the second of the matching elements (which is the third list item). Again the value of its `class` attribute is changed from `hot` to `cool`.

3: AFTER THE SECOND SET OF STATEMENTS

```
HTML                                          c05/query-selector.html

<ul>
  <li id="one" class="cool">
    <em>fresh</em> figs</li>
  <li id="two" class="hot">pine nuts</li>
  <li id="three" class="cool">honey</li>
  <li id="four">balsamic vinegar</li>
</ul>
```

3. When the second selector has done its job, the DOM tree now only holds one `<li>` element whose `class` attribute has a value of `hot`. Any further code looking for `<li>` elements whose `class` attribute has a value of `hot` would find only this one. However, if they were looking for `<li>` elements whose `class` attribute has a value of `cool`, they would find *two* matching element nodes.

REPEATING ACTIONS FOR AN ENTIRE NODELIST

When you have a NodeList, you can loop through each node in the collection and apply the same statements to each.

In this example, once a NodeList has been created, a **for** loop is used to go through each element in the NodeList.

All of the statements inside the **for** loop's curly braces are applied to each element in the NodeList one-by-one.

To indicate which item of the NodeList is currently being worked with, the counter **i** is used in the array-style syntax.

```
var hotItems = document.querySelectorAll('li.hot');
for (var i = 0; i < hotItems.length; i++) {
   hotItems[i].className = 'cool';
}
```

1

The variable **hotItems** contains a NodeList. It contains all list items whose **class** attribute has a value of **hot**. They are collected using the **querySelectorAll()** method.

2

The **length** property of the NodeList indicates how many elements are in the NodeList. The number of elements dictates how many times the loop should run.

3

Array syntax is used to indicate which item in the NodeList is currently being worked with: **hotItems[i]** It uses the counter variable inside the square brackets.

LOOPING THROUGH
A NODELIST

If you want to apply the same code to numerous elements, looping through a NodeList is a powerful technique.

It involves finding out how many items are in the NodeList, and then setting a counter to loop through them, one-by-one.

Each time the loop runs, the script checks that the counter is less than the total number of items in the NodeList.

```javascript
var hotItems = document.querySelectorAll('li.hot'); // Store NodeList in array

if (hotItems.length > 0) {                    // If it contains items

    for (var i=0; i<hotItems.length; i++) {    // Loop through each item
        hotItems[i].className = 'cool';       // Change value of class attribute
    }

}
```

RESULT

In this example, the NodeList is generated using querySelectorAll(), and it is looking for any <li> elements that have a class attribute whose value is hot.

The NodeList is stored in a variable called hotItems, and the number of elements in the list is found using the length property.

For each of the elements in the NodeList, the value of the class attribute is changed to cool.

LISTKING

BUY GROCERIES

- *fresh* figs
- pine nuts
- honey
- balsamic vinegar

START

is 0 < 3?   add 1 to 0

LISTKING

BUY GROCERIES

- *fresh* figs
- pine nuts
- honey
- balsamic vinegar

i = 0   i = 1

At the start of this example, there are three list items with a **class** attribute whose value is **hot** so the value of **hotItems.length** is 3.

At first, the value of the counter is set to **0,** so the first item from the NodeList (which has an index of **0**) is targeted and the value of its **class** attribute is set to **cool**.

```
for (var i = 0; i < hotItems.length; i++) {
    hotItems[i].className = 'cool';
}
```

is 1 < 3? add 1 to 1   is 2 < 3?   add 1 to 2   is 3 < 3?

i = 1   i = 2   i = 3   END

When the value of the counter is **1**, the second item from the NodeList (which has an index of **1**) is targeted and the value of its **class** attribute is set to **cool**.

When the value of the counter is **2**, the third item from the NodeList (which has an index of **2**) is targeted and the value of its **class** attribute is set to **cool**.

When the value of the counter is **3**, the condition no longer returns **true**, so the loops ends. The script then continues to the first line of code after the loop.

TRAVERSING THE DOM

When you have an element node, you can select another element in relation to it using these five properties. This is known as traversing the DOM.

parentNode

This property finds the element node for the containing (or parent) element in the HTML.

(1) If you started with the first `<li>` element, then its *parent node* would be the one representing the `<ul>` element.

previousSibling
nextSibling

These properties find the previous or next sibling of a node if there are siblings.

If you started with the first `<li>` element, it would not have a *previous sibling*. However, its *next sibling* **(2)** would be the node representing the second `<li>`.

firstChild
lastChild

These properties find the first or last child of the current element.

If you started with the `<ul>` element, the *first child* would be the node representing the first `<li>` element, and **(3)** the *last child* would be the last `<li>`.

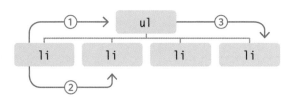

These are properties of the current node (not methods to select an element); therefore, they do not end in parentheses.

If you use these properties and they do not have a previous/next sibling, or a first/last child, the result will be `null`.

These properties are read-only; they can only be used to select a new node, not to update a parent, sibling, or child.

WHITESPACE NODES

Traversing the DOM can be difficult because some browsers add a text node whenever they come across whitespace between elements.

Most browsers, except IE, treat whitespace between elements (such as spaces or carriage returns) as a text node, so the properties below return different elements in different browsers:

```
previousSibling
nextSibling
firstChild
lastChild
```

Below, you can see all of the whitespace nodes added to the DOM tree for the list example. Each one is represented by a green square. You could strip all the whitespace out of a page before serving it to the browser. This would also make the page smaller and faster to serve/load. However, it would also make the code much harder to read.

Another way around this problem is to avoid using these DOM properties altogether.

One of the most popular ways to address this kind of problem is to use a JavaScript library such as jQuery, which helps deal with such problems. These types of browser inconsistencies were a big factor in jQuery's popularity.

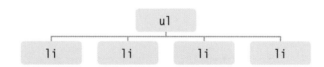

Internet Explorer (shown above) ignores whitespace and does not create extra text nodes.

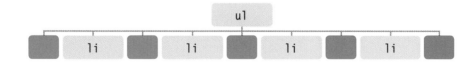

Chrome, Firefox, Safari, and Opera create text nodes from whitespace (spaces and carriage returns).

PREVIOUS & NEXT SIBLING

You have just seen that these properties can return inconsistent results in different browsers. However, it is safe to use them when there is no whitespace between elements.

For this example, all spaces between the HTML elements have been removed. In order to demonstrate these properties, the second list item is selected using getElementById().

From this element node, the previousSibling property will return the first <li> element, and the nextSibling property will return the third <li> element.

---

c05/sibling.html   `HTML`

```
<ul><li id="one" class="hot"><em>fresh</em> figs</li><li id="two"
class="hot">pine nuts</li><li id="three" class="hot">honey</li><li
id="four">balsamic vinegar</li></ul>
```

---

c05/js/sibling.js   `JAVASCRIPT`

```javascript
// Select the starting point and find its siblings
var startItem = document.getElementById('two');
var prevItem = startItem.previousSibling;
var nextItem = startItem.nextSibling;

// Change the values of the siblings' class attributes
prevItem.className = 'complete';
nextItem.className = 'cool';
```

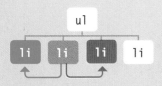

`RESULT`

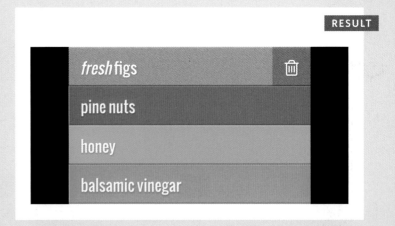

- ● START
- ● PREVIOUS SIBLING
- ● NEXT SIBLING

Note how references to sibling nodes are stored in new variables. This means properties such as className can be used on that node by adding the dot notation between the variable name and the property.

FIRST & LAST CHILD

These properties also return inconsistent results if there is whitespace between elements. In this example, a slightly different solution is used in the HTML – the closing tags are put next to the opening tags of the next element, making it a little more readable. The example starts by using the `getElementsByTagName()` method to select the `<ul>` element from the page. From this element node, the `firstChild` property will return the first `<li>` element, and the `lastChild` property will return the last `<li>` element.

HTML   c05/child.html

```html
<ul
  ><li id="one" class="hot"><em>fresh</em> figs</li
  ><li id="two" class="hot">pine nuts</li
  ><li id="three" class="hot">honey</li
  ><li id="four">balsamic vinegar</li
></ul>
```

JAVASCRIPT   c05/js/child.js

```javascript
// Select the starting point and find its children
var startItem = document.getElementsByTagName('ul')[0];
var firstItem = startItem.firstChild;
var lastItem = startItem.lastChild;

// Change the values of the children's class attributes
firstItem.setAttribute('class', 'complete');
lastItem.setAttribute('class', 'cool');
```

RESULT

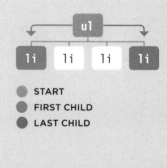

START
FIRST CHILD
LAST CHILD

HOW TO GET/UPDATE ELEMENT CONTENT

So far this chapter has focused on finding elements in the DOM tree. The rest of this chapter shows how to access/update element content. Your choice of techniques depends upon what the element contains.

Take a look at the three examples of `<li>` elements on the right. Each one adds some more markup and, as a result, the fragment of the DOM tree for each list item is very different.

- The first (on this page) just contains text.
- The second and third (on the right-hand page) contain a mix of text and an `<em>` element.

You can see that by adding something as simple as an `<em>` element, the DOM tree's structure changes significantly. In turn, this affects how you might work with that list item. When an element contains a mix of text and other elements, you are more likely to work with the containing element rather than the individual nodes for each descendant.

```
<li id="one">figs</li>
```

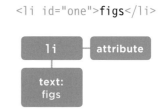

Above, the `<li>` element has:

- One *child* node holding the word that you can see in the list item: `figs`
- An attribute node holding the `id` attribute.

To work with the content of elements you can:

- **Navigate to the text nodes**. This works best when the element contains only text, no other elements.
- **Work with the containing element**. This allows you to access its text nodes and child elements. It works better when an element has text nodes and child elements that are siblings.

TEXT NODES

Once you have navigated from an element to its text node, there is one property that you will commonly find yourself using:

PROPERTY	DESCRIPTION
nodeValue	Accesses text from node (p214)

```
<li id="one"><em>fresh</em> figs</li>
```

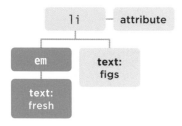

An **<em>** element is added. It becomes the *first child*.

- The **<em>** element node has its own *child* text node which contains the word **fresh**.
- The original text node is now a *sibling* of the node that represents the **<em>** element.

```
<li id="one">six <em>fresh</em> figs</li>
```

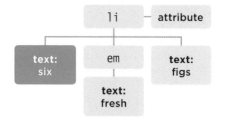

When text is added before the **<em>** element:

- The *first child* of the **<li>** element is a text node, which contains the word **six**.
- It has a *sibling* which is an element node for the **<em>** element. In turn, that **<em>** element node has a *child* text node containing the word **fresh**.
- Finally, there is a text node holding the word **figs**, which is a sibling of both the text node for the word "six" and the element node, **<em>**.

CONTAINING ELEMENT

When you are working with an element node (rather than its text node), that element can contain markup. You have to choose whether you want to retrieve (get) or update (set) the markup as well as the text.

PROPERTY	DESCRIPTION	
innerHTML	Gets/sets text & markup	(p220)
textContent	Gets/sets text only	(p216)
innerText	Gets/sets text only	(p216)

When you use these properties to update the content of an element, the new content will overwrite the entire contents of the element (both text and markup).

For example, if you used any of these properties to update the content of the **<body>** element, it would update the entire web page.

ACCESS & UPDATE A TEXT NODE WITH NODEVALUE

When you select a text node, you can retrieve or amend the content of it using the **nodeValue** property.

```
<li id="one"><em>fresh</em> figs</li>
```

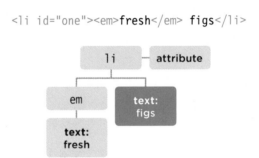

The code below shows how you access the second text node. It will return the result: **figs**

```
document.getElementById('one').firstChild.nextSibling.nodeValue;
```

In order to use **nodeValue**, you must be on a text node, not the element that contains the text.

This example shows that navigating from the element node to a text node can be complicated.

If you do not know whether there will be element nodes alongside text nodes, it is easier to work with the containing element.

1. The **<li>** element node is selected using the **getElementById()** method.
2. The *first child* of **<li>** is the **<em>** element.
3. The text node is the *next sibling* of that **<em>** element.
4. You have the text node and can access its contents using **nodeValue**.

ACCESSING & CHANGING
A TEXT NODE

To work with text in an element, first the element node is accessed and then its text node.

The text node has a property called **nodeValue** which returns the text in that text node.

You can also use the **nodeValue** property to update the content of a text node.

JAVASCRIPT   c05/js/node-value.js

```javascript
var itemTwo = document.getElementById('two');      // Get second list item

var elText  = itemTwo.firstChild.nodeValue;        // Get its text content

elText = elText.replace('pine nuts', 'kale');      // Change pine nuts to kale

itemTwo.firstChild.nodeValue = elText;             // Update the list item
```

RESULT

This example takes the text content of the second list item and changes it from pine nuts to kale.

The first line collects the second list item. It is stored in a variable called itemTwo.

Next the text content of that element is stored in a variable called elText.

The third line of text replaces the words 'pine nuts' with 'kale' using the String object's replace() method.

The last line uses the nodeValue property to update the content of the text node with the updated value.

ACCESS & UPDATE TEXT WITH TEXTCONTENT (& INNERTEXT)

The `textContent` property allows you to collect or update just the text that is in the containing element (and its children).

textContent

To collect the text from the `<li>` elements in our example (and ignore any markup inside the element) you can use the `textContent` property on the containing `<li>` element. In this case it would return the value: `fresh figs`.

You can also use this property to update the content of the element; it replaces the entire content of it (including any markup).

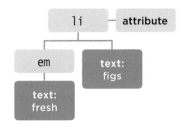

```
<li id="one"><em>fresh</em> figs</li>
```

```
document.getElementById('one').textContent;
```

One issue with the `textContent` property is that Internet Explorer did not support it until IE9. (All other major browsers support it.)

innerText

You may also come across a property called `innerText`, but you should generally avoid it for three key reasons:

SUPPORT

Although most browser manufacturers adopted the property, Firefox does not because `innerText` is not part of any standard.

OBEYS CSS

It will not show any content that has been hidden by CSS. For example, if there were a CSS rule that hid the `<em>` elements, the `innerText` property would return only the word `figs`.

PERFORMANCE

Because the `innerText` property takes into account layout rules that specify whether the element is visible or not, it can be slower to retrieve the content than the `textContent` property.

ACCESSING TEXT ONLY

In order to demonstrate the difference between **textContent** and **innerText**, this example features a CSS rule to hide the contents of the **<em>** element.

The script starts off by getting the content of the first list item using both the **textContent** property and **innerText**. It then writes the values after the list.

Finally, the value of the first list item is then updated to say **sourdough bread**. This is done using the **textContent** property.

JAVASCRIPT   c05/js/inner-text-and-text-content.js

```javascript
var firstItem = document.getElementById('one');      // Find first list item
var showTextContent = firstItem.textContent;         // Get value of textContent
var showInnerText = firstItem.innerText;             // Get value of innerText

// Show the content of these two properties at the end of the list
var msg = '<p>textContent: ' + showTextContent + '</p>';
    msg += '<p>innerText: ' + showInnerText + '</p>';
var el = document.getElementById('scriptResults');
el.innerHTML = msg;

firstItem.textContent = 'sourdough bread';           // Update the first list item
```

RESULT

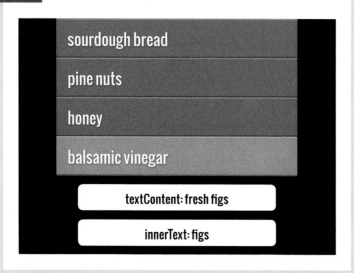

In most browsers:
- **textContent** collects the words **fresh figs**.
- **innerText** just shows **figs** (because **fresh** was hidden by the CSS).

But:
- In IE8 or earlier, the **textContent** property does not work.
- In Firefox, the **innerText** property will return **undefined** because it was never implemented in Firefox.

ADDING OR REMOVING HTML CONTENT

There are two very different approaches to adding and removing content from a DOM tree: the **innerHTML** property and DOM manipulation.

THE innerHTML PROPERTY

Note: there are security risks associated with using **innerHTML** - these issues are described on p228.

APPROACH

innerHTML can be used on any element node. It is used both to retrieve and replace content. To update an element, new content is provided as a string. It can contain markup for descendant elements.

ADDING CONTENT

To add new content:
1. Store new content (including markup) as a string in a variable.
2. Select the element whose content you want to replace.
3. Set the element's **innerHTML** property to be the new string.

REMOVING CONTENT

To remove all content from an element, you set **innerHTML** to an empty string. To remove one element from a DOM fragment, e.g., one **<li>** from a **<ul>**, you need to provide the entire fragment minus that element.

EXAMPLE: CHANGING A LIST ITEM

1: Create variable holding markup

```
var item;
item = '<em>Fresh</em> figs';
```

You can have as much or as little markup in the variable as you want. It is a quick way to add a lot of markup to the DOM tree.

2: Select element whose content you want to update

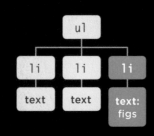

3: Update content of selected element with new markup

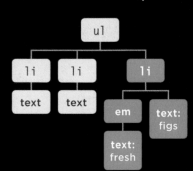

DOM manipulation easily targets individual nodes in the DOM tree, whereas **innerHTML** is better suited to updating entire fragments.

DOM MANIPULATION METHODS

DOM manipulation can be safer than using **innerHTML**, but it requires more code and can be slower.

APPROACH

DOM manipulation refers to a set of DOM methods that allow you to create element and text nodes, and then attach them to the DOM tree or remove them from the DOM tree.

ADDING CONTENT

To add content, you use a DOM method to create new content one node at a time and store it in a variable. Then another DOM method is used to attach it to the right place in the DOM tree.

REMOVING CONTENT

You can remove an element (along with any contents and child elements it may contain) from the DOM tree using a single method.

EXAMPLE: ADDING A LIST ITEM

1: Create new text node

2: Create new element node

li

3: Add text node to element node

4: Select element you want to add the new fragment to

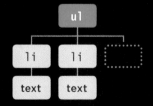

5: Append the new fragment to the selected element

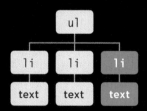

ACCESS & UPDATE TEXT & MARKUP WITH INNERHTML

Using the `innerHTML` property, you can access and amend the contents of an element, including any child elements.

innerHTML

When getting HTML from an element, the `innerHTML` property will get the content of an element and return it as one long string, including any markup that the element contains.

When used to set new content for an element, it will take a string that can contain markup and process that string, adding any elements within it to the DOM tree.

When adding new content using `innerHTML`, be aware that one missing closing tag could throw out the design of the entire page.

Even worse, if `innerHTML` is used to add content that your users created to a page, they could add malicious content. See p228.

```
<li id="one"><em>fresh</em> figs</li>
```

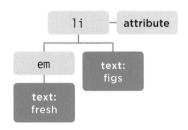

GET CONTENT

The following line of code collects the content of the list item and adds it to a variable called `elContent`:

```
var elContent = document.getElementById('one').innerHTML;
```

The `elContent` variable would now hold the string:
`'<em>fresh</em> figs'`

SET CONTENT

The following line of code adds the content of the `elContent` variable (including any markup) to the first list item:

```
document.getElementById('one').innerHTML = elContent;
```

UPDATE TEXT & MARKUP

This example starts by storing the first list item in a variable called `firstItem`.

It then retrieves the content of this list item and stores it in a variable called `itemContent`.

Finally, the content of the list item is placed inside a link. Note how the quotes are escaped.

JAVASCRIPT   c05/js/inner-html.js

```javascript
// Store the first list item in a variable
var firstItem = document.getElementById('one');

// Get the content of the first list item
var itemContent = firstItem.innerHTML;

// Update the content of the first list item so it is a link
firstItem.innerHTML = '<a href=\"http://example.org\">' + itemContent + '</a>';
```

RESULT

As the content of the string is added to the element using the `innerHTML` property, the browser will add any elements in the string to the DOM. In this example, an `<a>` element has been added to the page. (Any new elements will also be available to other scripts in the page.)

If you use attributes in your HTML code, escaping the quotation using the backslash character \ can make it clearer that those characters are not part of the script.

ADDING ELEMENTS USING DOM MANIPULATION

DOM manipulation offers another technique to add new content to a page (rather than innerHTML). It involves three steps:

1
CREATE THE ELEMENT
createElement()

You start by creating a new element node using the createElement() method. This element node is stored in a variable.

When the element node is created, it is not yet part of the DOM tree. It is not added to the DOM tree until step 3.

2
GIVE IT CONTENT
createTextNode()

createTextNode() creates a new text node. Again, the node is stored in a variable. It can be added to the element node using the appendChild() method.

This provides the content for the element, although you can skip this step if you want to attach an empty element to the DOM tree.

3
ADD IT TO THE DOM
appendChild()

Now that you have your element (optionally with some content in a text node), you can add it to the DOM tree using the appendChild() method.

The appendChild() method allows you to specify which element you want this node added to, as a child of it.

In the example at the end of the chapter, you will see another method that can be used to insert an element into the DOM tree. The insertBefore() method is used to add a new element before the selected DOM node.

DOM manipulation and innerHTML both have uses. You will see a discussion of when to choose each method on p226.

Note: You may see developers leave an empty element in their HTML pages in order to attach new content to that element, but this practice is best avoided unless absolutely necessary.

ADDING AN ELEMENT TO THE DOM TREE

createElement() creates an element that can be added to the DOM tree, in this case an empty `<li>` element for the list.

This new element is stored inside a variable called newEl until it is attached to the DOM tree later on.

createTextNode() allows you to create a new text node to attach to an element. It is stored in a variable called newText.

c05/js/add-element.js

JAVASCRIPT

```javascript
// Create a new element and store it in a variable.
var newEl = document.createElement('li');

// Create a text node and store it in a variable.
var newText = document.createTextNode('quinoa');

// Attach the new text node to the new element.
newEl.appendChild(newText);

// Find the position where the new element should be added.
var position = document.getElementsByTagName('ul')[0];

// Insert the new element into its position.
position.appendChild(newEl);
```

RESULT

The text node is added to the new element node using appendChild().

The getElementsByTagName() method selects the position in the DOM tree to insert the new element (the first `<ul>` element in the page).

Finally, appendChild() is used again - this time to insert the new element and its content into the DOM tree.

REMOVING ELEMENTS VIA DOM MANIPULATION

DOM manipulation can be used to remove elements from the DOM tree.

1
STORE THE ELEMENT TO BE REMOVED IN A VARIABLE

You start by selecting the element that is going to be removed and store that element node in a variable.

You can use any of the methods you saw in the section on DOM queries to select the element.

2
STORE THE PARENT OF THAT ELEMENT IN A VARIABLE

Next, you find the parent element that contains the element you want to remove and store that element node in a variable.

The simplest way to get this element is to use the `parentNode` property of this element.

3
REMOVE THE ELEMENT FROM ITS CONTAINING ELEMENT

The `removeChild()` method is used on the containing element that you selected in step 2.

The `removeChild()` method takes one parameter: the reference to the element that you no longer want.

When you remove an element from the DOM, it will also remove any child elements.

The example on the right is quite simple, but this technique can significantly alter the DOM tree.

Removing elements from the DOM will affect the index number of siblings in a NodeList.

REMOVING AN ELEMENT FROM THE DOM TREE

This example uses the `removeChild()` method to remove the fourth item from the list (along with its contents).

The first variable, `removeEl`, stores the actual element you want to remove from the page (the fourth list item).

The second variable, `containerEl`, stores the `<ul>` element that *contains* the element you want to remove.

c05/js/remove-element.js

```
var removeEl = document.getElementsByTagName('li')[3]; // The element to remove

var containerEl = removeEl.parentNode;                 // Its containing element

containerEl.removeChild(removeEl);                     // Removing the element
```

RESULT

The `removeChild()` method is used on the variable that holds the container node.

It requires one parameter: the element you want to remove (which is stored in the second variable).

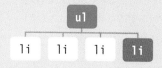

● CONTAINER ELEMENT
● ELEMENT TO BE REMOVED

COMPARING TECHNIQUES: UPDATING HTML CONTENT

So far, you have seen three techniques for adding HTML to a web page. It's time to compare when you should use each one.

In any programming language, there are often several ways to achieve the same task. In fact, if you asked ten programmers to write the same script, you may well find ten different approaches.

Some programmers can be rather opinionated and believe that their way is always the "right" way to do things – when there are often several right ways. If you understand why people prefer some approaches over others, then you are in a strong position to decide whether it meets the needs of your project.

document.write()

The document object's `write()` method is a simple way to add content that was not in the original source code to the page, but its use is rarely advised.

ADVANTAGES

- It is a quick and easy way to show beginners how content can be added to a page.

DISADVANTAGES

- It only works when the page initially loads.
- If you use it after the page has loaded it can:
  1. Overwrite the whole page
  2. Not add the content to the page
  3. Create a new page
- It can cause problems with XHTML pages that are strictly validated.
- This method is very rarely used by programmers these days and is generally frowned upon.

You can choose different techniques depending on the task (and keep in mind how the site might be developed in the future).

element.innerHTML

The innerHTML property lets you get/update the entire content of any element (including markup) as a string.

ADVANTAGES

- You can use it to add a lot of new markup using less code than DOM manipulation methods.
- It can be faster than DOM manipulation when adding a lot of new elements to a web page.
- It is a simple way to remove all of the content from one element (by assigning it a blank string).

DISADVANTAGES

- It should not be used to add content that has come from a user (such as a username or blog comment), as it can pose a significant security risk which is discussed over the next four pages.
- It can be difficult to isolate single elements that you want to update within a larger DOM fragment.
- Event handlers may no longer work as intended.

DOM MANIPULATION

DOM manipulation refers to using a set of methods and properties to access, create, and update elements and text nodes.

ADVANTAGES

- It is suited to changing one element from a DOM fragment where there are many siblings.
- It does not affect event handlers.
- It easily allows a script to add elements incrementally (when you do not want to alter a lot of code at once).

DISADVANTAGES

- If you have to make a lot of changes to the content of a page, it is slower than innerHTML.
- You need to write more code to achieve the same thing compared with innerHTML.

CROSS-SITE SCRIPTING (XSS) ATTACKS

If you add HTML to a page using `innerHTML` (or several jQuery methods), you need to be aware of **Cross-Site Scripting Attacks** or **XSS**; otherwise, an attacker could gain access to your users' accounts.

This book has several warnings about security issues when you add HTML to a page using `innerHTML`. (There are also notes about it when using jQuery.)

The next four pages describe the issues you need to be aware of, and how to make your site secure against these kinds of attacks.

HOW XSS HAPPENS

XSS involves an attacker placing malicious code into a site. Websites often feature content created by many different people. For example:

- Users can create profiles or add comments
- Multiple authors may contribute articles
- Data can come from third-party sites such as Facebook, Twitter, news tickers, and other feeds
- Files such as images and video may be uploaded

Data you do not have complete control over is known as **untrusted data**; it must be handled with care.

WHAT CAN THESE ATTACKS DO?

XSS can give the attacker access to information in:

- The DOM (including form data)
- That website's cookies
- Session tokens: information that identifies you from other users when you log into a site

This could let the attacker access a user account and:

- Make purchases with that account
- Post defamatory content
- Spread their malicious code further / faster

EVEN SIMPLE CODE CAN CAUSE PROBLEMS:

Malicious code often mixes HTML and JavaScript (although URLs and CSS can be used to trigger XSS attacks). The two examples below demonstrate how fairly simple code could help an attacker access a user's account.

This first example stores cookie data in a variable, which could then be sent to a third-party server:

```
<script>var adr='http://example.com/xss.php?cookie=' + escape(document.cookie);</script>
```

This code shows how a missing image can be used with an HTML attribute to trigger malicious code:

```
<img src="http://nofile" onerror="adr='http://example.com/xss.php?'+escape(document.cookie)";>
```

Any HTML from untrusted sources opens your site to XSS attacks. But the threat is only from certain characters.

DEFENDING AGAINST CROSS-SITE SCRIPTING

VALIDATE INPUT GOING TO THE SERVER

1. Only let visitors input the kind of characters they need to when supplying information. This is known as **validation**. Do not allow untrusted users to submit HTML markup or JavaScript.

2. Double-check validation on the server before displaying user content/storing it in a database. This is important because users could bypass validation in the browser by turning JavaScript off.

3. The database may safely contain markup and script from trusted sources (e.g., your content management system). This is because it does not try to process the code; it just stores it.

REQUESTS PAGES FROM
AND SENDS FORM DATA
TO WEB SERVER

COLLECTS INFORMATION
FROM BROWSER AND
PASSES IT TO DATABASE

STORES INFORMATION
CREATED BY WEBSITE
ADMINS AND USERS

BROWSER

PROCESSES HTML, CSS,
AND JAVASCRIPT FILES
SENT FROM WEB SERVER

WEB SERVER

GENERATES PAGES USING
DATA FROM DATABASE AND
INSERTS IT INTO TEMPLATES

DATABASE

RETURNS CONTENT NEEDED
TO CREATE WEB PAGES

ESCAPE DATA COMING FROM THE SERVER & DATABASE

6. Do not create DOM fragments containing HTML from untrusted sources. It should only be added as text once it has been escaped.

5. Make sure that you are only inserting content generated by users into certain parts of the template files (see p230).

4. As your data leaves the database, all potentially dangerous characters should be escaped (see p231).

So, you can safely use `innerHTML` to add markup to a page if you have written the code – but content from any untrusted sources should be escaped and added as text (not markup), using properties like `textContent`.

XSS: VALIDATION & TEMPLATES

Make sure that your users can only input characters they need to use and limit where this content will be shown on the page.

FILTER OR VALIDATE INPUT

The most basic defense is to prevent users from entering characters into form fields that they do not **need** to use when providing that kind of information.

For example, users' names and email addresses will not contain angled brackets, ampersands, or parentheses, so you can validate data to prevent characters like this being used.

This can be done in the browser, but must also be done on the server (in case the user has JavaScript turned off). You learn about validation in Chapter 13.

You may have seen that the comment sections on websites rarely allow you to enter a lot of markup (they sometimes allow a limited subset of HTML). This is to prevent people from entering malicious code such as `<script>` tags, or any other character with an event handling attribute.

Even the HTML editors used in many content management systems will limit the code that you are allowed to use within them, and will automatically try to correct any markup that looks malicious.

LIMIT WHERE USER CONTENT GOES

Malicious users will not *just* use `<script>` tags to try and create an XSS attack. As you saw on p228, malicious code can live in an event handler attribute without being wrapped in `<script>` tags. XSS can also be triggered by malicious code in CSS or URLs.

Browsers process HTML, CSS, and JavaScript in different ways (or execution contexts), and in each language different characters can cause problems. Therefore, you should only add content from untrusted sources as text (not markup), and place that text in elements that are visible in the viewport.

Never place any user's content in the following places without detailed experience of the issues involved (which are beyond the scope of this book):

Script tags:	`<script>not here</script>`
HTML comments:	`<!-- not here -->`
Tag names:	`<notHere href="/test" />`
Attributes:	`<div notHere="norHere" />`
CSS values:	`{color: not here}`

XSS: ESCAPING & CONTROLLING MARKUP

Any content generated by users that contain characters that are used in code should be escaped on the server. You must control any markup added to the page.

ESCAPING USER CONTENT

All data from untrusted sources should be escaped on the server before it is shown on the page. Most server-side languages offer helper functions that will strip-out or escape malicious code.

HTML

Escape these characters so that they are displayed as characters (not processed as code).

```
&    &amp;        '    &#x27; (not &apos;)
<    &lt;         "    &quot;
>    &gt;         /    &#x2F;
`    &#x60;
```

JAVASCRIPT

Never include data from untrusted sources in JavaScript. It involves escaping all ASCII characters with a value less than 256 that are not alphanumeric characters (and can be a security risk).

URLS

If you have links containing user input (e.g., links to a user profile or search queries), use the JavaScript `encodeURIComponent()` method to encode the user input. It encodes the following characters:
```
,  /  ?  :  @  &  =  +  $  #
```

ADDING USER CONTENT

When you add untrusted content to an HTML page, once it has been escaped on the server, it should still be added to the page as text. JavaScript and jQuery both offer tools for doing this:

JAVASCRIPT

DO use: `textContent` or `innerText` (see p216)
DO NOT use: `innerHTML` (see p220)

JQUERY

DO use: `.text()` (see p316)
DO NOT use: `.html()` (see p316)

You can still use the `innerHTML` property and jQuery `.html()` method to add HTML to the DOM, but you must make sure that:

- You control **all** of the markup being generated (do not allow user content that could contain markup).
- The user's content is escaped and added as text using the approaches noted above, rather than adding the user's content as HTML.

ATTRIBUTE NODES

Once you have an element node, you can use other properties and methods on that element node to access and change its attributes.

There are two steps to accessing and updating attributes.

First, select the element node that carries the attribute and follow it with a period symbol.

Then, use one of the methods or properties below to work with that element's attributes.

Finds the element node (works with any technique covered in this chapter)

Gets the value of the attribute that was given as a parameter of the method

DOM QUERY

METHOD

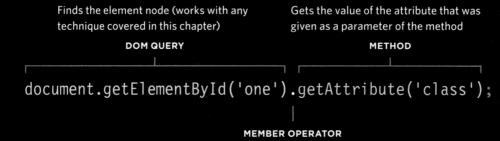

```
document.getElementById('one').getAttribute('class');
```

MEMBER OPERATOR

Indicates that the subsequent method will be used on the node specified to the left

METHOD	DESCRIPTION
getAttribute()	gets the value of an attribute
hasAttribute()	checks if element node has a specified attribute
setAttribute()	sets the value of an attribute
removeAttribute()	removes an attribute from an element node

PROPERTY	DESCRIPTION
className	gets or sets the value of the **class** attribute
id	gets or sets the value of the **id** attribute

You have seen that the DOM treats each HTML element as its own object in the DOM tree. The properties of the object correspond to the attributes that type of element can carry. On the left, you can see the **className** and **id** properties. (Others include **accessKey**, **checked**, **href**, **lang**, and **title**.)

CHECK FOR AN ATTRIBUTE AND GET ITS VALUES

Before you work with an attribute, it is good practice to check whether it exists. This will save resources if the attribute cannot be found.

The `hasAttribute()` method of any element node lets you check if an attribute exists. The attribute name is given as an argument in the parentheses.

Using `hasAttribute()` in an `if` statement like this means that the code inside the curly braces will run only if the attribute exists on the given element.

c05/js/get-attribute.js

```javascript
var firstItem = document.getElementById('one');      // Get first list item

if (firstItem.hasAttribute('class')) {               // If it has class attribute
    var attr = firstItem.getAttribute('class');      // Get the attribute

    // Add the value of the attribute after the list
    var el = document.getElementById('scriptResults');
    el.innerHTML = '<p>The first item has a class name: ' + attr + '</p>';

}
```

RESULT

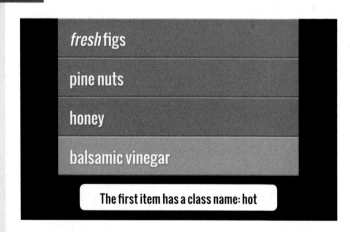

In this example, the DOM query `getElementById()` returns the element whose `id` attribute has a value of `one`.

The `hasAttribute()` method is used to check whether this element has a `class` attribute, and returns a Boolean. This is used with an `if` statement so that the code in the curly braces will run only if the `class` attribute does exist.

The `getAttribute()` method returns the value of the `class` attribute, which is then written to the page.

Browser Support: Both of these methods have good support in all major web browsers.

CREATING ATTRIBUTES & CHANGING THEIR VALUES

The `className` property allows you to change the value of the `class` attribute. If the attribute does not exist, it will be created and given the specified value.

You have seen this property used throughout the chapter to update the status of the list items. Below, you can see another way to achieve the task.

The `setAttribute()` method allows you to update the value of *any* attribute. It takes two parameters: the attribute name, and the value for the attribute.

```javascript
var firstItem = document.getElementById('one'); // Get the first item
firstItem.className = 'complete';               // Change its class attribute

var fourthItem = document.getElementsByTagName('li').item(3);// Get fourth item
fourthItem.setAttribute('class', 'cool');        // Add an attribute to it
```

c05/js/set-attribute.js

JAVASCRIPT

When there is a property (like the `className` or `id` properties), it is generally considered better to update the properties rather than use a method (because, behind the scenes, the method would just be setting the properties anyway).

When you update the value of an attribute (especially the `class` attribute) it can be used to trigger new CSS rules, and therefore change the appearance of the elements.

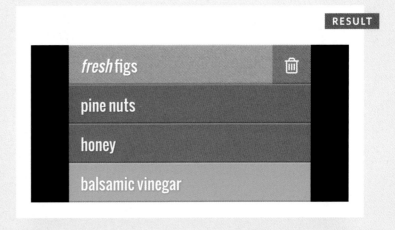

RESULT

Note: These techniques override the entire value of the `class` attribute. They do not add a new value to the existing value of the `class` attribute.

If you wanted to add a new value onto the existing value of the `class` attribute, you would need to read the content of the attribute first, then add the new text to that existing value of the attribute (or use the jQuery `.addClass()` method covered on p320).

REMOVING ATTRIBUTES

To remove an attribute from an element, first select the element, then call **removeAttribute()**. It has one parameter: the name of the attribute to remove.

Trying to remove an attribute that does not exist will not cause an error, but it is good practice to check for its existence before attempting to remove it.

In this example, the **getElementById()** method is used to retrieve the first item from this list, which has an **id** attribute with a value of **one**.

JAVASCRIPT   c05/js/remove-attribute.js

```javascript
var firstItem = document.getElementById('one'); // Get the first item
if (firstItem.hasAttribute('class')) {           // If it has a class attribute
    firstItem.removeAttribute('class');          // Remove its class attribute
}
```

RESULT

The script checks to see if the selected element has a **class** attribute and, if so, it is removed.

EXAMINING THE DOM IN CHROME

Modern browsers come with tools that help you inspect the page loaded in the browser and understand the structure of the DOM tree.

In the screenshot to the right, the `<li>` element is highlighted and the **Properties** panel (1) indicates that this is an:

- li element with an `id` attribute whose value is **one** and `class` whose value is **hot**
- an HTMLLIElement
- an HTMLElement
- an element
- a node
- an object

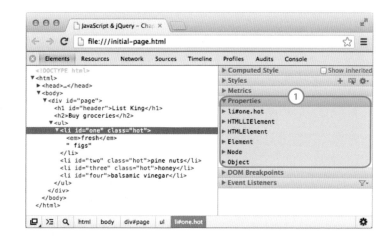

Each of these object names has an arrow next to it which you can use to expand that section.
It will tell you what properties are available to that kind of node.

They are separated because some properties are specific to list item elements, others to element nodes, others to all nodes, and others to all objects, and the different properties are listed under the corresponding type of node. But they do remind you of which properties you can access through the DOM node for that element.

To get the developer tools in Chrome on a Mac, go to the **View** menu, select **Developer** and then **Developer Tools**. On a PC, go to **Tools** (or **More Tools**) and select **Developer Tools**.

Or right-click on any element and select **Inspect Element**.

Select **Elements** from the menu that runs across the top of this tool. The source of the page will be shown on the left and several other options to the right.

Any element that has child elements has an arrow next to it that lets you expand and collapse the item to show and hide its content.

The **Properties** panel (on the right) tells you the type of object the selected element is. (In some versions of Chrome this is shown as a tab.) When you highlight different elements in the main left-hand window, you can see the values in the **Properties** panel on the right reflect that element.

EXAMINING THE DOM IN FIREFOX

Firefox has similar built-in tools, but you can also download a DOM inspector tool that shows the text nodes.

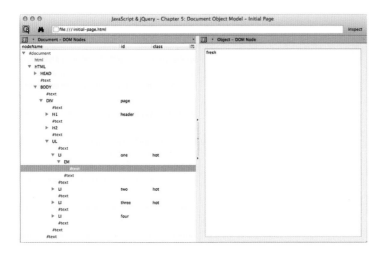

If you search online for "DOM Inspector", you will find the tool designed for Firefox shown on the left. In the screen shot, you can see a similar tree view to the one shown in Chrome, but it also shows you where there are whitespace nodes (they are shown as #text). In the panel to the right, you can see the value in the nodes; whitespace nodes have no value in this panel.

Another FIrefox extension worth trying is called Firebug.

Firefox also has a 3D view of the DOM, where a box is drawn around each element, and you can change the angle of the page to show which parts of it stick out more than others. The further they protrude the further into child elements they appear.

This can give you an interesting (and quick) glimpse into the complexity of the markup used on a page and the depth to which elements are nested.

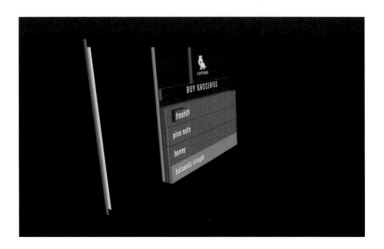

LISTKING

BUY GROCERIES 6

kale

fresh figs

pine nuts

honey

balsamic vinegar

EXAMPLE
DOCUMENT OBJECT MODEL

This example brings together a selection of the techniques you have seen throughout the chapter to update the contents of the list. It has three main aims:

1: Add a new item to the start and end of the list

Adding an item to the *start* of a list requires the use of a different method than adding an element to the *end* of the list.

2: Set a `class` attribute on all items

This involves looping through each of the `<li>` elements and updating the value of the `class` attribute to `cool`.

3: Add the number of list items to the heading

This involves four steps:
1. Reading the content of the heading
2. Counting the number of `<li>` elements in the page
3. Adding the number of items to the content of the heading
4. Updating the heading with this new content

EXAMPLE
DOCUMENT OBJECT MODEL

c05/js/example.js

```javascript
// ADDING ITEMS TO START AND END OF LIST
var list = document.getElementsByTagName('ul')[0];  // Get the <ul> element

// ADD NEW ITEM TO END OF LIST
var newItemLast = document.createElement('li');      // Create element
var newTextLast = document.createTextNode('cream');  // Create text node
newItemLast.appendChild(newTextLast);                // Add text node to element
list.appendChild(newItemLast);                       // Add element end of list

// ADD NEW ITEM START OF LIST
var newItemFirst = document.createElement('li');     // Create element
var newTextFirst = document.createTextNode('kale');  // Create text node
newItemFirst.appendChild(newTextFirst);              // Add text node to element
list.insertBefore(newItemFirst, list.firstChild);    // Add element to list
```

This part of the example adds two new list items to the <ul> element: one to the end of the list and one to the start of it. The technique used here is DOM manipulation and there are four steps to creating a new element node and adding it to the DOM tree:

1. Create the element node
2. Create the text node
3. Add the text node to the element node
4. Add the element to the DOM tree

To achieve step four, you must first specify the *parent* that will contain the new node. In both cases, this is the <ul> element. The node for this element is stored in a variable called list because it is used many times.

The appendChild() method adds new nodes as a child of the parent element. It has one parameter: the new content to be added to the DOM tree. If the parent element already has child elements, it will be added after the last of these (and will therefore be the last child of the parent element).

parent.appendChild(*newItem*);

(You have seen this method used several times both to add new elements to the tree and to add text nodes to element nodes.)

To add the item to the *start* of the list, the insertBefore() method is used. This requires one extra piece of information: the element you want to add the new content before (the target element).

parent.insertBefore(*newItem*, *target*);

EXAMPLE
DOCUMENT OBJECT MODEL

```javascript
var listItems = document.querySelectorAll('li');        // All <li> elements

// ADD A CLASS OF COOL TO ALL LIST ITEMS
var i;                                                   // Counter variable
for (i = 0; i < listItems.length; i++) {                // Loop through elements
 listItems[i].className = 'cool';                        // Change class to cool
}

// ADD NUMBER OF ITEMS IN THE LIST TO THE HEADING
var heading = document.querySelector('h2');             // h2 element
var headingText = heading.firstChild.nodeValue;         // h2 text
var totalItems = listItems.length;                      // No. of <li> elements
var newHeading = headingText + '<span>' + totalItems + '</span>'; // Content
heading.innerHTML = newHeading;                         // Update h2
```

The next step of this example is to loop through all of the elements in the list and update the value of their class attributes, setting them to cool.

This is achieved by first collecting all of the list item elements and storing them in a variable called listItems. A for loop is then used to go through each of them in turn. In order to tell how many times the loop should run, you use the length property.

Finally, the code updates the heading to include the number of list items. It updates it using the innerHTML property as opposed to the DOM manipulation techniques used earlier in the script.

This demonstrates how you can add to the content of an existing element by reading its current value and adding to it. You could use a similar technique if you needed to add a value to an attribute – without overwriting its existing value.

To update the heading with the number of items in the list, you need two pieces of information:
1. **The original content of the heading** so that you can add the number of list items to it. It is collected using the nodeValue property (although innerHTML or textContent would do the same).
2. **The number of list items**, which can be found using the length property on the listItems variable.

With this information ready, there are two steps to updating the content of the <h2> element:
1. **Creating the new heading** and storing it in a variable – the new heading will be made up of the original heading content, followed by the number of items in the list.
2. **Updating the heading**, which is done by updating the content of the heading element using the innerHTML property of that node.

SUMMARY
DOCUMENT OBJECT MODEL

▸ The browser represents the page using a DOM tree.

▸ DOM trees have four types of nodes: document nodes, element nodes, attribute nodes, and text nodes.

▸ You can select element nodes by their `id` or `class` attributes, by tag name, or using CSS selector syntax.

▸ Whenever a DOM query can return more than one node, it will always return a `NodeList`.

▸ From an element node, you can access and update its content using properties such as `textContent` and `innerHTML` or using DOM manipulation techniques.

▸ An element node can contain multiple text nodes and child elements that are siblings of each other.

▸ In older browsers, implementation of the DOM is inconsistent (and is a popular reason for using jQuery).

▸ Browsers offer tools for viewing the DOM tree.

6

EVENTS

When you browse the web, your browser registers different types of events. It's the browser's way of saying, "Hey, this just happened." Your script can then respond to these events.

Scripts often respond to these events by updating the content of the web page (via the Document Object Model) which makes the page feel more interactive. In this chapter, you will learn how:

INTERACTIONS CREATE EVENTS

Events occur when users click or tap on a link, hover or swipe over an element, type on the keyboard, resize the window, or when the page they requested has loaded.

EVENTS TRIGGER CODE

When an event occurs, or fires, it can be used to trigger a particular function. Different code can be triggered when users interact with different parts of the page.

CODE RESPONDS TO USERS

In the last chapter, you saw how the DOM can be used to update a page. The events can trigger the kinds of changes the DOM is capable of. This is how a web page reacts to users.

DIFFERENT EVENT TYPES

Here is a selection of the events that occur in the browser while you are browsing the web. Any of these events can be used to trigger a function in your JavaScript code.

UI EVENTS

Occur when a user interacts with the browser's user interface (UI) rather than the web page

EVENT	DESCRIPTION
load	Web page has finished loading
unload	Web page is unloading (usually because a new page was requested)
error	Browser encounters a JavaScript error or an asset doesn't exist
resize	Browser window has been resized
scroll	User has scrolled up or down the page

KEYBOARD EVENTS

Occur when a user interacts with the keyboard (see also input event)

EVENT	DESCRIPTION
keydown	User first presses a key (repeats while key is depressed)
keyup	User releases a key
keypress	Character is being inserted (repeats while key is depressed)

MOUSE EVENTS

Occur when a user interacts with a mouse, trackpad, or touchscreen

EVENT	DESCRIPTION
click	User presses and releases a button over the same element
dblclick	User presses and releases a button twice over the same element
mousedown	User presses a mouse button while over an element
mouseup	User releases a mouse button while over an element
mousemove	User moves the mouse (not on a touchscreen)
mouseover	User moves the mouse over an element (not on a touchscreen)
mouseout	User moves the mouse off an element (not on a touchscreen)

TERMINOLOGY

EVENTS FIRE OR ARE RAISED

When an event has occurred, it is often described as having **fired** or
been **raised**. In the diagram on the right, if the user is tapping on a link, a
`click` event would fire in the browser.

EVENTS TRIGGER SCRIPTS

Events are said to **trigger** a function or script. When the `click` event
fires on the element in this diagram, it could trigger a script that enlarges
the selected item.

FOCUS EVENTS

Occur when an element (e.g., a link or form field) gains or loses focus

EVENT	DESCRIPTION
focus / focusin	Element gains focus
blur / focusout	Element loses focus

FORM EVENTS

Occur when a user interacts with a form element

EVENT	DESCRIPTION
input	Value in any `<input>` or `<textarea>` element has changed (IE9+) or any element with the `contenteditable` attribute
change	Value in select box, checkbox, or radio button changes (IE9+)
submit	User submits a form (using a button or a key)
reset	User clicks on a form's reset button (rarely used these days)
cut	User cuts content from a form field
copy	User copies content from a form field
paste	User pastes content into a form field
select	User selects some text in a form field

MUTATION EVENTS*

Occur when the DOM structure has been changed by a script
* To be replaced by mutation observers (see p284)

EVENT	DESCRIPTION
DOMSubtreeModified	Change has been made to document
DOMNodeInserted	Node has been inserted as a direct child of another node
DOMNodeRemoved	Node has been removed from another node
DOMNodeInsertedIntoDocument	Node has been inserted as a descendant of another node
DOMNodeRemovedFromDocument	Node has been removed as a descendant of another node

HOW EVENTS TRIGGER JAVASCRIPT CODE

When the user interacts with the HTML on a web page, there are three steps involved in getting it to trigger some JavaScript code. Together these steps are known as **event handling**.

1

Select the **element** node(s) you want the script to respond to.

For example, if you want to trigger a function when a user clicks on a specific link, you need to get the DOM node for that link element. You do this using a DOM query (see Chapter 5).

2

Indicate which **event** on the selected node(s) will trigger the response.

Programmers call this **binding** an event to a DOM node.

The previous two pages showed a selection of the popular events that you can monitor for.

3

State the **code** you want to run when the event occurs.

When the event occurs, on a specified element, it will trigger a function. This may be a named or an anonymous function.

The UI events that relate to the browser window (rather than the HTML page loaded in it) work with the window object rather than an element node. Examples include the events that occur when a requested page has finished loading, or when the user scrolls. You will learn about using these on p272.

Some events work with most element nodes, such as the mouseover event, which is triggered when the user rolls over any element. Other events only work with specific element nodes, such as the submit event, which only works with a form.

Here you can see how event handling can be used to provide feedback to users filling in a registration form. It will show an error message if their username is too short.

1
SELECT ELEMENT

The element that users are interacting with is the text input where they enter the username.

2
SPECIFY EVENT

When users move out of the text input, it loses focus, and the blur event fires on this element.

3
CALL CODE

When the blur event fires on the username input, it will trigger a function called checkUsername(). This function checks if the username is less than 5 characters.

If there are not enough characters, it shows an error message that prompts the user to enter a longer username.

If there *are* enough characters, the element that holds the error message should be cleared.

This is because an error message may have been shown to the user already and they subsequently corrected their mistake. (If the error message was still visible when they had filled in the form correctly, it would be confusing.)

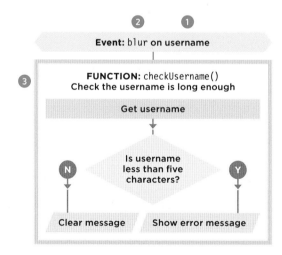

THREE WAYS TO BIND AN EVENT TO AN ELEMENT

Event handlers let you indicate which event you
are waiting for on any particular element.
There are three types of event handlers.

HTML EVENT HANDLERS

See p251

This is bad practice, but you need to be aware of it because you may see it in older code.

Early versions of HTML included a set of attributes that could respond to events on the element they were added to. The attribute names matched the event names. Their values called the function that was to run when that event occurred.

For example, the following:
`<a onclick="hide()">`
indicated that when a user clicked on this `<a>` element, the `hide()` function would be called.

This method of event handling is no longer used because it is better to separate the JavaScript from the HTML. You should use one of the other approaches shown on this page instead.

TRADITIONAL DOM EVENT HANDLERS

See p252

DOM **event handlers** were introduced in the original specification for the DOM. They are considered better than HTML event handlers because they let you separate the JavaScript from the HTML.

Support in all major browsers is very strong for this approach. The main drawback is that you can only attach a single function to any event. For example, the submit event of a form cannot trigger one function that checks the contents of a form, and a second to submit the form data if it passes the checks.

As a result of this limitation, if more than one script is used on the same page, and both scripts respond to the same event, then one or both of the scripts may not work as intended.

DOM LEVEL 2 EVENT LISTENERS

See p254

Event listeners were introduced in an update to the DOM specification (DOM level 2, released in the year 2000). They are now the favored way of handling events.

The syntax is quite different and, unlike traditional event handlers, these newer event listeners allow one event to trigger multiple functions. As a result, there are less likely to be conflicts between different scripts that run on the same page.

This approach does not work with IE8 (or earlier versions of IE) but you meet a workaround on p258. Differences in browser support for the DOM and events helped speed adoption of jQuery (but you need to know how events work to understand how jQuery uses them).

HTML EVENT HANDLER ATTRIBUTES (DO NOT USE)

Please note: This approach is now considered bad practice; however, you need to be aware of it because you may see it if you are looking at older code. (See previous page.)

In the HTML, the first `<input>` element has an attribute called `onblur` (triggered when the user leaves the element). The value of the attribute is the name of the function that it should trigger.

The value of the event handler attributes would be JavaScript. Often it would call a function that was written either in the `<head>` element or a separate JavaScript file (as shown below).

HTML   c06/event-attributes.html

```html
<form method="post" action="http://www.example.org/register">
  <label for="username">Create a username: </label>
  <input type="text" id="username" onblur="checkUsername()" />
  <div id="feedback"></div>

  <label for="password">Create a password: </label>
  <input type="password" id="password" />

  <input type="submit" value="Sign up!" />
</form>
...
<script type="text/javascript" src="js/event-attributes.js"></script>
```

JAVASCRIPT   c06/js/event-attributes.js

```javascript
function checkUsername() {                                 // Declare function
  var elMsg = document.getElementById('feedback');         // Get feedback element
  var elUsername = document.getElementById('username');// Get username input
  if (elUsername.value.length < 5) {                       // If username too short
    elMsg.textContent = 'Username must be 5 characters or more'; // Set msg
  } else {                                                 // Otherwise
    elMsg.textContent = '';                                // Clear message
  }
}
```

The names of the HTML event handler attributes are identical to the event names shown on p246 – p247, preceded by the word "on."

For example:
- `<a>` elements can have onclick, onmouseover, onmouseout
- `<form>` elements can have onsubmit
- `<input>` elements for text can have onkeypress, onfocus, onblur

TRADITIONAL DOM EVENT HANDLERS

All modern browsers understand this way of creating an event handler, but you can only attach one function to each event handler.

Here is the syntax to bind an event to an element using an event handler, and to indicate which function should execute when that event fires:

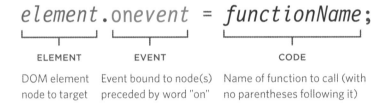

element.**onevent** = *functionName*;

ELEMENT   EVENT   CODE

DOM element node to target

Event bound to node(s) preceded by word "on"

Name of function to call (with no parentheses following it)

Below, the event handler is on the last line (after the function has been defined and the DOM element node(s) selected).

When a function is called, the parentheses that follow its name tell the JavaScript interpreter to "run this code now."

We don't want the code to run until the event fires, so the parentheses are omitted from the event handler on the last line.

The code starts by defining the named function.

A reference to the DOM element node is often stored in a variable.

```
function checkUsername() {
    // code to check the length of username
}
var el = document.getElementById('username');
el.onblur = checkUsername;
```

The event name is preceded by the word "on."

The function is called by the event handler on the last line, but the parentheses are omitted.

An example of an anonymous function and a function with parameters is shown on p256.

USING DOM EVENT HANDLERS

In this example, the event handler appears on the last line of the JavaScript. Before the DOM event handler, two things are put in place:

1. If you use a named function when the event fires on your chosen DOM node, write that function first. (You could also use an anonymous function.)

2. The DOM element node is stored in a variable. Here the text input (whose id attribute has a value of username) is placed into a variable called elUsername.

```
function checkUsername() {                                      // Declare function
  var elMsg = document.getElementById('feedback');             // Get feedback element
  if (this.value.length < 5) {                                 // If username too short
    elMsg.textContent = 'Username must be 5 characters or more';   // Set msg
  } else {                                                     // Otherwise
    elMsg.textContent = '';                                    // Clear message
  }
}

var elUsername = document.getElementById('username');  // Get username input
elUsername.onblur = checkUsername;  // When it loses focus call checkuserName()
```

When using event handlers, the event name is preceded by the word "on" (onsubmit, onchange, onfocus, onblur, onmouseover, onmouseout, etc).

3. On the last line of the code sample above, the event handler elUsername.onblur indicates that the code is waiting for the blur event to fire on the element stored in the variable called elUsername.

This is followed by an equal sign, then the name of the function that will run when the event fires on that element. Note that there are no parentheses on the function name. This means you cannot pass arguments to this function. (If you want to pass arguments to a function in an event handler, see p256.)

The HTML is the same as that shown on p251 but without the onblur event attribute. This means that the event handler is in the JavaScript, not the HTML.

Browser support: On line 3, the checkUsername() function uses the this keyword in the conditional statement to check the number of characters the user entered. It works in most browsers because they know this refers to the element the event happened on.

However, in Internet Explorer 8 or earlier, IE would treat this as the window object. As a result, it would not know which element the event occurred on and there would be no value that it checked the length of, so it would raise an error. You will learn a solution for this issue on p264.

EVENT LISTENERS

Event listeners are a more recent approach to handling events.
They can deal with more than one function at a time
but they are not supported in older browsers.

Here is the syntax to bind an event to an element using an event listener,
and to indicate which function should execute when that event fires:

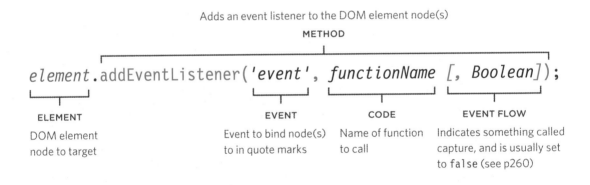

Adds an event listener to the DOM element node(s)

METHOD

```
element.addEventListener('event', functionName [, Boolean]);
```

ELEMENT

DOM element
node to target

EVENT

Event to bind node(s)
to in quote marks

CODE

Name of function
to call

EVENT FLOW

Indicates something called
capture, and is usually set
to `false` (see p260)

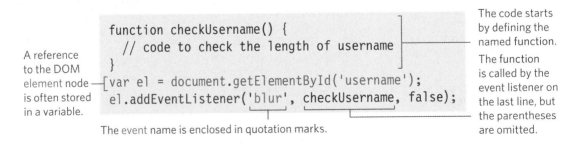

A reference
to the DOM
element node
is often stored
in a variable.

```
function checkUsername() {
    // code to check the length of username
}
var el = document.getElementById('username');
el.addEventListener('blur', checkUsername, false);
```

The event name is enclosed in quotation marks.

The code starts
by defining the
named function.

The function
is called by the
event listener on
the last line, but
the parentheses
are omitted.

An example of an anonymous function and a function with parameters is shown on p256.

USING EVENT LISTENERS

In this example, the event listener appears on the last line of the JavaScript. Before you write an event listener, two things are put in place:

1. If you use a named function when the event fires on your chosen DOM node, write that function first. (You could also use an anonymous function.)

2. The DOM element node(s) is stored in a variable. Here the text input (whose id attribute has a value of username) is placed into a variable called elUsername.

JAVASCRIPT   c06/js/event-listener.js

```
① function checkUsername() {                                              // Declare function
     var elMsg = document.getElementById('feedback');                     // Get feedback element
     if (this.value.length < 5) {                                         // If username too short
       elMsg.textContent = 'Username must be 5 characters or more'; // Set msg
     } else {                                                             // Otherwise
       elMsg.textContent = '';                                           // Clear msg
     }
   }

② var elUsername = document.getElementById('username');  // Get username input
   // When it loses focus call checkUsername()
   elUsername.addEventListener('blur', checkUsername, false);
```

          (i)   (ii)   (iii)

The addEventListener() method takes three properties:

i) The event you want it to listen for. In this case, the blur event.

ii) The code that you want it to run when the event fires. In this example, it is the checkUsername() function. Note that the parentheses are omitted where the function is called because they would indicate that the function should run as the page loads (rather than when the event fires).

iii) A Boolean indicating how events flow, see p260. (This is usually set to false.)

BROWSER SUPPORT

Internet Explorer 8 and earlier versions of IE do not support the addEventListener() method, but they do support a method called attachEvent() and you will see how to use this on p258.

Also, as with the previous example, IE8 and older versions of IE would not know what this referred to in the conditional statement. An alternative approach for dealing with it is shown on p270.

EVENT NAMES

Unlike the HTML and traditional DOM event handlers, when you specify the name of the event that you want to react to, the event name is not preceded by the word "on".

If you need to remove an event listener, there is a function called removeEventListener() which removes the event listener from the specified element (it has the same parameters).

USING PARAMETERS WITH EVENT HANDLERS & LISTENERS

Because you cannot have parentheses after the function names in event handlers or listeners, passing arguments requires a workaround.

Usually, when a function needs some information to do its job, you pass arguments within the parentheses that follow the function name.

When the interpreter sees the parentheses after a function call, it runs the code straight away. In an event handler, you want it to wait until the event triggers it.

Therefore, if you need to pass arguments to a function that is called by an event handler or listener, you wrap the function call in an **anonymous function**.

The named function includes parentheses containing the parameter after the function name.

Event name   Start of anonymous function

```
el.addEventListener('blur', function() {
    checkUsername(5);
}, false);
```

The anonymous function is used as the second argument. It "wraps around" the named function.

End of statement
End of addEventListener() method
Event flow Boolean (see p260)
End of anonymous function

The named function that requires the arguments lives inside the anonymous function.

Although the anonymous function has parentheses, it only runs when the event is triggered.

The named function can use arguments as it only runs if the anonymous function is called.

USING PARAMETERS WITH EVENT LISTENERS

The first line of this example shows the updated `checkUsername()` function. The `minLength` parameter specifies the minimum number of characters that the username should be.

The value that is passed into the `checkUsername()` function is used in the conditional statement to check if the name is long enough, and provide feedback if the username name is too short.

c06/js/event-listener-with-parameters.js

```javascript
var elUsername = document.getElementById('username');   // Get username input
var elMsg = document.getElementById('feedback');        // Get feedback element

function checkUsername(minLength) {                      // Declare function
  if (elUsername.value.length < minLength) {            // If username too short
    // Set the error message
    elMsg.textContent = 'Username must be ' + minLength + ' characters or more';
  } else {                                               // Otherwise
    elMsg.innerHTML = '';                                // Clear msg
  }
}

elUsername.addEventListener('blur', function() {         // When it loses focus
  checkUsername(5);                                      // Pass arguments here
}, false);
```

The event listener on the last three lines is longer than the previous example because the call to the `checkUsername()` function needs to include the value for the `minLength` parameter.

To receive this information, the event listener uses an anonymous function, which acts like a wrapper. Inside that wrapper the `checkUsername()` function is called, and passed an argument.

Browser support: On the next page you also see how to deal with the lack of support for event listeners in IE8 and earlier.

SUPPORTING OLDER VERSIONS OF IE

IE5-8 had a different event model and did not support addEventListener() but you can provide fallback code to make event listeners work with older versions of IE.

IE5-IE8 did not support the addEventListener() method. Instead, it used its own method called attachEvent() which did the same job, but was only available in Internet Explorer. If you want to use event listeners and need to support Internet Explorer 8 or earlier, you can use a conditional statement as illustrated below.

Using an if...else statement, you can check if the browser supports the addEventListener() method. The condition in the if statement will return true if the browser supports the addEventListener() method, and you can use it. If the browser does not support that method, it returns false, and the code will try to use the attachEvent() method.

If the browser supports addEventListener():

Run the code inside these curly braces

If it doesn't, do something else:

Run the code inside these curly braces

```
if (el.addEventListener) {
    el.addEventListener('blur', function() {
        checkUsername(5);
    }, false );
} else {
    el.attachEvent('onblur', function() {
        checkUsername(5);
    });
}
```

When attachEvent() is used, the event name should be preceded by the word "on" (e.g., blur becomes onblur). You will see another approach to supporting the older IE event model in Chapter 13 (using a utility file).

FALLBACK FOR USING EVENT LISTENERS IN IE8

The event handling code builds on the last example, but it is a lot longer this time because it contains the fallback for Internet Explorer 5-8.

After the checkUsername() function, an if statement checks whether addEventListener() is supported or not; it returns true if the element node supports this method, and false if it does not.

If the browser supports the addEventListener() method, the code inside the first set of curly braces is run using addEventListener().

If it is not supported, then the browser will use the attachEvent() method that older versions of IE will understand. In the IE version, note that the event name must be preceded by the word "on."

JAVASCRIPT   c06/js/event-listener-with-ie-fallback.js

```javascript
var elUsername = document.getElementById('username');  // Get username input
var elMsg = document.getElementById('feedback');       // Get feedback element

function checkUsername(minLength) {                     // Declare function
  if (elUsername.value.length < minLength) {           // If username too short
    // Set message
    elMsg.innerHTML = 'Username must be ' + minLength + ' characters or more';
  } else {                                             // Otherwise
    elMsg.innerHTML = '';                              // Clear message
  }
}

if (elUsername.addEventListener) {                     // If event listener supported
  elUsername.addEventListener('blur', function(){      // When username loses focus
    checkUsername(5);                                  // Call checkUsername()
  }, false );                                          // Capture during bubble phase
} else {                                               // Otherwise
  elUsername.attachEvent('onblur', function(){         // IE fallback: onblur
    checkUsername(5);                                  // Call checkUsername()
  });
}
```

If you need to support IE8 (or older), instead of writing this fallback code for *every* event you are responding to, it is better to write your own function (known as a helper function) that creates the appropriate event handler for you. You will see a demonstration of this in Chapter 13, which covers form enhancement and validation.

It is, however, important to understand this syntax, used by IE8 (and older) so that you know why the helper function is used and what it is doing.

As you will see in the next chapter, this is another type of cross-browser inconsistency that jQuery can take care of for you.

EVENT FLOW

HTML elements nest inside other elements. If you hover or click on a link, you will also be hovering or clicking on its parent elements.

Imagine a list item contains a link. When you hover over the link or click on it, JavaScript can trigger events on the **<a>** element, and also any elements the **<a>** element sits inside.

Event handlers/listeners can be bound to the containing **<li>**, **<ul>**, **<body>**, and **<html>** elements, plus the **document** object, and the **window** object. The order in which the events fire is known as **event flow**, and events flow in two directions.

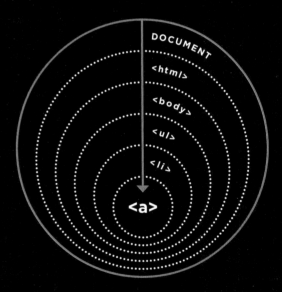

EVENT BUBBLING

The event starts at the *most* specific node and flows outwards to the *least* specific one. This is the default type of event flow with very wide browser support.

EVENT CAPTURING

The event starts at the *least* specific node and flows inwards to the *most* specific one. This is not supported in Internet Explorer 8 and earlier.

The example below has event listeners that respond to the **click** event on each of the following elements:

- One on the **<ul>** element
- One on the **<li>** element
- One on the **<a>** element in the list item

The event will show the HTML content of that element in an alert box, and event flow will tell you which element the click is registered upon first.

For traditional DOM event handlers (and HTML event attributes), all modern browsers default to using event bubbling rather than capturing. With event listeners, the final parameter in the **addEventListener()** method lets you choose the direction to trigger events:

- **true** = capturing phase
- **false** = bubbling phase (**false** is often a default choice because capturing was not supported in IE8 or earlier.)

The **event-flow.js** file (shown on the left, and available in the download code) demonstrates the difference between bubbling and capturing. In this example, the event handlers have a value of **false** for their last parameter indicating events should be followed in **bubbling** phase. So the first alert box shows the content of the innermost **<a>** element, and works its way out. You can also see the capturing version in the download code.

LISTKING

BUBBLE

*fresh*figs ☑

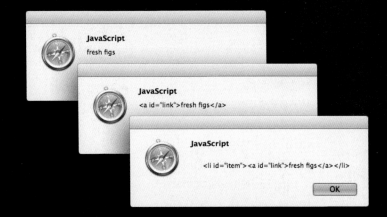

THE EVENT OBJECT

When an event occurs, the **event** object tells you information about the event, and the element it happened upon.

Every time an event fires, the **event** object contains helpful data about the event, such as:

- Which element the event happened on
- Which key was pressed for a **keypress** event
- What part of the viewport the user clicked for a **click** event (the viewport is the part of the browser window that shows the web page)

The **event** object is passed to any function that is the event handler or listener.

If you need to pass arguments to a named function, the **event** object will first be passed to the anonymous wrapper function (this happens automatically); then you must specify it as a parameter of the named function (as shown on the next page).

When the **event** object is passed into a function, it is often given the parameter name **e** (for event). It is a widely used shorthand (and you see it adopted throughout this book).

Note, however, that some programmers also use the parameter name **e** to refer to the error object; so **e** may mean **event** or **error** in some scripts.

Not only did IE8 have a different syntax for event listeners (as shown on p258), the **event** object in IE5-8 also had different names for the properties and methods shown in the tables below, and the example on p265.

PROPERTY	IE5-8 EQUIVALENT	PURPOSE
target	srcElement	The target of the event (most specific element interacted with)
type	type	Type of event that was fired
cancelable	not supported	Whether you can cancel the default behavior of an element

METHOD	IE5-8 EQUIVALENT PROPERTY	PURPOSE
preventDefault()	returnValue	Cancel default behavior of the event (if it can be canceled)
stopPropagation()	cancelBubble	Stops the event from bubbling or capturing any further

EVENT LISTENER WITH NO PARAMETERS

```
         ②  ←
function checkUsername(e) {
   ③ var target = e.target; // get target of event
}

var el = document.getElementById('username');
el.addEventListener('blur', checkUsername, false);
         ①
```

1. Without you doing anything, a reference to the **event** object is automatically passed from the number 1, where the event listener calls the function...

2. To here, where the function is defined. At this point, the parameter must be named. It Is often given the name **e** for **event**.

3. This name can then be used inside the function as a reference to the **event** object. You can now use the properties and methods of the **event** object.

EVENT LISTENER WITH PARAMETERS

```
         ③  ←
function checkUsername(e, minLength) {
   ④ var target = e.target; // get target of event
}

var el = document.getElementById('username');
el.addEventListener('blur', function(e){ ①
   checkUsername(e, 5);
}, false);        ②  ←
```

1. The reference to the **event** object is automatically passed to the anonymous function, but it must be named in the parentheses.

2. The reference to the **event** object can then be passed onto the named function. It is given as the first argument of the named function.

3. The named function receives the reference to the **event** object as the first parameter of the method. **4.** It can now be used by this name in the named function.

THE EVENT OBJECT IN IE5-8

Below you can see how you get the **event** object in IE5-8.
It is *not* passed automatically to event handler/listener functions;
but it *is* available as a child of the **window** object.

On the right, an **if** statement checks if the **event** object has been passed into the function. As you saw on p168, the existence of an object is treated as a truthy value, so the condition here is saying "if the event object *does not* exist..."

```
function checkUsername(e) {
  if (!e) {
    e = window.event;
  }
}
```

In IE8 and less, **e** will not hold an object, so the following code block runs and **e** is set to be the **event** object that is a child of the **window** object.

GETTING PROPERTIES

Once you have a reference to the **event** object, you can get its properties using the technique on the right. This works on short circuit evaluation (see p169).

```
var target;
target = e.target || e.srcElement;
```

A FUNCTION TO GET THE TARGET OF AN EVENT

If you need to assign event listeners to several elements, here is a function that will return a reference to the element the event happened on.

```
function getEventTarget(e) {
  if (!e) {
    e = window.event;
  }
  return e.target || e.srcElement;
}
```

USING EVENT LISTENERS WITH THE EVENT OBJECT

Here is the example that has been used throughout the chapter so far with some modifications:
1. The function is called `checkLength()` rather than `checkUsername()`. It can be used on any text input.
2. The **event** object is passed to the event listener. The code includes fallbacks for IE5-8 (Chapter 13 demonstrates using helper functions to do this).
3. In order to determine which element the user was interacting with, the function uses the **event** object's `target` property (and for IE5-8 it uses the equivalent `srcElement` property).

This function is now far more flexible than the previous code you have seen in this chapter because:
1. It can be used to check the length of any text input so long as that input is directly followed by an empty element that can hold a feedback message for the user. (There should not be space or carriage returns between the two elements; otherwise, some browsers might return a whitespace node.)
2. The code will work with IE5-8 because it tests whether the browser supports the latest features (or whether it needs to fallback to use older techniques).

```
JAVASCRIPT                                        c06/js/event-listener-with-event-object.js
```

```javascript
function checkLength(e, minLength) {        // Declare function
  var el, elMsg;                            // Declare variables
  if (!e) {                                 // If event object doesn't exist
    e = window.event;                       // Use IE fallback
  }
  el = e.target || e.srcElement;            // Get target of event
  elMsg = el.nextSibling;                   // Get its next sibling

  if (el.value.length < minLength) {        // If length is too short set msg
    elMsg.innerHTML = 'Username must be ' + minLength + ' characters or more';
  } else {                                  // Otherwise
    elMsg.innerHTML = '';                   // Clear message
  }
}

var elUsername = document.getElementById('username');// Get username input
if (elUsername.addEventListener) {          // If event listener supported
  elUsername.addEventListener('blur', function(e) {  // On blur event
    checkLength(e, 5);                      // Call checkLength()
  }, false);                                // Capture in bubble phase
} else {                                    // Otherwise
  elUsername.attachEvent('onblur', function(e){  // IE fallback onblur
    checkLength(e, 5);                      // Call checkLength()
  });
}
```

EVENT DELEGATION

Creating event listeners for a lot of elements can slow down a page, but event flow allows you to listen for an event on a parent element.

If users can interact with a lot of elements on the page, such as:
● a lot of buttons in the UI
● a long list
● every cell of a table
adding event listeners to each element can use a lot of memory and slow down performance.

Because events affect containing (or ancestor) elements (due to event flow – p260), you can place event handlers on a containing element and use the event object's target property to find which of its children the event happened on.

By attaching an event listener to a containing element, you are only responding to one element (rather than having an event handler for each child element).

You are delegating the job of the event listener to a parent of the elements. In the list shown here, if you place the event listener on the <ul> element rather than on links in each <li> element, you only need one event listener. This gives better performance, and if you add or remove items from the list it would still work the same. (The code for this example is shown on p269.)

ADDITIONAL BENEFITS OF EVENT DELEGATION

WORKS WITH NEW ELEMENTS

If you add new elements to the DOM tree, you do not have to add event handlers to the new elements because the job has been delegated to an ancestor.

SOLVES LIMITATIONS WITH this KEYWORD

Earlier in the chapter, the this keyword was used to identify an event's target, but that technique did not work in IE8, or when a function needed parameters.

SIMPLIFIES YOUR CODE

It requires fewer functions to be written, and there are fewer ties between the DOM and your code, which helps maintainability.

CHANGING DEFAULT BEHAVIOR

The **event** object has methods that change:
the default behavior of an element and how
the element's ancestors respond to the event.

preventDefault()

Some events, such as clicking on links and submitting forms, take the user to another page.

To prevent the default behavior of such elements (e.g., to keep the user on the same page rather than following a link or being taken to a new page after submitting a form), you can use the event object's `preventDefault()` method.

IE5-8 have an equivalent property called `returnValue` which can be set to `false`. A conditional statement can check if the `preventDefault()` method is supported, and use IE8's approach if it isn't:

```
if (event.preventDefault) {
  event.preventDefault();
} else {
  event.returnValue = false;
}
```

stopPropagation()

Once you have handled an event using one element, you may want to stop that event from bubbling up to its ancestor elements (especially if there are separate event handlers responding to the same events on the containing elements).

To stop the event bubbling up, you can use the **event** object's `stopPropogation()` method.

The equivalent in IE8 and earlier is the `cancelBubble` property which can be set to `true`. Again, a conditional statement can check if the `stopPropogation()` method is supported and use IE8's approach if not:

```
if (event.stopPropogation) {
  event.stopPropogation();
} else {
  event.cancelBubble = true;
}
```

USING BOTH METHODS

You will sometimes see the following used in similar situations that are in a function:
`return false;`

It prevents the default behavior of the element, and prevents the event from bubbling up or capturing further. It also works in all browsers, so it is popular.

Note, however, when the interpreter comes across the **return false** statement, it stops processing any subsequent code within that function and moves to the next statement after the function was called.

Since this blocks any further code within the function, it is often better to use the `preventDefault()` method of the **event** object rather than **return false**.

USING EVENT DELEGATION

This example will put together a lot of what you have learned in the chapter so far. Each list item contains a link. When the user clicks on that link (to indicate they have completed that task), the item will be removed from the list.

- There is a screen grab of the example on p266.
- On the right there is a flowchart that helps explain the order in which the code is processed.
- The right-hand page has the code for the example

1. The event listener will be added to the `<ul>` element, so this needs to be selected.
2. Check whether or not the browser supports `addEventListener()`.
3. If so, use it to call the `itemDone()` function when the user clicks anywhere on that list.
4. If not, use the `attachEvent()` method.
5. The `itemDone()` function will remove the item from the list. It requires three pieces of information.
6. Three variables are declared to hold the info.
7. `target` holds the element the user clicked on. To obtain this, the `getTarget()` function is called. This is created at the start of the script, and shown at the bottom of the flowchart.
8. `elParent` holds that element's parent (the `<li>`)
9. `elGrandparent` holds that element's grandparent
10. The `<li>` element is removed from the `<ul>` element.
11. Check if the browser supports `preventDefault()` to prevent the link taking the user to a new page.
12. If so, use it.
13. If not, use the older IE `returnValue` property.

In the HTML, the links would take you to `itemDone.php` if the browser did not support JavaScript. (The PHP file is not supplied with the code download because server-side languages are beyond the scope of this book.)

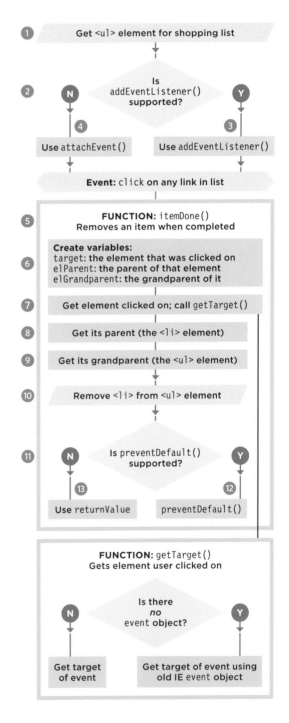

```html
<ul id="shoppingList">
  <li class="complete"><a href="itemDone.php?id=1"><em>fresh</em> figs</a></li>
  <li class="complete"><a href="itemDone.php?id=2">pine nuts</a></li>
  <li class="complete"><a href="itemDone.php?id=3">honey</a></li>
  <li class="complete"><a href="itemDone.php?id=4">balsamic vinegar</a></li>
</ul>
```

```javascript
function getTarget(e) {                          // Declare function
  if (!e) {                                      // If there is no event object
   e = window.event;                             // Use old IE event object
  }
  return e.target || e.srcElement;               // Get the target of event
}

function itemDone(e) {                            // Declare function
  // Remove item from the list
  var target, elParent, elGrandparent;           // Declare variables
  target = getTarget(e);                          // Get the item clicked link
  elParent = target.parentNode;                   // Get its list item
  elGrandparent = target.parentNode.parentNode;  // Get its list
  elGrandparent.removeChild(elParent);           // Remove list item from list

  // Prevent the link from taking you elsewhere
  if (e.preventDefault) {                         // If preventDefault() works
    e.preventDefault();                           // Use preventDefault()
  } else {                                        // Otherwise
    e.returnValue = false;                        // Use old IE version
  }
}

// Set up event listeners to call itemDone() on click
var el = document.getElementById('shoppingList');// Get shopping list
if (el.addEventListener) {                        // If event listeners work
  el.addEventListener('click', function(e) {      // Add listener on click
    itemDone(e);                                  // It calls itemDone()
  }, false);                                      // Use bubbling phase for flow
} else {                                          // Otherwise
  el.attachEvent('onclick', function(e){          // Use old IE model: onclick
    itemDone(e);                                  // Call itemDone()
  });
}
```

WHICH ELEMENT DID AN EVENT OCCUR ON?

When calling a function, the **event** object's **target** property is the best way to determine which element the event occurred on. But you may see the approach below used; it relies on the **this** keyword.

THE this KEYWORD

The **this** keyword refers to the owner of a function. On the right, **this** refers to the element that the event is on.

This works when no parameters are being passed to the function (and therefore it is not called from an anonymous function).

```
function checkUsername() {
  var elMsg = document.getElementById('feedback');
  if (this.value.length < 5) {
    elMsg.innerHTML = 'Not long enough';
  } else {
    elMsg.innerHTML = '';
  }
}
```

```
var el = document.getElementById('username');
el.addEventListener('blur', checkUsername, false);
```

It's like the function had been written here rather than higher up

USING PARAMETERS

If you pass parameters to the function, the **this** keyword no longer works because the owner of the function is no longer the element that the event listener was bound to, it is an anonymous function.
You could pass the element the event was called on as another parameter of the function.

In both cases, the **event** object is the preferred approach.

```
function checkUsername(el, minLength) {
  var elMsg = document.getElementById('feedback');
  if (el.value.length < minLength) {
    elMsg.innerHTML = 'Not long enough';
  } else {
    elMsg.innerHTML = '';
  }
}
```

```
var el = document.getElementById('username');
el.addEventListener('blur', function() {
  checkUsername(el, 5);
}, false);
```

DIFFERENT TYPES OF EVENTS

In the rest of the chapter, you learn about the different types of events you can respond to.

Events are defined in:
- The W3C DOM specification
- The HTML5 specification
- In Browser Object Models

Most are a result of the user interacting with the HTML, but there are a few that react to the browser or other DOM events.

We do not show every event, but the examples you see should teach you enough so that you can work with all types of events.

W3C DOM EVENTS

The DOM events specification is managed by the W3C (who also look after other specifications including HTML, CSS, and XML). Most of the events you will meet in this chapter are part of this DOM events specification.

Browsers implement all the events using the same **event** object that you already met. It also provides feedback such as which element the event occurred on, which key a user pressed, or where the cursor is positioned).

There are, however, some events that are not covered in the DOM event model – in particular those that deal with form elements. (They used to be part of the DOM, but got moved to the HTML5 specification.)

HTML5 EVENTS

The HTML5 specification (that is still being developed) details events that browsers are expected to support that are specifically used with HTML. For example, events that are fired when a form is submitted or form elements are changed (which you will meet on p282):

```
submit
input
change
```

There are also new events introduced with the HTML5 specification that are only supported by more recent browsers. Here are a few (which you will meet on p286):

```
readystatechange
DOMContentLoaded
hashchange
```

BOM EVENTS

Browser manufacturers also implement some events as part of their Browser Object Model (or BOM). Typically these are events not (yet) covered by W3C specifications (although some will be added to W3C specifications in the future). Several of these events dealt with touchscreen devices:

```
touchstart
touchend
touchmove
orientationchange
```

Other events are being added to capture gestures and take advantage of accelerometers. Care is needed using such features, as different browsers often create different implementations of similar functionality.

USER INTERFACE EVENTS

User interface (UI) events occur as a result of interaction with the browser window rather than the HTML page contained within it, e.g., a page having loaded or the browser window being resized.

The event handler / listener for UI events should be attached to the browser window.

In old HTML code, you may see these events used as attributes on the opening <body> tag. (For example, older code used the onload attribute to trigger code that would run when the page had loaded.)

EVENT	TRIGGER	BROWSER SUPPORT
load	Fires when the web page has finished loading. It can also fire on nodes of other elements that load, such as images, scripts, or objects.	The DOM Level 2 (Nov 2000) states that it fires on the document object, but prior to this it fired on the window object. Browsers support both for backwards compatibility, and developers often still attach load event handlers to the window (not document) object.
unload	Fires when the web page is unloading (usually because a new page has been requested). See also the beforeunload event (on p286) which fires before the user leaves a page.	The DOM Level 2 states that it fires on the node for the <body> element, but in older browsers it fired on the window object (this is often used for backwards compatibility).
error	Fires when the browser encounters a JavaScript error or an asset doesn't exist.	Support for this event is inconsistent across browsers and so it is not reliable for error handling, a topic you learn more about in Chapter 10.
resize	Fires when the browser window has been resized.	Browsers repeatedly fire the resize event as the window is being resized, so avoid using this event to trigger complicated code because this might make the page appear less responsive.
scroll	Fires when the user has scrolled up or down the page. It can relate to the entire page or a specific element on the page (such as a <textarea> that has scrollbars).	Browsers repeatedly fire the event as the window is scrolled, so avoid running complicated code as the user scrolls.

LOAD

The load event is commonly used to trigger scripts that access the contents of the page. In this example, a function called setup() gives focus to the text input when the page has loaded.

The event is automatically raised by the window object when a page has finished loading the HTML *and* all of its resources: images, CSS, scripts (even third party content e.g., banner ads).

The setup() function would not work before the page has loaded because it relies on finding the element whose id attribute has a value of username, in order to give it focus.

JAVASCRIPT   c06/js/load.js

```
function setup() {                         // Declare function
  var textInput;                           // Create variable
  textInput = document.getElementById('username');  // Get username input
  textInput.focus();                       // Give username focus
}

window.addEventListener('load', setup, false); // When page loaded call setup()
```

RESULT

Note that the event listener is attached to the window object (not the document object – as this can cause cross-browser compatibility issues).

If the <script> element is at the end of the HTML page, then the DOM would have loaded the form elements before the script runs, and there would be no need to wait for the load event. (See also: the DOMContentLoaded event on p286 and jQuery's document.ready() method on p312.)

Because the load event only fires when everything else on the page has loaded (images, scripts, even ads), the user already have started to use the page *before* the script has started to run.

Users particularly notice when a script changes the appearance of the page, changes focus, or selects form elements after they have started to use it. (It can make a site look slower to load.)

Imagine this form had more inputs; the user may be filling in the second or third box when the script fires - moving focus back to the first box too late and interrupting the user.

FOCUS & BLUR EVENTS

The HTML elements you can interact with, such as links and form elements, can gain focus. These events fire when they gain or lose focus.

If you can interact with an HTML element, then it can gain (and lose) focus. You can also tab between the elements that can gain focus (a technique often used by those with visual impairments).

In older scripts, the focus and blur events were often used to change the appearance of an element as it gained focus, but now the CSS :focus pseudo-class is a better solution (unless you need to affect an element *other* than the one that gained focus).

The focus and blur events are most commonly used on forms. They can be particularly helpful when:

- You want to show tips or feedback to users as they interact with an individual element within a form (the tips are usually shown in *other* elements and *not* the one they are interacting with)
- You need to trigger form validation as a user moves from one control to the next (rather than waiting for them to submit the entire form first)

EVENT	TRIGGER	FLOW
focus	When an element gains focus, the focus event fires for that DOM node.	Capture
blur	When an element loses focus, the blur event fires for that DOM node.	Capture
focusin	Same as focus (see above but not supported in Firefox at time of writing)	Bubble & capture
focusout	Same as blur (see above but not supported in Firefox at time of writing)	Bubble & capture

FOCUS & BLUR

In this example, as the text input gains and loses focus, feedback is shown to the user in the `<div>` element under the text input. The feedback is given using two functions.

`tipUsername()` is triggered when the text input gains focus. It changes the `class` attribute of the element containing the message, and updates the contents of the element.

`checkUsername()` is triggered when the text input loses focus. It adds a message and changes the `class` if the username is less than 5 characters; otherwise, it clears the message.

c06/js/focus-blur.js

```javascript
function checkUsername() {                          // Declare function
  var username = el.value;                          // Store username in variable
  if (username.length < 5) {                        // If username < 5 characters
    elMsg.className = 'warning';                     // Change class on message
    elMsg.textContent = 'Not long enough, yet...';  // Update message
  } else {                                          // Otherwise
    elMsg.textContent = '';                         // Clear the message
  }
}
function tipUsername() {                             // Declare function
    elMsg.className = 'tip';                         // Change class for message
    elMsg.innerHTML = 'Username must be at least 5 characters'; // Add message
}

var el = document.getElementById('username');       // Username input
var elMsg = document.getElementById('feedback');    // Element to hold message

// When the username input gains / loses focus call functions above:
el.addEventListener('focus', tipUsername, false);   // focus call tipUsername()
el.addEventListener('blur', checkUsername, false);  // blur call checkUsername()
```

RESULT

Create a username:

```
Max
```

⚠ Not long enough, yet...

MOUSE EVENTS

The mouse events are fired when the mouse is moved and also when its buttons are clicked.

All of the elements on a page support the mouse events, and all of these bubble. Note that actions are different on touchscreen devices.

Preventing a default behavior can have unexpected results. E.g., a click event only fires when both the mousedown and mouseup event have fired.

EVENT	TRIGGER	TOUCH
click	Fires when the user clicks on the primary mouse button (usually the left button if there is more than one). The click event will fire for the element that the mouse is currently over. It will also fire if the user presses the Enter key on the keyboard when an element has focus.	A tap on the touchscreen will be treated like a single left-click.
dblclick	Fires when the user clicks the primary mouse button twice in quick succession.	A double-tap will be treated as a double left click.
mousedown	Fires when the user clicks down on any mouse button. (Cannot be triggered by keyboard.)	You can use the touchstart event.
mouseup	Fires when the user releases a mouse button. (Cannot be triggered by keyboard.)	You can use the touchend event.
mouseover	Fires when the cursor was outside an element and is then moved inside it. (Cannot be triggered by keyboard.)	Fires when the cursor is moved over an element.
mouseout	Fires when the cursor is over an element, and then moves onto another element – outside of the current element or a child of it (Cannot be triggered by keyboard.)	Fires when the cursor is moved off an element.
mousemove	Fires when the cursor is moved around an element. This event is repeatedly fired. (Cannot be triggered by keyboard.)	Fires when the cursor is moved.

WHEN TO USE CSS

The mouseover and mouseout events were often used to change the appearance of boxes or to switch images as the user rolls over them. To change the appearance of the element, a preferable technique would be to use the CSS :hover pseudo-class.

WHY SEPARATE MOUSEDOWN & UP?

The mousedown and mouseup events separate out the press and release of a mouse button. They are commonly used for adding drag and drop functionality, or to add controls in game development.

CLICK

The aim of this example is to use the click event to remove the big note that has been added to the middle of the page. But first, the script has to create that note.

Because the note is over the top of the page, we only want to show it to users who have JavaScript enabled (otherwise they could not hide it).

When the click event fires on the close link the dismissNote() function is called. This function will remove the note that was added by the same script.

JAVASCRIPT   c06/js/click.js

```javascript
// Create the HTML for the message
var msg = '<div class=\"header\"><a id=\"close\" href="#">close X</a></div>';
msg += '<div><h2>System Maintenance</h2>';
msg += 'Our servers are being updated between 3 and 4 a.m. ';
msg += 'During this time, there may be minor disruptions to service.</div>';

var elNote = document.createElement('div');          // Create a new element
elNote.setAttribute('id', 'note');                   // Add an id of note
elNote.innerHTML = msg;                              // Add the message
document.body.appendChild(elNote);                   // Add it to the page

function dismissNote() {                              // Declare function
  document.body.removeChild(elNote);                 // Remove the note
}

var elClose = document.getElementById('close');      // Get the close button
elClose.addEventListener('click', dismissNote, false);// Click close-clear note
```

RESULT

ACCESSIBILITY

The click event can be applied to any element, but it is better to only use it on items that are usually clicked or it will not be accessible to people who rely upon keyboard navigation.

You may also be tempted to use the click event to run a script when a user clicks on a form element, but it is better to use the focus event because that fires when the user accesses that control using the tab key.

The **event** object can tell you where the cursor
was positioned when an event was triggered.

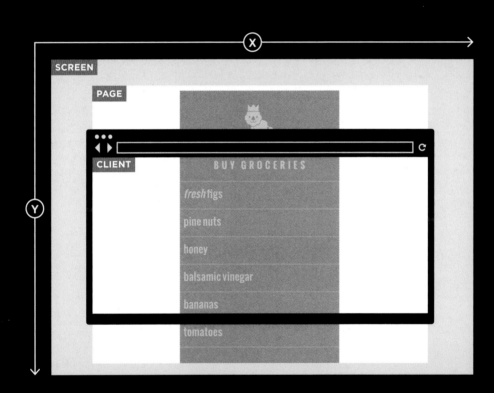

SCREEN

The **screenX** and **screenY**
properties indicate the position
of the cursor within the entire
screen on your monitor,
measuring from the top left
corner of the screen (rather than
the browser).

PAGE

The **pageX** and **pageY** properties
indicate the position of the
cursor within the entire page.
The top of the page may be
outside of the viewport so
even if the cursor is in the
same position, page and client
coordinates can be different.

CLIENT

The `clientX` and `clientY`
properties indicate the
position of the cursor within
the browser's viewport. If the
user has scrolled down and the
top of the page is no longer in
view, it will not affect the client
coordinates.

DETERMINING POSITION

In this example, as you move your mouse around the screen, the text inputs across the top of the page are updated with the current mouse position.

This demonstrates the three different positions you can retrieve when the mouse is moved or when one of the buttons is clicked.

Note how showPosition() is passed event as a parameter, which refers to the event object. The positions are all properties of this event object.

c06/js/position.js

```javascript
var sx = document.getElementById('sx');            // Element to hold screenX
var sy = document.getElementById('sy');            // Element to hold screenY
var px = document.getElementById('px');            // Element to hold pageX
var py = document.getElementById('py');            // Element to hold pageY
var cx = document.getElementById('cx');            // Element to hold clientX
var cy = document.getElementById('cy');            // Element to hold clientY

function showPosition(event) {                     // Declare function
  sx.value = event.screenX;                        // Update element with screenX
  sy.value = event.screenY;                        // Update element with screenY
  px.value = event.pageX;                          // Update element with pageX
  py.value = event.pageY;                          // Update element with pageY
  cx.value = event.clientX;                        // Update element with clientX
  cy.value = event.clientY;                        // Update element with clientY
}

var el = document.getElementById('body');              // Get body element
el.addEventListener('mousemove', showPosition, false); // Move updates position
```

RESULT

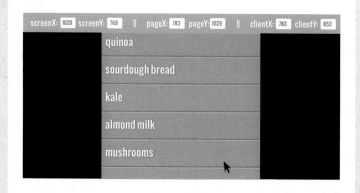

KEYBOARD EVENTS

The keyboard events are fired when a user interacts with the keyboard (they fire on any kind of device with a keyboard).

EVENT	TRIGGER
input	Fires when the value of an `<input>` or `<textarea>` element changes. First supported in IE9 (although it does not fire when deleting text in IE9). For older browsers, you can use **keydown** as a fallback.
keydown	Fires when the user presses any key on the keyboard. If the user holds down a key, the event continues to fire repeatedly. This is important because it mimics what would happen in a text input if the user holds down a key (the same character would be added repeatedly while the key is held down).
keypress	Fires when the user presses a key that would result in a character being shown on the screen. For example, this event would not fire when the user presses the arrow keys, whereas the **keydown** event would. If the user holds down a key, the event continues to fire repeatedly.
keyup	Fires when the user releases a key on the keyboard. The **keydown** and **keypress** events fire before a character shows on screen, whereas **keyup** fires after it appears.

The three events that begin key... fire in this order:
1. **keydown** – user presses key down
2. **keypress** – user has pressed or is holding a key that adds a character into the page
3. **keyup** – user releases key

WHICH KEY WAS PRESSED?

When you use the **keydown** or **keypress** events, the **event** object has a property called **keyCode**, which can be used to tell which key was pressed. However, it does not return the *letter* for that key (as you might expect); it returns an **ASCII code** that represents the lowercase character for that key. You can see a table of the characters and their ASCII codes in an online extra on the website accompanying this book.

If you want to get the letter or number as it would be displayed on the keyboard (rather than an ASCII equivalent), the **String** object has a built-in method called **fromCharCode()** which will do the conversion for you: `String.fromCharCode(event.keycode);`

WHICH KEY WAS PRESSED

In this example, the <textarea> element should only have 180 characters. When the user enters text, the script will show them how many characters they have left available to use.

The event listener checks for the keypress event on the <textarea> element. Each time it fires, the charCount() function updates the character count and shows the last character used.

The input event would work well to update the count when the user pastes in text or uses keys like backspace, but it does not tell you which key was the last to be pressed.

JAVASCRIPT

c06/js/keypress.js

```javascript
var el;                                                     // Declare variables

function charCount(e) {                                     // Declare function
  var textEntered, charDisplay, counter, lastkey;          // Declare variables
  textEntered = document.getElementById('message').value;  // User's text
  charDisplay = document.getElementById('charactersLeft');  // Counter element
  counter = (180 - (textEntered.length));                   // Num of chars left
  charDisplay.textContent = counter;                        // Show chars left

  lastkey = document.getElementById('lastkey');             // Get last key used
  lastkey.textContent = 'Last key in ASCII code: ' + e.keyCode; // Create msg
}
el = document.getElementById('message');                    // Get msg element
el.addEventListener('keypress', charCount, false);          // keypress event
```

RESULT

MY PROFILE

I like cooking and|

162
Last key in ASCII code: 68

FORM EVENTS

There are two events that are commonly used with forms.
In particular you are likely to see submit used in form validation.

EVENT	TRIGGER
submit	When a form is submitted, the submit event fires on the node representing the <form> element. It is most commonly used when checking the values a user has entered into a form before sending it to the server.
change	Fires when the status of several form elements change. For example, when: • a selection is made from a drop-down select box • a radio button is selected • a checkbox is selected or deselected It is often better to use the change event rather than the click event because clicking is not the only way users interact with form elements (for example, they might use the tab, arrow, or Enter keys).
input	The input event, which you saw on the previous page is commonly used with <input> and <textarea> elements.

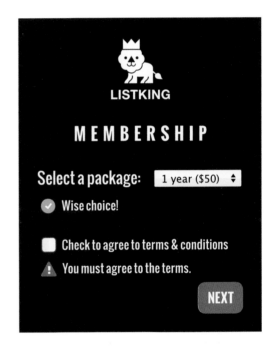

FOCUS AND BLUR

The focus and blur events (which you met on p274) are often used with forms, but they can also be used in conjunction with other elements, such as links (so they are not specifically related to forms).

VALIDATION

Checking form values is known as validation. If users miss required information or enter incorrect information, checking it using JavaScript is faster than sending the data to the server for it to be checked. Validation is covered in Chapter 13.

USING FORM EVENTS

When a user interacts with the drop-down select box, the change event will trigger the packageHint() function. This shows messages below the select box that reflect the choice.

When the form is submitted, the checkTerms() function is called. This tests to see if the user has checked the box that indicates they agree to the terms and conditions.

If not, the script will prevent the default behavior of the form element (and stop it from submitting the form data to the server) and it will show an error message to the user.

JAVASCRIPT   c06/js/form.js

```javascript
var elForm, elSelectPackage, elPackageHint, elTerms, elTermsHint;
elForm           = document.getElementById('formSignup'); // Store elements
elSelectPackage = document.getElementById('package');
elPackageHint    = document.getElementById('packageHint');
elTerms          = document.getElementById('terms');
elTermsHint      = document.getElementById('termsHint');

function packageHint() {                              // Declare function
  var pack = this.options[this.selectedIndex].value;  // Get selected option
  if (pack == 'monthly') {                            // If monthly package
    elPackageHint.innerHTML = 'Save $10 if you pay for 1 year!';//Show this msg
  } else {                                            // Otherwise
    elPackageHint.innerHTML = 'Wise choice!';         // Show this message
  }
}

function checkTerms(event) {                          // Declare function
  if (!elTerms.checked) {                             // If checkbox ticked
    elTermsHint.innerHTML = 'You must agree to the terms.'; // Show message
    event.preventDefault();                           // Don't submit form
  }
}

//Create event listeners: submit calls checkTerms(), change calls packageHint()
elForm.addEventListener('submit', checkTerms, false);
elSelectPackage.addEventListener('change', packageHint, false);
```

MUTATION EVENTS & OBSERVERS

Whenever elements are added to or removed from the DOM, its structure changes. This change triggers a mutation event.

When your script adds or removes content from a page it is updating the DOM tree. There are many reasons why you might want to respond to the DOM tree being updated, for example, you might want to tell the user that the page had changed.

Below are some events that are triggered when the DOM changes. These mutation events were introduced in Firefox 3, IE9, Safari 3, and all versions of Chrome. But they are already scheduled to be replaced by an alternative called mutation observers.

EVENT	TRIGGER
DOMNodeInserted	Fires when a node is inserted into the DOM tree. e.g. using `appendChild()`, `replaceChild()`, or `insertBefore()`.
DOMNodeRemoved	Fires when a node is removed from the DOM tree. e.g. using `removeChild()` or `replaceChild()`.
DOMSubtreeModified	Fires when the DOM structure changes. It fires after the two events listed above occur.
DOMNodeInsertedIntoDocument	Fires when a node is inserted into the DOM tree as a descendant of another node that is already in the document.
DOMNodeRemovedFromDocument	Fires when a node is removed from the DOM tree as a descendant of another node that is already in the document.

PROBLEMS WITH MUTATION EVENTS

If your script makes a lot of changes to a page, you end up with a lot of mutation events firing. This can make a page feel slow or unresponsive. They can also trigger other event listeners as they propagate through the DOM, which modify other parts of the DOM, triggering more mutation events. Therefore they are being replaced by mutation observers.

Browser support: Chrome, Firefox 3, IE 9, Opera 9, Safari 3

NEW MUTATION OBSERVERS

Mutation observers are designed to wait until a script has finished its task before reacting, then report the changes as a batch (rather than one at a time). You can also specify the type of changes to the DOM that you want them to react to. But at the time of writing, the browser support was not widespread enough to use them on public websites.

Browser support: IE 11, Firefox 14, Chrome 27 (or 18 with webkit prefix), Safari 6.1, Opera 15 On mobile: Android 4.4, Safari on iOS 7.

USING MUTATION EVENTS

In this example, two event listeners each trigger their own function. The first is on the last but one line, and it listens for when the user clicks the link to add a new list item. It then uses DOM manipulation events to add a new element (changing the DOM structure and triggering mutation events).

The second event listener waits for the DOM tree within the `<ul>` element to change. When the `DOMNodeInserted` event fires, it calls a function called `updateCount()`. This function counts how many items there are in the list, and then updates the list count at the top of the page accordingly.

`c06/js/mutation.js`

```javascript
var elList, addLink, newEl, newText, counter, listItems; // Declare variables

elList  = document.getElementById('list');         // Get list
addLink = document.querySelector('a');              // Get add item button
counter = document.getElementById('counter');       // Get item counter

function addItem(e) {                                // Declare function
  e.preventDefault();                               // Prevent link action
  newEl = document.createElement('li');             // New <li> element
  newText = document.createTextNode('New list item'); // New text node
  newEl.appendChild(newText);                       // Add text to <li>
  elList.appendChild(newEl);                        // Add <li> to list
}

function updateCount() {                            // Declare function
  listitems = list.getElementsByTagName('li').length; // Get total of <li>s
  counter.innerHTML = listitems;                    // Update counter
}

addLink.addEventListener('click', addItem, false);  // Click on button
elList.addEventListener('DOMNodeInserted', updateCount, false); // DOM updated
```

HTML5 EVENTS

Here are three page-level events that have been included in versions of the HTML5 spec that have become popular very quickly.

EVENT	TRIGGER	BROWSER SUPPORT
DOMContentLoaded	Event fires when the DOM tree is formed (images, CSS, and JavaScript might still be loading). Scripts start to run earlier than using the load event which waits for other resources such as images and advertisements to load. This makes the page seem faster to load. However, because it does not wait for scripts to load, the DOM tree will not contain any HTML that would have been generated by those scripts. It can be attached to the window or document objects.	Chrome 0.2, Firefox 1, IE9, Safari 3.1, Opera 9
hashchange	Event fires when the URL hash changes (without the entire window refreshing). Hashes are used on links to specific parts (sometimes known as anchors) within a page and also on pages that use AJAX to load content. The hashchange event handler works on the window object, and after firing, the event object will have oldURL and newURL properties that hold the url before and after the hashchange.	IE8, Firefox 20, Safari 5.1, Chrome 26, and Opera 12.1
beforeunload	Event fires on the window object before the page is unloaded. It should only be used to help the user (not to encourage them to stay on a website if they are trying to leave). For example, it can be helpful to let a user know that changes on a form they completed have not been saved. You can add a message to the dialog box that is shown by the browser, but you do not have control over the text shown before it or on the buttons the user can press (which can vary slightly between browsers and operating systems).	Chrome 1, Firefox 1, IE4, Safari 3, Opera 12

There are also several other events that are being introduced to support more recent devices (such as phones and tablets). They respond to events such as gestures and movements that are based upon an accelerometer (which detects the angle at which a device is being held).

USING HTML5 EVENTS

In this example, as soon as the DOM tree has been formed, focus is given to the text input with an `id` of `username`.

The `DOMContentLoaded` event fires before the `load` event (because the latter waits for all of the page's resources to load).

If users try to leave the page before they press the submit button, the `beforeunload` event checks that they want to leave.

06/js/html5-events.js

```javascript
function setup() {
  var textInput;
  textInput = document.getElementById('message');
  textInput.focus();
}

window.addEventListener('DOMContentLoaded', setup, false);

window.addEventListener('beforeunload', function(event){
  var message = 'You have changes that have not been saved...';
  (event || window.event).returnValue = message;
  return message;
});
```

RESULT

On the left, you can see the dialog box that is shown when you try to navigate away from the page.

The text before your message and on the buttons may change from browser to browser (you have no control over this).

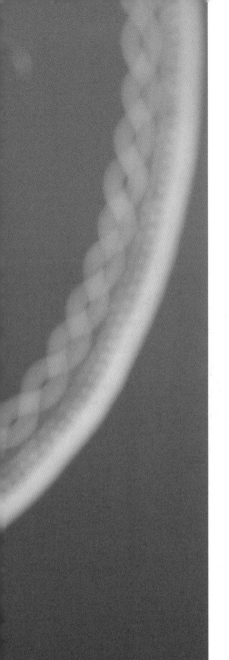

EXAMPLE
EVENTS

This example shows an interface for a user to record voice notes. The user can enter a name which is displayed in the heading, and they can press record (which changes the image that is shown).

When the user starts typing a name into the text box, the **keyup** event will trigger a function called **writeLabel()** which copies the text from the form input and writes it into the main heading under the logo for List King, replacing the words 'AUDIO NOTE'.

The record / pause button is a bit more interesting. The button has an attribute called **data-state**. When the page loads, its value is **record**. When the user presses the button, the value of this attribute changes to **pause** (this triggers a new CSS rule to indicate that it is now recording).

If you have not used HTML5's **data-** attributes, they allow you to store custom data on any HTML element. (The name of the attribute can be anything starting with **data-** as long as the name is lowercase.)

This demonstrates a new technique based upon event delegation. The event listener is placed upon the containing element whose **id** is **buttons**. The **event** object is used to determine the value of the **id** attribute on the element that was used. The value from that **id** attribute is then used in a **switch** statement to decide which function to call (depending on whether the button is in **record** state or **pause** state).

This is a good way to handle many buttons because it reduces the number of event listeners in your code.

The event listeners are written at the bottom of the page, and they have fallbacks for users who are running IE8 or less (which has a different event model).

EXAMPLE
EVENTS

The script starts by defining the variables that it will need to use, and then collecting the element nodes that are needed.

The player functions (shown on the right-hand page) would appear next, and at the bottom of this page you can see the event listeners.

The event listeners live inside a conditional statement so that the attachEvent() method can be used for visitors who have IE8 or less.

```
c06/js/example.js                                          JAVASCRIPT

var noteInput, noteName, textEntered, target;    // Declare variables

noteName = document.getElementById('noteName');  // Element that holds note
noteInput = document.getElementById('noteInput');// Input for writing the note

function writeLabel(e) {                          // Declare function
  if (!e) {                                       // If event object not present
    e = window.event;                             // Use IE5-8 fallback
  }
  target = e.target || e.srcElement;              // Get target of event
  textEntered = e.target.value;                   // Value of that element
  noteName.textContent = textEntered;             // Update note text
}

// This is where the record / pause controls and functions go...
// See right hand page

if (document.addEventListener) {                  // If event listener supported
  document.addEventListener('click', function(e){// For any click document
    recorderControls(e);                          // Call recorderControls()
  }, false);                                      // Capture during bubble phase
  // If input event fires on username input call writeLabel()
  username.addEventListener('input', writeLabel, false);
} else {                                           // Otherwise
  document.attachEvent('onclick', function(e){    // IE fallback: any click
    recorderControls(e);                          // Calls recorderControls()
  });
  // If keyup event fires on username input call writeLabel()
  username.attachEvent('onkeyup', writeLabel, false);
}
```

EXAMPLE
EVENTS

The `recorderControls()` function is automatically passed the **event** object. Not only does this offer code to support older versions of IE, but also stops the link from performing its default behavior (of taking the user to a new page).

The `switch` statement is used to indicate which function to run depending on whether the user is trying to record or stop the audio note. This technique of delegation is a good way to cope with multiple buttons in the UI.

```javascript
function recorderControls(e) {        // Declare recorderControls()
  if (!e) {                           // If event object not present
    e = window.event;                 // Use IE5-8 fallback
  }
  target = e.target || e.srcElement;  // Get the target element
  if (e.preventDefault) {             // If preventDefault() supported
    e.preventDefault();               // Stop default action
  } else {                            // Otherwise
    e.returnValue = false;            // IE fallback: stop default action
}

switch(target.getAttribute('data-state')) { // Get the data-state attribute
  case 'record':                      // If its value is record
    record(target);                   // Call the record() function
    break;                            // Exit function to where called
  case 'stop':                        // If its value is stop
    stop(target);                     // Call the stop() function
    break;                            // Exit function to where called
    // More buttons could go here...
  }
};

function record(target) {                    // Declare function
    target.setAttribute('data-state', 'stop'); // Set data-state attr to stop
    target.textContent = 'stop';             // Set text to 'stop'
}

function stop(target) {                       // Declare function
    target.setAttribute('data-state', 'record');//Set data-state attr to record
    target.textContent = 'record';           // Set text to 'record'
}
```

SUMMARY
EVENTS

▶ Events are the browser's way of indicating when something has happened (such as when a page has finished loading or a button has been clicked).

▶ Binding is the process of stating which event you are waiting to happen, and which element you are waiting for that event to happen upon.

▶ When an event occurs on an element, it can trigger a JavaScript function. When this function then changes the web page in some way, it feels interactive because it has responded to the user.

▶ You can use event delegation to monitor for events that happen on all of the children of an element.

▶ The most commonly used events are W3C DOM events, although there are others in the HTML5 specification as well as browser-specific events.

7

JQUERY

jQuery offers a simple way to achieve a variety of common JavaScript tasks quickly and consistently, across all major browsers and without any fallback code needed.

SELECT ELEMENTS

It is simpler to access elements using jQuery's CSS-style selectors than it is using DOM queries. The selectors are also more powerful and flexible.

PERFORM TASKS

jQuery's methods let you update the DOM tree, animate elements into and out of view, and loop through a set of elements, all in one line of code.

HANDLE EVENTS

jQuery includes methods that allow you to attach event listeners to selected elements without having to write any fallback code to support older browsers.

This chapter assumes that you have read the book up to this point or are familiar with the basics of JavaScript. As you will see, jQuery is powerful when combined with traditional JavaScript techniques, but you need to understand JavaScript to make full use of jQuery.

LISTKING

BUY GROCERIES

fresh figs

pine nuts

honey

balsamic vinegar

TYPOGRAPHIC IS TOO MUCH NOISE NOT ENOUGH TIME
THE JOURNAL OF THE INTERNATIONAL SOCIETY OF TYPOGRAPHIC DESIGNERS
DAVID JURY
HARRY MONTPERE

WHAT IS JQUERY?

jQuery is a JavaScript file that you include in your web pages.
It lets you find elements using CSS-style selectors and then do
something with the elements using jQuery methods.

1: FIND ELEMENTS USING CSS-STYLE SELECTORS

A function called **jQuery()** lets you find one or more elements in the page.
It creates an object called **jQuery** which holds references to those elements.
$() is often used as a shorthand to save typing **jQuery()**, as shown here.

FUNCTION (CREATES JQUERY OBJECT)

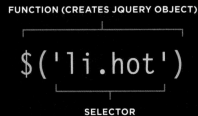

$('li.hot')

SELECTOR

The **jQuery()** function has one parameter: a CSS-style **selector**.
This selector finds all of the **<li>** elements with a **class** of **hot**.

SIMILARITIES TO DOM

- jQuery selectors perform a similar task to traditional DOM queries, but the syntax is much simpler.
- You can store the **jQuery** object in a variable, just as you can with DOM nodes.
- You can use jQuery methods and properties (like DOM methods and properties) to manipulate the DOM nodes that you select.

The jQuery object has many methods that you can use to work with the elements you select. The methods represent tasks that you commonly need to perform with elements.

2: DO SOMETHING WITH THE ELEMENTS USING JQUERY METHODS

Here a **jQuery** object is created by the **jQuery()** function. The object and the elements it contains is referred to as a **matched set** or a **jQuery selection**.

You can then use the methods of the **jQuery** object to update the elements that it contains. Here, the method adds a new value to the **class** attribute.

JQUERY OBJECT

METHOD

$('li.hot').addClass('complete');

MEMBER OPERATOR

PARAMETER(S)

The member operator indicates that the method on the right should be used to update the elements in the **jQuery** object on the left.

Each method has parameter(s) that provide details about how to update the elements. This parameter specifies a value to add to the **class** attribute.

KEY DIFFERENCES FROM DOM

- It's cross-browser, and there's no need to write fallback code.
- Selecting elements is simpler (because it uses CSS-style syntax) and is more accurate.
- Event handling is simpler as it uses one method that works in all major browsers.
- Methods affect all the selected elements without the need to loop through each one (see p310).
- Additional methods are provided for popular required tasks such as animation (see p332).
- Once you have made a selection, you can apply multiple methods to it.

A BASIC JQUERY EXAMPLE

The examples in this chapter revisit the list application used in the previous two chapters, and they will use jQuery to update the content of the page.

1. In order to use jQuery, the first thing you need to do is include the jQuery script in your page. You can see that it is included before the closing `</body>` tag.

2. Once jQuery has been added to the page, a second JavaScript file is included that uses jQuery selectors and methods to update the content of the HTML page.

```
c07/basic-example.html                                    HTML

<body>
  <div id="page"
    <h1 id="header">List</h1>
    <h2>Buy groceries</h2>
    <ul>
      <li id="one" class="hot"><em>fresh</em> figs</li>
      <li id="two" class="hot">pine nuts</li>
      <li id="three" class="hot">honey</li>
      <li id="four">balsamic vinegar</li>
    </ul>
  </div>
① <script src="js/jquery-1.11.0.js"></script>
② <script src="js/basic-example.js"></script>
</body>
```

WHERE TO GET JQUERY AND WHICH VERSION TO USE

Above, jQuery is included before the closing `</body>` tag just like other scripts. (Another way to include the script is shown on p355.) A copy of jQuery is included with the code for this book, or you can download it from http://jquery.org. The version number of jQuery should be kept in the file name. Here, it is `jquery-1.11.0.js`, but by the time you read this book, there may be a newer version. The examples should still work with newer versions.

You often see websites use a version of the jQuery file with the file extension `.min.js`. It means unnecessary spaces and carriage returns have been stripped from the file. e.g., `jquery-1.11.0.js` becomes `jquery-1.11.0.min.js`.

It is done using a process called **minification** (hence `min` is used in the file name). The result is a much smaller file which makes it faster to download. But minified files are much harder to read.

If you want to look at the jQuery file, you can open it with a text editor – it is just text like JavaScript, albeit very complicated JavaScript.

Most people who use jQuery do not try to understand how the jQuery JavaScript file achieves what it does. As long as you know how to select elements and how to use its methods and properties, you can reap the benefits of using jQuery without looking under the hood.

Here, the JavaScript file uses the `$()` shortcut for the `jQuery()` function. It selects elements and creates three jQuery objects that hold references to the elements.

The methods of the **jQuery** object fade the list items in, and remove them when they are clicked on. Don't worry if you don't understand the code yet.

First, you will learn how to *select* elements using jQuery selectors, and then how to *update* those elements using the methods and properties of the **jQuery** object.

c07/js/basic-example.js

```
① $(':header').addClass('headline');
② $('li:lt(3)').hide().fadeIn(1500);
  ┌ $('li').on('click', function() {
③ ┤     $(this).remove();
  └ });
```

1. The first line selects all of the `<h1>` – `<h6>` headings, and adds a value of `headline` to their `class` attributes.

2. The second line selects the first three list items and does two things:
- The elements are hidden (in order to allow the next step).
- The elements fade into view.

3. The last three lines of the script set an event listener on each of the `<li>` elements. When a user clicks on one, it triggers an anonymous function to remove that element from the page.

Here is a reminder of the colors used to convey the priority and status of each list item:

HOT COOL
NORMAL COMPLETE

fresh figs

pine nuts

honey

balsamic vinegar

WHY USE JQUERY?

jQuery doesn't do anything you cannot achieve with pure JavaScript. It is just a JavaScript file but estimates show it has been used on over a quarter of the sites on the web, because it makes coding simpler.

1: SIMPLE SELECTORS

As you saw in Chapter 5, which introduced the DOM, it is not always easy to select the elements that you want to. For example:

- Older browsers do not support the latest methods for selecting elements.
- IE does not treat whitespace between elements as text nodes, while other browsers do.

Such issues make it hard to select the right elements on a page across all major browsers.

Rather than learn a new way to select elements, jQuery uses a language that is already familiar to front-end web developers: CSS selectors. They:

- Are much faster at selecting elements
- Can be a lot more accurate about which elements to select
- Often require a lot less code than older DOM methods
- Are already used by most front-end developers

jQuery even adds some extra CSS-style selectors which offer additional functionality.

Since jQuery was created, modern browsers have implemented the `querySelector()` and `querySelectorAll()` methods to let developers select elements using CSS syntax. However, these methods are not supported in older browsers.

2: COMMON TASKS IN LESS CODE

There are some tasks that front-end developers need to do regularly, such as loop through the elements that have been selected.

jQuery has methods that offer web developers simpler ways to perform common tasks, such as:

- Loop through elements
- Add / remove elements from the DOM tree
- Handle events
- Fade elements into / out of view
- Handle Ajax requests

jQuery simplifies each of these tasks, and allows you to write less code to achieve them.

jQuery also offers chaining of methods (a technique which you will meet on p311). Once you have selected some elements, this allows you to apply multiple methods to the same selection.

jQuery's motto is "Write less, do more," because it allows you to achieve the same goals but in fewer lines of code than you would need to write with plain JavaScript.

3: CROSS-BROWSER COMPATIBILITY

jQuery automatically handles the inconsistent ways in which browsers select elements and handle events, so you do not need to write cross-browser fallback code (such as that shown in the previous two chapters).

To do this, jQuery uses **feature detection** to find the best way to achieve a task. It involves the use of many conditional statements: if the browser supports the ideal way to achieve a task, it uses that approach; otherwise, it tests to see if it supports the next best option to achieve the same task.

This was the technique used in the last chapter to determine whether or not the browser supported event listeners. If event listeners were not supported, an alternative approach was offered (aimed at users of Internet Explorer 8 and older versions of IE).

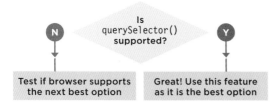

Here, a conditional statement checks if the browser supports querySelector(). If it does, that method is used. If it doesn't, it checks to see if the next best option is supported and uses that instead.

JQUERY 1.9.X+ OR 2.0.X+

As jQuery developed, it built up a lot of code to support IE6, 7, and 8; which made the script bigger and more complicated. As version 2.0 of jQuery was approaching, the development team decided to create a version that would drop support for older browsers in order to create a smaller, faster script.

The jQuery team was, however, aware that many people on the web still used these older browsers, and that developers therefore needed to support them. For this reason, they now maintain two parallel versions of jQuery:

jQuery 1.9+: Encompasses the same features as 2.0.x but still offers support for IE6, 7, and 8

jQuery 2.0+: Drops support for older browsers to make the script smaller and faster to use

The functionality of both versions is not expected to diverge significantly in the short term.

The jQuery file name should contain the version number in it (e.g., jquery-1.11.0.js or jquery-1.11.0.min.js). If you don't do this, a user's browser might try to use a cached version of the file that is either older *or* newer – which could prevent other scripts from working correctly.

FINDING ELEMENTS

Using jQuery, you usually select elements using CSS-style selectors. It also offers some extra selectors, noted below with a 'jQ'.

Examples of using these selectors are demonstrated throughout the chapter. The syntax will be familiar to those who have used selectors in CSS.

BASIC SELECTORS

*	All elements
element	All elements with that element name
#id	Elements whose id attribute has the value specified
.class	Elements whose class attribute has the value specified
selector1, selector2	Elements that match more than one selector (see also the .add() method, which is more efficient when combining selections)

HIERARCHY

ancestor descendant	An element that is a descendant of another element (e.g., li a)
parent > child	An element that is a direct child of another element (you can use * in the place of the child to select all child elements of the specified parent)
previous + next	Adjacent sibling selector only selects elements that are immediately followed by the previous element
previous ~ siblings	Sibling selector will select any elements that are a sibling of the previous element

BASIC FILTERS

not(*selector*)		All elements except the one in the selector (e.g., div:not('#summary'))
first	jQ	The first element from the selection
last	jQ	The last element from the selection
even	jQ	Elements with an even index number in the selection
odd	jQ	Elements with an odd index number in the selection
eq(*index*)	jQ	Elements with an index number equal to the one in the parameter
gt(*index*)	jQ	Elements with an index number greater than the parameter
lt(*index*)	jQ	Elements with an index number less than the parameter
header	jQ	All <h1> - <h6> elements
animated	jQ	Elements that are currently being animated
focus		The element that currently has focus

CONTENT FILTERS

`:contains('text')`		Elements that contain the specified text as a parameter
`:empty`		All elements that have no children
`:parent`	jQ	All elements that have a child node (can be text or element)
`:has(selector)`	jQ	Elements that contain at least one element that matches the selector (e.g., `div:has(p)` matches all `div` elements that contain a `<p>` element)

VISIBILITY FILTERS

`:hidden`	jQ	All elements that are hidden
`:visible`	jQ	All elements that consume space in the layout of the page
		Not selected if: `display: none`; `height / width: 0`; ancestor is hidden
		Selected if: `visibility: hidden`; `opacity: 0` because they would take up space in layout

CHILD FILTERS

`:nth-child(expr)`	The value here is not zero-based e.g. `ul li:nth-child(2)`
`:first-child`	First child from the current selection
`:last-child`	Last child from the current selection
`:only-child`	When there is only one child of the element (`div p:only-child`)

ATTRIBUTE FILTERS

`[attribute]`		Elements that carry the specified attribute (with any value)
`[attribute='value']`		Elements that carry the specified attribute with the specified value
`[attribute!='value']`	jQ	Elements that carry the specified attribute but not the specified value
`[attribute^='value']`		The value of the attribute begins with this value
`[attribute='value']`		The value of the attribute ends with this value
`[attribute*='value']`		The value should appear somewhere in the attribute value
`[attribute|='value']`		Equal to given string, or starting with string and followed by a hyphen
`[attribute~='value']`		The value should be one of the values in a space separated list
`[attribute][attribute2]`		Elements that match all of the selectors

FORM

`:input`	jQ	All input elements
`:text`	jQ	All text inputs
`:password`	jQ	All password inputs
`:radio`	jQ	All radio buttons
`:checkbox`	jQ	All checkboxes
`:submit`	jQ	All submit buttons
`:image`	jQ	All `<img>` elements
`:reset`	jQ	All reset buttons
`:button`	jQ	All `<button>` elements
`:file`	jQ	All file inputs
`:selected`	jQ	All selected items from drop-down lists
`:enabled`		All enabled form elements (the default for all form elements)
`:disabled`		All disabled form elements (using the CSS `disabled` property)
`:checked`		All checked radio buttons or checkboxes

DOING THINGS WITH YOUR SELECTION

Once you have seen the basics of how jQuery works, most of this chapter is dedicated to demonstrating these methods.

These two pages both offer an overview to the jQuery methods and will also help you find the methods you are looking for once you have read the chapter.

You often see jQuery method names written starting with a period (.) before the name. This convention is used in this book to help you easily identify those methods as being jQuery methods rather than built-in JavaScript methods, or methods of custom objects.

When you make a selection, the **jQuery** object that is created has a property called **length**, which will return the number of elements in the object.

If the jQuery selection did not find any matching elements, you will not get an error by calling any of these methods – they just won't do or return anything.

There are also methods that are specifically designed to work with Ajax (which lets you refresh part of the page rather than an

CONTENT FILTERS

Get or change content of elements, attributes, text nodes

GET/CHANGE CONTENT

ELEMENTS

ATTRIBUTES

FORM VALUES

FINDING ELEMENTS

Find and select elements to work with & traverse the DOM

GENERAL

FILTER/TEST

ORDER IN SELECTION

Once you have selected the elements you want to work with (and they are in a jQuery object), the jQuery methods listed on these two pages perform tasks on those elements.

DIMENSION/POSITION

Get or update the dimensions or position of a box

DIMENSION

`.height()`	p348
`.width()`	p348
`.innerHeight()`	p348
`.innerWidth()`	p348
`.outerHeight()`	p348
`.outerWidth()`	p348
`$(document).height()`	p350
`$(document).width()`	p350
`$(window).height()`	p350
`$(window).width()`	p350

POSITION

`.offset()`	p351
`.position()`	p351
`.scrollLeft()`	p350
`.scrollTop()`	p350

EFFECTS & ANIMATION

Add effects and animation to parts of the page

BASIC

`.show()`	p332
`.hide()`	p332
`.toggle()`	p332

FADING

`.fadeIn()`	p332
`.fadeOut()`	p332
`.fadeTo()`	p332
`.fadeToggle()`	p332

SLIDING

`.slideDown()`	p332
`.slideUp()`	p332
`.slideToggle()`	p332

CUSTOM

`.delay()`	p332
`.stop()`	p332
`.animate()`	p332

EVENTS

Create event listeners for each element in the selection

DOCUMENT/FILE

`.ready()`	p312
`.load()`	p313

USER INTERACTION

`.on()`	p326

There used to be methods for individual types of event, so you may see methods such as `.click()`, `.hover()`, `.submit()`. However, these have been dropped in favour of the `.on()` method to handle events.

A MATCHED SET / JQUERY SELECTION

When you select one or more elements, a jQuery object is returned. It is also known as a **matched set** or a **jquery selection**.

SINGLE ELEMENT

If a selector returns one element, the **jQuery** object contains a reference to just one element node.

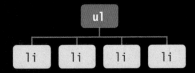

This selector picks the **<ul>** element from the page. So the **jQuery** object contains a reference to just one node (the only **<ul>** element in the page):

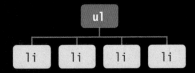

Each element is given an index number. Here there is just one element in the object.

INDEX	ELEMENT NODE
0	ul

MULTIPLE ELEMENTS

If a selector returns several elements, the **jQuery** object contains references to each element.

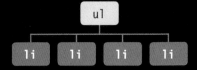

This selector picks all the **<li>** elements. Here, the **jQuery** object has references for each of the nodes that was selected (each **<li>** element):

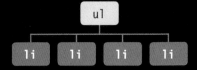

The resulting jQuery object contains four list items. Remember that index numbers start at zero.

INDEX	ELEMENT NODE
0	li#one.hot
1	li#two.hot
2	li#three.hot
3	li#four

JQUERY METHODS THAT GET AND SET DATA

Some jQuery methods both retrieve information from, and update the contents of, elements. But they do not always apply to all elements.

GET INFORMATION

If a jQuery selection holds more than one element, and a method is used to get information from the selected elements, it will **retrieve information from only the first element** in the matched set.

In the list example we have been using, the following selector chooses the four **<li>** elements from a list.

$$\$('li')$$

When you use the **.html()** method (which will be introduced on p316) to get information from an element, it will return the content of the first element in the matched set.

```
var content = $('li').html();
```

This will retrieve the content of the first list item, and store it in the variable called **content**.

To get a different element, you can use methods to traverse (p336) or filter (p338) the selection, or write a more specific selector (p302).

To get the content of all of the elements, see the **.each()** method (p324).

SET INFORMATION

If a jQuery selection holds more than one element, and a method is used to update information on the page, it will **update all of the elements** in the matched set, not just the first one.

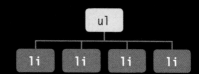

When you use the **.html()** method (which you meet on p316) to update the element, it will replace the contents of each element in the matched set. Here, it updates the content of each item in the list.

```
$('li').html('Updated');
```

This will update the content of all of the list items in the matched set with the word **Updated**.

To update just *one* element, you can use methods to traverse (p336) or filter (p338) the selection, or write a more specific selector (p302).

JQUERY OBJECTS STORE REFERENCES TO ELEMENTS

When you create a selection with jQuery, it stores a reference to the corresponding nodes in the DOM tree. It does not create copies of them.

As you have seen, when HTML pages load, the browser creates a model of the page in memory. Imagine your browser's memory is a set of tiles:

`<>` Nodes in the DOM take up a tile

`var` Variables take up a tile

`$` Complex JavaScript objects may take several tiles because they hold more data

In reality, the items in the browser's memory are not spread out as they are in this diagram, but the diagram helps explain the concept.

When you create a jQuery selection, the jQuery object holds **references** to the elements in the DOM – it does not create a copy of them.

When programmers say that a variable or object is storing a reference to something, what it is doing is storing the *location* a piece of information in the browser's memory. Here, the jQuery object would know that the list items are stored in A4, B4, and C4. Again, this is purely for illustration purposes; the browser's memory is not quite as simple as a checkerboard with these locations.

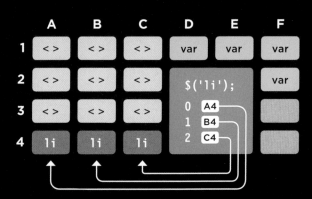

The jQuery object is an array-like object because it stores a list of the elements in the same order that they appear in the HTML document (unlike other objects where the order of the properties is not usually preserved).

CACHING JQUERY SELECTIONS IN VARIABLES

A jQuery object stores references to elements.
Caching a jQuery object stores a reference to it in a variable.

To create a jQuery object takes time, processing resources, and memory. The interpreter must:

1. Find the matching nodes in the DOM tree
2. Create the jQuery object
3. Store references to the nodes in the jQuery object

So, if the code needs to use the same selection more than once, it is better to use that same jQuery object again rather than repeat the above process. To do this, you store a reference to the jQuery object in a variable.

Below, a jQuery object is created. It stores the locations of the **<li>** elements in the DOM tree.

```
$('li');
```

A reference to this object is in turn stored in a variable called **$listItems**. Note that when a variable contains a jQuery object, it is often given a name beginning with the $ symbol (to help differentiate it from other variables in your script).

```
$listItems = $('li');
```

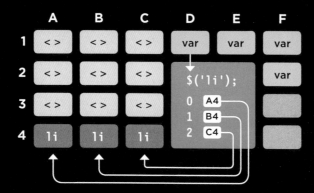

Caching jQuery selections is similar to the idea of storing a reference to a DOM node once you have made a DOM query (as you saw in Chapter 5).

LOOPING

In plain JavaScript, if you wanted to do the same thing to several elements, you would need to write code to loop through all of the elements you selected.

With jQuery, when a selector returns multiple elements, you can update all of them using the one method. There is no need to use a loop.

In this code, the same value is added to the class attribute for all of the elements that are found using the selector. It doesn't matter if there are one or many.

```
c07/js/looping.js
$('li em').addClass('seasonal');
$('li.hot').addClass('favorite');
```

In this example, the first selector applies only to one element and the class attribute's new value triggers a CSS rule that adds a calendar icon to the left of it.

The second selector applies to three elements. The new value added to the class attribute for each of these elements triggers a CSS rule that adds a heart icon on the right-hand side.

The ability to update all of the elements in the jQuery selection is known as **implicit iteration**.

When you want to get information from a series of elements, you can use the `.each()` method (which you meet on p324) rather than writing a loop.

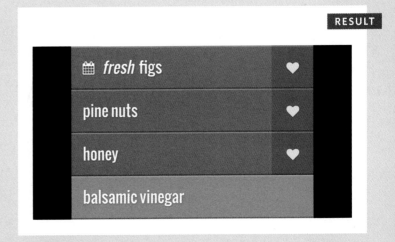

RESULT

CHAINING

If you want to use more than one jQuery method on the same selection of elements, you can list several methods at a time using dot notation to separate each one, as shown below.

In this one statement, three methods act on the same selection of elements:
`hide()` hides the elements
`delay()` creates a pause
`fadeIn()` fades in the elements

The process of placing several methods in the same selector is referred to as **chaining**. As you can see, it results in code that is far more compact.

JAVASCRIPT   c07/js/chaining.js

```javascript
$('li[id!="one"]').hide().delay(500).fadeIn(1400);
```

RESULT

To make your code easier to read, you can place each new method on a new line:

```javascript
$('li[id!="one"]')
  .hide()
  .delay(500)
  .fadeIn(1400);
```

Each line starts with the dot notation, and the semicolon at the end of the statement indicates that you have finished working with this selection.

Most methods used to **update** the jQuery selection can be chained. However the methods that **retrieve** information from the DOM (or about the browser) cannot be chained.

It is worth noting that if one method in the chain does not work, the rest will not run either.

CHECKING A PAGE IS READY TO WORK WITH

jQuery's `.ready()` method checks that the page is ready for your code to work with.

$(document) creates a jQuery object representing the page.

When the page is ready, the function inside the parentheses of the .ready() method is run.

JQUERY OBJECT

READY EVENT METHOD

```
$(document).ready(function() {
    // Your script goes here
});
```

As with plain JavaScript, if the browser has not yet constructed the DOM tree, jQuery will not be able to select elements from it.

If you place a script at the end of the page (just before the closing **</body>** tag), the elements will be loaded into the DOM tree.

If you wrap your jQuery code in the method above, it will still work when used elsewhere on the page or even in another file.

A shorthand for this is shown on the right-hand page. It is more commonly used than this longer version.

THE load EVENT

jQuery had a `.load()` method. It fired on the **load** event, but has been replaced by the `.on()`. As you saw on p272, the **load** event fires after the page and all of its resources (images, CSS, and scripts) have loaded.

You should use this when your script relies on assets to have loaded, e.g., if it needs to know the dimensions of an image.

It works in all browsers, and also provides function-level scope for the variables it contains.

VS

THE `.ready()` METHOD

jQuery's `.ready()` method checks if the browser supports the **DOMContentLoaded** event, because it fires as soon as the DOM has loaded (it does not wait for other assets to finish loading) and can make the page appear as if it is loading faster.

If **DOMContentLoaded** is supported, jQuery creates an event listener that responds to that event. But the event is only supported in modern browsers. In older browsers, jQuery will wait for the **load** event to fire.

VS

PLACING SCRIPTS BEFORE THE CLOSING </body> TAG

When you place your script at the end of the page (before the closing **</body>** tag), the HTML will have loaded into the DOM before the script runs.

You will, however, still see people using the `.ready()` method because scripts that use it will still work if someone moves the script tag elsewhere in the HTML page. (This is particularly common when that script is being made available for other people to use.)

SHORTCUT FOR READY EVENT METHOD ON DOCUMENT OBJECT

```
$(function() {
    // Your script goes here
});
```

Above, you can see the shorthand that is commonly used instead of `$(document).ready()`

A positive side-effect of writing jQuery code inside this method is that it creates function-level scope for its variables.

This function-level scope prevents naming collisions with other scripts that might use the same variable names.

Any statements inside the method automatically run when the page has loaded. This is the version that will be used in the examples in the rest of the chapter.

GETTING ELEMENT CONTENT

The `.html()` and `.text()` methods both retrieve and update the content of elements. This page will focus on how to retrieve element content. To learn how to update element content, see p316.

`.html()`

When this method is used to retrieve information from a jQuery selection, it retrieves only the HTML inside the *first* element in the matched set, along with any of its descendants.

For example, `$('ul').html();` will return this:

```
<li id="one"><em>fresh</em> figs</li>
<li id="two">pine nuts</li>
<li id="three">honey</li>
<li id="four">balsamic vinegar</li>
```

Whereas `$('li').html();` will return this:

```
<em>fresh</em> figs
```

Note how this returns only the content of the first `<li>` element.

If you want to retrieve the value of every element, you can use the `.each()` method (see p324).

`.text()`

When this method is used to retrieve the text from a jQuery selection, it returns the content from every element in the jQuery selection, along with the text from any descendants.

For example, `$('ul').text();` will return this:

```
fresh figs
pine nuts
honey
balsamic vinegar
```

Whereas `$('li').text();` will return this:

```
fresh figspine nutshoneybalsamic vinegar
```

Note how this returns the text content of all `<li>` elements (including spaces between words), but there are no spaces between the individual list items.

To get the content from `<input>` or `<textarea>` elements, use the `.val()` method shown on p343.

GETTING AT CONTENT

On this page you can see variations on how the `.html()` and `.text()` methods are used on the same list (depending on whether `<ul>` or `<li>` elements are used in the selector).

Please note: The `.append()` method (covered on p318) lets you add content to the page.

Please note: The `.append()` method (covered on p318) lets you add content to the page.

JAVASCRIPT   c07/js/get-html-fragment.js

```javascript
var $listHTML = $('ul').html();
$('ul').append($listHTML);
```

The selector returns the `<ul>` element. The `.html()` method gets all the HTML inside it (the four `<li>` elements). This is then appended to the end of the selection, in this case after the existing `<li>` elements.

JAVASCRIPT   c07/js/get-text-fragment.js

```javascript
var $listText = $('ul').text();
$('ul').append('<p>' + $listText  + '</p>');
```

The selector returns the `<ul>` element. The `.text()` method gets the text from all of the `<ul>` element's children. This is then appended to the end of the selection, in this case after the existing `<ul>` element.

JAVASCRIPT   c07/js/get-html-node.js

```javascript
var $listItemHTML = $('li').html();
$('li').append('<i>' + $listItemHTML + '</i>');
```

The selector returns the four `<li>` elements, but the `.html()` method returns only the contents of the first one. This is then appended to the end of the selection, in this case after each existing `<li>` element.

JAVASCRIPT   c07/js/get-text-node.js

```javascript
var $listItemText = $('li').text();
$('li').append('<i>' + $listItemText + '</i>');
```

The selector returns the four `<li>` elements. The `.text()` method gets the text from these. This is then appended to each of the `<li>` elements in the selection.

UPDATING ELEMENTS

Here are four methods that update the content
of all elements in a jQuery selection.

When the `.html()` and `.text()`
methods are used as setters (to
update content) they will replace
the content of each element in
the matched set (along with any
content and child elements).

The `.replaceWith()` and
`.remove()` methods replace and
remove the elements they match
(as well as their content and any
child elements).

The `.html()`, `.text()`, and
`.replaceWith()` methods can
take a string as a parameter.
The string can:
● Be stored in a variable
● Contain markup

When you add markup to the
DOM, be sure to escape all
untrusted content properly on
the server. Both the `.html()` and
`.replaceWith()` methods carry
the same security risks as using
the DOM's `innerHTML` property.
See p228 – p231 on XSS.

`.html()`

This method gives every element
in the matched set the same new
content. The new content may
include HTML.

`.replaceWith()`

This method replaces every
element in a matched set with
new content. It also returns the
replaced elements.

`.text()`

This method gives every element
in the matched set the same new
text content. Any markup would
be shown as text.

`.remove()`

This method removes all of the
elements in the matched set.

USING A FUNCTION TO UPDATE CONTENT

If you want to use *and* amend the content of the current selection,
these methods can take a function as a parameter. The function can be
used to create new content. Here the text from each element is placed
inside <em> tags.

```
$('li.hot').html(function() {
    return '<em>' + $(this).text() + '</em>';
});
    └─①─┘ └─②─┘    └──────③──────┘    └─②─┘
```

1. `return` indicates that content should be returned by the function.
2. <em> tags are placed around the text content of the list item.
3. `this` refers to the current list item. `$(this)` places that element in a
new jQuery object so that you can use jQuery methods on it.

CHANGING CONTENT

In this example, you can see three methods that allow you to update the content of the page.

When updating the content of an element, you can use a string, a variable, or a function.

```javascript
$(function() {
  $('li:contains("pine")').text('almonds');
  $('li.hot').html(function() {
    return '<em>' + $(this).text() + '</em>';
  });
  $('li#one').remove();
});
```

1. This line selects any list items that contain the word pine. It then changes the text of the matching element to almonds using the .text() method.

2. These lines select all list items whose class attribute contains the word hot, and uses the .html() method to update the content of each of them.

The .html() method uses a function to place the content of each element inside an <em> element. (See the bottom of the left-hand page for a closer look at the syntax.)

3. This line selects the <li> element that has an id attribute whose value is one, then uses the remove() method to remove it. (This does not require a parameter.)

When specifying new content, carefully choose when to use single quotes and when to use double quotes. If you append a new element that has attributes, use single quotes to surround the content. Then use double quotes for the attribute values themselves.

RESULT

almonds

honey

balsamic vinegar

INSERTING ELEMENTS

Inserting new elements involves two steps:
1: Create the new elements in a jQuery object
2: Use a method to insert the content into the page

You can create new jQuery objects to hold text and markup that you then add to the DOM tree using one of the methods listed in step 2 on the right.

If you create a selection that returns multiple elements, these methods will add the same content to each of the elements in the matched set.

When adding content to the DOM, make sure you have escaped all untrusted content properly on the server. (See p228 – p231 on XSS.)

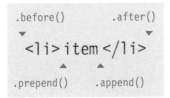

1: CREATING NEW ELEMENTS IN A JQUERY OBJECT

The following statement creates a variable called **$newFragment** and stores a jQuery object in it. The jQuery object is set to contain an empty `<li>` element: `var $newFragment = $('<li>');`

The following statement creates a variable called **$newItem** and stores a jQuery object in it. This jQuery object in turn contains an `<li>` element with a `class` attribute and some text:
`var $newItem = $('<li class="new">item</li>');`

2: ADDING THE NEW ELEMENTS TO THE PAGE

Once you have a variable holding the new content, you can use the following methods to add the content to the DOM tree:

.before()

This method inserts content before the selected element(s).

.after()

This method inserts content after the selected element(s).

.prepend()

This method inserts content inside the selected element(s), after the opening tag.

.append()

This method inserts content inside the selected element(s), before the closing tag.

There are also `.prependTo()` and `.appendTo()` methods. They work the other way around from `.prepend()` and `.append()`. So:

a.prepend(b) adds b to a
a.prependTo(b) adds a to b

a.append(b) adds b to a
a.appendTo(b) adds a to b

ADDING NEW CONTENT

In this example, you can see three jQuery selections are made. Each selection uses a different method to amend the content of the list.

The first adds a new notice before the list, the second adds a + symbol before the hot items, and the third adds a new element to the end of the list.

JAVASCRIPT

c07/js/adding-new-content.js

```
$(function() {
①    $('ul').before('<p class="notice">Just updated</p>');
②    $('li.hot').prepend('+ ');
③    var $newListItem = $('<li><em>gluten-free</em> soy sauce</li>');
     $('li:last').after($newListItem);
});
```

1. The `<ul>` element is selected, and the `.before()` method is used to insert a new paragraph before the list.

2. Selects all `<li>` elements whose `class` attribute contains a value of **hot** and uses the `.prepend()` method to add a plus symbol (+) before the text.

3. A new `<li>` element is created and stored in a variable. Then the last `<li>` element is selected, and the new element is added using the `.after()` method.

RESULT

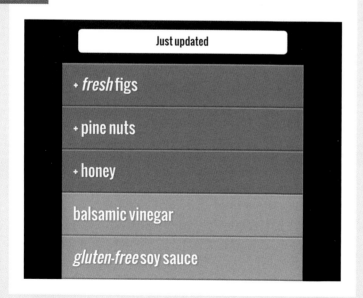

GETTING AND SETTING ATTRIBUTE VALUES

You can create attributes, or access and update their contents, using the following four methods.

You can work with any attribute on any element using the `attr()` and `removeAttr()` methods.

If you use the `attr()` method to update an attribute that does not exist, it will create the attribute and give it the specified value.

The value of the `class` attribute can hold more than one class name (each separated by a space). The `addClass()` and `removeClass()` methods are very powerful because they let you add or remove an *individual* class name within the value of the `class` attribute (and they do not affect any other class names).

.attr()

This method can get or set a specified attribute and its value. To get the value of an attribute, you specify the name of the attribute in the parentheses.

```
$('li#one').attr('id');
```

To update the value of an attribute, you specify both the attribute name and its new value.

```
$('li#one').attr('id','hot');
```

.addClass()

This method adds a new value to the existing value of the `class` attribute. It does not overwrite existing values.

.removeAttr()

This method removes a specified attribute (and its value). You just specify the name of the attribute that you want to remove from the element in the parentheses.

```
$('li#one').removeAttr('id');
```

.removeClass()

This method removes a value from the `class` attribute, leaving any other class names within that attribute intact.

These two methods are another good example of how jQuery adds helpful functionality commonly needed by web developers.

WORKING WITH ATTRIBUTES

The statements in this example use jQuery methods to change the class and id attributes of the specified HTML elements.

When the values of these attributes change, new CSS rules are applied to the elements, changing how they look.

Using events to trigger changes to attribute values that apply new CSS rules is a popular way to make a web page interactive.

c07/js/attributes.js

```
$(function() {
①    $('li#three').removeClass('hot');
②    $('li.hot').addClass('favorite');
③    $('ul').attr('id', 'group');
});
```

1. The first statement finds the third list item (it has an id attribute with a value of three) and removes hot from the class attribute on that element. This is important to note because it affects the next statement.

2. The second statement selects all <li> elements whose class attribute has a value of hot. It adds a new class name called favorite. Because step 1 updated the third list item, this statement affects only the first two.

3. The third statement selects the <ul> element and adds an id attribute, giving it a value of group (which triggers a CSS rule that will add a margin and border to the <ul> element).

RESULT

JQUERY (321)

GETTING & SETTING CSS PROPERTIES

The `.css()` method lets you retrieve and set the values of CSS properties.

To **get** the value of a CSS property, you indicate which property you want to retrieve in parentheses. If the matched set contains more than one element, it will return the value from the first element.

To **set** the values of a CSS property, you specify the property name as the first argument in the parentheses, then a comma, followed by its value as the second argument. This will update every element in the matched set. You can also specify multiple properties in the same method using object literal notation.

Note: In the method used to set an individual property, the property name and its value are separated by a comma (because all parameters in a method are separated by a comma).

In the object literal notation, properties and their values are separated by a colon.

HOW TO GET A CSS PROPERTY

This will store the background color of the first list item in a variable called `backgroundColor`. The color will be returned as an RGB value.

```
var backgroundColor = $('li').css('background-color');
```

HOW TO SET A CSS PROPERTY

This will set the background color of all list items. Note how the CSS property and its value are separated using a comma instead of a colon.

```
$('li').css('background-color', '#272727');
```

When dealing with dimensions that are specified in pixels, you can increase and decrease the values using the += and -= operators.

```
$('li').css('padding-left', '+=20');
```

SETTING MULTIPLE PROPERTIES

You can set multiple properties using **object literal notation**:
- Properties and values are placed in curly braces
- A colon is used to separate property names from their values
- A comma separates each pair (but there is not one after the last pair)

This sets the background color and typeface for all list items.

```
$('li').css({
  'background-color': '#272727',
  'font-family': 'Courier'
});
```

CHANGING CSS RULES

This example demonstrates how the `.css()` method can be used to select and update the CSS properties of elements.

The script checks what the background color of the first list item is when the page loads and then writes it after the list.

Next, it updates several CSS properties in all list items using the same `.css()` method with object literal notation.

JAVASCRIPT   c07/js/css.js

```
$(function() {
  var backgroundColor = $('li').css('background-color');
  $('ul').append('<p>Color was: ' + backgroundColor + '</p>');
  $('li').css({
    'background-color': '#c5a996',
    'border': '1px solid #fff',
    'color': '#000',
    'font-family': 'Georgia',
    'padding-left': '+=75'
  });
});
```

1. The `backgroundColor` variable is created. The jQuery selection contains all `<li>` elements, and the `.css()` method returns the value of the `background-color` property of the first list item.

2. The background color of the first list item is written into the page using the `.append()` method (which you met on p318). Here, it is used to add content after the `<ul>` element.

3. The selector picks all `<li>` elements, and then the `.css()` method updates several properties at the same time:

- The background color is changed to brown
- A white border is added
- The color of the text is changed to black
- The typeface is changed to Georgia
- Extra padding is added on the left

Note: It is better to change the value of a `class` attribute (to trigger new CSS rules in the style sheet) rather than to change CSS properties from within the JavaScript file itself.

RESULT

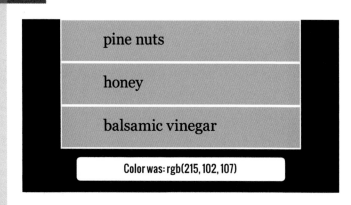

pine nuts

honey

balsamic vinegar

Color was: rgb(215, 102, 107)

WORKING WITH EACH ELEMENT IN A SELECTION

jQuery allows you to recreate the functionality of a loop on a selection of elements, using the `.each()` method.

You have already seen several jQuery methods that update all of the elements in a matched set without the need for a loop.

There are, however, times when you will want to loop through each of the elements in the selection. Often this will be to:

- Get information from each element in the matched set.
- Perform a *series* of actions on each of the elements.

The `.each()` method is provided for this purpose. The parameter of the `.each()` method is a function. This could be an anonymous function (as shown here) or a named function.

.each()

Allows you to perform one or more statements on each of the items in the selection of elements that is returned by a selector – rather like a loop in JavaScript.

It takes one parameter: a function containing the statements you want to run on each element.

```
   ┌─①─┐ ┌─②─┐
$('li').each(function() {
  var ids = this.id;
    $(this).append(' <em class="order">' + ids + '</em>');  ③
});
```

1. The jQuery selection contains all of the `<li>` elements.
2. `.each()` applies the same code to each element in the selection.
3. An anonymous function is run for each of the items in the list.

Since `this` refers to the current node, if you want to access a property of that node, e.g., that element's `id` or `class` attributes, it is better to use plain JavaScript to access those attributes:
`ids = this.id;`

this or $(this)

As the `.each()` method goes through the elements in a selection, you can access the current element using the `this` keyword.

You also often see `$(this)`, which uses the `this` keyword to create a new jQuery selection containing the current element. It allows you to use jQuery methods on the current element.

It is more efficient than writing `ids = $(this).attr('id');` because this would involve the interpreter creating a new jQuery object, and then using a method to access info that is available as a property.

USING .EACH()

This example creates a jQuery object containing all of the list items from the page.

The .each() method is then used to loop through the list items and run an anonymous function for each of them.

The anonymous function takes the value from the id attribute on the <li> element and adds it to the text in the list item.

JAVASCRIPT   c07/js/each.js

```
$(function() {
  $('li').each(function() {
    var ids = this.id;
    $(this).append(' <span class="order">' + ids + '</span>');
  });
});
```

1. The selector creates a jQuery object containing all <li> elements. The .each() method calls an anonymous function for each of the list items in the matched set.

2. The this keyword refers to the current element node in the loop. It is used to access the value of the current element's id attribute, which is stored in a variable called ids.

3. $(this) is used to create a jQuery object that contains the current element in the loop.

Having the element in a jQuery object enables you to use jQuery methods on that element. In this case the .append() method is used to add a new <span> element to the current list item.

The content of that element is the value of its id attribute, which was obtained in step 2.

RESULT

fresh figs one

pine nuts two

honey three

balsamic vinegar four

EVENT METHODS

The `.on()` method is used to handle all events.
Behind the scenes, jQuery handles all of the
cross-browser issues you saw in the last chapter.

Using the `.on()` method is no
different than using any other
jQuery method; you:

- Use a selector to create a
  jQuery selection.

- Use `.on()` to indicate which
  event you want to respond to.
  It adds an event listener to
  each element in the selection.

`.on()` was introduced in v 1.7
of jQuery. Prior to that, jQuery
used separate methods for
each event, e.g., `.click()`
and `.focus()`. You may come
across them in older code, but
you should only use the `.on()`
method now.

```
  ┌─①─┐ ┌②┐ ┌─③─┐
$('li').on('click', function() {  ⌉
  $(this).addClass('complete');  ④
});                               ⌋
```

1. The jQuery selection contains all of the `<li>` elements.
2. The `.on()` method is used to handle events. It needs two parameters:
3. The first parameter is the event you want to respond to. Here it is the
`click` event.
4. The second parameter is the code you want to run when that event
occurs on any element in the matched set. This could be a named
function or an anonymous function. Above, it is an anonymous function
that adds a value of `complete` to the `class` attribute.

You will see more advanced options for this method on p330.

JQUERY EVENTS

Some of the most popular events that `.on()` deals with are listed below.
jQuery also added some extras to make life easier, such as **ready**, which
fires when the page is ready to be worked with. These are noted with a
pink asterisk: *

UI	focus, blur, change
KEYBOARD	input, keydown, keyup, keypress
MOUSE	click, dblclick, mouseup, mousedown, mouseover, mousemove, mouseout, hover*
FORM	submit, select, change
DOCUMENT	ready*, load, unload*
BROWSER	error, resize, scroll

EVENTS

In this example, when the mouse moves over a list item, the content of its id attribute is written into the list item.

The same happens if the user clicks on a list item (because mouseover does not work on touchscreen devices).

The mouseout event also removes this extra information from the page to prevent the added content building up.

JAVASCRIPT   c07/js/events.js

```javascript
$(function() {
  var ids = '';
  var $listItems = $('li');

  $listItems.on('mouseover click', function() {
    ids = this.id;
    $listItems.children('span').remove();
    $(this).append(' <span class="priority">' + ids + '</span>');
  });

  $listItems.on('mouseout', function() {
    $(this).children('span').remove();
  });

});
```

① `var $listItems = $('li');`

② `$listItems.on('mouseover click', function() { ... });`

③ `$listItems.on('mouseout', function() { ... });`

1. The selector finds all list items on the page. The resulting jQuery object is used more than once, so it is stored in a variable called $listItems.

2. The .on() method creates an event listener, which waits for when the user moves a mouse over a list item or clicks on it. It triggers an anonymous function.

Note how the two events are specified in the same set of quote marks, with a space between them.

The anonymous function:
- Gets the value of the id attribute on that element.
- Removes <span> elements from all of the list items.
- Adds the value of the id attribute to the list item in a new <span> element.

3. The .mouseout() method triggers the removal of any child <span> elements to prevent build-up of added values.

RESULT

pine nuts two

honey

balsamic vinegar

THE EVENT OBJECT

Every event handling function receives an **event** object.
It has methods and properties related to the event that occurred.

Just like the JavaScript **event** object, the jQuery **event** object has properties and methods that tell you more about the event that took place.

If you look at the function that is called when the event occurs, the **event** object is named in the parentheses. Like any other parameter, this name is then used within the function to refer to the **event** object.

The example on the right uses the letter **e** as shorthand for the **event** object. However, as noted in the previous chapter, you should be aware that this shorthand is also often used for the **error** object.

①
```
$('li').on('click', function(e) {
  eventType = e.type;
});          ② ③
```

1. Give the **event** object a parameter name.
2. Use that name in the function to reference the **event** object.
3. Access the properties and methods of the object using the familiar dot notation (the member operator).

PROPERTY	DESCRIPTION
type	Type of event, (e.g., click, mouseover)
which	Button or key that was pressed
data	An object literal containing extra information passed to the function when the event fires (See right-hand page for an example)
target	DOM element that initiated the event
pageX	Mouse position from left edge of viewport
pageY	Mouse position from top of viewport
timeStamp	Number of milliseconds from Jan 1st, 1970, to when the event was triggered (this is known as Unix Time). Does not work in Firefox.

METHOD	DESCRIPTION
.preventDefault()	Prevents the default (e.g., submitting a form)
.stopPropagation()	Stops the event bubbling up to ancestors

EVENT OBJECT

In this example, when users click on a list item, the date that the event happened on is written next to that item, along with the type of event that triggered it.

To achieve this, two properties of the **event** object will be used: **timeStamp** states when the event occurred; **type** states the kind of event that triggered it.

To prevent the list from becoming cluttered with multiple date entries, whenever a list item is clicked, any <span> elements will be removed from the list.

c07/js/event-object.js

```
$(function() {

  $('li').on('click', function(e) {
①    $('li span').remove();
②    var date = new Date();
     date.setTime(e.timeStamp);
③    var clicked = date.toDateString();
④    $(this).append('<span class="date">' + clicked + ' ' + e.type + '</span>');
  });

});
```

1. Any <span> elements that already exist inside the <li> elements are removed.

2. A new **Date** object is created, and its time is set to the time at which the event was clicked.

3. The time the event was clicked is then converted into a date that can be read.

4. The date that the list item was clicked is written into the list item (along with the type of event that was used).

Note that the **timeStamp** property does not display in Firefox.

JQUERY 329

ADDITIONAL PARAMETERS FOR EVENT HANDLERS

The .on() method has two optional properties that let you:
Filter the initial jQuery selection to respond to a subset of the elements;
Pass extra information into the event handler using object literal notation.

Here you can see two additional properties that can be used with the .on() method.

When square brackets are used inside a method, they signify that the parameter is optional.

Leaving out a parameter written in square brackets will not stop the method working.

1. This is the event(s) that you want to respond to. If you want to respond to more than one event, you can provide a space-separated list of event names, e.g., 'focus click' will work on both focus *and* click.

2. If you just want to respond to the event happening on a *subset* of the elements in the initial jQuery selection, you can provide a second selector that will filter its descendants.

3. You can pass extra information to the function that is called when the event is triggered. This information is passed along with the **event** object (e).

$$.on(events[, selector][, data], function(e));$$

① ② ③ ④ ⑤

4. This is the function that should be run when the specified events occur on one of the elements in the matched set.

5. The function is automatically passed the **event** object as a parameter, as you saw on the previous two pages. (Remember, if you use it you must give it a name in the parentheses.)

Older jQuery scripts may use the .delegate() method for delegation. However, since jQuery 1.7 .on() is the preferred approach to delegation.

DELEGATING EVENTS

In this example, the event handler will run when users click or mouseover items in the list, *except* for the last list item.

It writes out the content of the element the user interacted with, a status message (using the data property), and the event type.

The information passed in the data property here uses object literal notation (so it could handle multiple properties).

c07/js/event-delegation.js

```javascript
$(function() {
  var listItem, itemStatus, eventType;

  $('ul').on(
    'click mouseover',
    ':not(#four)',
    {status: 'important'},
    function(e) {
      listItem = 'Item: ' + e.target.textContent + '<br />';
      itemStatus = 'Status: ' + e.data.status + '<br />';
      eventType = 'Event: ' + e.type;
      $('#notes').html(listItem + itemStatus + eventType);
    }
  );

});
```

RESULT

There is an extra element in the HTML for this example to hold the data that appears under the list.

1. The event handler is triggered by click and mouseover events.

2. The selector parameter filters *out* the element whose id attribute has a value of four.

3. Additional data that will be used by the event handler is passed in as an object literal.

4. The event handler uses the event object to display the content of the element the user interacts with, the information from the data that was passed into the function, and the event type, under the list in a white box.

EFFECTS

When you start using jQuery, the effects methods can enhance your web page with transitions and movement.

Here you can see some of the jQuery effects that show or hide elements and their content. You can animate them fading in and out, or slide them up and down.

When an element that was previously hidden is shown, faded in, or slides into view, the other elements on the page may move to make space for it.

When an element is hidden, has been faded out, or has slid out of view, the other elements on the page can move into the space these elements took up.

Methods with `toggle` in their name will look at the current state of the element (whether it is visible or hidden) and will switch to the opposite state.

Increasingly it is possible to create animations using CSS3. They are often faster than their jQuery counterparts, but they only work in recent browsers.

BASIC EFFECTS

METHOD	DESCRIPTION
.show()	Displays selected elements
.hide()	Hides selected elements
.toggle()	Toggles between showing and hiding selected elements

FADING EFFECTS

METHOD	DESCRIPTION
.fadeIn()	Fades in selected elements making them opaque
.fadeOut()	Fades out selected elements making them transparent
.fadeTo()	Changes opacity of selected elements
.fadeToggle()	Hides or shows selected elements by changing their opacity (the opposite of their current state)

SLIDING EFFECTS

METHOD	DESCRIPTION
.slideUp()	Shows selected elements with a sliding motion
.slideDown()	Hides selected elements with a sliding motion
.slideToggle()	Hides or shows selected elements with a sliding motion (in the opposite direction to its current state)

CUSTOM EFFECTS

METHOD	DESCRIPTION
.delay()	Delays execution of subsequent items in queue
.stop()	Stops an animation if it is currently running
.animate()	Creates custom animations (see p334)

BASIC EFFECTS

In this example, it appears as if list items are faded into view when the page loads. Each item is faded out when it is clicked on.

In fact, the items are loaded normally along with the rest of the page, but then immediately hidden using JavaScript.

Once hidden, only then are they faded into view. This is so they will still be visible in browsers that do not have JavaScript enabled.

c07/js/effects.js

```
$(function() {
①    $('h2').hide().slideDown();
     var $li = $('li');
     $li.hide().each(function(index) {
②      $(this).delay(700 * index).fadeIn(700);
     });
     $li.on('click', function() {
③      $(this).fadeOut(700);
     });
});
```

1. In the first statement, the selector picks the <h2> element and hides it so that it can be animated in. The chosen effect to show the heading is the `.slideDown()` method. Note how the methods are chained; there is no need to make a new selection for each of the tasks.

2. The second part causes the list of items to appear one by one. Again, before they can be faded in, they must be hidden. Then the `.each()` method is used to loop through each of the <li> elements in turn. You can see that this triggers an anonymous function.

Inside the anonymous function, the `index` property acts as a counter indicating which <li> element is the current one.

The `.delay()` method creates a pause before the list item is shown. The delay is set, multiplying the index number by 700 ms (otherwise all of the list items would appear at the same time). Then it is faded in using the `fadeIn()` method.

3. The final part creates an event listener that waits for the user to click on a list item. When they do, it will fade that item out to remove it from the list (the fade will take 700 milliseconds).

RESULT

ANIMATING CSS PROPERTIES

The `.animate()` method allows you to create some of your own effects and animations by changing CSS properties.

You can animate any CSS property whose value can be represented as a number, e.g., `height`, `width`, and `font-size`. But not those whose value would be a string, such as `font-family` or `text-transform`.

The CSS properties are written using camelCase notation, so the first word is all lowercase and each subsequent word starts with an uppercase character, e.g.: `border-top-left-radius` would become `borderTopLeftRadius`.

The CSS properties are specified using object literal notation (as you can see on the right-hand page). The method can also take three optional parameters, shown below.

```
.animate({
    // Styles you want to change
}[, speed][, easing][, complete]);
```
        ①   ②   ③

1. `speed` indicates the duration of the animation in milliseconds. (It can also take the keywords `slow` and `fast`.)

2. `easing` can have two values: `linear` (the speed of animation is uniform); or `swing` (speeds up in the middle of the transition, and is slower at start and end).

3. `complete` is used to call a function that should run when the animation has finished. This is known as a **callback function**.

EXAMPLES OF JQUERY EQUIVALENTS OF CSS PROPERTY NAMES

bottom	left	right	top	backgroundPositionX	backgroundPositionY	height	width
maxHeight	minHeight	maxWidth	minWidth	margin	marginBottom	marginLeft	marginRight
marginTop	outlineWidth	padding	paddingBottom	paddingLeft	paddingRight	paddingTop	
fontSize	letterSpacing	wordSpacing	lineHeight	textIndent	borderRadius	borderWidth	
borderBottomWidth	borderLeftWidth	borderRightWidth	borderTopWidth	borderSpacing			

USING ANIMATION

In this example, the `.animate()` method is used to gradually change the values of two CSS properties. Both of them have numerical values: `opacity` and `padding-left`.

When the user clicks on a list item, it fades out and the text content slides to the right. (This takes 500ms.) Once that is complete, a callback function removes the element.

You can increase or decrease numeric values by a specific amount. Here, `+=80` is used to increase the `padding` property by 80 pixels. (To decrease it by 80 pixels, you would use `-=80`.)

c07/js/animate.js

```javascript
$(function() {
  $('li').on('click', function() {
    $(this).animate({
      opacity: 0.0,
      paddingLeft: '+=80'
    }, 500, function() {
      $(this).remove();
    });
  });
});
```

① ② ③ ④

1. All list items are selected and, when a user clicks on one of them, an anonymous function runs. Inside it, `$(this)` creates a new jQuery object holding the element the user clicked on. The `.animate()` method is then called on that jQuery object.

2. Inside the `.animate()` method, the `opacity` and `paddingLeft` are changed. The value of the `paddingLeft` property is increased by 80 pixels, which makes it look like the text is sliding to the right as it fades out.

3. The `.animate()` method has two more parameters. The first is the speed of the animation in milliseconds (in this case, 500ms). The second is another anonymous function indicating what should happen when the animation finishes.

4. When the animation has finished, the callback function removes that list item from the page using the `.remove()` method.

If you want to animate between two colors, rather than using the `.animate()` method, there is a helpful jQuery color plugin here:

https://github.com/jquery/jquery-color

RESULT

TRAVERSING THE DOM

When you have made a jQuery selection, you can use these methods to access other element nodes relative to the initial selection.

Each method finds elements that have a different relationship to those that are in the current selection (e.g., parents or children of the current selection).

The .find() and .closest() methods both *require* a CSS-style selector as an argument.

For the other methods, the CSS-style selector is optional. But if a selector is provided, both the method and selector must match in order for the element to be added to the new selection.

For example, if you start with a selection that contains one list item, you could create a new selection containing the other items from the list using the .siblings() method.

If you added a selector into the method such as this:
.siblings('.important')
then it would find only siblings with a class attribute whose value included important.

SELECTOR REQUIRED

METHOD	DESCRIPTION
.find()	All elements within current selection that match selector
.closest()	Nearest ancestor (not just parent) that matches selector

SELECTOR OPTIONAL

METHOD	DESCRIPTION
.parent()	Direct parent of current selection
.parents()	All parents of current selection
.children()	All children of current selection
.siblings()	All siblings of current selection
.next()	Next sibling of current element
.nextAll()	All subsequent siblings of current element
.prev()	Previous sibling of current element
.prevAll()	All previous siblings of current element

If the original selection contains multiple elements, these methods will work on all of the elements in the selection (which can result in quite an odd selection of elements). You may need to narrow down your initial selection before traversing the DOM.

Behind the scenes, jQuery will handle the cross-browser inconsistencies involved in traversing the DOM (such as whitespace nodes being added by some browsers).

TRAVERSING

When the page loads, the list is hidden, and a link is added to the heading that indicates the users can display the list if they wish.

The link is added inside the heading and, if the user clicks anywhere on the <h2> element, the <ul> element is faded in.

Any child <li> elements that have a class attribute whose value is hot are also given an extra value of complete.

c07/js/traversing.js

JAVASCRIPT

```
$(function() {
  var $h2 = $('h2');
  $('ul').hide();
  $h2.append('<a class="show">show</a>');

  $h2.on('click', function() {
    $h2.next()
      .fadeIn(500)
      .children('.hot')
      .addClass('complete');
    $h2.find('a').fadeOut();
  });

});
```

① $h2.on('click', function() {
② $h2.next()
③ .fadeIn(500)
④ .children('.hot')
⑤ .addClass('complete');
⑥ $h2.find('a').fadeOut();

1. A click event anywhere in the <h2> element will trigger an anonymous function.
2. The .next() method is used to select the next sibling after the <h2> element, which is the <ul> element.

3. The <ul> is faded into view.
4. The .children() method then selects any child elements of the <ul> element, and the selector indicates that it should pick only those whose class attribute has a value of hot.

5. The .addClass() method is then used on those <li> elements to add a class name of complete. This shows how you can chain methods and traverse from one node to another.
6. In the last step, the .find() method can be used to select the <a> element that is a child of the <h2> element and fade it out because the list is now being shown to the users.

RESULT

ADD & FILTER ELEMENTS IN A SELECTION

Once you have a jQuery selection, you can add more elements to it, or you can filter the selection to work with a subset of the elements.

The `.add()` method allows you to add a new selection to an existing one.

The second table on the right shows you how to find a subset of your original selection.

The methods take another selector as a parameter and return a filtered matched set.

The items in this table that begin with a colon can be used wherever you would use a CSS-style selector.

The `:not()` and `:has()` selectors take another CSS-style selector as a parameter. There is also a selector called `:contains()` that lets you find elements that contain specific text.

The `.is()` method lets you use another selector to check whether the current selection matches a condition. If it does, it will return **true**. This is helpful in conditional statements.

ADDING ELEMENTS TO A SELECTION

METHOD	DESCRIPTION
`.add()`	Selects all elements that contain the text specified (parameter is case sensitive)

FILTERING WITH A SECOND SELECTOR

METHOD / SELECTOR	DESCRIPTION
`.filter()`	Finds elements in matched that in turn match a second selector
`.find()`	Finds descendants of elements in matched set that match the selector
`.not()` / `:not()`	Finds elements that do not match the selector
`.has()` / `:has()`	Finds elements from the matched set that have a descendant that matches the selector
`:contains()`	Selects all elements that contain the text specified (parameter is case sensitive)

The following two selectors are equivalent:
```
$('li').not('.hot').addClass('cool');
$('li:not(.hot)').addClass('cool');
```
In browsers that support querySelector() / querySelectorAll(), :not() is faster than .not() and :has() is faster than .has()

TESTING CONTENT

METHOD	DESCRIPTION
`.is()`	Checks whether current selection matches a condition (returns Boolean)

FILTERS IN USE

This example selects all list items and then uses different filters to select a subset of the items from the list to work with.

The example uses both the filtering methods as well as the CSS-style pseudo-selector :not().

Once the filters have selected a subset of the list items, other jQuery methods are used to update them.

```
   var $listItems = $('li');
①  $listItems.filter('.hot:last').removeClass('hot');
②  $('li:not(.hot)').addClass('cool');
③  $listItems.has('em').addClass('complete');

   $listItems.each(function() {
     var $this = $(this);
     if ($this.is('.hot')) {
④     $this.prepend('Priority item: ');
     }
   });

⑤  $('li:contains("honey")').append(' (local)');
```

1. The `.filter()` method finds the last list item with a `class` attribute whose value is `hot`. It then removes that value from the `class` attribute.

2. The `:not()` selector is used within the jQuery selector to find `<li>` elements without a value of `hot` in their `class` attribute and adds a value of `cool`.

3. The `.has()` method finds the `<li>` element that has an `<em>` element within it and adds the value `complete` to the `class` attribute.

4. The `.each()` method loops through the list items. The current element is cached in a jQuery object. The `.is()` method looks to see if the `<li>` element has a `class` attribute whose value is `hot`. If it does, `'Priority item: '` is added to the start of the item.

5. The `:contains` selector checks for `<li>` elements that contain the text `"honey"` and appends the text `" (local)"` to the end of those items.

RESULT

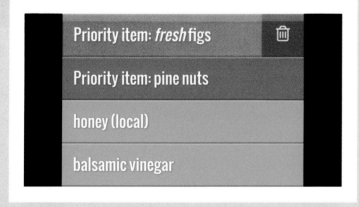

FINDING ITEMS BY ORDER

Each item returned by a jQuery selector is given an index number, which can be used to filter the selection.

The `jQuery` object is sometimes referred to as being an **array-like** object because it assigns a number to each of the elements that is returned by a selector. That number is an index number, which means it starts at 0.

You can filter the selected elements based on this number using methods or these additional CSS-style selectors that jQuery has added.

Methods are applied to the jQuery selection, whereas selectors are used as part of the CSS-style selector.

On the right, you can see a selector which picks all of the `<li>` elements from the list example used throughout this chapter. The table shows each list item and its corresponding index number. The example on the next page will use these numbers to select list items and update their `class` attributes.

FINDING ELEMENTS BY INDEX NUMBER

METHOD / SELECTOR	DESCRIPTION
`.eq()`	The element that matches the index number
`:lt()`	Elements with an index less than the number specified
`:gt()`	Elements with an index greater than the number specified

`$('li')`

INDEX	HTML
0	`<li id="one" class="hot"><em>fresh</em> figs</li>`
1	`<li id="two" class="hot">pine nuts</li>`
2	`<li id="three" class="hot">honey</li>`
3	`<li id="four">balsamic vinegar</li>`

USING INDEX NUMBERS

This example demonstrates how jQuery gives an index number to each of the elements in the jQuery selection.

The :lt() and :gt() selectors and the .eq() method are used to find elements based on their index numbers.

For each of the matching elements, the value of the class attributes are changed.

JAVASCRIPT

c07/js/index-numbers.js

```
$(function() {
①    $('li:lt(2)').removeClass('hot');
②    $('li').eq(0).addClass('complete');
③    $('li:gt(2)').addClass('cool');
});
```

1. The :lt() selector is used in the selector to pick list items with an index number less than 2. It removes the value hot from their class attribute.

2. The .eq() method selects the first item (using the number 0 because the index numbers start at zero). It adds the value of complete to the class attribute.

3. The :gt() selector is used in the jQuery selector to pick the list items with an index number higher than 2. It adds a value of cool to their class attribute.

RESULT

SELECTING FORM ELEMENTS

jQuery has selectors that are designed specifically to work with forms, however, they are not always the quickest way to select elements.

If you use one of these selectors on its own, jQuery will examine each element in the document to find a match (using code in the jQuery file, which is not as quick as CSS selectors).

Therefore, you should narrow down the part of the document the script needs to look through by placing an element name or other jQuery selector before using the selectors shown on this page.

You can also access elements in a form using the same selectors used to pick any element in jQuery. This will often be the faster option.

It is also worth noting that, because jQuery handles inconsistencies in the way browsers treat whitespace, it is easier to traverse between form elements using jQuery than it is when you are using plain JavaScript.

SELECTORS FOR FORM ELEMENTS

SELECTOR	DESCRIPTION
`:button`	`<button>` and `<input>` elements whose `type` attribute has a value of `button`
`:checkbox`	`<input>` elements whose `type` attribute has a value of `checkbox`. Note that you get better performance with `$('[type="checkbox"]')`
`:checked`	Checked elements from checkboxes and radio buttons (see `:selected` for select boxes)
`:disabled`	All elements that have been disabled
`:enabled`	All elements that are enabled
`:focus`	Element that currently has focus. Note that you get better performance with `$(document.activeElement)`
`:file`	All elements that are file inputs
`:image`	All image inputs. Note that you get better performance using `[type="image"]`
`:input`	All `<button>`, `<input>`, `<select>`, and `<textarea>` elements. Note that you get better performance from selecting elements, then using `.filter(":input")`
`:password`	All password inputs. Note that you get better performance using `$('input:password')`
`:radio`	All radio inputs. To select a group of radio buttons, you can use `$('input[name="gender"]:radio')`
`:reset`	All inputs that are reset buttons
`:selected`	All elements that are selected. Note that you get better performance using a CSS selector inside the `.filter()` method, e.g., `.filter(":selected")`
`:submit`	`<button>` and `<input>` elements whose `type` attribute has a value of `submit`. Note that you will get better performance using `[type="submit"]`
`:text`	Selects `<input>` elements with a `type` attribute whose value is text, or whose `type` attribute is not present. You will likely get better performance from `('input:text')`

FORM METHODS & EVENTS

RETRIEVE THE VALUE OF ELEMENTS

METHOD	DESCRIPTION
`.val()`	Primarily used with `<input>`, `<select>`, and `<textarea>` elements. It can be used to get the value of the first element in a matched set, or update the value of all of them.

OTHER METHODS

METHOD	DESCRIPTION
`.filter()`	Used to filter a jQuery selection using a second selector (especially form-specific filters)
`.is()`	Often used with filters to check whether a form input is selected/checked
`$.isNumeric()`	Checks whether the value represents a numeric value and returns a Boolean. It returns **true** for the following: `$.isNumeric(1)` `$.isNumeric(-3)` `$.isNumeric("2")` `$.isNumeric(4.4)` `$.isNumeric(+2)` `$.isNumeric(0xFF)`

EVENTS

METHOD	DESCRIPTION
`.on()`	Used to handle all events

EVENT	DESCRIPTION
blur	When an element loses focus
change	When the value of an input changes
focus	When an element gains focus
select	When the option for a `<select>` element is changed
submit	When a form is submitted

When submitting a form, there is also a helpful method called `.serialize()` which you will learn about on p394–p395.

The `.val()` method gets the value of the first `<input>`, `<select>`, or `<textarea>` element in a jQuery selection. It can also be used to set the value for all matching elements.

The `.filter()` and `.is()` methods are commonly used with form elements. You met them on p338.

`$.isNumeric()` is a global method. It is not used on a jQuery selection; rather, the value you want to test is passed as an argument.

All of the event methods on the left correspond to JavaScript events that you might use to trigger functions. As with other jQuery code, they handle the inconsistencies between browsers behind the scenes.

jQuery also makes it easier to work with a group of elements (such as radio buttons, checkboxes, and the options in a select box), because, once you have selected the elements, you can simply apply individual methods to each of them without having to write a loop.

There is an example using forms on the next page, and there are more examples in Chapter 13.

WORKING WITH FORMS

In this example, a button and form have been added under the list. When the user clicks on the button to add a new item, the form will come into view.

The form lets users add a new item to the list with a single text input and a submit button. (The new item button is hidden when the form is in view.)

When the user presses the submit button, the new item is added to the bottom of the list. (The form is also hidden and the new item button is shown again.)

```html
<!-- list goes here -->...</ul>
<div id="newItemButton"><button href="#" id="showForm">new item</button></div>
<form id="newItemForm">
  <input type="text" id="itemDescription" placeholder="Add description..." />
  <input type="submit" id="addButton" value="add" />
</form>
```

RESULT

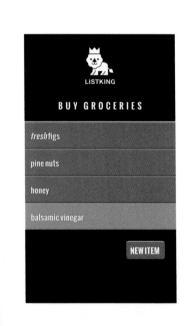
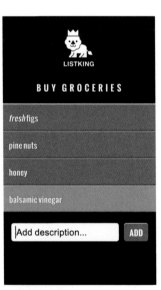
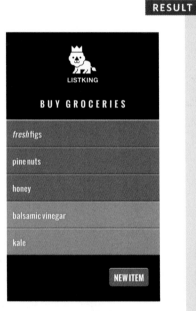

1. New jQuery objects are created to hold the new item button, the form to add new items, and the add button. These are cached in variables.

2. When the page loads, the CSS hides the new item button (and shows the form), so jQuery methods show the new item button and hide the form.

3. If a user clicks on the new item button (the **<button>** element whose **id** attribute has a value of **showForm**), the new item button is hidden and the form is shown.

c07/js/form.js

```javascript
$(function() {

  var $newItemButton = $('#newItemButton');
  var $newItemForm = $('#newItemForm');
  var $textInput = $('input:text');

  $newItemButton.show();
  $newItemForm.hide();

  $('#showForm').on('click', function(){
    $newItemButton.hide();
    $newItemForm.show();
  });

  $newItemForm.on('submit', function(e){
    e.preventDefault();
    var newText = $('input:text').val();
    $('li:last').after('<li>' + newText + '</li>');
    $newItemForm.hide();
    $newItemButton.show();
    $textInput.val('');
  });

});
```

4. When the form is submitted, an anonymous function is called. It is passed the **event** object.
5. The **.preventDefault()** method can stop the form being submitted.

6. The **:text** selector picks the **<input>** element whose **type** attribute has a value of **text**, and the **.val()** method gets the value the user entered into it. This value is stored in a variable called **newText**.

7. A new item is added to the end of the list using the **.after()** method.
8. The form is hidden, the new item button is shown again, and the content of the text input is emptied (so the user can add a new entry if they want to).

CUTTING & COPYING ELEMENTS

Once you have a jQuery selection, you can use these methods to remove those elements or make a copy of them.

The `.remove()` method deletes the matched elements and all of their descendants from the DOM tree.

The `.detach()` method also removes the matched elements and all of their descendants from the DOM tree; however, it retains any event handlers (and any other associated jQuery data) so they can be inserted back into the page.

The `.empty()` and `.unwrap()` methods remove elements in relation to the current selection.

The `.clone()` method creates a copy of the matched set of elements (and any descendants). If you use this method on HTML that contains `id` attributes, the value of the `id` attributes would need updating otherwise they would no longer be unique. If you want to pass any event handlers, you should add `true` between the parentheses.

CUT

METHOD	DESCRIPTION
`.remove()`	Removes matched elements from DOM tree (including any descendants and text nodes)
`.detach()`	Same as `.remove()` but keeps a copy of them in memory
`.empty()`	Removes child nodes and descendants from any elements in matched set
`.unwrap()`	Removes parents of matched set, leaving matched elements

COPY

METHOD	DESCRIPTION
`.clone()`	Creates a copy of the matched set (including any descendants and text nodes)

PASTE

You saw how to add elements into the DOM tree on p318.

CUT, COPY, PASTE

In this example, you can see parts of the DOM tree being removed, duplicated, and placed elsewhere on the page.

The HTML has an extra <p> element after the list, which contains a quote. It is moved to a new position under the heading.

In addition, the first list item is detached from the list and moved to the end of it.

JAVASCRIPT   c07/js/cut-copy-paste.js

```
$(function() {
①    var $p = $('p');
②    var $clonedQuote = $p.clone();
③    $p.remove();
④    $clonedQuote.insertAfter('h2');

⑤    var $moveItem = $('#one').detach();
⑥    $moveItem.appendTo('ul');
});
```

RESULT

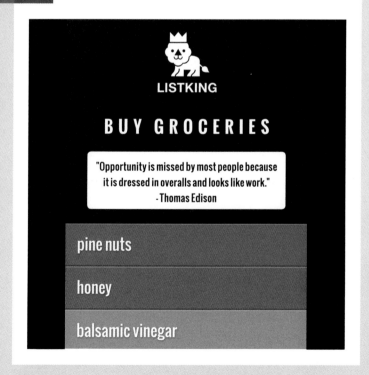

1. A jQuery selection is made containing the <p> element at the end of the page, and this is cached in a variable called $p.

2. That element is copied using the `.clone()` method (along with its content and child elements). It is stored in a variable called $clonedQuote.

3. The paragraph is removed.

4. The cloned version of the quote is inserted after the <h2> element at the top of the page.

5. The first list item is detached from the DOM tree and stored in a variable called $moveItem (effectively removing it from the DOM tree).

6. That list item is then appended to the end of the list.

BOX DIMENSIONS

These methods allow you to discover or update the width and height of all boxes on the page.

CSS treats each element on a web page as if it were in its own box. A box can have padding, a border, and a margin. If you set the width or height of the box in CSS, it does not include any padding, border, or margin – they are added to the dimensions.

The methods shown here allow you to retrieve the width and height of the first element in the matched set. The first two also allow you to update the dimensions of all boxes in the matched set.

The remaining methods give different measurements depending on whether you want to include padding, border, and a margin. Note how the `.outerHeight()` and `.outerWidth()` methods take a parameter of `true` if you want the margin included.

When retrieving dimensions, these methods return a number in pixels.

RETRIEVE OR SET BOX DIMENSIONS

METHOD	DESCRIPTION
`.height()`	Height of box (no margin, border, padding)
`.width()`	Width of box (no margin, border, padding) **(1)**

RETRIEVE BOX DIMENSIONS ONLY

METHOD	DESCRIPTION
`.innerHeight()`	Height of box plus padding
`.innerWidth()`	Width of box plus padding **(2)**
`.outerHeight()`	Height of box plus padding and border
`.outerWidth()`	Width of box plus padding and border **(3)**
`.outerHeight(true)`	Height of box plus padding, border, and margin
`.outerWidth(true)`	Width of box plus padding, border, and margin **(4)**

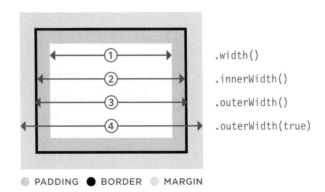

`.width()`
`.innerWidth()`
`.outerWidth()`
`.outerWidth(true)`

PADDING   BORDER   MARGIN

CHANGING DIMENSIONS

This example demonstrates how the `.height()` and `.width()` methods can be used to retrieve and update box dimensions.

The page displays the height of the container. It then changes the width of the list items using percentages and pixels.

c07/js/dimensions.js

```
$(function() {
①    var listHeight = $('#page').height();
②    $('ul').append('<p>Height: ' + listHeight + 'px</p>');
③    $('li').width('50%');
④ ┌  $('li#one').width(125);
   └  $('li#two').width('75%');
});
```

1. A variable called `listHeight` is created to store the height of the page container. It is obtained using the `.height()` method.

2. The height of the page is written at the end of the list using the `.append()` method and may vary between browsers.

3. The selector picks all the `<li>` elements and sets their width to 50% of their current width using the `.width()` method.

4. These two statements set the width of the first list item to 125 pixels and the width of the second list item to be 75% of the width it was when the page loaded.

Measurements in percentages or ems should be given as a string, with the suffix % or em. Pixels do not require a suffix and are not enclosed in quotes.

RESULT

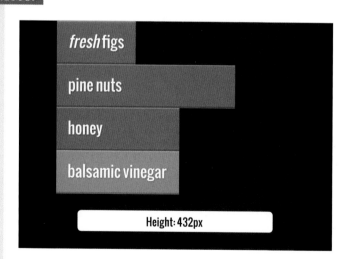

JQUERY (349)

WINDOW & PAGE DIMENSIONS

The `.height()` and `.width()` methods can be used to determine the dimensions of both the browser window and the HTML document. There are also methods to get and set the position of the scroll bars.

On p348, you saw that you can get and set the height or width of a box using the `.height()` and `.width()` methods.

These can also be used on a jQuery selection containing the **window** or **document** objects.

The browser can display scroll bars if the height or width of:

- A box's content is larger than its allocated space.
- The current page represented by the **document** object is larger than the dimensions of the browser window's viewable area (viewport).

The `.scrollLeft()` and `.scrollTop()` methods allow you to get and set the position of the scroll bars.

When retrieving dimensions, these methods return a number in pixels.

METHOD	DESCRIPTION
`.height()`	Height of the jQuery selection
`.width()`	Width of the jQuery selection
`.scrollLeft()`	Gets the horizontal position of the scroll bar for the first element in the jQuery selection, or sets the horizontal scroll bar position for matched nodes
`.scrollTop()`	Gets the vertical position of the scroll bar for the first element in the jQuery selection, or sets the vertical scroll bar position for matched nodes

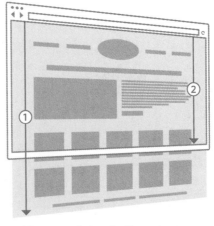

`$(window).height();`

This method will often return the incorrect value unless a DOCTYPE declaration is specified for the HTML page.

`$(document).height();`

POSITION OF ELEMENTS ON THE PAGE

The `.offset()` and `.position()` methods can be used to determine the position of elements on the page.

METHOD	DESCRIPTION
`.offset()`	Gets or sets coordinates of the element relative to the top left-hand corner of the **document** object **(1)**
`.position()`	Gets or sets coordinates of the element relative to any ancestor that has been taken out of normal flow (using CSS box offsets). If no ancestor is out of normal flow, it will return the same as `.offset()` **(2)**

The two methods on the left help you to determine the position of an element:

- Within the page.
- In relation to an ancestor that is offset from normal flow.

Each of them returns an object that has two properties:

`top` – the position from the top of the document or containing element.

`left` – the position from the left of the document or containing element.

As with other jQuery methods, when used to retrieve information, they return the co-ordinates of the first element in the matched set.

If they are used to set the position of elements, they will update the position of all elements in the matched set (putting them in the same spot).

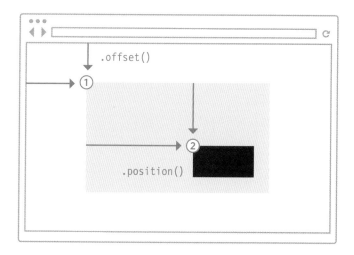

To get the offset or position, store the object that is returned by these methods in a variable. Then use the `left` or `right` properties of the object to retrieve their position.

```
var offset = $('div').offset();
var text = 'Left: ' + offset.left + ' Right: ' + offset.right;
```

DETERMINING POSITION OF ITEMS ON THE PAGE

In this example, as the user scrolls down the page, a box slides into view if they get within 500 pixels of the footer.

We will call this part of the page the end zone, and you need to work out the height at which the endZone starts.

Every time the user scrolls, you then check the position of the scroll bar from the top of the page.

If the scroll bar is further down the page than the start of the end zone, the box is animated into the page. If not, then the box is hidden.

The HTML for this example contains an extra `<div>` element at the end of the page containing the advert. A lot of items have been added to the list to create a long page that scrolls.

```
...<li>quinoa</li>
</ul>
<p id="footer">&copy; ListKing</p>
<div id="slideAd">
  Buy ListKing Pro for only $1.99
</div>
</div>
<script src="js/jquery-1.11.0.js"></script>
<script src="js/position.js"></script>
```

RESULT

1. Cache the window and advert.

2. The height of the end zone is calculated, and stored in a variable called endZone.

3. The scroll event triggers an anonymous function every time the user scrolls up or down.

4. A conditional statement checks if the user's position is further from the top of the page than the start of the end zone.

5. If the condition returns true, the box slides in from the right-hand edge of the page. This takes 250 milliseconds.

6. If the condition is false or the box is in the middle of animating, it is stopped using the .stop() method. The advert then slides off the right-hand edge of the page. Again, this animation will take 250 milliseconds.

JAVASCRIPT   c07/js/position.js

```
$(function() {
  var $window = $(window);
  var $slideAd = $('#slideAd');
  var endZone = $('#footer').offset().top - $window.height() - 500;

  $window.on('scroll', function() {

    if ( (endZone) < $window.scrollTop() ) {
      $slideAd.animate({ 'right': '0px' }, 250);
    } else {
      $slideAd.stop(true).animate({ 'right': '-360px' }, 250);
    }

  });

});
```

CALCULATING THE END ZONE

Calculate the height at which the box should come into view by:

a) Getting the height from the top of the page to the top of the footer (the gray bar) in pixels.

b) Subtracting the height of the viewport from this result.

c) Subtracting a further 500px for the area where the box will come into view (shown in pink).

You can tell how far the user has scrolled down the page using:

`$(window).scrollTop();`

If the distance extends down further than the height at which the end zone should show, the box should be made visible.

If not, then the box should move off the page.

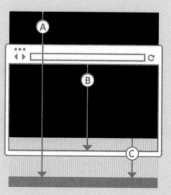

WAYS TO INCLUDE
JQUERY IN YOUR PAGE

In addition to hosting the jQuery file with the rest of your website, you can also use a version that is hosted by other companies. However, you should still include a fallback version.

At the time of writing, the main CDNs to offer jQuery are jQuery CDN (powered by Max CDN), Google, and Microsoft.

● ORIGIN ● CDN ● USER

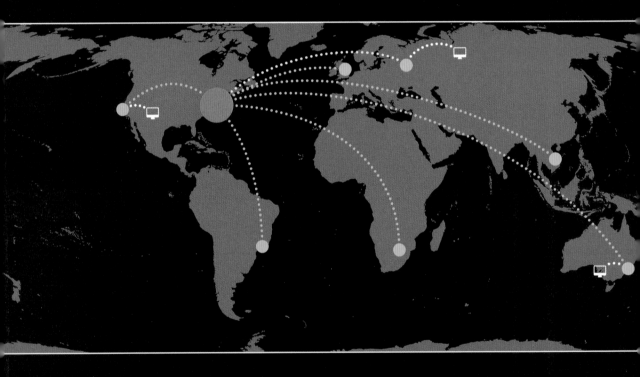

A Content Delivery Network (or CDN) is a series of servers spread out around the world. They are designed to serve static files (such as HTML, CSS, JavaScript, images, audio, and video files) very quickly.

The CDN tries to find a server near you, then sends files from that server so the data does not travel as far. With jQuery, users might have already downloaded and cached the file from a CDN when visiting another site.

When including jQuery in your pages, you can try to load it from one of these CDNs. Then you check if it loaded, and if not, you can include a version that is stored on your own servers (this is known as a fallback).

LOADING JQUERY
FROM A CDN

When a page loads jQuery from a CDN, you will often see a syntax like the one shown below. It starts with a `<script>` tag that tries to load the jQuery file from the CDN. But note that the URL for the script starts with two forward slashes (not `http:`).

This is known as a **protocol relative URL**. If the user is looking at the current page through `https`, then they will not see an error that tells them there are unsecure items on the page. **Note:** This does not work locally with the `file://` protocol.

This is often followed by a second `<script>` tag that contains a logical operator, which checks to see if jQuery has loaded. If it has not loaded, the browser tries to load the jQuery script from the same server as the rest of the website.

HTML

```html
<script src="//ajax.googleapis.com/ajax/libs/jquery/1.10.2/jquery.min.js">
</script>

<script>
window.jQuery || document.write('<script src="js/jquery-1.10.2.js"><\/script>')
</script>
```

The logical operator looks for the `jQuery` object that the jQuery script makes available. If it exists, then a truthy value is returned and the logical operator short circuits (see p157).

If jQuery has not loaded, then the `document.write()` method is used to add a new `<script>` tag into the page. This will load a version of jQuery from the same server as the rest of the website.

The fallback option is important because the CDN may be unavailable, the file may have moved, and some countries ban some domain names (such as Google).

WHERE TO PLACE YOUR SCRIPTS

The position of `<script>` elements can affect how quickly a web page seems to load.

SPEED

In the early days of the web, developers were told to place the `<script>` tags in the `<head>` of the page as you do with style sheets. However, this can make pages seem slower to load.

Your web page may use files from several different locations (e.g., images or CSS files might be loaded from one CDN, jQuery could be loaded from the jQuery or Google CDNs, and fonts might be loaded from another third party).

Usually a browser will collect up to two files at a time from each different server. However, when a browser starts to download a JavaScript file, it stops all other downloads and pauses laying out the page until the script has finished loading and been processed.

Therefore, if you place the script at the end of the page before the closing `</body>` tag, it will not affect the rendering of the rest of the page.

HTML LOADED INTO THE DOM TREE

Whenever a script is accessing the HTML within a web page, it also needs to have loaded that HTML into the DOM tree before the script can work. (This is often referred to as the DOM having loaded.)

You can use the `load` event to trigger a function so that you know the HTML has loaded. However, it fires only when the page and all of its resources load. You can also use the HTML5 `DOMContentLoaded` event, but it does not work in older browsers.

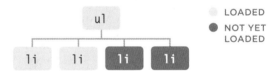

If the script tries to access an element before it has loaded, it causes an error. In the diagram above, the script could access the first two `<li>` elements, but not the third or fourth.

Where possible, do consider using alternatives to scripts. For example, use CSS for animations or HTML5's `autofocus` attribute rather than using the `load` event to bring focus to an element.

If your page is slow to load and you only want to include a small amount of code before the rest of the page has loaded, you can place a `<script>` tag within the body of the page.

At the time of writing, this technique was commonly used by Google for speed advantages, but it is acknowledged that it makes code much harder to maintain.

```html
<!DOCTYPE html>
<html>
  <head>
    <title>Sample Page</title>
    <link rel="stylesheet" href="sample.css" />
    <script src="js/sample.js"></script>
  <head>
  <body>
    <h1>Sample Page</h1>
    <div id="page">Main content here...</div>
  </body>
</html>
```

```html
<!DOCTYPE html>
<html>
  <head>
    <title>Sample Page</title>
    <link rel="stylesheet" href="sample.css" />
  <head>
  <body>
    <h1>Sample Page</h1>
    <script src="js/sample.js"></script>
    <div id="page">Main content here...</div>
  </body>
</html>
```

```html
<!DOCTYPE html>
<html>
  <head>
    <title>Sample Page</title>
    <link rel="stylesheet" href="sample.css" />
  <head>
  <body>
    <h1>Sample Page</h1>
    <div id="page">Main content here...</div>
    <script src="js/sample.js"></script>
  </body>
</html>
```

IN THE HEAD

This location is best avoided as:
1. Pages seem slower to load.
2. DOM content is not loaded, when the script is executed so you have to wait for an event like **load** or **DOMContentLoaded** to trigger your functions.

If you must use a **<script>** element within the head of the page, it should be just before the closing **</head>** tag.

IN THE PAGE

As with scripts in the **<head>**, those in the middle of the page will slow the rest of the page down when it is loading.

If you use **document.write()**, the **<script>** element has to be placed where you want that content to appear. This is one of several good reasons to avoid using **document.write()**.

BEFORE THE CLOSING </body> TAG

This is an ideal location as:
1. The script is not blocking other things from downloading.
2. The DOM has already loaded by the time the script is executed.

JQUERY
DOCUMENTATION

For an exhaustive list of the functionality
provided in jQuery, visit `http://api.jquery.com`

It is not possible to teach you everything about
jQuery in one (albeit long) chapter. But you have
seen many of the most popular features, and
you should now know enough about jQuery to
understand how it works and how to make use of it
in your scripts.

Throughout the remaining chapters of this book, you
will see many more examples that use jQuery.

What you have learned should also give you enough
experience to work with the comprehensive jQuery
documentation available online at:
`http://api.jquery.com`

This site lists each method and property available to
you, along with new functionality added in the latest
versions, and notes that indicate which features are
scheduled to be dropped.

HOW THE DOCUMENTATION WORKS

On the left-hand side of the page, you will see the
different types of functionality that you can explore.

When you click on any of the methods in the main
column, you will see a list of the parameters that it
can take. When parameters are optional, they are
shown in square brackets.

You will also find deprecated methods. This
means that you are no longer advised to use this
markup because it is likely to be removed from
future versions of jQuery (if it has not already been
removed).

EXTENDING JQUERY
WITH PLUGINS

Plugins are scripts that extend the functionality of the jQuery library.
Hundreds have been written and are available for you to use.

Plugins offer functionality that is not included in the jQuery library. They usually deal with a particular task such as creating slideshows or video players, performing animations, transforming data, enhancing forms, and displaying new data from a remote server.

To get an idea of the number and range of plugins available, see `http://plugins.jquery.com`. All of these are free for you to download and use on your own sites. You may also find other sites listing jQuery plugins for sale (such as `codecanyon.net`).

Plugins are written so that new methods extend the `jQuery` object and can, therefore, be used on a jQuery selection. As long as you know how to do the following with jQuery:

- Make a selection of elements
- Call a method and use parameters

You can use a lot of the functionality of these plugins without having to write the code yourself. In Chapter 11, you will see an example of how to create a basic jQuery plugin.

HOW TO CHOOSE A PLUGIN

When you are choosing a plugin to work with, it can be worth checking that it is still being maintained or whether other people have experienced problems using it. Finding out the following can help:

- When was the plugin last updated?
- How many people are watching the plugin?
- What do the bug reports say?

If you ask a question or find a bug in a script, bear in mind that their authors may have a day job and only maintain these plugins in their spare time to help others and to give back to the community.

JAVASCRIPT LIBRARIES

jQuery is an example of what programmers call a JavaScript library.
It is a JavaScript file that you include in your page, which then lets you
use the functions, objects, methods, and properties it contains.

The concept of a library is that it allows you to borrow code from one file and use its functions, objects, methods, and properties in another script.

Once you have included the script in your page, its functionality is available to use. The documentation for the library will tell you how to use it.

jQuery is the most widely used library on the web, but when you have learned it, you might like to explore some of the other libraries listed below.

Popular libraries have the advantage that they will be well-tested, and some have a whole team of developers who work on them in their spare time.

One of the main drawbacks with a library is that they will usually contain functionality that you will not need to use. This means users have to download code that will not be needed (which can slow your site down). You may find that you can strip out the subset of the library you need or indeed write your own script to do that job.

DOM & EVENTS

Zepto.js
YUI
Dojo.js
MooTools.js

USER INTERFACE

jQuery UI
jQuery Mobile
Twitter Bootstrap
YUI

GRAPHICS & CHARTS

Chart.js
D3.js
Processing.js
Raphael.js

TEMPLATING

Mustache.js
Handlebars.js
jQuery Mobile

WEB APPLICATIONS

Angular.js
Backbone.js
Ember.js

COMPATIBILITY

Modernizr.js
YepNope.js
Require.js

PREVENTING CONFLICTS WITH OTHER LIBRARIES

Earlier in the chapter, you saw that $() was shorthand for jQuery().
The $ symbol is used by other libraries such as prototype.js, MooTools,
and YUI. To avoid conflicts with those scripts, use these techniques.

INCLUDING JQUERY AFTER OTHER LIBRARIES

Here, jQuery's meaning of $ takes precedence:

```
<script src="other.js"></script>
<script src="jquery.js"></script>
```

You can use the .noConflict() method at the start
of your script, to tell jQuery to release the $ shortcut
so that other scripts can use it. Then you can use the
full name rather than the shortcut:

```
jQuery.noConflict();
jQuery(function() {
    jQuery('div').hide();
});
```

You can wrap your script in an IIFE and still use $:

```
jQuery.noConflict();
(function($) {
    $('div').hide();
})(jQuery);
```

Or you can specify your own alias instead, e.g., $j:

```
var $j = jQuery.noConflict();
$j(document).ready(function() {
    $j('div').hide();
});
```

INCLUDING JQUERY BEFORE OTHER LIBRARIES

Here, the other scripts' use of $ takes precedence:

```
<script src="jquery.js"></script>
<script src="other.js"></script>
```

$ will have the meaning defined in the other library.
There is no need to use the .noConflict() method
because it will have no effect. But you can continue
to use the full name jQuery:

```
jQuery(document).ready(function() {
    jQuery('div').hide();
});
```

You can pass $ as an argument to the anonymous
function called by the .ready() method like so:

```
jQuery(document).ready(function($) {
    $('div').hide();
});
```

This is equivalent to the code shown above:

```
jQuery(function($){
    $('div').hide();
});
```

TYPOGRAPHIC 58: TOO MUCH NOISE NOT ENOUGH TIME
THE JOURNAL OF THE INTERNATIONAL SOCIETY OF TYPOGRAPHIC DESIGNERS
DAVID JURY
HARRY MCINTOSH

LISTKING

BUY GROCERIES ❹

fresh figs

pine nuts

honey

balsamic vinegar

NEW ITEM

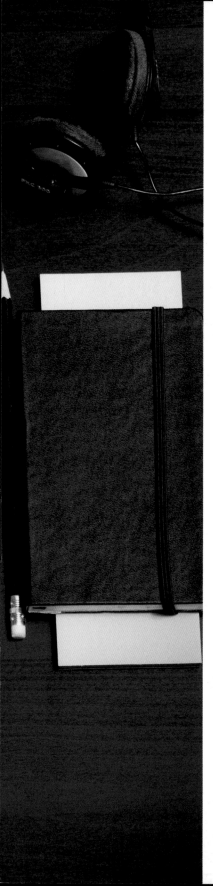

EXAMPLE
JQUERY

This example brings together a number of the techniques you have seen in this chapter to create a list that users can add items to and remove items from.

- Users can add new list items.
- They can also click to indicate that an item is complete (at which point it is moved to the bottom of the list and marked as complete).
- Once an item is marked as complete, a second click on the item will remove it from the list.

An updated count of the number of items there are in the list will be shown in the heading.

As you will see, the code using jQuery is more compact than it would be if you were writing this example in plain JavaScript, and it will work across browsers even though there is no explicit fallback code.

Because new items can be added to the list, the events are handled using event delegation. When the user clicks anywhere on the <ul> element, the .on() event method handles the event. Inside the event handler, there is a conditional statement to check whether the list item is:

- Not complete – in which case, the click is used to change the item to complete, move it to the bottom of the list, and update the counter.
- Complete – in which case, the second click on the item fades it out and removes it from the list altogether.

The use of conditional statements and custom functions (used for the counter) illustrate how jQuery techniques are used in combination with traditional JavaScript that you have been learning throughout the book.

The appearance and removal of the elements is also animated, and these animations demonstrate how methods can be chained together to create complex interactions based on the same selection of elements.

EXAMPLE
JQUERY

`JAVASCRIPT`

```javascript
$(function() {

  // SETUP
  var $list, $newItemForm, $newItemButton;
  var item = '';                                // item is an empty string
  $list = $('ul');                              // Cache the unordered list
  $newItemForm = $('#newItemForm');             // Cache form to add new items
  $newItemButton = $('#newItemButton');         // Cache button to show form

  $('li').hide().each(function(index) {         // Hide list items
    $(this).delay(450 * index).fadeIn(1600);    // Then fade them in
  });

  // ITEM COUNTER
  function updateCount() {                       // Declare function
    var items = $('li[class!=complete]').length; // Number of items in list
    $('#counter').text(items);                   // Added into counter circle
  }
  updateCount();                                 // Call the function

  // SETUP FORM FOR NEW ITEMS
  $newItemButton.show();                         // Show the button
  $newItemForm.hide();                           // Hide the form
  $('#showForm').on('click', function() {        // When new item clicked
    $newItemButton.hide();                       // Hide the button
    $newItemForm.show();                         // Show the form
  });
```

The entire script will wait until the DOM is ready before running, because it is inside the shorthand for the `document.ready()` method. Variables are created that will be used in the script, including jQuery selections that need to be cached.

The `updateCount()` function checks how many items are in the list and writes it into the heading. It is called straight away to calculate how many list items are on the page when it loads, and then write that number next to the heading.

The form to add new items is hidden when the page loads, and is shown when the user clicks on the add button. When the user clicks on the add button a new item is added to the form and the `updateCount()` is called.

```javascript
// ADDING A NEW LIST ITEM
$newItemForm.on('submit', function(e) {      // When a new item is submitted
  e.preventDefault();                        // Prevent form being submitted
  var text = $('input:text').val();          // Get value of text input
  $list.append('<li>' + text + '</li>');     // Add item to end of the list
  $('input:text').val('');                   // Empty the text input
  updateCount();                             // Update the count
});

// CLICK HANDLING - USES DELEGATION ON <ul> ELEMENT
$list.on('click', 'li', function() {
  var $this = $(this);                       // Cache the element in a jQuery object
  var complete = $this.hasClass('complete'); // Is item complete

  if (complete === true) {                   // Check if item is complete
    $this.animate({                          // If so, animate opacity + padding
      opacity: 0.0,
      paddingLeft: '+=180'
    }, 500, 'swing', function() {            // Use callback when animation completes
      $this.remove();                        // Then completely remove this item
    });
  } else {                                   // Otherwise indicate it is complete
    item = $this.text();                     // Get the text from the list item
    $this.remove();                          // Remove the list item
    $list                                    // Add back to end of list as complete
      .append('<li class=\"complete\">' + item + '</li>')
      .hide().fadeIn(300);                   // Hide it so it can be faded in
    updateCount();                           // Update the counter
  }                                          // End of else option
});                                          // End of event handler

});
```

The `.on()` event method listens for the user clicking anywhere on the list because this script uses event delegation. When they do, the element that was clicked on is stored in a jQuery object and cached in a variable called `$this`.

Next, the code checks if that element has a class name of `complete`. If it does, then the list item is animated out of view and removed. If it was not already complete, then it is moved to the end of the list.

When it is added to the end of the list, its `class` attribute is given a value of `complete`.

Finally, `updateCount()` is called to update the number of items left to do on the list.

SUMMARY
JQUERY

▸ jQuery is a JavaScript file you include in your pages.

▸ Once included, it makes it faster and easier to write cross-browser JavaScript, based on two steps:

   1. Using CSS-style selectors to collect one or more nodes from the DOM tree.

   2. Using jQuery's built-in methods to work with the elements in that selection.

▸ jQuery's CSS-style selector syntax makes it easier to select elements to work with. It also has methods that make it easier to traverse the DOM.

▸ jQuery makes it easier to handle events because the event methods work across all browsers.

▸ jQuery offers methods that make it quick and simple to achieve a range of tasks that JavaScript programmers commonly need to perform.

8

AJAX & JSON

Ajax is a technique for loading data into part of a page without having to refresh the entire page. The data is often sent in a format called JavaScript Object Notation (or JSON).

The ability to load new content into part of a page improves the user experience because the user does not have to wait for an entire page to load if only part of it is being updated. This has led to a rise in so-called single page web applications (web-based tools that feel more like software applications, even though they run in the browser). This chapter covers:

WHAT AJAX IS

Ajax allows you to request data from a server and load it without having to refresh the entire page.

DATA FORMATS

Servers typically send back HTML, XML, or JSON, so you will learn about these formats.

JQUERY & AJAX

jQuery makes it easier to create Ajax requests and process the data the server returns.

WHAT IS AJAX?

You may have seen Ajax used on many websites,
even if you were not aware that it was being used.

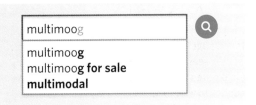

Live search (or autocomplete) commonly uses Ajax.
You may have seen it used on the Google website.
When you type into the search bar on the home
page, sometimes you will see results coming up
before you have finished typing.

Moog Music Inc. @moogmusicinc

Born today in 1896: Leon Theremin,
physicist, spy & inventor of one of the
earliest electronic musical instruments.
pic.twitter.com/theremin

Websites with user-generated content (such
as Twitter and Flickr) may allow you to display
your information (such as your latest tweets or
photographs) on your own website. This involves
collecting data from their servers.

Sometimes when you are shopping online and add
items to your shopping cart, it is updated without
you leaving the page. At the same time, the site may
display a message confirming the item was added.

Choose your username

minimoog

This username is taken. Try another?
Available: minimoog70

If you are registering for a website, a script may
check whether your username is available before
you have completed the rest of the form.

Sites may also use Ajax to load data behind the scenes so that they can use or show that data later on.

WHY USE AJAX?

Ajax uses an asynchronous processing model. This means the user can do other things while the web browser is waiting for the data to load, speeding up the user experience.

USING AJAX WHILE PAGES ARE LOADING

When a browser comes across a `<script>` tag, it will typically stop processing the rest of the page until it has loaded and processed that script. This is known as a **synchronous processing model**.

When a page is loading, if a script needs to collect data from a server (e.g., if it collects financial exchange rates or status updates), then the browser would not just wait for the script to be loaded and processed; it would also have to wait for a server to send the data that the script is going to display.

With Ajax, the browser can request some data from a server and – once that data has been requested – continue to load the rest of the page and process the user's interactions with the page. It is known as an **asynchronous** (or **non-blocking**) **processing model**.

The browser does not wait for the third party data in order to show the page. When the server responds with the data, an event is fired (like the `load` event that fires when a page has loaded). This event can then call a function that processes the data.

USING AJAX WHEN PAGES HAVE LOADED

Once a page has loaded, if you want to update what the user sees in the browser window, typically you would refresh the entire page. This means that the user has to wait for a whole new page to download and be rendered by the browser.

With Ajax, if you only want to update a *part* of the page, you can just update the content of one element. This is done by intercepting an event (such as the user clicking on a link or submitting a form) and requesting the new content from the server using an asynchronous request.

While that data is loading, the user can continue to interact with the rest of the page. Then, once the server has responded, a special Ajax event will trigger another part of the script that reads the new data from the server and updates just that one part of the page.

Because you do not have to refresh the whole page, the data will load faster and the user can still use the rest of the page while they are waiting.

Historically, AJAX was an acronym for the technologies used in asynchronous requests like this. It stood for Asynchronous JavaScript And XML. Since then, technologies have moved on and the term Ajax is now used to refer to a *group* of technologies that offer asynchronous functionality in the browser.

When using Ajax, the browser requests information from a web server. It then processes the server's response and shows it within the page.

1

THE REQUEST

The browser requests information from the server.

2

THE RESPONSE

The browser processes the content and adds it to the page.

ON THE SERVER

The server responds with data (usually HTML, XML, or JSON).

The browser requests data from the server. The request may include information that the server needs – just like a form might send data to a server.

Browsers implement an object called **XMLHttpRequest** to handle Ajax requests. Once a request has been made, the browser does not wait for a response from the server.

What happens on the server is not part of what is called Ajax.

Server-side technologies such as ASP.net, PHP, NodeJS, or Ruby can generate web pages for each user. When there is an Ajax request, the server might send back HTML, or it might send data in a different format such as JSON or XML (which the browser turns into HTML).

When the server has finished responding to the request, the browser will fire an event (just like it can fire an event when a page has finished loading).

This event can be used to trigger a JavaScript function that will process the data and incorporate it into one part of the page (without affecting the rest of the page).

HANDLING AJAX REQUESTS & RESPONSES

To create an Ajax request, browsers use the XMLHttpRequest object. When the server responds to the browser's request, the same XMLHttpRequest object will process the result.

THE REQUEST

```
① var xhr = new XMLHttpRequest();
② xhr.open('GET', 'data/test.json', true);
③ xhr.send('search=arduino');
```

1. An instance of the **XMLHttpRequest** object is created using object constructor notation (which you met on p106). It uses the **new** keyword and stores the object in a variable. The variable name **xhr** is short for **XMLHttpRequest** (the name of the object).

2. The **XMLHttpRequest** object's **open()** method prepares the request. It has three parameters (which you meet on p379):
i) The HTTP method
ii) The url of the page that will handle your request
iii) A Boolean indicating if it should be asynchronous

3. The **send()** method is the one that sends the prepared request to the server. Extra information can be passed to the server in the parentheses. If no extra information is sent, you may see the keyword **null** used (although it is not strictly needed): **xhr.send(null)**.

THE RESPONSE

```
① xhr.onload = function() {
②   if (xhr.status === 200) {
      // Code to process the results from the server
    }
  }
```

1. When the browser has received and loaded a response from the server, the **onload** event will fire. This will trigger a function (here, it is an anonymous function).

2. The function checks the **status** property of the object. This is used to make sure the server's response was okay. (If this property is blank, check the setup of the server.)

Note that IE9 was the first version of IE to support this way of dealing with Ajax responses. To support older browsers, you can use jQuery (see p388).

DATA FORMATS

The response to an Ajax request usually comes in one of three formats: HTML, XML, or JSON. Below is a comparison of these formats. XML and JSON are introduced over the next three pages.

HTML

You are probably most familiar with HTML, and, when you want to update a section of a web page, it is the simplest way to get data into a page.

BENEFITS

- It is easy to write, request, and display.
- The data sent from the server goes straight into the page. There's no need for the browser to process it (as with the other two methods).

DRAWBACKS

- The server must produce the HTML in a format that is ready for use on your page.
- It is not well-suited for use in applications other than web browsers. It does not have good **data portability**.
- The request must come from the same domain* (see below).

XML

XML looks similar to HTML, but the tag names are different because they describe the data that they contain. The syntax is also more strict than HTML.

BENEFITS

- It is a flexible data format and can represent complex structures.
- It works well with different platforms and applications.
- It is processed using the same DOM methods as HTML.

DRAWBACKS

- It is considered a verbose language because the tags add a lot of extra characters to the data being sent.
- The request must come from the same domain as the rest of the page* (see below).
- It can require a lot of code to process the result.

JSON

JavaScript Object Notation (JSON) uses a similar syntax to object literal notation (which you met on p102) in order to represent data.

BENEFITS

- It can be called from any domain (see JSON-P/CORS).
- It is more concise (less verbose) than HTML/XML.
- It is commonly used with JavaScript (and is gaining wider use across web applications).

DRAWBACKS

- The syntax is not forgiving. A missed quote, comma, or colon can break the file.
- Because it is JavaScript, it can contain malicious content (see XSS on p228). Therefore, you should only use JSON that has been produced by trusted sources.

* Browsers only let Ajax load HTML and XML from the same domain name as the rest of the page (e.g., if the page is on `www.example.com`, the Ajax request must return data from `www.example.com`).

XML: EXTENSIBLE
MARKUP LANGUAGE

XML looks a lot like HTML, but the tags contain different words.
The purpose of the tags is to describe the kind of data that they hold.

```xml
<?xml version="1.0" encoding="utf-8" ?>
<events>
  <event>
    <location>San Francisco, CA</location>
    <date>May 1</date>
    <map>img/map-ca.png</map>
  </event>
  <event>
    <location>Austin, TX</location>
    <date>May 15</date>
    <map>img/map-tx.png</map>
  </event>
  <event>
    <location>New York, NY</location>
    <date>May 30</date>
    <map>img/map-ny.png</map>
  </event>
</events>
```

In the same way that HTML is a markup language that can be used to describe the structure and semantics of a web page, XML can be used to create markup languages for other types of data – anything from stock reports to medical records.

The tags in an XML file should describe the data they contain. As a result, even if you have never seen the code to the left, you can see that the data describes information about several events. The `<events>` element contains several individual events. Each individual event is represented in its own `<event>` element.

XML works on any platform and gained wide popularity in the early 2000s because it made it easy to transfer data between different types of applications. It is also a very flexible data format because it is capable of representing complex data structures.

You can process an XML file using the same DOM methods as HTML. Because different browsers deal with whitespace in HTML/XML documents in different ways, it is easier to process XML using jQuery rather than plain JavaScript (just as it can be with HTML).

JSON: JAVASCRIPT OBJECT NOTATION

Data can be formatted using JSON (pronounced "Jason").
It looks very similar to object literal syntax, but it is not an object.

JSON data looks like the object literal notation which you met on p102; however, it is just plain text data (not an object).

The distinction may sound small but remember that HTML is just plain text, and the browser converts it into DOM objects.

You cannot transfer the actual objects over a network. Rather, you send text which is converted into objects by the browser.

```
{
    "location": "San Francisco, CA",
    "capacity": 270,
    "booking":  true
}
```

KEY (in double quotes)　　VALUE

KEYS

In JSON, the key should be placed in **double quotes** (not single quotes).

The key (or name) is separated from its value by a colon.

Each key/value pair is separated by a comma. However, note that there is *no* comma after the last key/value pair.

VALUES

The value can be any of the following data types (some of these are demonstrated above; others are shown on the right-hand page):

DATA TYPE	DESCRIPTION
string	Text (must be written in quotes)
number	Number
Boolean	Either true or false
array	Array of values – this can also be an array of objects
object	JavaScript object – this can contain child objects or arrays
null	This is when the value is empty or missing

WORKING WITH
JSON DATA

JavaScript's JSON object can turn JSON data into a JavaScript object.
It can also convert a JavaScript object into a string.

```
{
    "events": [
        {
            "location": "San Francisco, CA",
            "date": "May 1",
            "map": "img/map-ca.png"
        },
        {
            "location": "Austin, TX",
            "date": "May 15",
            "map": "img/map-tx.png"
        },
        {
            "location": "New York, NY",
            "date": "May 30",
            "map": "img/map-ny.png"
        }
    ]
}
```

● OBJECT ● ARRAY

An object can also be written on one line, as you can see here:

The object on the left represents a series of three events, stored in an array called **events**. The array uses square bracket notation, and it holds three objects (one for each event).

JSON.stringify() converts JavaScript objects into a string, formatted using JSON. This allows you to send JavaScript objects from the browser to another application.

JSON.parse() processes a string containing JSON data. It converts the JSON data into a JavaScript objects ready for the browser to use.

Browser support: Chrome 3, Firefox 3.1, IE8, and Safari 4

```
{
    "events": [
        { "location": "San Francisco, CA", "date": "May 1", "map": "img/map-ca.png" },
        { "location": "Austin, TX", "date": "May 15", "map": "img/map-tx.png" },
        { "location": "New York, NY", "date": "May 30", "map": "img/map-ny.png" }
    ]
}
```

LOADING HTML
WITH AJAX

HTML is the easiest type of data to add into a page using Ajax.
The browser renders it just like any other HTML.
The CSS rules for the rest of the page are applied to the new content.

Below, the example loads data about three events using Ajax. (The result will look the same for the next four examples.)

The page users open does not hold the event data (highlighted in pink). Ajax is used to load it into the page from another file.

Browsers will only let you use this technique to load HTML that comes from the same domain name as the rest of the page.

Whether HTML, XML, or JSON is being returned from the server, the process of setting up the Ajax request and checking whether the file is ready to be worked with is the same. What changes is how you deal with the data that is returned.

In the example on the right-hand page, the code to display the new HTML is placed inside a conditional statement.

Please note: These examples do not work locally in Chrome. They should work locally in Firefox and Safari. Internet Explorer support is mixed.

Later in the chapter, you will see that jQuery offers better cross-browser support for Ajax.

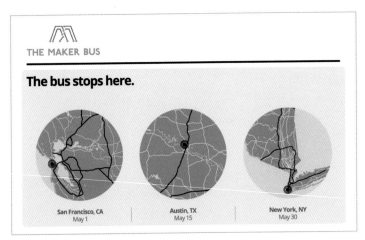

HIGHLIGHTED AREA LOADED USING AJAX

When a server responds to any request, it should send back a status message, to indicate if it completed the request. The values can be:

200   The server has responded and all is ok
304   Not modified
404   Page not found
500   Internal error on the server

If you run the code locally, you will not get a server status property, so this check must be commented out, and return true for the condition. If a server fails to return a status property, check the server setup.

1. An XMLHttpRequest object is stored in a variable called xhr.

2. The XMLHttpRequest object's open() method prepares the request. It has three parameters:
i) Either HTTP GET or POST to specify how to send the request
ii) The path to the page that will handle the request
iii) Whether or not the request is asynchronous (this is a Boolean)

3. Up to this point, the browser has not yet contacted the server to request the new HTML.

This does not happen until the script gets to the last line that calls the XMLHttpRequest object's send() method. The send() method requires an argument to be passed. If there is no data to send, you can just use null.

4. The object's onload event will fire when the server responds. It triggers an anonymous function.

5. Inside the function, a conditional statement checks if the status property of the object is 200, indicating the server responded successfully. If the example is run locally, there will be no response so you cannot perform this check.

JAVASCRIPT   c08/js/data-html.js

```
① var xhr = new XMLHttpRequest();                        // Create XMLHttpRequest object

④ xhr.onload = function() {                              // When response has loaded
     // The following conditional check will not work locally - only on a server
⑤   if(xhr.status === 200) {                             // If server status was ok
⑥     document.getElementById('content').innerHTML = xhr.responseText; // Update
     }
   };

② xhr.open('GET', 'data/data.html', true);              // Prepare the request
③ xhr.send(null);                                        // Send the request
```

6. Finally, the page is updated: document.getElementById('content').innerHTML = xhr.responseText;
                                   └─────────── A ───────────┘ └── B ──┘ └────── C ──────┘

A) The element that will contain the new HTML is selected. (Here it is an element whose id attribute has a value of content.)

B) The innerHTML property replaces the content of that element with the new HTML that has been sent from the server.

C) The new HTML is retrieved from the XMLHttpRequest object's responseText property.

Remember that innerHTML should only be used when you know that the server will not return malicious content. All content that has been created by users or third parties should be escaped on the server (see p228).

LOADING XML
WITH AJAX

Requesting XML data is very similar to requesting HTML. However, processing the data that is returned is more complicated because the XML must be converted into HTML to be shown on the page.

On the right-hand page, you can see that the code to request an XML file is almost identical to the code to request an HTML file shown on the previous page. What changes is the part *inside* the conditional statement that processes the response (points 1-4 on the right-hand page). The XML must be turned into HTML. The structure of the HTML for each event is shown below.

1. When a server responds with XML, it can be obtained using the `responseXML` property of the `XMLHttpRequest` object. Here, the XML returned is stored in a variable called **response**.

2. This is followed by the declaration of a new variable called **events**, which holds all of the `<event>` elements from the XML document. (You saw the XML file on p375.)

3. The XML file is then processed using the DOM methods you learned about in Chapter 5. First, the `for` loop goes through each of the `<event>` elements, collecting the data stored in their child elements, and placing it into new HTML elements.

Each of those HTML elements is then added into the page.

4. Inside the `for` loop, you will see the `getNodeValue()` function is called several times. Its purpose is to get the contents from each of the XML elements. It takes two parameters:

i) `obj` is an XML fragment.
ii) `tag` is the name of the tag you want to collect the information from.

The function looks for the matching tag within the XML fragment (using the DOM's `getElementsByTagName()` method). It then gets the text from the first matching element within that fragment.

The XML for each event is being transformed into the following HTML structure:

```html
<div class="event">
  <img src="file.png" alt="Location" />
  <p><b>Location</b><br />Event date</p>
</div>
```

```javascript
var xhr = new XMLHttpRequest();           // Create XMLHttpRequest object

xhr.onload = function() {                 // When response has loaded
 // The following conditional check will not work locally - only on a server
 if (xhr.status === 200) {                // If server status was ok

 // THIS PART IS DIFFERENT BECAUSE IT IS PROCESSING XML NOT HTML
 var response = xhr.responseXML;                    // Get XML from the server
 var events = response.getElementsByTagName('event'); // Find <event> elements

 for (var i = 0; i < events.length; i++) {          // Loop through them
  var container, image, location, city, newline;    // Declare variables
  container = document.createElement('div');         // Create <div> container
  container.className = 'event';                     // Add class attribute

  image = document.createElement('img');             // Add map image
  image.setAttribute('src', getNodeValue(events[i], 'map'));
  image.appendChild(document.createTextNode(getNodeValue(events[i], 'map')));
  container.appendChild(image);

  location = document.createElement('p');            // Add location data
  city = document.createElement('b');
  newline = document.createElement('br');
  city.appendChild(document.createTextNode(getNodeValue(events[i], 'location')));
  location.appendChild(newline);
  location.insertBefore(city, newline);
  location.appendChild(document.createTextNode(getNodeValue(events[i], 'date')));
  container.appendChild(location);

  document.getElementById('content').appendChild(container);
 }
 function getNodeValue(obj, tag) {                    // Gets content from XML
  return obj.getElementsByTagName(tag)[0].firstChild.nodeValue;
 }

  // THE FINAL PART IS THE SAME AS THE HTML EXAMPLE BUT IT REQUESTS AN XML FILE
  }
};
xhr.open('GET', 'data/data.xml', true);              // Prepare the request
xhr.send(null);                                      // Send the request
```

LOADING JSON
WITH AJAX

The request for JSON data uses the same syntax you saw in the requests for HTML and XML data. When the server responds, the JSON will be converted into HTML.

When JSON data is sent from a server to a web browser, it is transmitted as a string.

When it reaches the browser, your script must then convert the string into a JavaScript object. This is known as **deserializing** an object.

This is done using the `parse()` method of a built-in object called JSON. This is a global object, so you can use it without creating an instance of it first.

Once the string has been parsed, your script can access the data in the object and create HTML that can be shown in the page.

The HTML is added to the page using the `innerHTML` property. Therefore, it should only be used when you are confident that it will not contain malicious code (see XSS on p228).

This example will look the same as the last two examples when you view it in a web browser.

The JSON object also has a method called `stringify()`, which converts objects into a string using JSON notation so it can be sent from the browser back to a server. This is also known as **serializing** an object.

This method can be used when the user has interacted with the page in a way that has updated the data held in the JavaScript object (e.g., filling in a form), so that it can then update the information stored on the server.

Here you can see the JSON data that is being processed again (it was introduced on p377). Note how it is saved with the `.json` file extension.

```
c08/data/data.json                                                    JAVASCRIPT
```

```javascript
{
  "events": [
    { "location": "San Francisco, CA", "date": "May 1", "map": "img/map-ca.png" },
    { "location": "Austin, TX", "date": "May 15", "map": "img/map-tx.png" },
    { "location": "New York, NY", "date": "May 30", "map": "img/map-ny.png"}
  ]
}
```

1. The JSON data from the server is stored in a variable called `responseObject`. It is made available by the `XMLHttpRequest` object's `responseText` property

When it comes from the server, the JSON data is a string, so it is converted into a JavaScript object using the `JSON` object's `parse()` method.

2. The `newContent` variable is created to hold the new HTML data. It is set to an empty string outside the loop so that the code in the loop can add to the string.

3. Loop through the objects that represent each event using a `for` loop. The data in the objects are accessed using dot notation, just like you access other objects.

Inside the loop, the contents of the object are added to the `newContent` variable, along with their corresponding HTML markup.

4. When the loop has finished running through the `event` objects in `responseObject`, the new HTML is added to the page using the `innerHTML` property.

```javascript
    var xhr = new XMLHttpRequest();                      // Create XMLHttpRequest object

    xhr.onload = function() {                            // When readystate changes
     if(xhr.status === 200) {                            // If server status was ok
①    responseObject = JSON.parse(xhr.responseText);

     // BUILD UP STRING WITH NEW CONTENT (could also use DOM manipulation)
②    var newContent = '';
     for (var i = 0; i < responseObject.events.length; i++) {//Loop through object
       newContent += '<div class="event">';
       newContent += '<img src="' + responseObject.events[i].map + '" ';
③     newContent += 'alt="' + responseObject.events[i].location + '" />';
       newContent += '<p><b>' + responseObject.events[i].location + '</b><br>';
       newContent += responseObject.events[i].date + '</p>';
       newContent += '</div>';
     }

     // Update the page with the new content
④    document.getElementById('content').innerHTML = newContent;

     }
    };

    xhr.open('GET', 'data/data.json', true);             // Prepare the request
    xhr.send(null);                                       // Send the request
```

WORKING WITH DATA FROM OTHER SERVERS

Ajax works smoothly with data from your own server but – for security reasons – browsers do not load Ajax responses from other domains (known as cross-domain requests). There are three common workarounds.

A PROXY FILE ON THE WEB SERVER

The first way to load data from a remote server is to create a file on *your* server that collects the data from the remote server (using a server-side language such as ASP.net, PHP, NodeJS, or Ruby). The other pages on your site then request the data from the file on your server (which in turn gets it from the remote server). This is called a **proxy**, because it acts on behalf of the other page.

Because this relies upon creating pages in server-side languages, it is beyond the scope of this book.

JSONP (JSON WITH PADDING)

JSONP (sometimes written JSON-P) involves adding a `<script>` element into the page, which loads the JSON data from another server. This works because there are no restrictions on the source of script in a `<script>` element.

The script contains a call to a function, and the JSON-formatted data is provided as an argument to that function. The function that is called is defined in the page that requests the data, and is used to process and display the data. See next page.

CROSS-ORIGIN RESOURCE SHARING

Every time a browser and server communicate, they send information to each other using HTTP headers. **Cross-Origin Resource Sharing** or **CORS** involves adding extra information to the HTTP headers to let the browser and server know that they should be communicating with each other.

CORS is a W3C specification, but is only supported by the most recent browsers and – because it requires setting up of HTTP headers on the server – is beyond the scope of this book.

ALTERNATIVES

Many people use jQuery when making requests for remote data, as it simplifies the process and handles backward compatibility for older browsers. As you can see in the next column, support for new approaches is an issue.

CORS SUPPORT

Standard support is as follows: Chrome 4, FF 3.5, IE10, Safari 4 Android 2.1, iOS 3.2

IE8+9 used a non-standard XDomainRequest object to handle cross-origin requests.

HOW JSONP WORKS

First, the page must include a function to process the JSON data. It then requests the data from the server using a `<script>` element.

The server returns a file that calls the function that processes the data. The JSON data is provided as an argument to that function.

BROWSER

The HTML page will use two pieces of JavaScript:

1. A function that will process the JSON data that the server sends. In the example on the next page, the function is called showEvents().

2. A `<script>` element whose src attribute will request the JSON data from the remote server.

```
<script>
function showEvents(data) {
  // Code to process data and
  // display it in the page here
}
</script>

<script src="http://example.org/jsonp">
</script>
```

SERVER

When the server responds, the script contains a call to the named function that will process the data (that function was defined in step 1). This function call is the "padding" in JSONP. The JSON-formatted data is sent as an argument to this function.

So, in this case, the JSON data sits inside the call to the showEvents() function.

```
showEvents({
  "events": [
    {
      "location": "San Francisco, CA",
      "date": "May 1",
      "map": "img/map-ca.png"
    }...
  ]
});
```

It is important to note that there is no need to use the JSON object's parse() or stringify() methods when working with JSONP. Because the data is being sent as a script file (not as a string), it will be treated as an object.

The file on the server is often written so that you can specify the name of the function that will process the data that is returned. The name of the function is usually given in the query string of a URL:
http://example.org/upcomingEvents.php?callback=showEvents

USING JSONP

This example looks the same as the JSON example, but the event details come from a remote server. Therefore, the HTML uses two `<script>` elements.

The first `<script>` element loads a JavaScript file that contains the `showEvents()` function. This will be used to display the deals information.

The second `<script>` element loads the information from a remote server. The name of the function that processes the data is given in the query string.

c08/data-jsonp.html

```html
  <script src="js/data-jsonp.js"></script>
  <script src="http://wagonbooks.com/js/jsonp.js?callback=showEvents"></script>
 </body>
</html>
```

c08/js/data-jsonp.js

```javascript
 function showEvents(data) {                          // Callback when JSON loads
   var newContent = '';                               // Variable to hold HTML

  // BUILD UP STRING WITH NEW CONTENT (could also use DOM manipulation)
   for (var i = 0; i < data.events.length; i++) {     // Loop through data
     newContent += '<div class="event">';
     newContent += '<img src="' + data.events[i].map + '"';
     newContent += ' alt="' + data.events[i].location + '" />';
     newContent += '<p><b>' + data.events[i].location + '</b><br>';
     newContent += data.events[i].date + '</p>';
     newContent += '</div>';
   }

   // Update the page with the new content
   document.getElementById('content').innerHTML = newContent; }
```

① (marker pointing to the for loop)

1. The code in the `for` loop (which is used to process the JSON data and create the HTML) and the line that writes it into the page are the same as the code that processed the JSON data from the same server.

There are three key differences:
i) It is wrapped in a function called `showEvents()`.
ii) The JSON data comes in as an argument of the function call.
iii) The data does not need to be parsed with `JSON.parse()`. In the for loop, it is just referred to by the parameter name `data`.

Instead of using a second `<script>` element in the HTML pages, you can use JavaScript to write that `<script>` element into the page (just like you would add any other element into the page). That would place all the functionality for the external data in the one JavaScript file.

JSONP loads JavaScript, and any JavaScript data may contain malicious code. For this reason, you should load data only from trusted sources.

Since JSONP is loading data from a different server, you might add timer to check if the server has replied within a fixed time (and, if not, show an error message).

You will see more about handling errors in Chapter 10, and there is an example of a timer in Chapter 11 (where you create a content slider).

```javascript
showEvents({
  "events": [
    {
      "location": "San Francisco, CA",
      "date": "May 1",
      "map": "img/map-ca.png"
    },
    {
      "location": "Austin, TX",
      "date": "May 15",
      "map": "img/map-tx.png"
    },
    {
      "location": "New York, NY",
      "date": "May 30",
      "map": "img/map-ny.png"
    }
  ]
});
```

RESULT

The bus stops here.

San Francisco, CA
May 1

Austin, TX
May 15

New York, NY
May 30

The file that is returned from the server wraps the JSON-formatted data inside the call to the showEvents() function. So the showEvents() function is only called when the browser has loaded this remote data.

JQUERY & AJAX: REQUESTS

jQuery provides several methods that handle Ajax requests.
Just like other examples in this chapter, the process involves two steps: making a request and handling the response.

Here you can see the six ways jQuery lets you make Ajax requests. The first five are all shortcuts for the **$.ajax()** method, which you meet last.

The **.load()** method operates on a jQuery selection (like most jQuery methods). It loads new HTML content into the selected element(s).

You can see that the other five methods are written differently. They are methods of the global **jQuery** object, which is why they start with **$**. They only request data from a server; they do not automatically use that data to update the elements of a matched set, which is why the **$** symbol is not followed by a selector.

When the server returns data, the script needs to indicate what to do with it.

METHOD / SYNTAX	DESCRIPTION
`.load()`	Loads HTML fragments into an element It is the simplest method for retrieving data
`$.get()`	Loads data using the HTTP GET method Used to **request** data from the server
`$.post()`	Loads data using the HTTP POST method Used to **send** data that updates data on server
`$.getJSON()`	Loads JSON data using a GET request Used for JSON data
`$.getScript()`	Loads and executes JavaScript data using GET Used for JavaScript (e.g., JSONP) data
`$.ajax()`	This method is used to perform all requests The above methods all use this under the hood

JQUERY & AJAX: RESPONSES

When using the `.load()` method, the HTML returned from the server is inserted into a jQuery selection. For the other methods, you specify what should be done when the data that is returned using the `jqXHR` object.

JQXHR PROPERTIES	DESCRIPTION
responseText	Text-based data returned
responseXML	XML data returned
status	Status code
statusText	Status description (typically used to display information about an error if one occurs)

jQuery has an object called `jqXHR`, which makes it easier to handle the data that is returned from the server. You will see its properties and methods (shown in the tables on the left) used over the next few pages.

JQXHR METHODS	DESCRIPTION
.done()	Code to run if request was successful
.fail()	Code to run if request was unsuccessful
.always()	Code to run if request succeeded or failed
.abort()	Halt the communication

Because jQuery lets you chain methods, you can use the `.done()`, `.fail()`, and `.always()` methods to run different code depending on the outcome of loading the data.

RELATIVE URLS

If the content you load via Ajax contains relative URLs (e.g., images and links) those URLs get treated as if they are relative to the *original* page that was loaded.

If the new HTML is in a different folder from the original page, the relative paths could be broken.

1. This HTML file uses Ajax to load content from a page in the folder shown in step 2.
2. The page in the this folder has an image whose path is a relative link to the second folder:
`<img src="img/box.gif" />`
3. The HTML file cannot find the image as the path is no longer correct – it is not in a child folder.

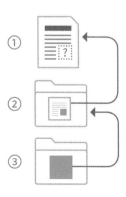

LOADING HTML INTO A PAGE WITH JQUERY

The `.load()` method is the simplest of the jQuery Ajax methods. It can only be used to load HTML from the server, but when the server responds, the HTML is then loaded into the jQuery Selection for you.

JQUERY SELECTOR
You start by selecting the element that you want the HTML code to appear inside.

URL OF THE PAGE
Then you use the `.load()` method to specify the URL of the HTML page to load.

SELECTOR
You can specify that you want to load only part of the page (rather than the whole page).

```
$('#content').load('jq-ajax3.html #content');
         ①                    ②            ③
```

1. This creates a jQuery object with the element whose `id` attribute has a value of `content`.

2. This is the URL of the page you want to load the HTML from. There must be a space between the URL and the selector in step 3.

3. This is the fragment of the HTML page to show. Again, it is the section whose `id` attribute has a value of `content`.

Here, links in the top right corner take the user to other pages. If the user has JavaScript enabled, when they click on a link, code inside the `.on()` event method stops it from loading a whole new page. Instead, the `.load()` method will replace the area highlighted in pink (whose `id` attribute has a value of `content`) with the equivalent area from the page that the user just requested. Only the pink area is refreshed – not the whole page.

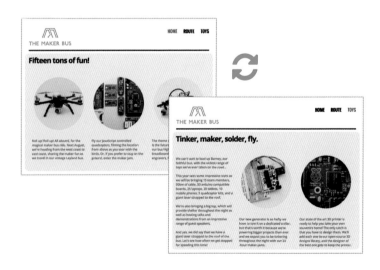

LOADING CONTENT

When users click on any of the links in the <nav> element, one of two things will occur:

If they have JavaScript enabled, a click event will trigger an anonymous function that loads new content into the page.

If they do not have JavaScript enabled, they will move from page to page as normal.

Inside the anonymous function, five things happen:

1. e.preventDefault() stops the link taking users to a new page.

2. A variable called url holds the URL of the page to load. This is collected from the href attribute of the link the user clicked on. It indicates which page to load.

3. The class attributes on the links are updated to indicate which page is the current page.

4. The element holding the content is removed.

5. The container element is selected and .load() fetches new the new content. It is hidden straight away using .hide() so that fadeIn() can fade it in.

JAVASCRIPT c08/js/jq-load.js

```javascript
$('nav a').on('click', function(e) {          // User clicks nav link
①  e.preventDefault();                         // Stop loading new link
②  var url = this.href;                        // Get value of href

③  $('nav a.current').removeClass('current');   // Clear current indicator
    $(this).addClass('current');               // New current indicator

④  $('#container').remove();                   // Remove old content
⑤  $('#content').load(url + ' #content').hide().fadeIn('slow'); // New content
});
```

HTML c08/jq-load.html

```html
<nav>
  <a href="jq-load.html" class="current">Home</a>
  <a href="jq-load2.html">Route</a>
  <a href="jq-load3.html">Toys</a>
</nav>
<section id="content">
  <div id="container">
      <!-- Page content lives here -->
  </div>
</section>
```

The links still work if JavaScript is not enabled. If JavaScript is enabled, jQuery will load content into the <div> whose id has a value of content from the target URL. The rest of the page does not need to be reloaded.

JQUERY'S AJAX SHORTHAND METHODS

jQuery provides four shorthand methods to handle specific types of Ajax requests.

The methods below are all shorthand methods. If you looked at the source code for jQuery, you would see that they all use the $.ajax() method.

You will meet each one over the next few pages because they introduce key aspects of the $.ajax() method.

These methods do not work on a selection like other jQuery methods, which is why you prefix them with only the $ symbol rather than a jQuery selection. They are usually triggered by an event, such as the page having loaded or the user interacting with the page (e.g., clicking on a link, or submitting a form).

With an Ajax request, you will often want to send data to the server, which will in turn affect what the server sends back to the browser.

As with HTML forms (and the Ajax requests you met earlier in the chapter), you can send the data using HTTP GET or POST.

METHOD / SYNTAX	DESCRIPTION
$.get(*url*[, *data*][, *callback*][, *type*])	HTTP GET request for data
$.post(*url*[, *data*][, *callback*][, *type*])	HTTP POST to update data on the server
$.getJSON(*url*[, *data*][, *callback*])	Loads JSON data using a GET request
$.getScript(*url*[, *callback*])	Loads and executes JavaScript (e.g., JSONP) using a GET request

The parameters in square brackets are optional.

$ shows that this is a method of the **jQuery** object.
url specifies where the data is fetched from.
data provides any extra information to send to the server.
callback indicates that the function should be called when data is returned (can be named or anonymous).
type shows the type of data to expect from the server.

Note: The examples in this section only work on a web server (and not on local file systems). Server-side languages and server setup are beyond the scope of this book, but you can try out the examples on our website. PHP files have been included with the download code, but they are for demonstration purposes only.

REQUESTING DATA

Here, users vote for their favorite t-shirt without leaving the page.
1. If users click on a t-shirt an anonymous function is triggered.
2. `e.PreventDefault()` stops the link opening a new page.
3. The user's choice is the value of the `id` attribute on the image. It is stored in a variable called `queryString` in the format of a query string, e.g., `vote=gray`

4. The `$.get()` method is called using three parameters:
i) The page that will handle the request (on the same server).
ii) The data being sent to the server (here it is a query string, but it could be JSON).
iii) The function that handles the result the server sends back; in this case it is an anonymous function.

When the server responds, the anonymous callback function handles the data. In this case, the code in that function selects the element that the held the t-shirts and replaces it with the HTML sent back from the server. This is done using jQuery's `.html()` method.

JAVASCRIPT   c08/js/jq-get.js

```
① $('#selector a').on('click', function(e) {
②   e.preventDefault();
③     var queryString = 'vote=' + event.target.id;
④     $.get('votes.php', queryString, function(data) {
⑤       $('#selector').html(data);
      });
    });
```

HTML GENERATED AT START OF JAVASCRIPT FILE

```
<div class="third"><a href="vote.php?vote=gray">
  <img src="img/t-gray.png" id="gray" alt="gray" /></a></div>
<div class="third"><a href="vote.php?vote=yellow">
  <img src="img/t-yellow.png" id="yellow" alt="yellow" /></a></div>
<div class="third"><a href="vote.php?vote=green">
  <img src="img/t-green.png" id="green" alt="green" /></a></div>
```

RESULT

Note: The t-shirt links are created in the JavaScript file to ensure they only show if the browser supports JavaScript (the resulting HTML structure is shown above). When the server responds, it does not have to send back HTML; it can return any kind of data that the browser can process and use.

SENDING FORMS USING AJAX

To send data to the server, you are likely to use the `.post()` method. jQuery also provides the `.serialize()` method to collect form data.

SENDING FORM DATA

The HTTP POST method is often used when sending form data to a server and it has a corresponding function, the `.post()` method. It takes the same three parameters as the `.get()` method:

i) The name of the file on the (same) server that will process the data from the form
ii) The form data that you are sending
iii) The callback function that will handle the response from the server

On the right-hand page you can see the `$.post()` method used with a method called `.serialize()`, which is very helpful when working with forms. Together they send the form data to the server.

COLLECTING FORM DATA

jQuery's `.serialize()` method:
- Selects all of the information from the form
- Puts it into a string ready to send to the server
- Encodes characters that cannot be used in a query string

Typically it will be used on a selection containing a `<form>` element (although it can be used on individual elements or a subsection of a form).

It will only send *successful* form controls, which means it will not send:
- Controls that have been disabled
- Controls where no option has been selected
- The submit button

SERVER-SIDE

When a server-side page handles a form, you might want the same page to work whether:
- It was a normal request for a web page (in which case you would send the whole page); or
- It was an Ajax request (where you might respond with just a fragment of the page)

On the server, you can check whether a page is being requested by an Ajax call using the `X-Requested-With` header.

If it is set and has a value of `XMLHttpRequest`, you know that the request was an Ajax request.

SUBMITTING FORMS

1. When users submit the form, an anonymous function runs.

2. `e.PreventDefault()` stops the form from submitting.

3. The form data is collected by the `.serialize()` method and stored in the `details` variable.

4. The `$.post()` method is called using all three parameters:

i) The url of the page that the data is being sent to
ii) The data that was just collected from the form
iii) A callback function that will display the results to the user

5. When the server responds, the content of the element whose `id` attribute has a value of `register` is overwritten with new HTML sent from the server.

JAVASCRIPT   c08/js/jq-post.js

```
① $('#register').on('submit', function(e) {          // When form is submitted
② e.preventDefault();                                // Prevent it being sent
③ var details = $('#register').serialize();          // Serialize form data
④ $.post('register.php', details, function(data) {   // Use $.post() to send it
⑤   $('#register').html(data);                        // Where to display result
  });
});
```

HTML   c08/jq-post.html

```
<form id="register" action="register.php" method="post">
 <h2>Register</h2>
 <label for="name">Username</label><input type="text" id="name" name="name" />
 <label for="pwd">Password</label><input type="password" id="pwd" name="pwd" />
 <label for="email">Email</label><input type="email" id="email" name="email" />
 <input type="submit" value="Join" />
</form>
```

RESULT

This example needs to be run on a web server. The server-side page will return a confirmation message (but it does not validate the data submitted nor send a confirmation email).

LOADING JSON & HANDLING AJAX ERRORS

You can load JSON data using the $.getJSON() method.
There are also methods that help you deal with the response if it fails.

LOADING JSON

If you want to load JSON data, there is a method called $.getJSON() which will retrieve JSON from the same server that the page is from. To use JSONP you should use the method called $.getScript().

AJAX AND ERRORS

Occasionally a request for a web page will fail and Ajax requests are no exception. Therefore, jQuery provides two methods that can trigger code depending on whether the request was successful or unsuccessful, along with a third method that will be triggered in both cases (successful or not).

Below is an example that will demonstrate these concepts. It loads fictional exchange rates.

SUCCESS / FAILURE

There are three methods you can chain after $.get(), $.post(), $.getJSON(), and $.ajax() to handle success / failure. These methods are:

.done() – an event method that fires when the request has successfully completed
.fail() – an event method that fires when the request did not complete successfully
.always() – an event method that fires when the request has completed (whether it was successful or not)

Older scripts may use the .success(), .error(), and .complete() methods instead of these methods. They do the same thing, but these newer methods have been the preferred option since jQuery 1.8.

Exchange Rates

UK: 20.00
US: 35.99
AU: 39.99

Last update: 15:34

Exchange Rates

Sorry, we cannot load rates.

JSON & ERRORS

1. In this example, JSON data representing currency exchange rates is loaded into the page by a function called `loadRates()`.

2. On the first line of the script an element is added to the page to hold the exchange rate data.

3. The function is called on the last line of the script.

4. Inside `loadRates()`, the `$.getJSON` method tries to load some JSON data. There are three methods chained after this method. They do not all run.

5. `.done()` only runs if the data is retrieved successfully. It contains an anonymous function that shows exchange rates and the time they were displayed.

6. `.fail()` only runs if the server cannot return the data. Its job is to display an error message to the user.

7. `.always()` will run whether or not the answer was returned. It adds a refresh button to the page, along with an event handler that triggers the `loadRates()` function again.

```javascript
$('#exchangerates').append('<div id="rates"></div><div id="reload"></div>');

function loadRates() {
  $.getJSON('data/rates.json')                                      // SERVER RETURNS DATA
  .done( function(data){                                            // SERVER RETURNS DATA
    var d = new Date();                                             // Create date object
    var hrs = d.getHours();                                         // Get hours
    var mins = d.getMinutes();                                      // Get mins
    var msg = '<h2>Exchange Rates</h2>';                            // Start message
    $.each(data, function(key, val) {                              // Add each rate
      msg += '<div class="' + key + '">' + key + ': ' + val + '</div>';
    });
    msg += '<br>Last update: ' + hrs + ':' + mins + '<br>';        // Show update time
    $('#rates').html(msg);                                          // Add rates to page
  }).fail( function() {                                             // THERE IS AN ERROR
    $('aside').append('Sorry, we cannot load rates.');             // Show error message
  }).always( function() {                                          // ALWAYS RUNS
    var reload = '<a id="refresh" href="#">';                      // Add refresh link
    reload += '<img src="img/refresh.png" alt="refresh" /></a>';   // Add refresh link
    $('#reload').html(reload);                                      // Add refresh link
    $('#refresh').on('click', function(e) {                        // Add click handler
      e.preventDefault();                                          // Stop link
      loadRates();                                                 // Call loadRates()
    });
  });
}

loadRates();                                                       // Call loadRates()
```

AJAX REQUESTS WITH FINE-GRAINED CONTROL

The `$.ajax()` method gives you greater control over Ajax requests. Behind the scenes, this method is used by all of jQuery's Ajax shorthand methods.

Inside the jQuery file, the `$.ajax()` method is used by the other Ajax helper methods that you have seen so far (which are offered as a simpler way of making Ajax requests).

This method offers greater control over the entire process, with over 30 different settings that you can use to control the Ajax request. You can see a selection of these settings in the table below. These settings are provided using object literal notation (the object is referred to as the settings object).

The example on the right-hand page looks and works like the one that demonstrated the `.load()` method on p390. But it uses the `$.ajax()` method instead.

- The settings can appear in any order, as long as they use valid JavaScript literal notation.
- The settings that take a function can use a named function or an anonymous function written inline.
- `$.ajax()` does not let you load just one part of the page so the jQuery `.find()` method is used to select the required part of the page.

SETTING	DESCRIPTION
type	Can take values GET or POST depending on whether the request is made using HTTP GET or POST
url	The page the request is being sent to
data	The data that is being sent to the server with the request
success	A function that runs if the Ajax request completes successfully (similar to the `.done()` method)
error	A function that runs if there is an error with the Ajax request (similar to the `.fail()` method)
beforeSend	A function (anonymous or named) that is run before the Ajax request starts In the example on the right, this is used to trigger a loading icon
complete	Runs after success/error events In the example on the right, this removes a loading icon
timeout	The number of milliseconds to wait before the event should fail

CONTROLLING AJAX

When the user clicks on a link in the <nav> element, new content is loaded into the page. This is very similar to the example on p390 for the .load() method, but that shorthand method only required one line.

1. Here the click event handler triggers the $.ajax() method.

This example sets seven settings for the $.ajax() method. The first three are properties, the final four are anonymous functions triggered at different points in the Ajax request.

2. This example sets the timeout property to wait two seconds for the Ajax response.

3. The code also adds elements into the page to show that data is loading. You may not see them appear if the request is handled quickly, but you will see them if the page is slower to load.

4. If the Ajax request fails, then an error message will be shown to the user.

JAVASCRIPT   c08/js/jq-ajax.js

```
① $('nav a').on('click', function(e) {
     e.preventDefault();
     var url = this.href;                                    // URL to load
     var $content = $('#content');                           // Cache selection

     $('nav a.current').removeClass('current');              // Update links
     $(this).addClass('current');
     $('#container').remove();                               // Remove content

     $.ajax({
       type: "POST",                                         // GET or POST
       url: url,                                             // Path to file
②     timeout: 2000,                                        // Waiting time
       beforeSend: function() {                              // Before Ajax
③       $content.append('<div id="load">Loading</div>');    // Load message
       },
       complete: function() {                                // Once finished
         $('#loading').remove();                             // Clear message
       },
       success: function(data) {                             // Show content
         $content.html( $(data).find('#container') ).hide().fadeIn(400);
       },
       fail: function() {                                    // Show error msg
④       $('#panel').html('<div class="loading">Please try again soon.</div>');
       }
     });

   });
```

EXAMPLE
AJAX & JSON

This example shows information about three events. The data used comes from three different sources.

1) When the page loads, event locations are coded into the HTML. Users click on an event in the left-hand column; it updates the timetable in the middle column.

In the left column, the links have an id attribute whose value is a two-letter identifier for the state the event is in:
```
<a id="tx" href="tx.html">... Austin, TX</a>
```

2) The timetables are stored in a JSON object, in an external file collected when the DOM has loaded. When users click on a session in the middle column, its description is shown in the right-hand column.

In the middle column showing timetables, the title of each session is used inside a link that will show the description for the session.
```
<a href="descriptions.html#Circuit-Hacking">
Circuit Hacking</a>
```

3) Descriptions of all sessions are stored in one HTML file. Individual descriptions are selected using jQuery's .load() method (and the # selector shown on p390).

In the right column, the session description is taken from an HTML file. Each session is stored in an element whose id attribute contains the title of the session (with spaces replaced by dashes).
```
<div id="Intro-to-3D-Modeling">
  <h3>Intro to 3D Modeling</h3>
  <p>Come learn how to create 3D models of ...</p>
</div>
```

Because links are added and removed, event delegation is used.

EXAMPLE
AJAX & JSON

This example uses data from three separate sources to demonstrate Ajax techniques.

In the left-hand column you can see three locations for an event. These are written into the HTML for the timetable page. Each one is a link.

1. Clicking on an event loads the session times for that event. They are stored in a file called `example.json`, which is collected when the DOM has loaded.

2. Clicking on a session will load its description. They are stored in `descriptions.html`, which is loaded when a user clicks on a session title.

THE MAKER BUS

HOME   ROUTE   TOYS   TIMETABLE

Roll up! Roll up! It's the maker bus...

①   ②

 SAN FRANCISCO, CA

 AUSTIN, TX

 NEW YORK, NY

9:00	Arduino Antics
10:00	Brain Hacking
11:30	Intro to 3D Modeling
1:00	The Printed Lunch
2:00	Droning On
3:00	Circuit Hacking
4:30	Make The Future

Arduino Antics

Learn how to program and use an Arduino! This easy-to-learn open source microcontroller board takes all sorts of sensor inputs, follows user-generated programs, and outputs data and power. Arduinos are commonly used in robotics, mechatronics, and all manners of electronics projects around the world. Taught by Elsie Denney, professional software developer with a long previous career as a technical artist in the video game industry, electronics enthusiast and instructor.

```html
<body>
  <header>
    <h1>THE MAKER BUS</h1>
    <nav>
      <a href="jq-load.html">HOME</a>
      <a href="jq-load2.html">ROUTE</a>
      <a href="jq-load3.html">TOYS</a>
      <a href="example.html" class="current">TIMETABLE</a>
    </nav>
  </header>

  <section id="content">
    <div id="container">
      <div class="third">
        <div id="event">
          <a id="ca" href="ca.html">
            <img src="img/map-ca.png" alt="SF, CA" />San Francisco, CA</a>
          <a id="tx" href="tx.html">
            <img src="img/map-tx.png" alt="Austin, TX" />Austin, TX</a>
          <a id="ny" href="ny.html">
            <img src="img/map-ny.png" alt="New York, NY" />New York, NY</a>
        </div>
      </div>
      <div class="third">
        <div id="sessions">Select an event from the left</div>
      </div>
      <div class="third">
        <div id="details">Details</div>
      </div>
    </div><!-- #container -->
  </section><!-- #content -->

  <script src="js/jquery-1.11.0.min.js"></script>
  <script src="js/example.js"></script>
</body>
```

Here you can see the HTML page. It has a header, followed by three columns. Two scripts appear before the closing **</body>** tag.

Left column: list of the events
Middle column: timetable of the sessions
Right column: description of the sessions

EXAMPLE
AJAX & JSON

cNN/data/example.json   JAVASCRIPT

```
{
    "CA": [
        {
            "time": "09.00",
            "title": "Intro to 3D Modeling"
        },
        {
            "time": "10.00",
            "title": "Circuit Hacking"
        },
        {
            "time": "11.30",
            "title": "Arduino Antics"
        }...
```

c08/descriptions.html   HTML

```html
<div id="Intro-to-3D-Modeling">
   <h3>Intro to 3D Modeling</h3>
   <p>Come learn how to create 3D models of parts you can then make...</p>
</div>
<div id="Circuit-Hacking">
   <h3>Circuit Hacking</h3>
   <p>Head to the Electro-Tent for a free introductory soldering...</p>
</div>
<div id="Arduino-Antics">
   <h3>Arduino Antics</h3>
   <p>Learn how to program and use an Arduino! This easy-to-learn...</p>
</div>
```

When the script is run, the `loadTimetable()` function loads the timetables for all three events from a file formatted using JSON, stored in `example.json`. The data is cached in a variable called `times`.

Events are identified by a two-letter code for the state. You can see a sample of the JSON-formatted data above and a sample of the HTML that will be created using that data.

EXAMPLE
AJAX & JSON

```
①  $(function() {                          // When the DOM is ready

②    var times;                            // Declare global variable
      $.ajax({                             // Setup request
        beforeSend: function(xhr){         // Before requesting data
          if (xhr.overrideMimeType) {      // If supported
③          xhr.overrideMimeType("application/json"); // set MIME to prevent errors
          }
        }
      });

      // FUNCTION THAT COLLECTS DATA FROM THE JSON FILE
④    function loadTimetable() {            // Declare function
        $.getJSON('data/example.json')     // Try to collect JSON data
⑤      .done( function(data){             // If successful
          times = data;                    // Store it in a variable
⑥      }).fail( function() {              // If a problem: show message
          $('#event').html('Sorry! We could not load the timetable at the moment');
        });
      }

⑦    loadTimetable();                      // Call the function
```

1. The script that does all the work is in **example.js**. It runs when the DOM has loaded.

2. The **times** variable will be used to store the session timetables for all of the events.

3. Before the browser requests the JSON data, the script checks if the browser supports the **overrideMimeType()** method. This is used to indicate that the response from the server should be treated as JSON data. This method can be used in case the server is accidentally set up to indicate that the data being returned is in any other format.

4. Next you can see a function called **loadTimetable()**, which is used to load the timetable data from a file called **example.json**.

5. If the data loads successfully, the data for the timetables will be stored in a variable called **times**.

6. If it fails to load, an error message will be shown to the users.

7. The **loadTimetable()** function is then called to load the data.

EXAMPLE
AJAX & JSON

```
c08/js/example.js                                              JAVASCRIPT

      // CLICK ON THE EVENT TO LOAD A TIMETABLE
①    $('#content').on('click', '#event a', function(e) {   // User clicks on place

②      e.preventDefault();                              // Prevent loading page
③      var loc = this.id.toUpperCase();                 // Get value of id attr

④      var newContent = '';                             // To build up timetable
        for (var i = 0; i < times[loc].length; i++) {    // loop through sessions
⑤        newContent += '<li><span class="time">' + times[loc][i].time + '</span>';
⑥        newContent += '<a href="descriptions.html#';
⑦        newContent += times[loc][i].title.replace(/ /g, '-') + '">';
⑧        newContent += times[loc][i].title + '</a></li>';
        }

⑨      $('#sessions').html('<ul>' + newContent + '</ul>'); // Display time

⑩      $('#event a.current').removeClass('current');     // Update selected link
        $(this).addClass('current');

⑪      $('#details').text('');                          // Clear third column
      });
```

1. A jQuery event helper method waits for users to click on the name of an event. It will load the timetable for that event into the middle column.

2. The preventDefault() method prevents the link from opening a page (because it is will show the AJAX data instead).

3. A variable called loc is created to hold the name of the event location. It is collected from the id attribute of the link that was clicked.

4. The HTML for the timetables will be stored in a variable called newContent. It is set to a blank string.

5. Each session is stored inside an <li> element, which starts by displaying the time of the session.

6. A link is added to the timetable, which will be used to load the description. The link points to the descriptions.html file. It is followed by a # symbol so it links to the correct part of the page.

7. The session title is added after the # symbol. The .replace() method replaces spaces in the title with a dash to match the value of the id attribute in the descriptions.html file for each session.

8. Inside the link you can see the title of the session.

9. The new content is added into the middle column.

10. The class attributes on the event links are updated to shows which event is the current event.

11. The third column is emptied if it had content.

EXAMPLE
AJAX & JSON

```
     // CLICK ON A SESSION TO LOAD THE DESCRIPTION
①   $('#content').on('click', '#sessions li a', function(e) { // Click on session
②     e.preventDefault();                                     // Prevent loading
③     var fragment = this.href;                               // Title is in href

④     fragment = fragment.replace('#', ' #');                 // Add space after#
⑤     $('#details').load(fragment);                           // To load info

⑥     $('#sessions a.current').removeClass('current');        // Update selected
       $(this).addClass('current');
     });

     // CLICK ON PRIMARY NAVIGATION
     $('nav a').on('click', function(e) {                     // Click on nav
       e.preventDefault();                                    // Prevent loading
       var url = this.href;                                   // Get URL to load

⑦     $('nav a.current').removeClass('current');              // Update nav
       $(this).addClass('current');

       $('#container').remove();                              // Remove old
       $('#content').load(url + ' #container').hide().fadeIn('slow'); // Add new
     });

   });
```

1. Another jQuery event helper method is set up to respond when a user clicks on a session in the middle column. It loads a description of the session.

2. `preventDefault()` stops the link opening.

3. A variable called `fragment` is created to hold the link to the session. This is collected from the `href` attribute of the link that was clicked.

4. A space is added before the # symbol so that it is the correct format for the jQuery `load()` method to collect part (not all) of the HTML page, e.g., `description.html #Arduino-Antics`

5. A jQuery selector is used to find the element whose id attribute has a value of `details` in the third column. The `.load()` method is then used to load the session description into that element.

6. The links are updated so that they highlight the appropriate session in the middle column.

7. The main navigation is set up as shown on p391.

SUMMARY
AJAX & JSON

▸ Ajax refers to a group of technologies that allow you to update just one part of the page (rather than reload a whole page).

▸ You can incorporate HTML, XML, or JSON data into your pages. (JSON is becoming increasingly popular.)

▸ To load JSON from a different domain, you can use JSONP but only if the code is from a trusted source.

▸ jQuery has methods that make it easier to use Ajax.

▸ `.load()` is the simplest way to load HTML into your pages and allows you to update just a part of the page.

▸ `.ajax()` is more powerful and more complex. (Several shorthand methods are also offered.)

▸ It is important to consider how the site will work if the user does not have JavaScript enabled, or if the page is not able to access the data from a server.

9

APIS

User interfaces allow humans to interact with programs. Application Programming Interfaces (APIs) let programs (including scripts) talk to each other.

Browsers, scripts, websites, and other applications frequently open up some of their functionality so that programmers can interact with them. For example:

BROWSERS

The DOM is an API. It allows scripts to access and update the contents of a web page while loaded in the browser. In this chapter you will meet some HTML5 JavaScript APIs that provide access to other browser features.

SCRIPTS

jQuery is a JavaScript file with an API. It allows you to select elements, then use its methods to work with those elements. It is just one of many scripts that let you to perform powerful tasks using their code.

PLATFORMS

Sites such as Facebook, Google, and Twitter open up their platforms so that you can access and update data they store (via websites and apps). In this chapter you see how Google lets you to add their maps to your sites.

You do not need to know *how* the other script or program achieves its task; you only need to know what it does, how to ask it to do something, and how to understand its replies. Therefore, this chapter will familiarize you with the form in which APIs are described.

Tell your friends to join us for an awesome day of tinkering with The Maker Bus...

To:

Sophie

Message:

Let's go make some robots...

send message

ALL ABOARD! ROLL UP! ROLL UP!
THE MERRY MAKER BUS

SOPHIE!
Let's go make some robots...

PLAYING NICELY
WITH OTHERS

You do not always need to know *how* a script or program works, as long
you know how to ask it to do something, and how to process its response.
The questions you can ask and the format of the answers form the API.

WHAT THE API CAN DO

If there is a script or program
that offers functionality you
need, consider using it rather
than writing something from
scratch.

Because each script, program, or
platform has different features,
the first thing you need to do is
understand what the API allows
you to do. For example:

- The DOM and jQuery APIs
  allow you to access and
  update a web page that is
  loaded in the browser and
  respond to events.
- Facebook, Google+, and
  Twitter APIs let you to access
  and update profiles and
  create status updates on their
  platforms.

When you know what the API
allows you to do, you can decide
if it is the right tool for the job.

HOW TO ACCESS IT

Next you need to know how to
access the functionality of the
API in order to use it.

The DOM's functionality is built
into the JavaScript interpreter in
the browser.

With jQuery you need to include
the jQuery script from your
server or a CDN in your pages.

Facebook, Google+, Twitter, and
other sites provide various ways
to access the functionality of
their platforms using APIs.

THE SYNTAX

Finally, you need to learn how to
ask the API to do something and
the format in which you should
expect any replies.

As long as you know how to
call a function, create an object,
and access the properties and
methods of an object, you will be
able to use any JavaScript API.

This chapter introduces you to
a range of APIs so you gain the
confidence to learn more about
them and other APIs.

HTML5 JAVASCRIPT APIS

First, we will look at some of the new HTML5 APIs.
Along with the markup in the HTML5 specification, a set of APIs define that describe how to interact with features of web browsers.

WHY HTML5 HAS APIS

As technologies evolve, so does the browsing experience. For example, smartphones may have smaller screens and less power than the latest desktop computers; but they include features that are rarely found on desktop machines such as accelerometers and GPS.

The HTML5 specification has not only added new markup, but also includes a new set of JavaScript APIs that standardize how you can make use of these new features in any device that implements them.

WHAT THEY COVER

Each of the HTML5 APIs focuses on one or more objects that browsers implement to deliver specific functionality.

For example, the geolocation API describes a `geolocation` object that lets you ask users for their location and two objects that handle the browsers response.

There are also APIs that offer improvements over existing functionality. For example, the web storage API lets you store information within the browser without relying on cookies.

WHAT YOU'LL LEARN

There is not space for an exhaustive reference of each of the HTML5 APIs (there have been whole books dedicated to these new HTML5 features). But you will meet three of the APIs and see examples of how to work with them.

This should get you used to using the HTML5 APIs so that you can then go on and learn more about them as you need them. You will also learn how you can test to see whether or not a browser supports the functionality in any of the APIs.

API	DESCRIPTION	
`geolocation`	How to tell where the user is located	p418
`localStorage`	Store information in the browser (even when user closes tab/window)	p420
`sessionStorage`	Store information in the browser while a tab/window is open	
`history`	How to access items from the browser's history	p424

FEATURE DETECTION

When you write code that uses the HTML5 APIs (or any other new feature in a web browser), you may need to check if the browser supports that feature before your code tries to use it.

The HTML5 APIs describe objects that browsers use to implement new functionality. For example, you are about to meet an object called the geolocation object that is used to determine a user's location. However, this object is only supported in modern browsers, so you need to check whether a browser supports this it before trying to use the object.

It is possible to check whether a browser supports an object using a conditional statement.

If the browser supports the object, then the condition will return a truthy value and the first set of statements are run. If it is not implemented, the second set of statements is run.

```
if (navigator.geolocation) {
  // Returns truthy so it is supported
  // Run statements in this code block
} else {
  // Not supported / turned off
  // Or user rejected request
}
```

You may not be surprised to hear that there are some cross-browser issues with feature detection.

For example, in the case of the code above, there was a bug in IE9 which could result in a memory leak when you check for the geolocation object. This could slow down your pages.

Luckily, there is a library called Modernizr, which takes away the hassles of cross-browser issues (like jQuery for feature detection). It is a better way to check if the browser supports recent features. The script is regularly updated and refined to deal with cross-browser issues as they are discovered, so they are less likely to affect you.

MODERNIZR

Modernizr is a script you can use in your pages to tell whether the browser supports features of HTML, CSS, and JavaScript.
It will be used in the coming HTML5 API examples.

HOW TO GET MODERNIZR

First, you need to download the script from the Modernizr.com website, where you will see:

- A development version of the script.
  It is uncompressed and features every check that the script is capable of performing.
- A tool (see screenshot below) that lets you select which features you want to test for.
  You can then download a custom version of the script that only contains the checks you *need*.
  On a live site, you should not test for features that you do not use as it would slow your site down.

In our examples, Modernizr is used near the end of the page just before the script that uses it. But you may see Modernizr included in the <head> of an HTML page (if the content of the page is uses features that you are testing for).

HOW MODERNIZR WORKS

When you include the Modernizr script in your page, it adds an object called `Modernizr`, which tests whether the browser supports the features that you specified that it should test for. Each feature you want it to test becomes a property of the `Modernizr` object. Their values are a Boolean (`true` or `false`) that tell you if a feature is supported.

You can use Modernizr as a condition like this:
If `Modernizr`'s `geolocation` property returns `true` run the code in the curly braces:

```
if (Modernizr.geolocation) {
  // Geolocation is supported
}
```

MODERNIZR PROPERTIES

In the screenshot on the left, you can see some of the features that Modernizr can check for. To see a full list of `Modernizr`'s properties, visit:
modernizr.github.io/Modernizr/test/index.html

GEOLOCATION API: FINDING USERS' LOCATIONS

An increasing number of sites offer extra functionality to users who disclose their location. The users' location can be requested using the geolocation API.

WHAT THE GEOLOCATION API DOES

Browsers that implement the geolocation API let users share their location with websites. The location data is provided in the form of longitude and latitude points. There are several ways for the browser to determine its location, including using data from its IP address, wireless network connection, cell towers, or GPS hardware.

In some devices, the geolocation API can give you more data along with longitude and latitude. But, we focus on these features because they have the most support. Having seen how to use them, if you need to work with the other features, you will be able to.

HOW TO ACCESS GEOLOCATION

The geolocation API is available by default in any browser that supports it (just like the DOM is). It was first supported in IE9, Firefox 3.5, Safari 5, Chrome 5, Opera 10.6, iOS3, and Android 2.

Browsers that support geolocation allow users to turn the feature on and off. If it is on, the browser will ask users if they want to share data for each individual web site that requests that information.

The way in which the browser asks the user if they will share location data differs from one browser to the next and one device to the next.

CHROME ON MAC

IOS ON IPHONE

FIREFOX ON PC

REQUESTING A USER'S LOCATION

PROCESSING THE RESPONSE

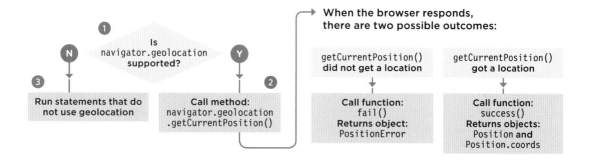

The geolocation API relies on an object called geolocation. If you want to try and make use of the user's location, first you need to check if the browser supports this object. This example will use the Modernizr script is used to perform this check.

1. A conditional statement is used to check whether the browser supports geolocation.

2. If geolocation is supported, the browser returns a truthy value and the first set of statements run. They request the user's location using the geolocation object's getCurrentPosition() method.

3. If geolocation is not supported, then a second set of statements is run.

```
if (Modernizr.geolocation) {
  // Returns truthy so it is supported
  // Run statements in this code block
} else {
  // Not supported / turned off
  // Or user rejected request
}
```

Once you call the getCurrentPosition() method, the code continues onto the next line because it is an asynchronous request (like the Ajax calls in the last chapter). The request is asynchronous because the browser will take a while to determine the user's location (and you do not want the rest of the page to stop loading while the browser works out where the user is). Therefore, the method has two parameters:
getCurrentPosition(*success*, *fail*)

success is the name of a function to call if the longitude and latitude are successfully returned. This method will automatically be passed an object called position, which holds the user's location.

fail is the name of a function called if the details cannot be obtained. This method will automatically be passed an object called PositionError containing details about the error.

So in all, there are three new objects you need to use in order to work with the geolocation API: geolocation, position, and PositionError. Their syntax is shown on the next page.

THE GEOLOCATION API

There are three objects involved in adding geolocation to your web page. The tables demonstrate how API documentation typically describes the objects, properties, and the methods you can use.

geolocation OBJECT

The geolocation object is used to request location data. It is a child of the navigator object.

METHOD	RETURNS
getCurrentPosition(*success, fail*)	Requests the position of the user and, if the user permits, returns the user's latitude / longitude plus other location information *success* is the name of a function to call if coordinates are retrieved *fail* is the name of a function to call if coordinates are not returned

Position OBJECT

If a user's location is found, a Position object is sent to the callback function. It has a child object called coords whose properties hold the user's location. If a device supports geolocation, it must provide a minimum amount of data (see the required column); other properties are optional (they may depend on the device's capabilities).

PROPERTY	RETURNS	REQUIRED
Position.coords.latitude	Latitude in decimal degrees	Yes
Position.coords.longitude	Longitude in decimal degrees	Yes
Position.coords.accuracy	Accuracy of latitude and longitude in meters	Yes
Position.coords.altitude	Meters above sea level	Yes (value can be null)
Position.coords.altitudeAccuracy	Accuracy of altitude in meters	Yes (value can be null)
Position.coords.heading	Degrees clockwise from north	No (up to device)
Position.coords.speed	Speed traveling in meters per second	No (up to device)
Position.coords.timestamp	Time since created (formatted as Date object)	No (up to device)

PositionError OBJECT

If location is not determined, the callback function is passed the PositionError object.

PROPERTY	RETURNS	REQUIRED
PositionError.code	An error number with the following values: 1 Permission denied 2 Unavailable 3 Timeout	Yes
PositionError.message	A message (not intended for the end user)	Yes

WORKING WITH LOCATION

1. In this example, Modernizr checks if geolocation is supported by the browser and enabled by the user.
2. When `getCurrentPosition()` is called, the user will be asked for permission to share their location.
3. If the location is gained, the user's latitude and longitude are written into the page.

4. If it is not supported, then the user will see a message that shows their location could not be found.
5. If the location is not gained (for any reason), again the message will say that a location cannot be found. The error code is logged to the browser console.

JAVASCRIPT   c09/js/geolocation.js

```
    var elMap = document.getElementById('loc');          // HTML element
    var msg = 'Sorry, we were unable to get your location.';   // No location msg

①  if (Modernizr.geolocation) {                          // Is geo supported
②    navigator.geolocation.getCurrentPosition(success, fail);  // Ask for location
     elMap.textContent = 'Checking location...';         // Say checking...
    } else {                                             // Not supported
④    elMap.textContent = msg;                            // Add manual entry
    }

   function success(position) {                          // Got location
     msg = '<h3>Longitude:<br>';                         // Create message
     msg += position.coords.longitude + '</h3>';         // Add longitude
③   msg += '<h3>Latitude:<br>';                          // Create message
     msg += position.coords.latitude + '</h3>';          // Add latitude
     elMap.innerHTML = msg;                              // Show location
   }

   function fail(msg) {                                  // Not got location
     elMap.textContent = msg;                            // Show text input
⑤   console.log(msg.code);                               // Log the error
   }
```

HTML   c09/geolocation.html

```
    <script src="js/geolocation.js"></script>
```

If you are unable to see a result on a desktop browser, try the example on a smart phone.
You can try all examples directly from the website for the book, http://www.javascriptbook.com/.
To support older browsers, search for a script called geoPosition.js

WEB STORAGE API: STORING DATA IN BROWSERS

Web storage (or HTML5 storage) lets you store data in the browser. There are two different types of storage: **local** and **session** storage.

HOW TO ACCESS THE STORAGE API

Before HTML5, cookies were the main mechanism for storing information in the browser. But cookies have several limitations, most notably they are:

- Not able to hold much data.
- Sent to the server every time you request a page from that domain.
- Not considered secure.

Therefore, HTML5 introduced a **storage object**. There are two different flavors of the storage object, `localStorage` and `sessionStorage`. Both use the same methods and properties. The differences are how long the data is stored for and whether all tabs can access the data that is being stored.

STORAGE	LOCAL	SESSION
Is the data stored when you close a window/tab?	✔	✘
Can all open windows/tabs access the data?	✔	✘

Commonly, browsers store 5MB of data per domain in a storage object. If a site tries to store more than 5mb of data, the browser will usually ask the user whether they want to allow this site to store more information (never rely on users agreeing to give a site more space).

The data is stored as properties of the storage objects (using in key/value pairs). The value in the pair is always a string. To protect the information that a website stores in these storage objects, browsers employ a **same origin policy**, which means data can only be accessed by other pages in the same domain.

```
http://www.google.com:80
   └──①──┘ ② └────③────┘ ④
```

These four parts of the URL must match:
1. **Protocol:** The protocol must be a match. If data was stored by a page that starts `http`, the storage object cannot be accessed via `https`.
2. **Subdomain:** The subdomain name must match. For example, `maps.google.com` cannot access data stored by `www.google.com`.
3. **Domain:** The domain name must match. For example, `google.com` cannot access local storage from `facebook.com`.
4. **Port:** The port number must match. Web servers can have many ports. Usually a port number is not specified in a URL, and the site uses port 80 for web pages, but the port number *can* be changed.

The storage objects are just one of the new HTML5 APIs for storing data. Others include access to the file system (through the FileSystem API) and client side databases such as the Web SQL database.

HOW TO ACCESS THE STORAGE API

Both of these objects are implemented on the `window` object, so you do not need to prefix the method names with any other object name.

To save an item into the storage object, you use the `setItem()` method, which takes two parameters: the name of the key and the value associated with it.

To retrieve a value from the storage object you use the `getItem()` method, passing it the key.

```
// Store information
localStorage.setItem('age', '12');
localStorage.setItem('color', 'blue');
// Access information and store in variable
var age   = localStorage.getItem('age');
var color = localStorage.getItem('color');
// Number of items stored
var items = localStorage.length;
```

You can also set and retrieve keys and values of the storage objects as you might with other objects using dot notation.

The storage objects are commonly used to store JSON-formatted data. The JSON object's:
- `parse()` method is used to turn the JSON-formatted data into a JavaScript object
- `stringify()` method is used to transform objects into JSON-formatted strings

```
// Store information (object notation)
localStorage.age   = 12;
localStorage.color = 'blue';
// Access information (object notation)
var age = localStorage.age;
var color = localStorage.color;
// Number of items stored
var items = localStorage.length;
```

Data for the storage objects is stored and accessed in a synchronous manner: all other processing stops while the script accesses or saves the data. Therefore, if a lot of data is regularly accessed or stored, the site can appear slower to use.

Below, you can see a table that shows the methods and property of the storage objects. This table is very similar to the one you saw for the geolocation API and is indicative of the types of tables you see in documentation for APIs.

METHOD	DESCRIPTION
setItem(*key, value*)	Creates a new key/value pair
getItem(*key*)	Gets the value for the specified key
removeItem(*key*)	Removes the key/value pair for the specified key
clear()	Clears all information from that storage object

PROPERTY	DESCRIPTION
length	Number of keys

LOCAL STORAGE

The examples on this page and the right-hand page store what the user enters into text boxes, but both examples store it for different lengths of time.

1. A conditional statement is used to check if the browser supports the relevant storage API.
2. References to the inputs for the username and answer are stored in variables.

3. The script checks to see if the storage object has a value for either of these elements using the getItem() method. If so, it is written into the appropriate input by updating its value property.
4. Each time an input event fires on one of the inputs, the form will save the data to the localStorage or sessionStorage object. It will automatically be shown if you refresh the page.

c09/js/local-storage.js   JAVASCRIPT

```
① if (window.localstorage) {

②   var txtUsername = document.getElementById('username');// Get form elements
     var txtAnswer = document.getElementById('answer');

③   txtUsername.value = localStorage.getItem('username'); // Elements populated
     txtAnswer.value = localStorage.getItem('answer');     // by localStorage data

     txtUsername.addEventListener('input', function () {   // Data saved
       localStorage.setItem('username', txtUsername.value);
     }, false);
④
     txtAnswer.addEventListener('input', function () {     // Data saved
       localStorage.setItem('answer', txtAnswer.value);
     }, false);
   }
```

c09/local-storage.html (The only difference in session-storage.html is the link to the script.)   HTML

```
<div class="two-thirds">
  <form id="application" action="apply.php">
    <label for="username">Name</label>
    <input type="text" id="username" name="username" /><br>
    <label for="answer">Answer</label>
    <textarea id="answer" name="answer"></textarea>
    <input type="submit" />
  </form>
</div>
<script src="js/local-storage.js"></script>
```

SESSION STORAGE

sessionStorage is more suited to information that:

- Changes frequently (each time the user visits the site – such as whether they are logged in or location data).
- Is personal and should not be viewed by other users of the device.

localStorage is best suited to information that:

- Only changes at set intervals (such as timetables / price lists), which can be helpful to store offline.
- The user might want to come back and use again (such as saving preferences / settings).

JAVASCRIPT   c09/js/session-storage.js

```
① if (window.sessionstorage) {

②   var txtUsername = document.getElementById('username');  // Get form elements
     var txtAnswer = document.getElementById('answer');

③   txtUsername.value = sessionStorage.getItem('username'); // Elements populated
     txtAnswer.value = sessionStorage.getItem('answer');    // by sessionStorage

④   txtUsername.addEventListener('input', function () {     // Save data
       sessionStorage.setItem('username', txtUsername.value);
     }, false);

     txtAnswer.addEventListener('input', function () {      // Save data
       sessionStorage.setItem('answer', txtAnswer.value);
     }, false);
   }
```

RESULT

What would you like to make?

Name

Answer

Submit

HISTORY API
& PUSHSTATE

If you move from one page to another, the browser's history remembers which pages you visited. But Ajax applications do not load new pages, so they can use the `history` API to update the location bar and history.

WHAT THE HISTORY API DOES

Each tab or window in the browser keeps its own history of pages you have viewed. When you visit a new page in that tab or window, the URL is added to the list of pages you have visited in the history.

Because of this, you can use the back and forward buttons in a browser to move between pages you have visited in that tab or window. However, on sites that use Ajax to load information, the URL is not automatically updated (and the back button might not show the last thing that the user was viewing).

HTML5's history API can help fix this problem. It lets you interact with the browser's `history` object:

- You can update the browser history stack using the `pushState()` and `replaceState()` methods.
- Extra information can be stored with each item.

As you will see, information can be added to the `history` object when an Ajax request is made, and the user can be shown the right content when they press back or forward buttons.

FIRST LINK:

The first page you visit is added to history stack

`one.html`

SECOND LINK:

Click a link: that page goes to the top of history stack

`two.html`

`one.html`

THIRD LINK:

Click a link: that page goes to the top of history stack

`three.html`

`two.html`

`one.html`

BACK BUTTON:

Pressing back takes you down the history stack

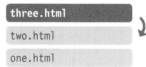

`three.html`

`two.html`

`one.html`

Browsing pages:
As you browse, the URL in your web browser's address bar updates. The page is also added to the top of something called the **history stack**.

Pressing back: takes you back down the stack
Pressing forward: takes you up the stack (where possible)
New page: if you request a new page, it will replace anything above the current page in the stack

State refers to the condition that something is in at a particular time. The browser history is like a pile (or stack) of states, one on top of the other. The three methods on this page allow you to manipulate the state in browsers.

ADDING INFORMATION TO THE HISTORY OBJECT

pushState() adds an entry to the history object. replaceState() updates the current entry. Both take the same three parameters (below), each of which updates the history object.

Because the history object is a child of the window object, you can use its name directly in the script; you can write history.pushState(), you do not need to write window.history.pushState().

$$history.pushState(state, title, url);$$
$$①\qquad②\qquad③$$

1. The history object can store information with each item in the history. This is provided in the state parameter and can be retrieved when you go back to that page.

2. Currently unused by most browsers, the title parameter is intended to change the title of the page. (You can specify a string for this value, ready for when browsers support it.)

3. The URL that you want the browser to show for this page. It must be on the same origin as the current URL and it should show the correct content if the user goes back to that URL.

GETTING INFORMATION FROM THE HISTORY OBJECT

Adding content to the browser history is only part of the solution; the other half is loading the right content when the user presses the back or forward buttons. To help show the right content, the onpopstate event fires whenever the user requests a new page.

This onpopstate event is used to trigger a function that will load the appropriate content into the page. There are two ways to determine what content should be loaded into the page:

- The location object (which represents the browser's location bar)
- The state information in the history object

The location object:
If the user presses back or forward, the address bar will update itself, so you can get the URL for the page that should be loaded using location.pathname (the location object is a child of the window object and its pathname property is the current URL). This works well when you are updating an entire page.

The state:
Because the first parameter of the pushState() method stores data with the history object for that page, you can use it to store JSON-formatted data. That data can then be loaded directly into the page. (This is used when the new content loads data rather than a traditional web page.)

THE HISTORY OBJECT

The HTML5 history API describes the functionality of the history object in modern web browsers. It lets you access and update the browser history (but only for pages the user visited on your site).

Even if the visitor is not taken to a new page in the browser window (for example, when only a part of the page is updated using Ajax), you can modify the history object to ensure that the back and forward buttons work as the user would expect them to on non-Ajax pages.

Again, the table below is indicative of the kind you might see in API documentation. As you become comfortable using the methods, properties, and events of an object you will find it easier to work with all kinds of APIs.

history OBJECT

METHOD	DESCRIPTION
history.back()	Takes you back in the history, like the browser's back button
history.forward()	Takes you forward in the history, like the browser's forward button
history.go()	Takes you to a specific page in the history. It is an index number, starting at 0. .go(1) is like clicking the forward button and .go(-1) is like clicking back
history.pushState()	Adds an item to the history stack (Clicking on a relative link in a page usually triggers a hashchange event, rather than load, but no event fires if you use pushState() and the url contains a hash)
history.replaceState()	Does the same as pushState() except it modifies the current history entry

PROPERTY	DESCRIPTION
length	Tells you how many items are in the history object

EVENT	DESCRIPTION
window.onpopstate	Used to handle the user moving backwards or forwards

WORKING WITH HISTORY

1. The `loadContent()` function uses jQuery's `.load()` method (see p390) to load content into the page.
2. If a link is clicked on, an anonymous function runs.
3. The page to load is held in a variable called `href`.

4. The current links are updated.
5. The `loadContent()` function is called (see step 1).
6. The `pushState()` method of the `history` object updates the history stack.

c09/js/history.js

JAVASCRIPT

```javascript
  $(function() {                                 // DOM has loaded
    function loadContent(url){                    // Load new content into page
      $('#content').load(url + ' #container').hide().fadeIn('slow');
    }

    $('nav a').on('click', function(e) {          // Click handler
      e.preventDefault();                          // Stop link loading new page
      var href = this.href;                        // Get href attribute of link
      var $this = $(this);                         // Store link in jQuery object
      $('a').removeClass('current');               // Remove current from links
      $this.addClass('current');                   // Update current link
      loadContent(href);                           // Call function: loads content
      history.pushState('', $this.text, href);     // Update history
    });

    window.onpopstate = function() {              // Handle back/forward buttons
      var path = location.pathname;                // Get the file path
      loadContent(path);                           // Call function to load page
      var page = path.substring(location.pathname.lastIndexOf('/') + 1);
      $('a').removeClass('current');               // Remove current from links
      $('[href="' + page + '"]').addClass('current'); // Update current link
    };
  });
```

RESULT

1ST	2ND	3RD

First prize is the DJI Phantom - a small, all-in one quadcopter designed for aerial photography enthusiasts. It comes fully configured and ready to fly. Both compact and stylish, the highly integrated design means that it's easy to carry wherever you go, ready at a moment's notice.

7. When the user clicks backwards or forwards, the `onpopstate` event fires. This is used to trigger an anonymous function.
8. The browser's location bar will display the corresponding page from the history stack, so `location.pathname` is used to obtain the path for the page that needs to be loaded.
9. The `loadContent()` function (in step 1) is called again, to retrieve the specified page.
10. The file name is retrieved so that the current link can be updated.

SCRIPTS WITH APIS

There are hundreds of scripts available for free on the web.
Many have an API you need to use to get them to work for you.

SCRIPT APIS

Lots of developers share their scripts through a range of websites. Some are relatively simple scripts with a single purpose (such as sliders, lightboxes, and table sorters). Others are far more complicated and can be used for a range of purposes (such as jQuery).

In this section, you will meet two different types of scripts whose code you can make use of when you have learned their API:

- A set of jQuery plugins known as jQuery UI.
- A script that makes it easier to create web apps called AngularJS.

THIRD-PARTY SCRIPTS

Before writing your own script it can pay to check if someone else has already done the hard work for you (there is no point reinventing the wheel).

JQUERY PLUGINS

Many developers have written code that adds extra functionality to jQuery. These scripts add methods to extend the jQuery object, which are known as **jQuery plugins**.

When you use these plugins, first you include the jQuery script, followed by the plugin script. Then, when you select elements (as you do with standard in jQuery methods), the plugin allows you to apply new methods that it has defined to that selection, offering new functionality that was not in the original jQuery script.

It is always a good idea to check:
- Whether it has been updated fairly recently
- That the JavaScript is separate from the HTML
- Reviews of the script if they are available

ANGULAR

Angular.js is another JavaScript library, but it is *very* different from jQuery. Its purpose is to make it easier to develop web applications.

One of the most striking things is that it allows you to access and update the contents of a page without writing code to handle events, select elements, or update the content of an element. We only have space to provide a very basic introduction to Angular in this chapter, but it does help demonstrate the variety of scripts available.

This helps to ensure that the script uses modern practices and is still being updated. It is also worth noting that the instructions for using a script are not always called an API.

JQUERY UI

The jQuery foundation maintain its own set of jQuery plugins called
jQuery UI. They help create user interfaces.

WHAT JQUERY UI DOES

jQuery UI is a suite of jQuery
plugins that extends jQuery with
a set of methods to create:

- Widgets (such as accordions
  and tabs)
- Effects (that make elements
  appear and disappear)
- Interactions (such as drag
  and drop functionality)

jQuery UI not only provides
JavaScript you can use, but it
also comes with a set of themes
that help control how the plugins
look on the page.

If you want fine-grained control
over how the jQuery plugins look
in the browser, you can also use
the **theme roller**, which gives you
more precise control over the
appearance of the elements.

HOW TO ACCESS IT

To use jQuery UI, first you must
include jQuery in your page; then
you must include the jQuery UI
script (after the jQuery file).

Versions of jQuery UI are
available on the same CDNs as
the main jQuery file. But, if you
only need part of the jQuery
UI functionality, you can just
download the relevant parts
from the `jqueryui.com` website.
This creates a smaller JavaScript
file, which in turn makes the
script faster to download.

SYNTAX

Once you have included the
jQuery and jQuery UI scripts
in the page, the syntax is very
similar to using other jQuery
methods. You create a jQuery
selection and then call a method
that will be defined in the plugin.

As you will see, the jQuery UI
documentation not only has to
explain the JavaScript methods
and properties it uses, but also
how to structure your HTML
if you want to use many of its
widgets and interactions.

JQUERY UI ACCORDION

Creating an accordion with jQuery UI is very simple. You only need to know:

- How to structure your HTML
- What element(s) should be used in the jQuery selector
- The jQuery UI method to call

1. In this example, the HTML for an accordion is contained within a `<div>` element (its `id` attribute has a value of `prizes`, which will be used in the script). Each panel of the accordion has:

2. An `<h3>` element for the clickable heading
3. A `<div>` element for the content of that panel

4. Before the closing `</body>` tag the jQuery and jQuery UI scripts are both included in the page.

5. Finally, you can see a third `<script>` element containing an anonymous function that runs when the page has loaded.

6. Inside that function, a standard jQuery selector picks the containing `<div>` element that contains the accordion (using the value of its `id` attribute). The accordion functionality is triggered by calling the `.accordion()` method on that selection.

c09/jqui-accordion.html `HTML`

```html
<body>
  <div id="prizes">
    <h3>1st Prize</h3>
    <div><p>First prize is the DJI...</p></div>
    <h3>2nd Prize</h3>
    <div><p>Second prize is the...</p></div>
    <h3>3rd Prize</h3>
    <div><p>Third prize is a...</p></div>
  </div>
  <script src="js/jquery-1.11.0.min.js"></script>
  <script src="js/1.10.3/jquery-ui.js"></script>
  <script>
    $(function() {
      $('#prizes').accordion();
    });
  </script>
</body>
```

`RESULT`

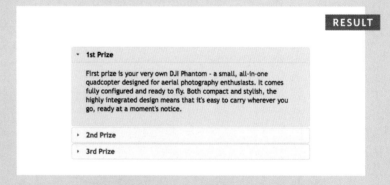

You do not need to know how the jQuery plugin achieves this, as long as you know how to:
- Structure your HTML
- Create the jQuery selection
- Call the new method defined in the jQuery plugin

Note: On a live site, the JavaScript should be kept in an external file to maintain a separation of concerns. It is shown here for convenience and to show how little work needs to be done to achieve this effect.

JQUERY UI TABS

c09/jqui-tabs.html

```
① <div id="prizes">
    <ul>
      <li><a href="#tab-1">1st Prize</a></li>
② ┌  <li><a href="#tab-2">2nd Prize</a></li>
   └  <li><a href="#tab-3">3rd Prize</a></li>
    </ul>
③   <div id="tab-1"><p>First prize is...</p></div>
    <div id="tab-2"><p>Second prize is...</p></div>
    <div id="tab-3"><p>Third prize is...</p></div>
  </div>
  <script src="js/jquery-1.11.0.min.js"></script>
  <script src="js/jquery-ui.js"></script>
  <script>
    $(function() {
④     $('#prizes').tabs();
    });
  </script>
```

RESULT

1st Prize	2nd Prize	3rd Prize

First prize is the DJI Phantom - a small, all-in-one quadcopter designed for aerial photography enthusiasts. It comes fully configured and ready to fly. Both compact and stylish, the highly integrated design means that it's easy to carry wherever you go, ready at a moment's notice.

This structure is common in most jQuery plugins:
1. jQuery is loaded.
2. The plugin is loaded.
3. An anonymous function runs when the page is ready.

The anonymous function will create a jQuery selection and applies the method defined in the jQuery plugin to that selection. Some methods will also require parameters in order to do their job.

The tabs are a similar concept to the accordion.

1. They are kept in a containing <div> element that will be used in the jQuery selector. The content, however, is slightly different.

2. The tabs are created using an unordered list. The link inside each list item points to a <div> element lower down the page that holds content for that tab.

3. Note that the id attributes on the <div> elements must match the value of the href attribute on the tabs.

Once you have included jQuery and jQuery UI in the page, there is a third script tag with an anonymous function that runs when the DOM has loaded.

4. A jQuery selector picks the element whose id attribute has a value of prizes (this is the containing element for the tabs). Then it calls the .tabs() method is called on that selection.

On a live site, the JavaScript should be kept in an external file to maintain a separation of concerns, but it is shown here for convenience and to show how little work needs to be done to achieve this effect.

JQUERY UI FORM

jQuery UI introduces several form controls that make it easier for people to enter data into forms. This example demonstrates two of them:

Slider input: This allows people to select a numeric value using a draggable slider. This slider has two handles that allow the user to set a range between two numbers. As you can see on the right, the HTML for the slider is made up of two components:
1. A normal label and text input that would allow users to enter a number.
2. An extra `<div>` element used to hold the slider that you see on the page.

Date picker: This allows people to pick a date from a pop-up calendar, which helps ensure that users provide the date in the correct format that you need.
3. It is just a text input, and does not need any additional markup.

Before the closing `</body>` tag, you can see that there are three `<script>` elements: the first is the jQuery script, the second is jQuery UI, and the third contains the instructions to setup these two form controls (see right-hand page). If JavaScript is not enabled, these controls look like normal form controls without the jQuery's enhancements.

c09/jqui-form.html   `HTML`

```html
<body> ...
  <h2>Find Accommodation</h2> ...
  <p id="price">
    <label for="amount">Price range:</label>
    <input type="text" id="amount" />
  </p>
  <div id="price-range"></div>
  <p>
    <label for="arrival">Arrival date:</label>
    <input type="text" id="arrival" />
  </p>
  <input type="submit" value="Find a hotel"/>

  <script src="js/jquery-1.9.1.js"></script>
  <script src="js/jquery-ui.js"></script>
  <script src="js/form-init.js"></script>
</body>
```

① (lines for label/input Price range)
② (line for div price-range)
③ (line for input arrival)

`RESULT`

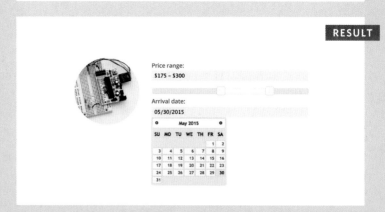

Most jQuery scripts live within the `.ready()` function or its shortcut (used on the next page). As you saw in Chapter 7, this ensures that the script only runs when the DOM has loaded.

If you include more than one jQuery plugin, each of which uses the `.ready()` method, you do not repeat the function - you combine the code from inside both functions into the one.

432 APIS

1. The JavaScript is contained within the shortcut for the jQuery `.ready()` method. It contains the setup instructions for both of the form controls.

2. To turn a text input into a date picker, all you need to do is select the text input and then call the `datepicker()` method on that selection.

3. Cache the inputs for price.

4. The slider uses an object literal to set the properties of the `.slider()` method (see below).

JAVASCRIPT   c09/js/form-init.js

```javascript
①  $(function() {

②    $('#arrival').datepicker();            // Turn input to JQUI datepicker

③    var $amount = $('#amount');            // Cache the price input
      var $range = $('#price-range');        // Cache the <div> for the price range

      $('#price-range').slider({             // Turn price-range input into a slider
        range: true,                         // If it is a range it gets two handles
        min: 0,                              // Minimum value
        max: 400,                            // Maximum value
④      values: [175, 300],                  // Values to use when the page loads
        slide: function(event, ui) {         // When slider used update amount element
          $amount.val('$' + ui.values[0] + ' - $' + ui.values[1]);
        }
      });
      $amount                                // Set initial values of amount element
⑤      .val('$' + $range.slider('values', 0)     // A $ sign then lower range
        + ' - $' + $range.slider('values', 1));   // A $ sign then higher range

    });
```

5. When the form loads, the text input that shows the amount as text needs to know the initial range for the slider. The value of that input is made up of:

a) A dollar sign: $ followed by the lower range value.

b) A dash and dollar sign: - $ followed by the higher range value.

The script is called **form-init. js**. Programmers often use **init** as a shorthand for initialize; and this script is used to set an initial state for the form.

When a jQuery plugin has settings that vary each time it is used, it is common to pass the settings in an object literal. You can see this with the `.slider()` method; it is passed several parameters and a method:

PROPERTY	DESCRIPTION
range	A Boolean to give the slider two handles (not just a single value)
min	The minimum value for the slider
max	The maximum value for the slider
values	An array containing two values to specify an initial range in the slider when the page first loads

METHOD	DESCRIPTION
slider()	Updates the text input which shows the text values for the slider (the documentation shows examples for this)

ANGULARJS

AngularJS is a framework that makes it easier to create web apps. In particular, it assists in creating apps that write, read, update, and delete data in a database on a server.

Angular is based on a software development approach called **model view controller** or **MVC**. (It is actually variant on MVC, not strict MVC). To use Angular, first you include the `angular.js` script in your page, and then it makes a set of tools available to you (just like jQuery does).

The point of MVC is that it separates out parts of a web application, in the same way that front-end developers should separate content (HTML), presentation (CSS), and behavior (JavaScript).

We do not have space to go into Angular in *detail*, but it introduces another example of a very different script with an API, as well as concepts such as the MVC approach, templating, and data binding. You can download Angular and view the full API at `http://angularjs.org`.

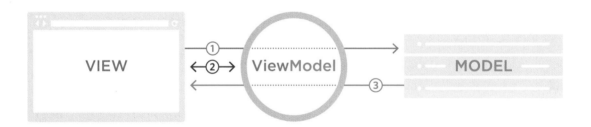

The **View** is what the user sees. In a web app, it is the HTML page. Angular lets you create templates with spaces for particular types of content. If the user changes values in the view, **commands (1)** are sent to up the chain to update the model. There can be different views of the same data, e.g., users and administrators.

This **ViewModel** (or *controller*) will update the view if there are changes to the model, and will update the model if there are changes in the view. The task of keeping data synchronized between the two is known as **data binding** (2). For example, if a form in the view is updated, it reflects the changes and updates the server.

In a web app, the **Model** is usually stored in the database, and managed by server-side code that can access and update the model.

When the model has been updated, change notifications (3) are sent to the ViewModel. This info can be passed onto the View to keep it updated.

USING ANGULAR

```
<!DOCTYPE html>
<html ng-app>
<head> ...
  <script src="https://ajax.googleapis.com/ajax/
  libs/angularjs/1.0.2/angular.min.js"></script>
</head>
<body> ...
  <form>
    To:<br>
    <input ng-model="name" type="text"/><br>
    Message:<br>
    <textarea ng-model="message"></textarea>
    <input type="submit" value="send message" />
  </form> ...
  <div class="postcard">
    <div>{{ name }}</div>
    <p>{{ message }}</p>
  </div> ...
</body>
</html>
```

RESULT

THE MAKER BUS

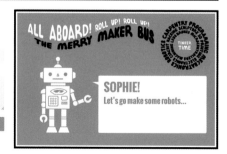

This example takes the content of the <input> and <textarea> elements and writes it into another part of the page (where you can see the double curly braces in the HTML file).

First, include the Angular script in your page. You can store it locally or use the version on Google's CDN. Until you understand more about Angular, place it in the <head> element.

Note the new markup in the HTML. There are attributes that start with ng- (which is short for Angular). These are called **directives**. There is one on the opening <html> tag and one on each of the form elements. The value of the ng-model attribute on the text inputs matches the values inside the double curly braces. Angular *automatically* takes the content of the form elements and writes it into the page where the corresponding curly braces are.

No more JavaScript is needed to achieve this, whereas in jQuery, this would involve four steps:
1. Writing an event handler for the form elements
2. Using that to trigger code to get the elements' content
3. Selecting new element nodes that represent the postcard
4. Writing the data into the page

VIEW & VIEWMODEL

Below, look at the `angular-controller.js` file.
It uses a a constructor function to create an object called `BasketCtrl`. This object is known as a **controller** or **ViewModel**. It is passed another object called `$scope` as an argument. Properties of the `$scope` object are set in the constructor function.

1. Note the object's name (`BasketCtrl`) matches the value of the `ng-controller` attribute on the opening `<table>` tag. In this example, there is no database, so the controller will also act as the model: sharing data with the view.

The HTML file (the view) gets its data from the `BasketCtrl` object in the JavaScript controller. In the HTML, note how the names in curly braces, e.g., `{{ cost }}` and `{{ qty }}`, match the properties of the `$scope` object in the JavaScript.

The HTML file is now called a **template** because it will display whatever data is in the corresponding controller. The names in curly braces are like variables that match the data in the object. If the JavaScript object had different values, the HTML would show those values.

```
c09/angular-controller.html                                                    HTML

    <!DOCTYPE html>
    <html ng-app>
      <head>
        <title>JavaScript &amp; jQuery - Chapter 9 ...</title>
        <script src="https://ajax.googleapis.com/.../angular.min.js"></script>
        <script src="js/angular-controller.js"></script>
        <link rel="stylesheet" href="css/c09.css">
      </head>
      <body> ...
①      <table ng-controller="BasketCtrl">
          <tr><td>Item:</td><td>{{ description }}</td></tr>
②        <tr><td>Cost:</td><td>${{ cost }}</td></tr>
          <tr><td>Qty:</td><td><input type="number" ng-model="qty"></td></tr>
③        <tr><td>Subtotal:</td><td>{{qty * cost | currency}}</td></tr>
        </table> ...
      </body>
    </html>
```

```
c09/js/angular-controller.js                                              JAVASCRIPT

① function BasketCtrl($scope) {
     $scope.description = 'Single ticket';
②    $scope.cost = 8;
     $scope.qty = 1;
③ }
```

DATA BINDING & SCOPE

2. It is also possible to evaluate expressions inside the curly braces. In step 3, the subtotal is calculated in the template. This is then formatted as a currency. Furthermore, if you update the quantity in the form, the underlying data model (in the JavaScript object) is updated along with the subtotal. Try updating the values in the JavaScript file, then refreshing the HTML to see the connection. This is an example of something programmers call **data binding**; the data in the JavaScript file is bound to the HTML and vice-versa. If the ViewModel changes, the view updates. If the view changes, the ViewModel updates.

As this shows, Angular is particularly helpful when you load data from a separate file into the view. A page can have multiple controllers, each of which has its own **scope**. In the HTML, the `ng-controller` attribute is used on an element to define the scope of that controller. This is similar to variable scope. For example, a different element might have a different controller (e.g., `StoreCtrl`), and both controllers would be able to have a property called `description`. Because the scope is only within that element, each controller's `description` property would only be used within that controller's scope.

RESULT

THE MAKER BUS

Buy tickets

Item:	Single ticket
Cost:	$8
Qty:	1
Subtotal:	$8.00

GETTING EXTERNAL DATA

Here, the controller (the JavaScript file) collects the model (the JSON data) from a file on the server. (In a web app, the JSON data would usually come from a database.) This updates the view in the HTML.

To collect the data, Angular uses what it calls the **$http service**. Inside the angular.js file, the code uses the XMLHttpRequest object to make Ajax requests (like those you saw in Chapter 8).

1. The path to the JSON file is relative to the HTML template, *not* the JavaScript file (even though the path is written in the JavaScript).

Just like jQuery's .ajax() method, the $http service has several shortcuts to make it easier to create some requests. To fetch data it uses get(), post(), and jsonp(); to delete data it uses delete(); and to create new records: put(). This example uses get().

c09/angular-external-data.html `HTML`

```html
<table ng-controller="TimetableCtrl">
  <tr><th>time</th><th>title</th><th>detail</th></tr>
  <tr ng-repeat="session in sessions">
    <td>{{ session.time }}</td>
    <td>{{ session.title }}</td>
    <td>{{ session.detail }}</td>
  </tr>
</table>
```
(5)

c09/js/angular-external-data.js `JAVASCRIPT`

```javascript
function TimetableCtrl($scope, $http) {
  $http.get('js/items.json')
    .success(function(data) { $scope.sessions = data.sessions; })
    .error(function(data) { console.log('error') });
    // The error could show a friendly message to users...
  }
```
(1)
(2)
(3)

c09/js/items.json `JAVASCRIPT`

```json
{
  "sessions": [
    {"time": "09.00", "title": "Intro to 3D Modeling", "detail": "Come..."}
    {"time": "10.00", "title": "Circuit Hacking", "detail": "Head to the..."}
    {"time": "11.30", "title": "Arduino Antics", "detail": "Learn how..."}
  ]
}
```
(4)

LOOP THROUGH RESULTS

2. If the request successfully fetches data, the code in the `success()` function runs. In this case, if it is successful the `$scope` object is passed the data from the JSON object. This allows the template to display the data.

3. If it fails, the `error()` function is run instead. This would to show an error message to users. Here it writes to the console (which you meet on p464).

4. The JSON data contains several objects, each of which is displayed in the page. Note, there is no JavaScript loop written in the controller. Instead, the HTML template (or view) is where the loop occurs.

5. The `ng-repeat` directive on the opening `<tr>` tag indicates that the table row should act like a loop. It should go through each object in the `sessions` array and create a new table row for each of them.

RESULT

Session Times

TIME	TITLE	DETAIL
09.00	Intro to 3D Modeling	Come learn how to create 3D models of parts you can then make on our bus! You'll get to know the same 3D modeling software that used worldwide in professional settings like engineering, product design, and more. Develop and test ideas in a fun and informative session hosted by Bella Stone, professional roboticist.
10.00	Circuit Hacking	Head to the Electro-Tent for a free introductory soldering lesson. There will be electronics kits on hand for those who wish to make things, and experienced hackers and engineers around to answer all your

In the HTML, the value of the `ng-repeat` directive is:
`session in sessions`

- `sessions` matches the JSON data; it corresponds with the object name.
- `session` is the identifier used in the template to indicate the name of each individual object within the `sessions` object.

If the `ng-repeat` attribute used different names than `session`, the value in the curly braces in the HTML would have to change to reflect that name. For example, if it said `lecture in sessions`, then the curly braces would change to reflect that:
`{{ lecture.time }}`, `{{ lecture.title }}`, etc.

This is just a very high-level introduction to Angular, but does demonstrate some popular techniques when using JavaScript to develop web apps, such as:

- The use of templates that take content from JavaScript and update the HTML page.
- The rise in MVC-influenced frameworks for web-based application development.
- The use of libraries to save developers having to write so much code.

For more on Angular, see `http://angularjs.org`

Another very popular alternative is Backbone `http://backbonejs.org`

PLATFORM APIS

Many large websites expose their APIs that allow you to access and update the data on their sites, including Facebook, Google, and Twitter.

WHAT YOU CAN DO

Each site offers different capabilities, for example:

- Facebook offers features such as allowing people to like sites or add comments and discussion to the bottom of a web page.
- Google Maps lets you to include various types of maps in your pages.
- Twitter allows you to display your latest tweets on your web pages or send new tweets.

By exposing some of the functionality of their platforms these companies are advertising their sites and encouraging people back to them. This in turn increase their total amount of activity (and their revenue).

Be aware that companies can change either how you access APIs or change what you are allowed to use the APIs for.

HOW TO ACCESS

On the web, you can access several of these platform APIs by including a script they provide in your page. That script will typically create an object (just like the jQuery script adds a jQuery object). In turn, that object will have methods and properties that you can use to access (and sometimes update) the data on that platform.

Most sites that offer an API will also provide documentation that explains how to use its objects, methods, and properties (along with some basic examples).

Some of the larger sites provide pages where you can get code that you can copy and paste into your site without even needing to understand the API.

Facebook, Google, and Twitter have all made changes to both how you access their APIs *and* what you can use them for.

THE SYNTAX

The syntax of an API will vary from platform to platform. But they will be documented using tables of objects, methods, and properties like those you saw in the first section of this chapter. You may also see sample code that demonstrates tasks people commonly use the API for (like the examples you have seen in this chapter).

Some platforms offer APIs in multiple languages, so that you can interact with them using server-side languages such as PHP / C# as well as using JavaScript.

In the rest of this chapter we will be focusing on the Google Maps API as an example of what you can do with platform APIs.

If you work on a site for a client, make them aware that APIs can change (and that could result in recoding pages that use them).

GOOGLE MAPS API

Currently, one of the most popular APIs in use on the web is the Google Maps API, which allows you to add maps to web pages.

WHAT IT DOES

The Google Maps JavaScript API allows you to show Google maps in your web pages. It also allows you to customize the look of the maps and what information is shown on them.

You may find it helpful to look at the documentation for the Google Maps API while going through this example. It will show you other things that you can do with the API. https://developers.google.com/maps/

WHAT YOU'LL SEE

We only have space to show a few of the features of the Google Maps API, as it is very powerful and contains a lot of advanced features. But the examples in this chapter will get you used to working with its API.

You will start by seeing how to add a map to your web pages, then you will see how to change the controls, and finally how to change the colors and add markers on top of the map.

API KEY

Some APIs require that you register and request an API key in order to get data from their servers. An API key is a set of letters and numbers that uniquely identify you to the application so the owners of the site can track how much you use the API and what you use it for.

At the time of writing, Google allowed websites to call their maps API 25,000 times per day for free without an API key, but sites that consistently make more requests are required to use a key and pay for the service.

If you run a busy site, or the map is part of the core application, it is good practice to use an API key with Google Maps because:
- You can see how many times your site requests the API
- Google can contact you if they change terms of service or charge for use

To get a Google API key, see https://cloud.google.com/console

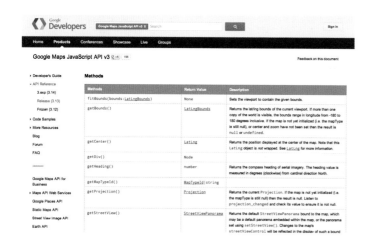

BASIC MAP SETTINGS

Once you have included the Google Maps script in your page, you can use their maps object. It lets you display Google maps in your pages.

CREATING A MAP

The maps object is stored within an object called google. This creates scope for all Google objects.

To add a map to your page, you create a new map object using a constructor: Map(). The constructor is part of the maps object, and it has two parameters:
- The element into which you want the map drawn
- A set of map options that control how it is displayed given using object literal notation

Zoom level is typically set using a number between 0 (the full earth) and 16. (Some cities can go higher.)

MAP OPTIONS

The settings that control how the map should look are stored inside another JavaScript object called mapOptions. It is created as an object literal before you call the Map() constructor. In the JavaScript on the right, you can see that the mapOptions object uses three pieces of data:
- Longitude and latitude of the center of the map
- The zoom level for the map
- The type of map data you want to show

The images that make up the map are called tiles. Four map types each show a different style of map.

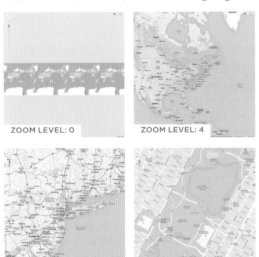

ZOOM LEVEL: 0 ZOOM LEVEL: 4

ZOOM LEVEL: 8 ZOOM LEVEL: 16

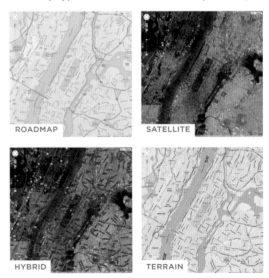

ROADMAP SATELLITE

HYBRID TERRAIN

A BASIC GOOGLE MAP

c09/google-map.html

```html
    <div id="map"></div> <!-- Dimensions of map are set in CSS -->
    <script src="js/google-map.js"></script>
  </body>
```

c09/js/google-map.js

```javascript
  function init() {
      var mapOptions = {                                    // Set up the map options
        center: new google.maps.LatLng(40.782710,-73.965310),
        mapTypeId: google.maps.MapTypeId.ROADMAP,
        zoom: 13
      };
      var venueMap;                                         // Map() draws a map
      venueMap = new google.maps.Map(document.getElementById('map'), mapOptions);
  }

  function loadScript() {
      var script = document.createElement('script');       // Create <script> element
      script.src = 'http://maps.googleapis.com/maps/api/js?
                        sensor=false&callback=init';
      document.body.appendChild(script);                   // Add element to page
  }

  window.onload = loadScript;                              // Onload call
```

(3) (4) (2) (1)

RESULT

THE MAKER BUS

Naumberg Bandshell
Central Park
New York, NY 10019

1. Starting at the bottom of the script, when the page has loaded, the `onload` event will call the `loadScript()` function.

2. `loadScript()` creates a `<script>` element to load the Google Maps API. When it has loaded, it calls `init()`, to initialize the map.

3. `init()` loads the map into the HTML page. First it creates a `mapOptions` object with three properties.

4. Then it uses the `Map()` constructor to create a map and draw the map into the page. The constructor takes two parameters:
- The element that the map will appear inside
- The `mapOptions` object

CHANGING CONTROLS

VISIBILITY OF MAP CONTROLS

POSITION OF MAP CONTROLS

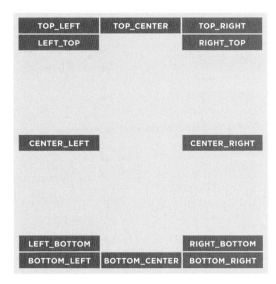

To show or hide the controls, use the control name followed by a value of true (to show it) or false (to hide it). Although Google Maps tries to prevent overlaps, use judgement to position controls on your map.

CONTROL	DESCRIPTION	DEFAULT
zoomControl (1)	Sets the zoom level of the map. It uses a slider (for large maps) "+/-" buttons (for small maps)	On
panControl (2)	Allows panning across the map	On for non-touch devices
scaleControl (3)	Shows the scale of the map	Off
mapTypeControl (4)	Switch map types (e.g., ROADMAP and SATELLITE)	On
streetViewControl (5)	A Pegman icon that can be dragged and dropped onto the map to show a street view	On
rotateControl	Rotates maps that have oblique imagery (not shown)	On when available
overviewMapControl	A thumbnail showing a larger area, that reflects where the current map is within that wider area (not shown)	On when map is collapsed, e.g., street view

GOOGLE MAP WITH CUSTOM CONTROLS

APPEARANCE OF CONTROLS

To alter the appearance and position of map controls, you add to the `mapOptions` object.

1. To show or hide a control, the key is the name of the control, and the value is a Boolean (`true` will show the control; `false` will hide it).

POSITION OF EACH CONTROL

2. Each control has its own options object used to control its style and position. The word `Options` follows the control name, e.g., `zoomControlOptions`. Styles are discussed below. The diagram on the left-hand page shows options for the `position` property.

Note: this is an excerpt of the JavaScript file - c09/js/google-map-controls.js

`JAVASCRIPT`

```
  var mapOptions = {
    zoom: 14,
    center: new google.maps.LatLng(40.782710,-73.965310),
    mapTypeId: google.maps.MapTypeId.ROADMAP,

①    panControl: false,
①    zoomControl: true,
     zoomControlOptions: {
③      style: google.maps.ZoomControlStyle.SMALL,
②      position: google.maps.ControlPosition.TOP_RIGHT
     },
①    mapTypeControl: true,
     mapTypeControlOptions: {
③      style: google.maps.MapTypeControlStyle.DROPDOWN_MENU,
②      position: google.maps.ControlPosition.TOP_LEFT
     },
①    scaleControl: true,
     scaleControlOptions: {
②      position: google.maps.ControlPosition.TOP_CENTER
     },
①    streetViewControl: false,
①    overviewMapControl: false
  };
```

STYLE OF MAP CONTROLS

3. You can change the appearance of the zoom and map type controls using the following options:

zoomControlStyle:		MapTypeControlStyle:	
SMALL	Small +/- buttons	HORIZONTAL_BAR	Buttons side-by-side
LARGE	Vertical slider	DROPDOWN_MENU	Dropdown select box
DEFAULT	The default for that device	DEFAULT	The default for that device

STYLING A GOOGLE MAP

To style the map you need to specify three things:

- **featureTypes**: the map feature you want to style: e.g., roads, parks, waterways, public transport.
- **elementTypes**: the part of that feature you want to style, such as its geometry (shapes) or labels.
- **stylers**: properties that allow you to adjust the color or visibility of items on the map.

The **styles** property in the **mapOptions** object sets the map style. It's value is an array of objects. Each object affects a different feature fo the map.

The first **stylers** property alters the colors of the map as a whole. It, too, contains an array of objects.

- **hue** property adjusts color, its value is a hex code
- **lightness** or **saturation** can take a value from -100 to 100

Then each feature that shows up on the map can have its own object, and its own **stylers** property. In it, the **visibility** property can have three values:

- **on** to show the feature type
- **off** to hide it
- **simplified** to show a more basic version

```
c09/js/google-map-styled.js - Note: this is an excerpt of the JavaScript file          JAVASCRIPT

styles: [                                // styles property is an array of objects
  {
    stylers: [                           // stylers property holds array of objects
      { hue: "#00ff6f" },                // Overall map colors
      { saturation: -50 }                // Overall map saturation
    ]
  }, {
    featureType: "road",                 // Road features
    elementType: "geometry",             // Their geometry (lines)
    stylers: [
      { lightness: 100 },                // Lightness of roads
      { visibility: "simplified" }       // Level of road detail
    ]
  }, {
    featureType: "transit",              // Public transport features
    elementType: "geometry",             // Their geometry (lines)
    stylers: [
      { hue: "#ff6600" },                // Color of public transport
      { saturation: +80 }                // Saturation of public transport
    ]
  }, {
    featureType: "transit",              // Public transport features
    elementType: "labels",               // Their labels
    stylers: [
      { hue: "#ff0066" },                // Label color
      { saturation: +80 }                // Label saturation
    ]
  } ...                                  // More stylers shown in the code download
```

ADDING MARKERS

Here you can see how to add a **marker** to a map. The map has been created, and its name is **venueMap**.

1. Create a `LatLng` object to store the position of the marker using object constructor syntax. Below that object is called `pinLocation`.
2. The `Marker()` constructor creates a `marker` object. It has one parameter: an object that contains settings using object literal notation.

The `settings` object contains three properties:

3. `position` is the object storing the location of the marker (`pinLocation`).
4. `map` is the map that the marker should be added to (because a page can have more than one map).
5. `icon` is the path to the image that should be displayed as the marker on the map (this should be provided relative to the HTML page).

```
① var pinLocation = new google.maps.LatLng(40.782710,-73.965310);

② var startPosition = new google.maps.Marker({        // Create a new marker
③   position: pinLocation,                            // Set its position
④   map: venueMap,                                    // Specify the map
⑤   icon: "img/go.png"                                // Path to image from HTML
  });
```

`RESULT`

THE MAKER BUS

Naumberg Bandshell
Central Park
New York, NY 10019

SUMMARY

APIS

▶ APIs are used in browsers, scripts, and by websites that share functionality with other programs or sites.

▶ APIs let you write code that will make a **request**, asking another program or script to do something.

▶ APIs also specify the format in which the **response** will be given (so that the response can be understood).

▶ To use an API on your website, you will need to include a script in the relevant web pages.

▶ An API's documentation will usually feature tables of objects, methods, and properties.

▶ Providing you know how to create an object and call its methods, access its properties, and respond to its events, you should be able to learn any JavaScript API.

10

ERROR HANDLING & DEBUGGING

JavaScript can be hard to learn and everyone makes mistakes when writing it. This chapter will help you learn how to find the errors in your code. It will also teach you how to write scripts that deal with potential errors gracefully.

When you are writing JavaScript, do not expect to write it perfectly the first time. Programming is like problem solving: you are given a puzzle and not only do *you* have to solve it, but you also need to create the instructions that allow the *computer* to solve it, too.

When writing a long script, nobody gets everything right in their first attempt. The error messages that a browser gives look cryptic at first, but they can help you determine what went wrong in your JavaScript and how to fix it. In this chapter you will learn about:

THE CONSOLE & DEV TOOLS

Tools built into the browser that help you hunt for errors.

COMMON PROBLEMS

Common sources of errors, and how to solve them.

HANDLING ERRORS

How code can deal with potential errors gracefully.

ORDER OF EXECUTION

To find the source of an error, it helps to know how scripts are processed. The order in which statements are executed can be complex; some tasks cannot complete until another statement or function has been run:

```
function greetUser() {
②    return 'Hello ' + getName();
   }

   function getName() {
③     var name = 'Molly';
      return name;
   }

① var greeting = greetUser();
④ alert(greeting);
```

This script above creates a greeting message, then writes it to an alert box (see right-hand page). In order to create that greeting, two functions are used: greetUser() and getName().

You might think that the **order of execution** (the order in which statements are processed) would be as numbered: one through to four. However, it is a little more complicated.

To complete step one, the interpreter needs the results of the functions in steps two *and* three (because the message contains values returned by those functions). The order of execution is more like this: 1, 2, 3, 2, 1, 4.

1. The greeting variable gets its value from the greetUser() function.

2. greetUser() creates the message by combining the string 'Hello ' with the result of getName().

3. getName() returns the name to greetUser().

2. greetUser() now knows the name, and combines it with the string. It then returns the message to the statement that called it in step 1.

1. The value of the greeting is stored in memory.

4. This greeting variable is written to an alert box.

EXECUTION CONTEXTS

The JavaScript interpreter uses the concept of **execution contexts**. There is one global execution context; plus, each function creates a new new execution context. They correspond to variable scope.

EXECUTION CONTEXT

Every statement in a script lives in one of three execution contexts:

○ **GLOBAL CONTEXT**
Code that is in the script, but not in a function. There is only one global context in any page.

FUNCTION CONTEXT
Code that is being run within a function. Each function has its own function context.

○ **EVAL CONTEXT (NOT SHOWN)**
Text is executed like code in an internal function called `eval()` (which is not covered in this book).

VARIABLE SCOPE

The first two execution contexts correspond with the notion of scope (which you met on p98):

○ **GLOBAL SCOPE**
If a variable is declared outside a function, it can be used anywhere because it has global scope. If you do not use the `var` keyword when creating a variable, it is placed in global scope.

FUNCTION-LEVEL SCOPE
When a variable is declared within a function, it can only be used within that function. This is because it has function-level scope.

THE STACK

The JavaScript interpreter processes one line of code at a time. When a statement needs data from another function, it **stacks** (or piles) the new function on top of the current task.

When a statement has to call some other code in order to do its job, the new task goes to the top of the pile of things to do.

Once the new task has been performed, the interpreter can go back to the task in hand.

Each time a new item is added to the stack, it creates a new execution context.

Variables defined in a function (or execution context) are only available in that function.

If a function gets called a second time, the variables can have different values.

You can see how the code that you have been looking at so far in this chapter will end up with tasks being stacked up on each other in the diagram to the right.

(The code is shown at the top of the right-hand page.)

> greetUser() returns 'Hello ' and the result of getName()

> Creates greeting variable and calls greetUser() to get the value

> Waiting...

The value for the **greeting** variable is obtained by calling the **greetUser()** function. So the variable cannot be assigned until the **greetUser()** function has done its job.

The statement is effectively put on hold, and the **greetUser()** task gets stacked on top it. In turn, the **greetUser()** function cannot return a value until the **getName()** function has completed *its* task.

```
function greetUser() {
    return 'Hello ' + getName();
}

function getName() {
    var name = 'Molly';
    return name;
}

var greeting = greetUser();
alert(greeting);
```

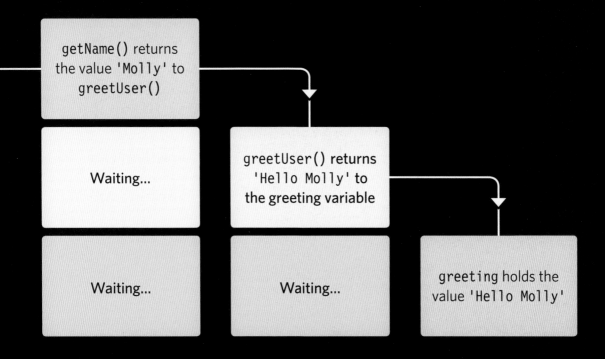

getName() returns the value 'Molly' to greetUser()

Waiting...

Waiting...

greetUser() returns 'Hello Molly' to the greeting variable

Waiting...

greeting holds the value 'Hello Molly'

So, **getName()** is stacked on top of the **greetUser()** function. You can see the stack starting to build up. When **getName()** has done its job, a value is returned back to the **greetUser()** function.

Since **getName()** has done its job, it is removed from the stack. In turn, the **greetUser()** function can now finish its job and return a value to the **greeting** variable.

The **greetUser()** function has finished its work and it is removed from the stack and the value is finally assigned to the **greeting** variable.

EXECUTION CONTEXT & HOISTING

Each time a script enters a new execution context, there are two phases of activity:

1: PREPARE

- The new scope is created
- Variables, functions, and arguments are created

2: EXECUTE

- Now it can assign values to variables
- Reference functions and run their code
- Execute statements

Understanding that these two phases happen helps with understanding a concept called **hoisting**. You may have seen that you *can*:

- Call functions *before* they have been declared (if they were created using function declarations – not function expressions, see p96)
- Assign a value to a variable that has not yet been declared

This is because any variables and functions within each execution context are created before they are executed.

The preparation phase is often described as taking all of the variables and functions and hoisting them to the top of the execution context. Or you can think of them as having been *prepared*.

Each execution context also creates its own **variables object**. This object contains details of all of the `variables`, functions, and parameters for that execution context.

You may expect the following to fail, because `greetUser()` is called before it has been defined:

```
var greeting = greetUser();
function greetUser() {
  // Create greeting
}
```

It works because the function and first statement are in the same execution context, so it is treated like this:

```
function greetUser() {
  // Create greeting
}
var greeting = greetUser();
```

The following would would fail because `greetUser()` is created within the `getName()` function's context:

```
var greeting = greetUser();
function getName() {
  function greetUser() {
    // Create greeting
  }
  // Return name with greeting
}
```

UNDERSTANDING SCOPE

In the interpreter, each execution context has its own `variables` object. It holds the variables, functions, and parameters available within it. Each execution context can also access its parent's `variables` object.

Functions in JavaScript are said to have **lexical scope**. They are linked to the object they were defined *within*. So, for each execution context, the scope is the current execution context's `variables` object, *plus* the `variables` object for each parent execution context.

Imagine that each function is a nesting doll. The children can ask the parents for information in their variables. But the parents cannot get variables from their children. Each child will get the same answer from the same parent.

```
var greeting = (function() {
  var d = new Date();
  var time = d.getHours();
  var greeting = greetUser();

  function greetUser() {
    if (time < 12) {
      var msg = 'Good morning ';
    } else {
      var msg = 'Welcome ';
    }
    return = msg + getName();

    function getName() {
      var name = 'Molly';
      return name;
    }

  }

});
alert(greeting);
```

If a variable is not found in the `variables` object for the current execution context, it can look in the `variables` object of the parent execution context. But it is worth knowing that looking further up the stack can affect performance, so ideally you create variables inside the functions that use them.

If you look at the example on the left, the inner functions can access the outer functions and their variables. For example, the `greetUser()` function can access the `time` variable that was declared in the outer `greeting()` function.

Each time a function is called, it gets its own execution context and `variables` object.

Each time an outer function calls an inner function, the inner function can have a new `variables` object. But variables in the outer function remain the same.

Note: you cannot access this `variables` object from your code; it is something the interpreter is creating and using behind the scenes. But understanding what goes on helps you understand scope.

UNDERSTANDING ERRORS

If a JavaScript statement generates an error, then it throws an **exception**. At that point, the interpreter stops and looks for exception-handling code.

If you are anticipating that something in your code may cause an error, you can use a set of statements to **handle** the error (you meet them on p480). This is important because if the error is not handled, the script will just stop processing and the user will not know why. So exception-handling code should inform users when there is a problem.

Whenever the interpreter comes across an error, it will look for error-handling code. In the diagram below, the code has the same structure as the code you saw in the diagrams at the start of the chapter. The statement at step 1 uses the function in step 2, which in turn uses the function in step 3. Imagine that there has been an error at step 3.

```
   function greetUser() {
2  // Interpreter looks here
   }

   function getName() {
   // Imagine this had an error
3  // It was caused by greetUser()
   }

1  var greeting = greetUser();
4  alert(greeting);
```

When an exception is thrown, the interpreter stops and checks the current execution context for exception-handling code. So if the error occurs in the getName() function (3), the interpreter starts to look for error handling code in that function.

If an error happens in a function and the function does not have an exception handler, the interpreter goes to the line of code that called the function. In this case, the getName() function was called by greetUser(), so the interpreter looks for exception-handling code in the greetUser() function (2). If none is found, it continues to the next level, checking to see if there is code to handle the error in that execution context. It can continue until it reaches the global context, where it would have to it terminate the script, and create an Error object.

So it is going through the stack looking for error-handling code until it gets to the global context. If there is still no error handler, the script stops running and the Error object is created.

ERROR OBJECTS

Error objects can help you find where your mistakes are and browsers have tools to help you read them.

When an **Error** object is created, it will contain the following properties:

PROPERTY	DESCRIPTION
name	Type of execution
message	Description
fileNumber	Name of the JavaScript file
lineNumber	Line number of error

When there is an error, you can see all of this information in the JavaScript console / Error console of the browser.

You will learn more about the console on p464, but you can see an example of the console in Chrome in the screen shot below.

There are seven types of built-in error objects in JavaScript. You'll see them on the next two pages:

OBJECT	DESCRIPTION
Error	Generic error – the other errors are all based upon this error
SyntaxError	Syntax has not been followed
ReferenceError	Tried to reference a variable that is not declared/within scope
TypeError	An unexpected data type that cannot be coerced
RangeError	Numbers not in acceptable range
URIError	encodeURI(), decodeURI(), and similar methods used incorrectly
EvalError	eval() function used incorrectly

Q Elements Network Sources Timeline Profiles Resources Audits Console ⊘1 ⟩≡ ⚙ ▢ ×

⊘ ▼ <top frame> ▼

⊗ Uncaught SyntaxError: Unexpected token ILLEGAL   errors.js:4

>   **1**   **2**

1. In the red on the left, you can see this is a **SyntaxError**. An unexpected character was found.

2. On the right, you can see that the error happened in a file called **errors.js** on line 4.

ERROR OBJECTS CONTINUED

Please note that these error messages are from the Chrome browser. Other browsers' error messages may vary.

SyntaxError

SYNTAX IS NOT CORRECT
This is caused by incorrect use of the rules of the language. It is often the result of a simple typo.

MISMATCHING OR UNCLOSED QUOTES
```
document.write("Howdy ' );
```
> SyntaxError: Unexpected EOF

MISSING CLOSING BRACKET
```
document.getElementById('page'
```
> SyntaxError: Expected token ')'

MISSING COMMA IN ARRAY
Would be same for missing] at the end
```
var list = ['Item 1', 'Item 2' 'Item 3'];
```
> SyntaxError: Expected token ']'

MALFORMED PROPERTY NAME
It has a space but is not surrounded by quote marks
```
user = {first name: "Ben", lastName: "Lee"};
```
> SyntaxError: Expected an identifier but found 'name' instead

ReferenceError

VARIABLE DOES NOT EXIST
This is caused by a variable that is not declared or is out of scope.

VARIABLE IS UNDECLARED
```
var width = 12;
var area = width * height;
```
> ReferenceError: Can't find variable: height

NAMED FUNCTION IS UNDEFINED
```
document.write( randomFunction() );
```
> ReferenceError: Can't find variable: randomFunction

EvalError

INCORRECT USE OF eval() FUNCTION
The eval() function evaluates text through the interpreter and runs it as code (it is not discussed in this book). It is rare that you would see this type of error, as browsers often throw other errors when they are supposed to throw an EvalError.

URIError

INCORRECT USE OF URI FUNCTIONS
If these characters are not escaped in URIs, they will cause an error: / ? & # : ;

CHARACTERS ARE NOT ESCAPED
```
decodeURI('http://bbc.com/news.php ? a=1');
```
> URIError: URI error

These two pages show JavaScript's seven different types of error objects and some common examples of the kinds of errors you are likely to see. As you can tell, the errors shown by the browsers can be rather cryptic.

TypeError
VALUE IS UNEXPECTED DATA TYPE
This is often caused by trying to use an object or method that does not exist.

INCORRECT CASE FOR document OBJECT
```
Document.write('Oops!');
```
```
TypeError: 'undefined' is not a function
(evaluating 'Document.write('Oops!')')
```

INCORRECT CASE FOR write() METHOD
```
document.Write('Oops!');
```
```
TypeError: 'undefined' is not a function
(evaluating 'document.Write('Oops!')')
```

METHOD DOES NOT EXIST
```
var box = {};       // Create empty object
box.getArea();      // Try to access getArea()
```
```
TypeError: 'undefined' is not a function
(evaluating 'box.getArea()')
```

DOM NODE DOES NOT EXIST
```
var el = document.getElementById('z');
el.innerHTML = 'Mango';
```
```
TypeError: 'null' is not an object
(evaluating 'el.innerHTML = 'Mango'')
```

Error
GENERIC ERROR OBJECT
The generic Error object is the template (or prototype) from which all other error objects are created.

RangeError
NUMBER OUTSIDE OF RANGE
If you call a function using numbers outside of its accepted range.

CANNOT CREATE ARRAY WITH -1 ITEMS
```
var anArray = new Array(-1);
```
```
RangeError: Array size is not a small
enough positive integer
```

NUMBER OF DIGITS AFTER DECIMAL IN toFixed() CAN ONLY BE 0-20
```
var price = 9.99;
price.toFixed(21);
```
```
RangeError: toFixed() argument must be
between 0 and 20
```

NUMBER OF DIGITS IN toPrecision() CAN ONLY BE 1-21
```
num = 2.3456;
num.toPrecision(22);
```
```
RangeError: toPrecision() argument must
be between 1 and 21
```

NaN
NOT AN ERROR
Note: If you perform a mathematical operation using a value that is not a number, you end up with the value of NaN, not a type error.

NOT A NUMBER
```
var total = 3 * 'Ivy';
```

HOW TO DEAL WITH ERRORS

Now that you know what an error is and how the browser treats them, there are two things you can do with the errors.

1: DEBUG THE SCRIPT TO FIX ERRORS

If you come across an error while writing a script (or when someone reports a bug), you will need to debug the code, track down the source of the error, and fix it.

You will find that the developer tools available in every major modern browser will help you with this task. In this chapter, you will learn about the developer tools in Chrome and Firefox. (The tools in Chrome are identical to those in Opera.)

IE and Safari also have their own tools (but there is not space to cover them all).

2: HANDLE ERRORS GRACEFULLY

You can handle errors gracefully using try, catch, throw, and finally statements.

Sometimes, an error *may* occur in the script for a reason beyond your control. For example, you might request data from a third party, and their server may not respond. In such cases, it is particularly important to write error-handling code.

In the latter part of the chapter, you will learn how to gracefully check whether something will work, and offer an alternative option if it fails.

A DEBUGGING WORKFLOW

Debugging is about deduction: eliminating potential causes of an error. Here is a workflow for techniques you will meet over the next 20 pages. Try to narrow down where the problem might be, then look for clues.

WHERE IS THE PROBLEM?

First, should try to can narrow down the area where the problem seems to be. In a long script, this is especially important.

1. Look at the error message, it tells you:
- The relevant script that caused the problem.
- The line number where it became a problem for the interpreter. (As you will see, the *cause* of the error may be earlier in a script; but this is the point at which the script could not continue.)
- The type of error (although the underlying cause of the error may be different).

2. Check how far the script is running.
Use tools to write messages to the console to tell how far your script has executed.

3. Use breakpoints where things are going wrong. They let you pause execution and inspect the values that are stored in variables.

If you are stuck on an error, many programmers suggest that you try to describe the situation (talking out loud) to another programmer. Explain what should be happening and where the error appears to be happening. This seems to be an effective way of finding errors in all programming languages. (If nobody else is available, try describing it to yourself.)

WHAT EXACTLY IS THE PROBLEM?

Once you think that you might know the rough area in which your problem is located, you can then try to find the actual line of code that is causing the error.

1. When you have set breakpoints, you can see if the variables around them have the values you would expect them to. If not, look earlier in the script.

2. Break down / break out parts of the code to test smaller pieces of the functionality.
- Write values of variables into the console.
- Call functions from the console to check if they are returning what you would expect them to.
- Check if objects exist and have the methods / properties that you think they do.

3. Check the number of parameters for a function, or the number of items in an array.

And be prepared to repeat the whole process if the above solved one error just to uncover another...

If the problem is hard to find, it is easy to lose track of what you *have* and *have not* tested. Therefore, when you start debugging, keep notes of what you have tested and what the result was. No matter how stressful the circumstances are, if you can, stay calm and methodical, the problem will feel less overwhelming and you will solve it faster.

BROWSER DEV TOOLS & JAVASCRIPT CONSOLE

The JavaScript console will tell you when there is a problem with a script, where to look for the problem, and what kind of issue it seems to be.

These two pages show instructions for opening the console in all of the main browsers (but the rest of this chapter will focus on Chrome and Firefox).

Browser manufacturers occasionally change how to access these tools. If they are not where stated, search the browser help files for "console."

CHROME / OPERA

On a PC, press the F12 key or:
1. Go to the options menu (or three line menu icon)
2. Select **Tools** or **More tools**.
3. Select **JavaScript Console** or **Developer Tools**
On a Mac press Alt + Cmd + J. Or:
4. Go to the **View** menu.
5. Select **Developer**.
6. Open the **JavaScript Console** or **Developer Tools** option and select **Console**.

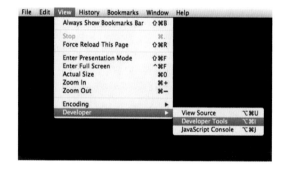

INTERNET EXPLORER

Press the F12 key or:
1. Go to the settings menu in the top-right.
2. Select **developer tools**.

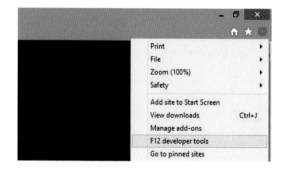

The JavaScript console is just one of several developer tools that are found in all modern browsers.

When you are debugging errors, it can help if you look at the error in more than one browser as they can show you different error messages.

If you open the `errors.html` file from the sample code in your browser, and then open the console, you will see an error is displayed.

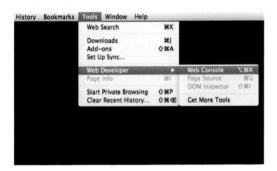

FIREFOX

On a PC, press Ctrl + Shift + K or:
1. Go to the **Firefox** menu.
2. Select **Web Developer**.
3. Open the **Web Console**.
On a Mac press Alt + Cmd + K. Or:
1. Go to the **Tools** menu.
2. Select **Web Developer**.
3. Open the **Web Console**.

SAFARI

Press Alt + Cmd + C or:
1. Go to the **Develop** menu.
2. Select **Show Error Console**.
If the **Develop** menu is not shown:
1. Go to the **Safari** menu.
2. Select **Preferences**.
3. Select **Advanced**.
4. Check the box that says **"Show Develop menu in menu bar."**

HOW TO LOOK AT ERRORS IN CHROME

The console will show you when there is an error in your JavaScript. It also displays the line where it became a problem for the interpreter.

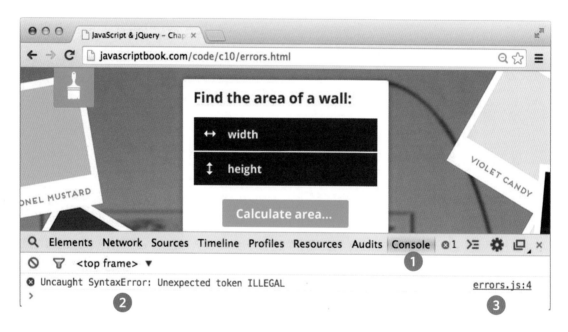

1. The **Console** option is selected.
2. The type of error and the error message are shown in red.
3. The file name and the line number are shown on the right-hand side of the console.

Note that the line number does not always indicate where the error is. Rather, it is where the interpreter noticed there was a problem with the code.

If the error stops JavaScript from executing, the console will show only one error – there may be more to troubleshoot once this error is fixed.

HOW TO LOOK AT ERRORS
IN FIREFOX

1. The **Console** option is selected.
2. Only the **JavaScript** and **Logging** options need to be turned on. The **Net**, **CSS**, and **Security** options show other information.

3. The type of error and the error message are shown on the left.
4. On the right-hand side of the console, you can see the name of the JavaScript file and the line number of the error.

Note that when debugging any JavaScript code that has been minified, it will be easier to understand if you expand it first.

TYPING IN THE CONSOLE IN CHROME

You can also just type code into the console and it will show you a result.

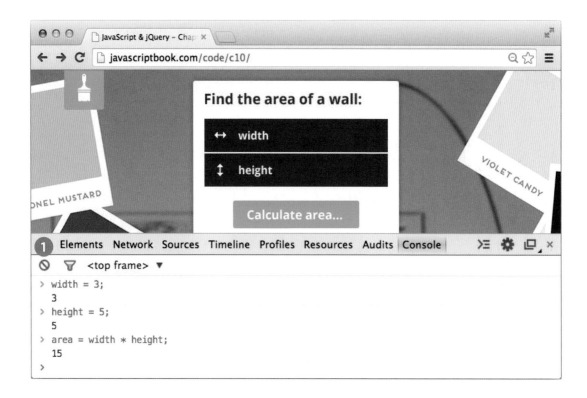

Above, you can see an example of JavaScript being written straight into the console. This is a quick and handy way to test your code.

Each time you write a line, the interpreter may respond. Here, it is writing out the value of each variable that has been created.

Any variable that you create in the console will be remembered until you clear the console.
1. In Chrome, the **no-entry sign** is used to clear the console.

TYPING IN THE CONSOLE IN FIREFOX

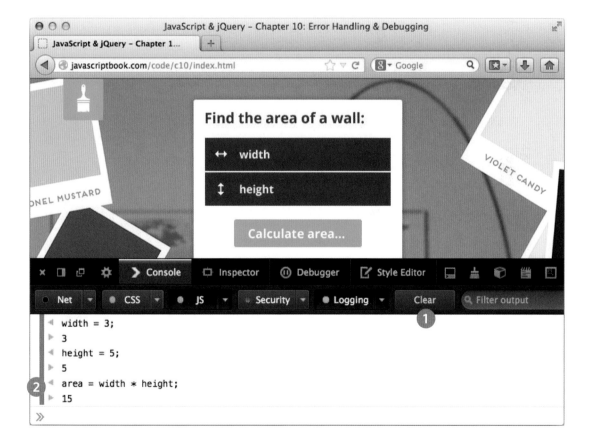

1. In Firefox, the **_Clear_** button will clear the contents of the console. This tells the interpreter that it no longer needs to remember the variables you have created.

2. The left and right arrows show which lines _you_ have written, and which are from the interpreter.

WRITING FROM THE SCRIPT TO THE CONSOLE

Browsers that have a console have a `console` object, which has several methods that your script can use to display data in the console. The object is documented in the Console API.

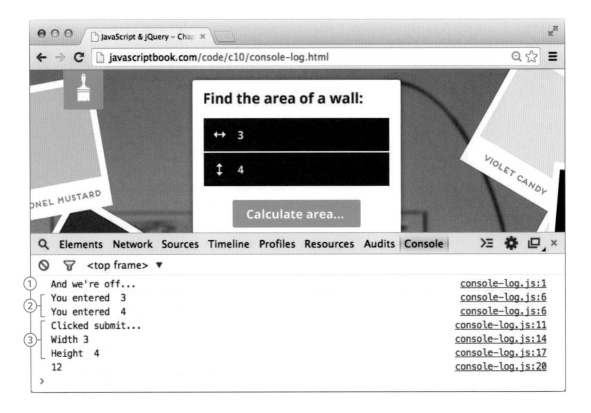

1. The `console.log()` method can write data from a script to the console. If you open `console-log.html`, you will see that a note is written to the console when the page loads.

2. Such notes can tell you how far a script has run and what values it has received. In this example, the `blur` event causes the value entered into a text input to be logged in the console.

3. Writing out variables lets you see what values the interpreter holds for them. In this example, the console will write out the values of each variable when the form is submitted.

LOGGING DATA TO THE CONSOLE

This example shows several uses of the `console.log()` method.

1. The first line is used to indicate the script is running.

2. Next an event handler waits for the user leaving a text input, and logs the value that they entered into that form field.

When the user submits the form, four values are displayed:

3. That the user clicked submit
4. The value in the width input
5. The value in the height input
6. The value of the **area** variable

They help check that you are getting the values you expect.

The `console.log()` method can write several values to the console at the same time, each separated by a comma, as shown when displaying the height (5).

You should always remove this kind of error handling code from your script before you use it on a live site.

```javascript
① console.log('And we\'re off...');              // Indicates script is running
   var $form, width, height, area;
   $form = $('#calculator');

② $('form input[type="text"]').on('blur', function() { // When input loses focus
     console.log('You entered ', this.value );     // Write value to console
   });

   $('#calculator').on('submit', function(e) {     // When the user clicks submit
     e.preventDefault();                           // Prevent the form submitting
③    console.log('Clicked submit...');             // Indicate button was clicked

     width = $('#width').val();
④    console.log('Width ' + width);                // Write width to console

     height = $('#height').val();
⑤    console.log('Height ', height);               // Write height to console

     area = width * height;
⑥    console.log(area);                            // Write area to console

     $form.append('<p>' + area + '</p>')
   });
```

MORE CONSOLE METHODS

To differentiate between the types of messages you write to the console, you can use three different methods. They use various icons and/or colors to distinguish them.

1. `console.info()` can be used for general information
2. `console.warn()` can be used for warnings
3. `console.error()` can be used to hold errors

This technique is particularly helpful to show the nature of the information that you are writing to the screen. (In Firefox, make sure you have the logging option selected.)

`c10/js/console-methods.js`

```javascript
① console.info('And we\'re off...');                      // Info: script running

   var $form, width, height, area;
   $form = $('#calculator');

  ┌$('form input[type="text"]').on('blur', function() {   // On blur event
② │  console.warn('You entered ', this.value);            // Warn: what was entered
  └});

   $('#calculator').on('submit', function(e) {            // When form is submitted
     e.preventDefault();

     width = $('#width').val();
     height = $('#height').val();

     area = width * height;
③    console.error(area);                                 // Error: show area

     $form.append('<p class="result">' + area + '</p>');
   });
```

```
Q   Elements  Network  Sources  Timeline  Profiles  Resources  Audits  »   ⊗1 ⚠2 ⟫≡ ⚙ ⬛ ×
⃠  ▽   <top frame> ▼
ⓘ And we're off...                                                    console-methods.js:1
⚠ You entered  12                                                    console-methods.js:7
⚠ You entered  14                                                    console-methods.js:7
⊗ ▶ 168                                                              console-methods.js:17
>
```

GROUPING MESSAGES

1. If you want to write a set of related data to the console, you can use the `console.group()` method to group the messages together. You can then expand and contract the results.

It has one parameter; the name that you want to use for the group of messages. You can then expand and collapse the contents by clicking next to the group's name as shown below.

2. When you have finished writing out the results for the group, to indicate the end of the group the `console.groupEnd()` method is used.

`c10/js/console-group.js`

```
var $form = $('#calculator');

$form.on('submit', function(e) {          // Runs when submit is pressed
  e.preventDefault();
  console.log('Clicked submit...');       // Show the button was clicked

  var width, height, area;
  width = $('#width').val();
  height = $('#height').val();
  area = width * height;

  console.group('Area calculations');     // Start group
    console.info('Width ', width);        // Write out the width
    console.info('Height ', height);      // Write out the height
    console.log(area);                    // Write out the area
  console.groupEnd();                     // End group

  $form.append('<p>' + area + '</p>');
});
```

① (next to `console.group('Area calculations');`)
② (next to `console.groupEnd();`)

```
Q   Elements  Network  Sources  Timeline  Profiles  Resources  Audits  | Console |      >≡  ⚙  ⧉ ⌄  ×
⊘   ▽    <top frame> ▼
  Clicked submit...                                                        console-group.js:5
▼ Area calculations                                                       console-group.js:12
  ❶ Width  12                                                             console-group.js:13
  ❶ Height  14                                                            console-group.js:14
    168                                                                   console-group.js:15
  >
```

WRITING TABULAR DATA

In browsers that support it, the `console.table()` method lets you output a table showing:
- objects
- arrays that contain other objects or arrays

The example below shows data from the `contacts` object. It displays the city, telephone number, and country. It is particularly helpful when the data is coming from a third party.

The screen shot below shows the result in Chrome (it looks the same in Opera). Safari will show expanding panels. At the time of writing Firefox and IE did not support this method.

`c10/js/console-table.js`

```javascript
var contacts = {                          // Store contact info in an object literal
  "London": {
    "Tel": "+44 (0)207 946 0128",
    "Country": "UK"},
  "Sydney": {
    "Tel": "+61 (0)2 7010 1212",
    "Country": "Australia"},
  "New York": {
     "Tel": "+1 (0)1 555 2104",
     "Country": "USA"}
}

console.table(contacts);                      // Write data to console

var city, contactDetails;                     // Declare variables for page
contactDetails = '';                          // Hold details written to page

$.each(contacts, function(city, contacts) {   // Loop through data to
  contactDetails += city + ': ' + contacts.Tel + '<br />';
});
$('h2').after('<p>' + contactDetails + '</p>'); // Add data to the page
```

(1) next to `console.table(contacts);`

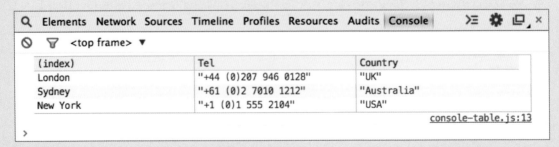

(index)	Tel	Country
London	"+44 (0)207 946 0128"	"UK"
Sydney	"+61 (0)2 7010 1212"	"Australia"
New York	"+1 (0)1 555 2104"	"USA"

console-table.js:13

WRITING ON A CONDITION

Using the `console.assert()` method, you can test if a condition is met, and write to the console only if the expression evaluates to `false`.

1. Below, when users leave an input, the code checks to see if they entered a value that is 10 or higher. If not, it will write a message to the screen.

2. The second check looks to see if the calculated area is a numeric value. If not, then the user must have entered a value that was not a number.

JAVASCRIPT   c10/js/console-assert.js

```javascript
var $form, width, height, area;
$form = $('#calculator');

$('form input[type="text"]').on('blur', function() {
  // The message only shows if user has entered number less than 10
  console.assert(this.value > 10, 'User entered less than 10');
});

$('#calculator').on('submit', function(e) {
  e.preventDefault();
  console.log('Clicked submit...');

  width = $('#width').val();
  height = $('#height').val();
  area = width * height;
  // The message only shows if user has not entered a number
  console.assert($.isNumeric(area), 'User entered non-numeric value');

  $form.append('<p>' + area + '</p>');
});
```

(1) marks the first `console.assert` line; (2) marks the second `console.assert` line.

| Q | Elements | Network | Sources | Timeline | Profiles | Resources | Audits | Console | ⊗2 | ⟩≡ | ⚙ | ⊡ | × |

🚫 ▽ <top frame> ▼

2 ▼ Assertion failed: User entered less than 10   console-assert.js:6
    (anonymous function)   console-assert.js:6
    x.event.dispatch   jquery.js:5095
    v.handle   jquery.js:4766
  Clicked submit...   console-assert.js:11

>

BREAKPOINTS

You can pause the execution of a script on any line using breakpoints. Then you can check the values stored in variables at that point in time.

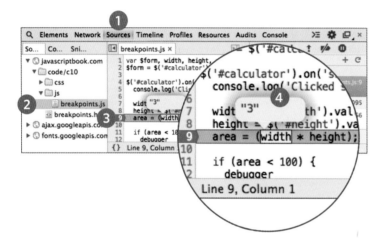

CHROME

1. Select the **Sources** option.
2. Select the script you are working with from the left-hand pane. The code will appear to the right.
3. Find the line number you want to stop on and click on it.
4. When you run the script, it will stop on this line. You can now hover over any variable to see its value at that time in the script's execution.

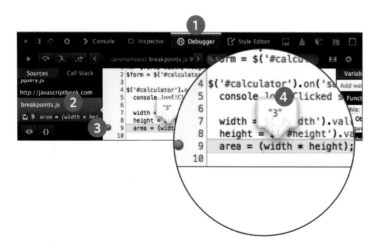

FIREFOX

1. Select the **Debugger** option.
2. Select the script you are working with from the left-hand pane. The code will appear to the right.
3. Find the line number you want to stop on and click on it.
4. When you run the script, it will stop on this line. You can now hover over any variable to see its value at that time in the script's execution.

STEPPING THROUGH CODE

If you set multiple breakpoints, you can step through them one-by-one to see where values change and a problem might occur.

When you have set breakpoints, you will see that the debugger lets you step through the code line by line and see the values of variables as your script progresses.

When you are doing this, if the debugger comes across a function, it will move onto the next line after the function. (It does not move to where the function is defined.) This behavior is sometimes called **stepping over** a function.

If you want to, it is possible to tell the debugger to **step into** a function to see what is happening inside the function.

Chrome and Firefox both have very similar tools for letting you step through the breakpoints.

1. A pause sign shows until the interpreter comes across a breakpoint. When the interpreter stops on a breakpoint, a play-style button is then shown. This lets you tell the interpreter to resume running the code.

2. Go to the next line of code and **step through** the lines one-by-one (rather than running them as fast as possible).

3. **Step into** a function call. The debugger will move to the first line in that function.

4. **Step out** of a function that you stepped into. The remainder of the function will be executed as the debugger moves to its parent function.

CONDITIONAL BREAKPOINTS

You can indicate that a breakpoint should be triggered only if a condition that you specify is met. The condition can use existing variables.

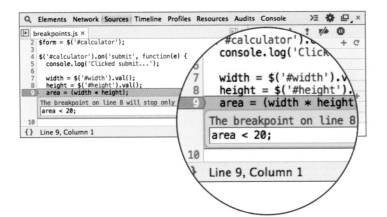

CHROME

1. Right-click on a line number.
2. Select **Add Conditional Breakpoint...**
3. Enter a condition into the popup box.
4. When you run the script, it will only stop on this line if the condition is true (e.g., if area is less than 20).

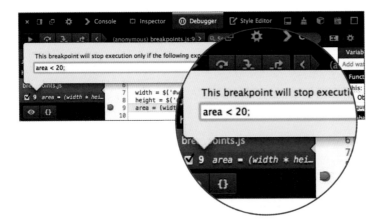

FIREFOX

1. Right-click on a line of code.
2. Select **Add conditional breakpoint**.
3. Enter a condition into the popup box.
4. When you run the script, it will stop on this line only if the condition is true (e.g., if area is less than 20).

DEBUGGER KEYWORD

You can create a breakpoint in your code using just the **debugger** keyword. When the developer tools are open, this will automatically create a breakpoint.

You can also place the **debugger** keyword within a conditional statement so that it only triggers the breakpoint if the condition is met. This is demonstrated in the code below.

It is particularly important to remember to remove these statements before your code goes live as this could stop the page running if a user has developer tools open.

JAVASCRIPT

c10/js/breakpoints.js

```javascript
var $form, width, height, area;
$form = $('#calculator');

$('#calculator').on('submit', function(e) {
  e.preventDefault();
  console.log('Clicked submit...');

  width = $('#width').val();
  height = $('#height').val();
  area = (width * height);

  if (area < 100) {
    debugger;              // A breakpoint is set if the developer tools are open
  }

  $form.append('<p>' + area + '</p>');
});
```

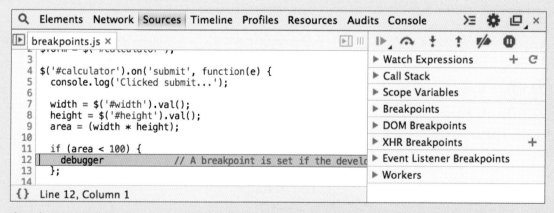

If you have a development server, your debugging code can be placed in conditional statements that check whether it is running on a specific server (and the debugging code only runs if it is on the specified server).

HANDLING EXCEPTIONS

If you know your code might fail, use `try`, `catch`, and `finally`.
Each one is given its own code block.

```
try {
  // Try to execute this code
} catch (exception) {
  // If there is an exception, run this code
} finally {
  // This always gets executed
}
```

TRY

First, you specify the code that you think might throw an exception within the `try` block.

If an exception occurs in this section of code, control is automatically passed to the corresponding `catch` block.

The `try` clause must be used in this type of error handling code, and it should always have either a `catch`, `finally`, or both.

If you use a `continue`, `break`, or `return` keyword inside a `try`, it will go to the `finally` option.

CATCH

If the `try` code block throws an exception, `catch` steps in with an alternative set of code.

It has one parameter: the error object. Although it is optional, you are not *handling* the error if you do not catch an error.

The ability to catch an error can be very helpful if there is an issue on a live website.

It lets you tell users that something has gone wrong (rather than not informing them why the site stopped working).

FINALLY

The contents of the `finally` code block will run either way – whether the `try` block succeeded or failed.

It even runs if a `return` keyword is used in the `try` or `catch` block. It is sometimes used to clean up after the previous two clauses.

These methods are similar to the `.done()`, `.fail()`, and `.always()` methods in jQuery.

You can nest checks inside each other (place another `try` inside a `catch`), but be aware that it can affect performance of a script.

TRY, CATCH, FINALLY

This example displays JSON data to the user. But, imagine that the data is coming from a third party and there have been occasional problems with it that could cause the page to fail.

This script checks if the JSON can be parsed using a try block before trying to display the information to the users.

If the try statement throws an error (because the data cannot be parsed), the code in the catch code block will be run, and the error will not prevent the rest of the script from being executed.

The catch statement creates a message using the name and message properties of the Error object.

The error will be logged to the console, and a friendly message will be shown to the users of the site. You could also send the error message to the server using Ajax so that it could be recorded. Either way, the finally statement adds a link that allows users to refresh the data they are seeing.

JAVASCRIPT   c10/js/try-catch-finally.js

```javascript
var feed = document.getElementById('feed');
response = ' {"deals": [{"title": "Farrow and Ball",... ' // JSON data

if (response) {
    try {
        var dealData = JSON.parse(response);             // Try to parse JSON
        showContent(dealData);                           // Show JSON data
    } catch(e) {
        var errorMessage = e.name + ' ' + e.message;     // Create error msg
        console.log(errorMessage);                       // Show devs msg
        feed.innerHTML = '<em>Sorry, could not load deals'</em>; // Users msg
    } finally {
        var link = document.createElement('a');          // Add refresh link
        link.innerHTML = ' <a href="try-catch-finally.html">reload</a>';
        feed.appendChild(link);
    }
}

// Function showContent() to display deals goes here
```

| Q | Elements | Network | Sources | Timeline | Profiles | Resources | Audits | Console | | >≡ | ⚙ | ▢ | × |

🚫 🔽 <top frame> ▼

SyntaxError Unexpected end of input   try-catch-finally.js:14

>

THROWING ERRORS

If you know something might cause a problem for your script, you can generate your own errors before the interpreter creates them.

To create your own error, you use the following line:

```
throw new Error('message');
```

This creates a new **Error** object (using the default **Error** object). The parameter is the message you want associated with the error. This message should be as descriptive as possible.

Being able to throw an error at the time you know there might be a problem can be better than letting that data cause errors further into the script.

If you are working with data from a third party, you may come across problems such as:

- JSON that contains a formatting error
- Numeric data that occasionally has a non-numeric value
- An error from a remote server
- A set of information with one missing value

Bad data might not cause an error in the script straight away, but it could cause a problem later on. In such cases, it helps to report the problem straight away. It can be much harder to find the source of the problem if the data causes an error in a different part of the script.

For example, if a user enters a string when you expect a number, it might not throw an error immediately.

However, if you know that the application will try to use that value in a mathematical operation at some point in the future, you know that it will cause a problem later on.

If you add a number to a string, it will result in a string. If you use a string in any other mathematical calculations, the result would be **NaN**. In itself, **NaN** is not an error; it is a value that is not a number.

Therefore, if you throw an error when the user enters a value you cannot use, it prevents issues at some other point in the code. You can create an error that explains the problem, before the user gets further into the script.

THROW ERROR FOR NaN

If you try to use a string in a mathematical operation (other than in addition), you do not get an error, you get a special value called NaN (not a number).

In this example, a **try** block attempts to calculate the area of a rectangle. If it is given numbers to work with, the code will run. If it does not get numbers, a custom error is thrown and the **catch** block displays the error.

By checking that the results are numeric, the script can fail at a specific point and you can provide a detailed error about what caused the problem (rather than letting it cause a problem later in the script).

c10/js/throw.js

```javascript
var width = 12;                                    // width variable
var height = 'test';                               // height variable

function calculateArea(width, height) {
  try {
    var area = width * height;                     // Try to calculate area
    if (!isNaN(area)) {                            // If it is a number
      return area;                                 // Return the area
    } else {                                       // Otherwise throw an error
      throw new Error('calculateArea() received invalid number');
    }
  } catch(e) {                                     // If there was an error
    console.log(e.name + ' ' + e.message);         // Show error in console
    return 'We were unable to calculate the area.'; // Show users a message
  }
}

// TRY TO SHOW THE AREA ON THE PAGE
document.getElementById('area').innerHTML = calculateArea(width, height);
```

There are two different errors shown: one in the browser window for the users and another in the console for the developers.

This not only catches an error that would not have been thrown otherwise, but it also provides a more descriptive explanation of what caused the error.

Ideally, form validation, which you learn about in Chapter 13, would solve this kind of issue. It is more likely to occur when data comes from a third party.

DEBUGGING TIPS

Here are a selection of practical tips that you can try to use when debugging your scripts.

ANOTHER BROWSER

Some problems are browser-specific. Try the code in another browser to see which ones are causing a problem.

ADD NUMBERS

Write numbers to the console so you can see which the items get logged. It shows how far your code runs before errors stop it.

STRIP IT BACK

Remove parts of code, and strip it down to the minimum you need. You can do this either by removing the code altogether, or by just commenting it out using multi-line comments:

```
/* Anything between these
characters is a comment */
```

EXPLAINING THE CODE

Programmers often report finding a solution to a problem while explaining the code to someone else.

SEARCH

Stack Overflow is a Q+A site for programmers.

Or use a traditional search engine such as Google, Bing, or DuckDuckGo.

CODE PLAYGROUNDS

If you want to ask about problematic code on a forum, in addition to pasting the code into a post, you could add it to a code playground site (such as JSBin.com, JSFiddle.com, or Dabblet.com) and then post a link to it from the forum.

(Other popular playgrounds include CSSDeck.com and CodePen.com – but these sites place more emphasis on show and tell.)

VALIDATION TOOLS

There are a number of online validation tools that can help you try to find errors in your code:

JAVASCRIPT
```
http://www.jslint.com
http://www.jshint.com
```

JSON
```
http://www.jsonlint.com
```

JQUERY
There is a jQuery debugger plugin available for Chrome which can be found in the Chrome web store.

COMMON ERRORS

Here is a list of common errors you might find with your scripts.

GO BACK TO BASICS

JavaScript is case sensitive so check your capitalization.

If you did not use `var` to declare the variable, it will be a global variable, and its value could be overwritten elsewhere (either in your script or by another script that is included in the page).

If you cannot access a variable's value, check if it is out of scope, e.g., declared within a function that you are not within.

Do not use reserved words or dashes in variable names.

Check that your single / double quotes match properly.

Check that you have escaped quotes in variable values.

Check in the HTML that values of your `id` attributes are unique.

MISSED / EXTRA CHARACTERS

Every statement should end in a semicolon.

Check that there are no missing closing braces } or parentheses).

Check that there are no commas inside a `,}` or `,)` by accident.

Always use parentheses to surround a condition that you are testing.

Check the script is not missing a parameter when calling a function.

`undefined` is not the same as `null`: `null` is for objects, `undefined` is for properties, methods, or variables.

Check that your script has loaded (especially CDN files).

Look for conflicts between different script files.

DATA TYPE ISSUES

Using = rather than == will assign a value to a variable, not check that the values match.

If you are checking whether values match, try to use strict comparison to check datatypes at the same time. (Use === rather than ==.)

Inside a `switch` statement, the values are not loosely typed (so their type will not be coerced).

Once there is a match in a switch statement, all expressions will be executed until the next `break` or `return` statement is executed.

The `replace()` method only replaces the first match. If you want to replace all occurrences, use the global flag.

If you are using the `parseInt()` method, you might need to pass a radix (the number of unique digits including zero used to represent the number).

SUMMARY
ERROR HANDLING & DEBUGGING

▶ If you understand execution contexts (which have two stages) and stacks, you are more likely to find the error in your code.

▶ Debugging is the process of finding errors. It involves a process of deduction.

▶ The console helps narrow down the area in which the error is located, so you can try to find the exact error.

▶ JavaScript has 7 different types of errors. Each creates its own error object, which can tell you its line number and gives a description of the error.

▶ If you know that you may get an error, you can handle it gracefully using the `try`, `catch`, `finally` statements. Use them to give your users helpful feedback.

11

CONTENT PANELS

Content panels allow you to showcase extra information within a limited space. In this chapter, you will see several examples of content panels that also give you practical insight into creating your own scripts using jQuery.

In this chapter, you will see how to create many types of content panels: accordions, tabbed panels, modal windows (also known as a lightboxes), a photo viewer, and a responsive slider. Each example of a content panel also demonstrates how to apply the code you have learned throughout the book so far in a practical setting.

Throughout the chapter, reference will be made to more complex jQuery plugins that extend the functionality of the examples shown here. But the code samples in this chapter also show how it is possible to achieve techniques you will have seen on popular websites in relatively few lines of code (without needing to rely on plugins written by other people).

ACCORDION

An accordion features titles which, when clicked, expand to show a larger panel of content.

TABBED PANEL

Tabs automatically show one panel, but when you click on another tab, the panel is changed.

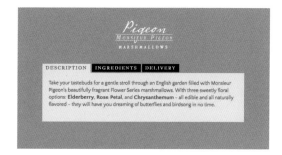

MODAL WINDOW

When you click on a link for a modal window (or "lightbox"), a hidden panel will be displayed.

PHOTO VIEWER

Photo viewers display different images within the same space when the user clicks on the thumbnails.

RESPONSIVE SLIDER

The slider allows you to show panels of content that slide into view as the user navigates between them.

CREATING A JQUERY PLUGIN

The final example revisits the accordion (the first example) and turns it into a jQuery plugin.

SEPARATION
OF CONCERNS

As you saw in the introduction to this book, it is considered good practice
to separate your content (in HTML markup), presentation (in CSS rules),
and behaviors (in JavaScript).

In general, your code should reflect that:
- HTML is responsible for structuring content
- CSS is responsible for presentation
- JavaScript is responsible for behavior

Enforcing this separation produces code that is
easier to maintain and reuse. While this may already
be a familiar concept to you, it's important to
remember as it is very easy to mix these concerns in
with your JavaScript. As a rule, editing your HTML
templates or stylesheets should not necessitate
editing your scripts and vice versa.

You can also place event listeners and calls to
functions in JavaScript files rather than adding them
to the end of an HTML document.

If you need to change the styles associated with an
element, rather than having styles written in the
JavaScript, you can update the value of the class
attributes for those elements. In turn, they can
trigger new rules from the CSS file that change the
appearance of those elements.

When your scripts access the DOM, you can
uncouple them from the HTML by using class
selectors rather than tag selectors.

ACCESSIBILITY & NO JAVASCRIPT

When writing any script, you should think about those who might be using a web page in different situations than you.

ACCESSIBILITY

Whenever a user can interact with an element:
- If it is a link, use <a>
- If it acts like a button, use a button

Both can gain focus, so users can move between them focusable elements using the Tab key (or other non-mouse solution). And although any element can become focusable by setting its `tabindex` attribute, only <a> elements and some input elements fire a `click` event when users press the Enter key on their keyboard (the ARIA `role="button"` attribute will not simulate this event).

NO JAVASCRIPT

This chapter's accordion menu, tabbed panels, and responsive slider all hide some of their content by default. This content would be inaccessible to visitors that do not have JavaScript enabled if we didn't provide alternative styling. One way to solve this is by adding a `class` attribute whose value is `no-js` to the opening <html> tag. This class is then removed by JavaScript (using the `replace()` method of the String object) if JavaScript is enabled.

The `no-js` class can then be used to provide styles targeted to visitors who do not have JavaScript enabled.

HTML
`c11/no-js.html`

```html
<!DOCTYPE html>
<html class="no-js">
<!-- Head and CSS go here (required for script to work) -->
  <body>
    <div class="js-warning">You must enable JavaScript to buy from us</div>
    <!-- Turn off your JavaScript to see the difference -->
    <script src="js/no-js.js"></script>
  </body>
</html>
```

JAVASCRIPT
`c11/js/no-js.js`

```javascript
var elDocument = document.documentElement;
elDocument.className = elDocument.className.replace(/(^|\s)no-js(\s|$)/, '$1');
```

ACCORDION

When you click on the title of an accordion, its corresponding panel expands to reveal the content.

An accordion is usually created within an unordered list (in a `<ul>` element). Each `<li>` element is a new item in the accordion. The items contain:

- A visible label (in this example, it is a `<button>`)
- A hidden panel holding the content (a `<div>`)

Clicking a label prompts the associated panel to be shown (or to be hidden if it is in view). To just hide or show a panel, you could change the value of the `class` attribute on the associated panel (triggering a new CSS rule to show or hide it). But, in this case, jQuery will be used to animate the panel into view or hide it.

HTML5 introduces `<details>` and `<summary>` elements to create a similar effect, but (at the time of writing) browser support was not widespread. Therefore, a script like this would still be used for browsers that do not support those features.

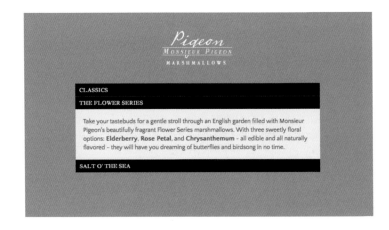

Other tabs scripts include liteAccordion and zAccordion. They are also included in jQuery UI and Bootstrap.

ACCORDION WITH ALL PANELS COLLAPSED

LABEL 1	COLLAPSED
LABEL 2	COLLAPSED
LABEL 3	COLLAPSED

ACCORDION WITH SECOND PANEL EXPANDED

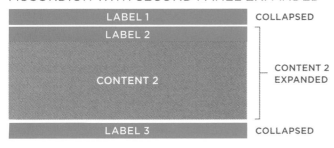

LABEL 1 — COLLAPSED

LABEL 2
CONTENT 2 — CONTENT 2 EXPANDED

LABEL 3 — COLLAPSED

When the page loads, CSS rules are used to hide the panels.

Clicking a label prompts the hidden panel that follows it to animate and reveal its full height. This is done using jQuery.

Clicking on the label again would hide the panel.

ANIMATING CONTENT WITH SHOW, HIDE, AND TOGGLE

jQuery's `.show()`, `.hide()`, and `.toggle()` methods animate the showing and hiding of elements.

jQuery calculates the size of the box, including its content, and any margins and padding. This helps if you do not know what content appears in a box.

(To use CSS animation, you would need to calculate the box's height, margin and padding.)

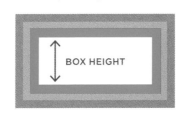

BOX HEIGHT

● MARGIN ● BORDER ● PADDING

`.toggle()` saves you writing conditional code to tell whether the box is already being shown or not. (If a box is shown, it hides it, and if hidden, it will show it.)

The three methods are all shorthand for the `animate()` method. For example, the `show()` method is shorthand for:

```
$('.accordion-panel')
.animate({
    height: 'show',
    paddingTop: 'show',
    paddingBottom: 'show',
    marginTop: 'show',
    marginBottom: 'show'
});
```

CREATING AN ACCORDION

Below you can see a diagram, rather like a flowchart. These diagrams have two purposes. They help you:

i) Follow the code samples; the numbers on the diagram correspond with the steps on the right, and the script on the right-hand page. Together, the diagrams, steps, and comments in the code should help you understand how each example works.

ii) Learn how to plan a script before coding it.

This is not a "formal" diagram style, but it gives you a visual idea of what is going on with the script. The diagrams show how a collection of small, individual instructions achieve a larger goal, and if you follow the arrows you can see how the data flows around the parts of the script.

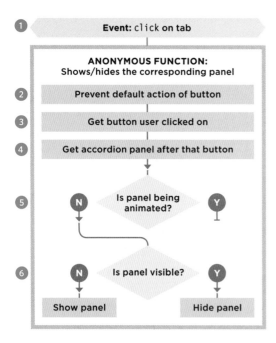

Some programmers use Unified Modeling Language or class diagrams - but they have a steeper learning curve, and these flowcharts are here to help you see how the interpreter moves through the script.

Now let's take a look at how the diagram is translated into code. The steps below correspond to the numbers next to the JavaScript code on the right-hand page and the diagram on the left.

1. A jQuery collection is created to hold elements whose `class` attribute has a value of `accordion`. In the HTML you can see that this corresponds to the unordered list element (there could be several lists on the page, each acting as an accordion). An event listener waits for the user to click on one of the buttons whose `class` attribute has a value of `accordion-control`. This triggers an anonymous function.

2. The `preventDefault()` method prevents browsers treating the the button like a submit button. It can be a good idea to use the `preventDefault()` method early in a function so that anyone looking at your code knows that the form element or link does not do what they might expect it to.

3. Another jQuery selection is made using the `this` keyword, which refers to the element the user clicked upon. Three jQuery methods are applied to that jQuery selection holding the element the user clicked on.

4. `.next('.accordion-panel')` selects the next element with a class of `accordion-panel`.

5. `.not(':animated')` checks that it is not in the middle of being animated. (If the user repeatedly clicks the same label, this stops the `.slideToggle()` method from queuing multiple animations.)

6. `.slideToggle()` will show the panel if it is currently hidden and will hide the panel if it is currently visible.

```html
<ul class="accordion">
  <li>
    <button class="accordion-control">Classics</button>
    <div class="accordion-panel">Panel content goes here...</div>
  </li>
  <li>
    <button class="accordion-control">The Flower Series</button>
    <div class="accordion-panel">Panel content goes here...</div>
  </li>
  <li>
    <button class="accordion-control">Salt O' the Sea</button>
    <div class="accordion-panel">Panel content goes here...</div>
  </li>
</ul>
```

```css
.accordion-panel {
  display: none;}
```

```javascript
① $('.accordion').on('click', '.accordion-control', function(e){ // When clicked
②   e.preventDefault();                      // Prevent default action of button
③   $(this)                                  // Get the element the user clicked on
④     .next('.accordion-panel')              // Select following panel
⑤     .not(':animated')                      // If it is not currently animating
⑥     .slideToggle();                        // Use slide toggle to show or hide it
  });
```

Note how steps 4, 5, and 6 are chained off the same jQuery selection.
You saw a screenshot of the accordion example on p492, at the start of this section.

TABBED PANEL

When you click on one of the tabs, its corresponding panel is shown. Tabbed panels look a little like index cards.

You should be able to see all of the tabs, but:

- Only one tab should look *active*.

- Only the panel that corresponds to the active tab should be shown (all other panels should be hidden).

The tabs are typically created using an unordered list. Each `<li>` element represents a tab and within each tab is a link.

The panels follow the unordered list that holds the tabs, and each panel is stored in a `<div>`.

To associate the tab to the panel:

- The link in the tab, like all links, has an `href` attribute.

- The panel has an `id` attribute.

Both attributes share the same value. (This is the same principle as creating a link to another location within an HTML page.)

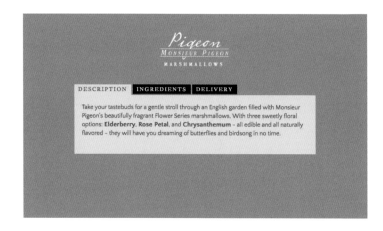

Other tabs scripts include Tabslet and Tabulous. They are also included in jQuery UI and Bootstrap.

FIRST TAB SELECTED

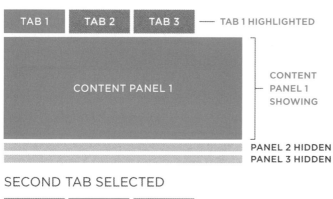

TAB 1 HIGHLIGHTED

CONTENT PANEL 1 SHOWING

PANEL 2 HIDDEN
PANEL 3 HIDDEN

SECOND TAB SELECTED

TAB 2 HIGHLIGHTED

PANEL 1 HIDDEN

CONTENT PANEL 2 SHOWING

PANEL 3 HIDDEN

When the page loads, CSS is used to make the tabs sit next to each other and to indicate which one is considered active.

CSS also hides the panels, except for the one that corresponds with the active tab.

When the user clicks on the link inside a tab, the script uses jQuery to get the value of the `href` attribute from the link. This corresponds to the `id` attribute on the panel that should be shown.

The script then updates the values in the `class` attribute on that tab and panel, adding a value of `active`. It also removes that value from the tab and panel that had previously been active.

If the user does not have JavaScript enabled, the link in the tab takes the user to the appropriate part of the page.

CREATING TAB PANELS

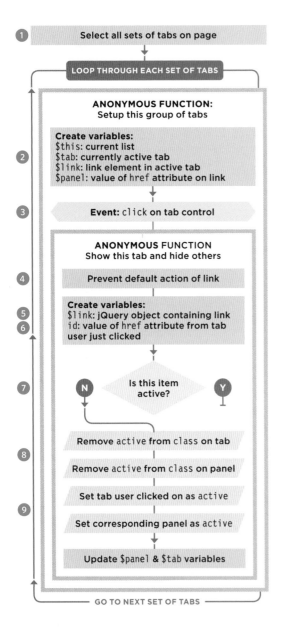

① Select all sets of tabs on page

LOOP THROUGH EACH SET OF TABS

ANONYMOUS FUNCTION:
Setup this group of tabs

② **Create variables:**
$this: current list
$tab: currently active tab
$link: link element in active tab
$panel: value of href attribute on link

③ **Event:** click on tab control

ANONYMOUS FUNCTION
Show this tab and hide others

④ Prevent default action of link

⑤ **Create variables:**
⑥ $link: jQuery object containing link
id: value of href attribute from tab
user just clicked

⑦ N — **Is this item active?** — Y

Remove active from class on tab

⑧ Remove active from class on panel

Set tab user clicked on as active

⑨ Set corresponding panel as active

Update $panel & $tab variables

GO TO NEXT SET OF TABS

The flowchart shows the steps that are involved in creating tabs when they are found in the HTML. Below, you can see how these steps can be translated into code:

1. A jQuery selection picks all sets of tabs within the page. The `.each()` method calls an anonymous function that is run for each set of tabs (like a loop). The code in the anonymous function deals with one set of tabs at a time, and the steps would be repeated for each set of tabs on the page.
2. Four variables hold details of the active tab:
i) `$this` holds the current set of tabs.
ii) `$tab` holds the currently active tab.
The `.find()` method selects the active tab.
iii) `$link` holds the <a> element within that tab.
iv) `$panel` holds the value of the `href` attribute for the active tab (this variable will be used to hide the panel if the user selects a different one).
3. An event listener is set up to check for when the user clicks on any tab within that list. When they do, it runs another anonymous function.
4. `e.preventDefault()` prevents the link that users clicked upon taking them to that page.
5. Creates a variable called `$link` to hold the current link inside a jQuery object.
6. Creates a variable called `id` to hold the value of the `href` attribute from the tab that was clicked. It is called `id` because it is used to select the matching content panel (using its `id` attribute).
7. An `if` statement checks whether the `id` variable contains a value, and the current item is **not** active. If both conditions are met:
8. The previously active tab and panel have the `class` of `active` removed (which deactivates the tab and hides the panel).
9. The tab that was clicked on and its corresponding panel both have `active` added to their `class` attributes (which makes the tab look active and displays its corresponding panel, which was hidden). At the same time, references to these elements are stored in the `$panel` and `$tab` variables.

```html
<ul class="tab-list">
  <li class="active"><a class="tab-control" href="#tab-1">Description</a></li>
  <li><a class="tab-control" href="#tab-2">Ingredients</a></li>
  <li><a class="tab-control" href="#tab-3">Delivery</a></li>
</ul>
<div class="tab-panel active" id="tab-1">Content 1...</div>
<div class="tab-panel" id="tab-2">Content 2...</div>
<div class="tab-panel" id="tab-3">Content 3...</div>
```

```css
.tab-panel {
  display: none;}
.tab-panel.active {
  display: block;}
```

```javascript
① $('.tab-list').each(function(){          // Find lists of tabs
②   var $this     = $(this);               // Store this list
    var $tab      = $this.find('li.active'); // Get the active list item
    var $link     = $tab.find('a');        // Get link from active tab
    var $panel    = $($link.attr('href')); // Get active panel

③   $this.on('click', '.tab-control', function(e) { // When click on a tab
④     e.preventDefault();                  // Prevent link behavior
⑤     var $link = $(this);                 // Store the current link
⑥     var id    = this.hash;               // Get href of clicked tab

⑦     if (id && !$link.is('.active')) {    // If not currently active
⑧       $panel.removeClass('active');      // Make panel inactive
        $tab.removeClass('active');        // Make tab inactive

⑨       $panel = $(id).addClass('active'); // Make new panel active
        $tab   = $link.parent().addClass('active'); // Make new tab active
      }
    });
  });
```

MODAL WINDOW

A modal window is any type of content that appears "in front of" the rest of the page's content. It must be "closed" before the rest of the page can be interacted with.

In this example, a modal window is created when the user clicks on the heart button in the top left-hand corner of the page.

The modal window opens in the center of the page, allowing users to share the page on social networks.

The content for the modal window will typically sit within the page, but it is hidden when the page loads using CSS.

JavaScript then takes that content and displays it inside `<div>` elements that create the modal window on top of the existing page.

Sometimes modal windows will dim out the rest of the page behind them. They can be designed to either appear automatically when the page has finished loading or they can be triggered by the user interacting with the page.

Other examples of modal window scripts include Colorbox (by Jack L. Moore), Lightbox 2 (by Lokesh Dhakar), and Fancybox (by Fancy Apps). They are also included in jQuery UI and Bootstrap.

A **design pattern** is a term programmers use to describe a common approach to solving a range of programming tasks.

This script uses the **module pattern**. It is a popular way to write code that contains both **public** and **private** logic.

Once the script has been included in the page, other scripts can use its public methods: open(), close(), or center(). But users do not need to access the variables that create the HTML, so they remain private (on p505 the private code is shown on green).

Using modules to build parts of an application has benefits:
- It helps organize your code.
- You can test and reuse the individual parts of the app.
- It creates scope, preventing variable /method names clashing with other scripts.

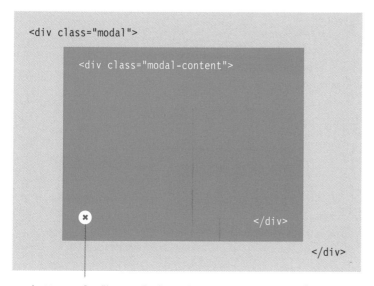

```
<div class="modal">

    <div class="modal-content">




          ✖                          </div>

                                   </div>
```

<button role="button" class="modal-close">close</button>

This modal window script creates an object (called modal), which, in turn, provides three new methods you can use to create modal windows:

open() opens a modal window
close() closes the window
center() centers it on the page

Another script would be used to call the open() method and specify what content should appear in the modal window.

Users of this script only need to know how the open() method works because:
- close() is called by an event listener when the user clicks on the close button.
- center() is called by the open() method and also by an event listener if the user resizes the window.

When you call the open() method, you specify the content that you want the modal window to contain as a parameter (you can also specify its width and height if you want).

In the diagram, you can see that the script adds the content to the page inside <div> elements.

div.modal acts as a frame around the modal window.

div.modal-content acts as a container for the content being added to the page.

button.modal-close allows the user to close the modal window.

CREATING MODALS

The modal script needs to do two things:
1. Create the HTML for the modal window
2. Return the `modal` object itself, which consists of the `open()`, `close()`, and `center()` methods

Including the script in the HTML page does not have any visible effect (rather like including jQuery in your page does not affect the appearance of the page).

But it does allow any other script you write to use the functionality of the `modal` object and call its `open()` method to create a modal window (just like including jQuery script includes the `jQuery` object in your page and allows you to use its methods).

This means that people who use the script only need to know how to call the `open()` method and tell it what they want to appear in the modal window.

In the example on the right, the modal window is called by a script called `modal-init.js`. You will see how to create the `modal` object and its methods on the next double page spread, but for now consider that including this script is the equivalent of adding the following to your own script. It creates an object called `modal` and adds three methods to the object:

```
var modal = {
  center: function() {
    // Code for center() goes here
  },
  open: function(settings) {
    // Code for open() goes here
  },
  close: function() {
    // Code for close() goes here
  }
};
```

The `modal-init.js` file removes the share content from the HTML page. It then adds an event handler to call the `modal` object's `open()` method to open a modal window containing the content it just removed from the page. `init` is short for initialize and is commonly used in the name of files and functions that set up a page or other part of a script.

1. First the script gets the contents of the element that has an `id` attribute whose value is `share-options`. Note how the jQuery `.detach()` method removes this content from the page.
2. Next an event handler is set to respond to when the user clicks on the share button. When they do, an anonymous function is run.
3. The anonymous function uses the `open()` method of the `modal` object. It takes parameters in the form of an object literal:
- `content`: the content to be shown in the modal window. Here it is the content of the element whose `id` attribute has a value of `share-options`.
- `width`: the width of the modal window.
- `height`: the height of the modal window.

Step 1 uses the `.detach()` method because it keeps the elements and event handlers in memory so they can be used again later. jQuery also has a `.remove()` method but it removes the items completely.

① **Create variable:**
$content: part of page to appear in modal

Hide that part of page by detaching it

② **Event:** `click` on share button

ANONYMOUS FUNCTION:
Show content in modal window

③ **Call `open()` method of modal object, then pass it the $content variable as a parameter, along with the modal's width and height**

USING THE MODAL SCRIPT

HTML

```
① <div id="share-options">
     <!-- This is where the message and sharing buttons go -->
   </div>
   <script src="js/jquery.js"></script>
② <script src="js/modal-window.js"></script>
③ <script src="js/modal-init.js"></script>
  </body>
</html>
```

In the HTML above, you should note three things:
1. A `<div>` that contains the sharing options.
2. A link to the script that creates the `modal` object (`modal-window.js`).
3. A link to the script that will open a modal window using the `modal` object (`modal-init.js`), using it to display the sharing options.

The `modal-init.js` file below opens the modal window. Note how the `open()` method is passed three pieces of information in JSON format:
i) `content` for modal (required)
ii) `width` of modal (optional - overrides default)
iii) `height` of modal (optional - overrides default)

JAVASCRIPT   c11/js/modal-init.js

```
   (function(){
①    var $content = $('#share-options').detach();   // Remove modal from page

②    $('#share').on('click', function() {            // Click handler to open modal
③      modal.open({content: $content, width:340, height:300});
     });                          (i)          (ii)        (iii)
   }());
```

The `z-index` of the modal window must be very high so that it appears on top of any other content.

These styles ensure the modal window sits on top of the page (there are more styles in the full example).

CSS   c11/css/modal-window.css

```
.modal {
  position: absolute;
  z-index: 1000;}
```

MODAL OBJECT

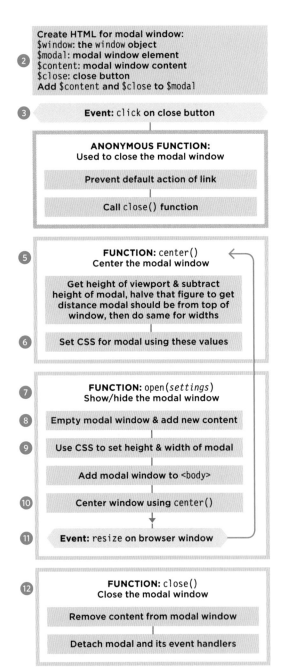

2 Create HTML for modal window:
$window: the window **object**
$modal: modal window element
$content: modal window content
$close: close button
Add $content and $close to $modal

3 Event: click on close button

ANONYMOUS FUNCTION:
Used to close the modal window

Prevent default action of link

Call close() function

5 FUNCTION: center()
Center the modal window

Get height of viewport & subtract
height of modal, halve that figure to get
distance modal should be from top of
window, then do same for widths

6 Set CSS for modal using these values

7 FUNCTION: open(*settings*)
Show/hide the modal window

8 Empty modal window & add new content

9 Use CSS to set height & width of modal

Add modal window to <body>

10 Center window using center()

11 Event: resize on browser window

12 FUNCTION: close()
Close the modal window

Remove content from modal window

Detach modal and its event handlers

Below are the steps for creating the modal object. Its methods are used to create modal windows.

1. The modal object is declared. The methods of this object are created by an Immediately Involved Function Expression or IIFE (see p97). (This step is not shown in the flowchart.)

2. Store the current window object in a jQuery selection, then create the three HTML elements needed for the modal window. Assemble the modal window and store it in $modal.

3. Add an event handler to the close button which calls the modal object's close() method.

4. Following the return keyword, there is a code block in curly braces. It creates three public methods of the modal object. **Please note:** This step is not shown in the flowchart.

5. The center() method creates two variables:
i) top: takes the height of the browser window and subtracts the height of the modal window. This number is divided by two, giving the distance of the modal from the top of the browser window.
ii) left: takes the width of the browser window and subtracts the width of modal window. This number is divided by two, giving the distance of the modal from the left of the browser window.

6. The jQuery .css() method uses these variables to position the modal in the center of the page.

7. open() takes an object as a parameter; it is referred to as settings (the data for this object was shown on the previous page).

8. Any existing content is cleared from the modal, and the content property of the settings object is added to the HTML created in steps 1 and 2.

9. The width and height of the modal are set using values from the settings object. If none were given, auto is used. Then the modal is added to the page using the appendTo() method.

10. center() is used to center the modal window.

11. If the window is resized, call center() again.

12. close() empties the modal, detaches the HTML from the page, and removes any event handlers.

In the code below, the lines that are highlighted in green are considered **private**. These lines of code are only used within the object. (This code cannot be accessed directly from outside the object.)

When this script has been included in a page, the center(), open(), and close() methods in steps 5-12 are available on the modal object for other scripts to use. They are referred to as **public**.

```
① var modal = (function() {                          // Declare modal object
     var $window = $(window);
     var $modal = $('<div class="modal"/>');          // Create markup for modal
②    var $content = $('<div class="modal-content"/>');
     var $close = $('<button role="button" class="modal-close">close</button>');

     $modal.append($content, $close);                 // Add close button to modal

     $close.on('click', function(e) {                 // If user clicks on close
③      e.preventDefault();                            // Prevent link behavior
        modal.close();                                // Close the modal window
     });

④   return {                                          // Add code to modal
       center: function() {                           // Define center() method
⑤        // Calculate distance from top and left of window to center the modal
          var top = Math.max($window.height() - $modal.outerHeight(), 0) / 2;
          var left = Math.max($window.width() - $modal.outerWidth(), 0) / 2;
          $modal.css({                                // Set CSS for the modal
⑥           top: top + $window.scrollTop(),           // Center vertically
            left: left + $window.scrollLeft()         // Center horizontally
          });
       },
⑦     open: function(settings) {                      // Define open() method
⑧       $content.empty().append(settings.content);    // Set new content of modal

         $modal.css({                                 // Set modal dimensions
⑨          width: settings.width || 'auto',           // Set width
           height: settings.height || 'auto'          // Set height
         }).appendTo('body');                         // Add it to the page

⑩       modal.center();                               // Call center() method
⑪       $(window).on('resize', modal.center);         // Call it if window resized
       },
       close: function() {                            // Define close() method
         $content.empty();                            // Remove content from modal
⑫       $modal.detach();                              // Remove modal from page
         $(window).off('resize', modal.center);       // Remove event handler
       }
     };
   }());
```

PHOTO VIEWER

The photo viewer is an example of an image gallery. When you click on a thumbnail, the main photograph is replaced with a new image.

In this example, you can see one main image with three thumbnails underneath it.

The HTML for the photo viewer consists of:

- One large `<div>` element that will hold the main picture. The images that sit in the `<div>` are centered and scaled down if necessary to fit within the allocated area.

- A second `<div>` element that holds a set of thumbnails that show the other images you can view. These thumbnails sit inside links. The `href` attribute on those links point to the larger versions of their images.

Other gallery scripts include Galleria, Gallerific, and TN3Gallery.

FIRST PHOTO SELECTED

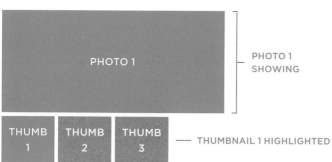

PHOTO 1 SHOWING

THUMBNAIL 1 HIGHLIGHTED

SECOND PHOTO SELECTED

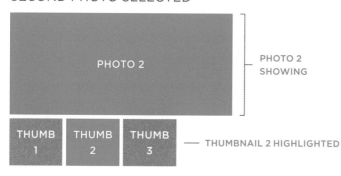

PHOTO 2 SHOWING

THUMBNAIL 2 HIGHLIGHTED

When you click on a thumbnail, an event listener triggers an anonymous function that:

1. Looks at the value of the `href` attribute (which points to the large image)
2. Creates a new `<img>` element to hold that image
3. Makes it invisible
4. Adds it to the big `<div>` element

Once the image has loaded, a function called `crossfade()` is used to fade between the existing image and the new one that has been requested.

USING THE PHOTO VIEWER

In order to use the photo viewer, you create a `<div>` element to hold the main image. It is empty, and its `id` attribute has a value of `photo-viewer`.

The thumbnails sit in another `<div>`. Each one is in an `<a>` element with three attributes:

- `href` points to the larger version of the image

- `class` always has a value of `thumb` and the current main image has a value of `active`
- `title` describes the image (it will be used for `alt` text)

c11/photo-viewer.html HTML

```html
<div id="photo-viewer"></div>
<div id="thumbnails">
  <a href="img/photo-1.jpg" class="thumb active" title="Elderberry mallow">
    <img src="img/thumb-1.jpg" alt="Elderberry Marshmallow" /></a>
  <a href="img/photo-2.jpg" title="Rose Marshmallow" class="thumb">
    <img src="img/thumb-2.jpg" alt="Rose Marshmallow" /></a>
  <a href="img/photo-3.jpg" title="Chrysanthemum  Marshmallow" class="thumb">
    <img src="img/thumb-3.jpg" alt="Chrysanthemum Marshmallow" /></a>
</div>
```

The script comes before the closing `</body>` tag. As you will see, it simulates the user clicking on the first thumbnail.

The `<div>` that holds the main picture uses relative positioning. This removes the element from normal flow, so a `height` for the viewer must be specified.

While images are loading, a `class` of `is-loading` is added to them (it displays an animated loading gif). When the image has loaded, `is-loading` is removed.

If the images are larger than the viewer the `max-width` and `max-height` properties will scale them to fit. To center the image within the viewer a mix of CSS and JavaScript will be used. See p511 for detailed explanation.

c11/css/photo-viewer.css CSS

```css
#photo-viewer {
  position: relative;
  height: 300px;
  overflow: hidden;}

#photo-viewer.is-loading:after {
  content: url(images/load.gif);
  position: absolute;
  top: 0;
  right: 0;}

#photo-viewer img {
  position: absolute;
  max-width: 100%;
  max-height: 100%;
  top: 50%;
  left: 50%;}

a.active {
  opacity: 0.3;}
```

ASYNCHRONOUS LOADING & CACHING IMAGES

This script (shown on the next page) shows two interesting techniques:
1. Dealing with asynchronous loading of content
2. Creating a custom **cache** object

SHOWING THE RIGHT IMAGE WHEN LOADING IMAGES ASYNCHRONOUSLY

PROBLEM:
The larger images are only loaded into the page when the user clicks on a thumbnail, and the script waits for the image to fully load before displaying it.

Because larger images take longer to load, if a user clicks on two different images in quick succession:
1. The second image could load faster than the first one and be displayed in the browser.
2. It would be replaced by the *first* image the user clicked on when that image had loaded. This could make users think the wrong image has loaded.

SOLUTION:
When the user clicks on a thumbnail:
- A function-level variable called **src** stores the path to this image.
- A global variable called **request** is also updated with the path to this image.
- An event handler is set to call an anonymous function when *this* image has loaded.

When the image loads, the event handler checks if the **src** variable (which holds the path to *this* image) matches the **request** variable. If the user had clicked on another image since the one that just loaded, the **request** variable would no longer match the **src** variable and the image should not be shown.

CACHING IMAGES THAT HAVE ALREADY LOADED IN THE BROWSER

PROBLEM:
When the user requests a big image (by clicking on the thumbnail), a new <img> element is created and added to the frame.

If the user goes back to look at an image they have already selected, you do not want to create a new element and load the image all over again.

SOLUTION:
A simple object is created, and it is called **cache**. Every time a new <img> element is created, it will be added to the **cache** object.

That way, each time an image is requested, the code can check if the corresponding <img> element is already in the cache (rather than creating it again).

PHOTO VIEWER SCRIPT (1)

This script introduces some new concepts, so it will be spread over four pages. On these two pages you see the global variables and `crossfade()` function.

1 **Store in variables:**
request: last image that was requested
$current: image currently being shown
cache: object to remember loaded images
$frame: container for image
$thumbs: container for thumbnails

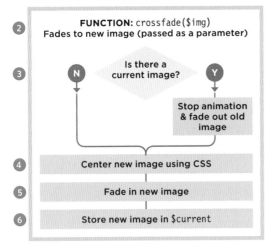

2 **FUNCTION:** crossfade($img)
Fades to new image (passed as a parameter)

3 N — Is there a current image? — Y

Stop animation & fade out old image

4 Center new image using CSS

5 Fade in new image

6 Store new image in $current

1. A set of global variables is created. They can be used throughout the script – both in the `crossfade()` function (on this page) and the event handlers (on p512).
2. The `crossfade()` function will be called when the user has clicked on a thumbnail. It is used to fade between the old image and the new one.
3. An `if` statement checks to see if there is an image loaded at the moment. If there is, two things happen: the `.stop()` method will stop any current animation and then `.fadeOut()` will fade the image out.
4. To center the image in the viewer element, you set two CSS properties on the image. Combined with the CSS rules you saw on p508, these CSS properties will center the image in its container. (See the diagrams on the bottom of p511.)
i) `marginleft`: gets the width of the image using the `.width()` method, divides it by two, and uses that number as a negative margin.
ii) `marginTop`: gets the height of the image, using the `.height()` method, divides it by two, and makes that number a negative margin.
5. If the new image is currently being animated, the animation is stopped and the image is faded in.
6. Finally, the new image becomes the current image and is stored in the `$current` variable.

THE CACHE OBJECT

The idea of a cache object might sound complicated, but all objects are just sets of key/value pairs. You can see what the cache object might look like on the right. When an image is requested by clicking on a new thumbnail, a new property is added to the cache object:

- The key added to the cache object is the path to the image (below this is referred to as *src*). Its value is another object with two properties.
- *src*.`$img` holds a reference to a jQuery object that contains the newly created `<img>` element.
- *src*.`isLoading` is a property indicating whether or not it is currently loading (its value is a Boolean).

```
var cache = {
  "c11/img/photo-1.jpg": {
    "$img": jQuery object,
    "isLoading": false
  },
  "c11/img/photo-2.jpg": {
    "$img": jQuery object,
    "isLoading": false
  },
  "c11/img/photo-3.jpg": {
    "$img": jQuery object,
    "isLoading": false
  }
}
```

```
  ┌ var request;                        // Latest image to be requested
  │ var $current;                       // Image currently being shown
①┤ var cache   = {};                    // Cache object
  │ var $frame  = $('#photo-viewer');   // Container for image
  └ var $thumbs = $('.thumb');          // Container for image

② function crossfade($img) {            // Function to fade between images
                                        // Pass in new image as parameter
  ┌   if ($current) {                   // If there is currently an image showing
③┤       $current.stop().fadeOut('slow'); // Stop animation and fade it out
  └   }

  ┌   $img.css({                        // Set the CSS margins for the image
④┤     marginLeft: -$img.width() / 2,   // Negative margin of half image's width
  │     marginTop: -$img.height() / 2   // Negative margin of half image's height
  └   });

⑤   $img.stop().fadeTo('slow', 1);      // Stop animation on new image & fade in

⑥   $current = $img;                    // New image becomes current image

  }
```

CENTERING THE IMAGE

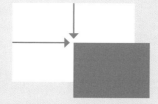

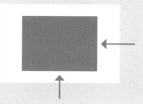

i) Centering the image involves three steps. In the style sheet, absolute positioning is used to place it in the top-left corner of the containing element.

ii) In the style sheet, the image is moved down and right by 50% of the **container's** width and height:
width: 800px ÷ **2** = 400 px
height: 500px ÷ **2** = 250 px

iii) In the script, negative margins move the image up and left by half the **image's** width and height:
width: 500 px ÷ **2** = 250 px
height: 400px ÷ **2** = 200 px

PHOTO VIEWER SCRIPT (2)

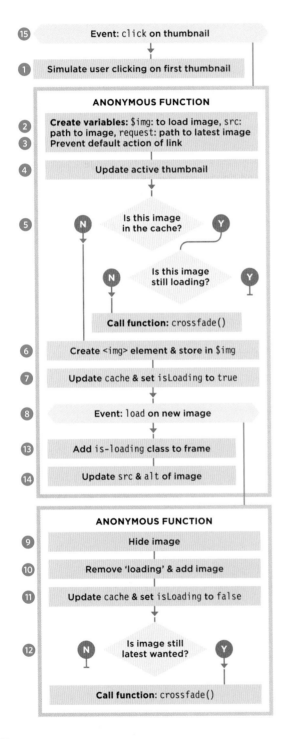

15 Event: `click on thumbnail`

1 Simulate user clicking on first thumbnail

ANONYMOUS FUNCTION

2
3 **Create variables:** `$img`: to load image, `src`: path to image, `request`: path to latest image **Prevent default action of link**

4 Update active thumbnail

5 **N** / **Y** Is this image in the cache?

N / **Y** Is this image still loading?

Call function: `crossfade()`

6 Create `<img>` element & store in `$img`

7 Update `cache` & set `isLoading` to `true`

8 Event: `load` on new image

13 Add `is-loading` class to frame

14 Update `src` & `alt` of image

ANONYMOUS FUNCTION

9 Hide image

10 Remove 'loading' & add image

11 Update `cache` & set `isLoading` to `false`

12 **N** / **Y** Is image still latest wanted?

Call function: `crossfade()`

---

1. The thumbnails are wrapped in links. Every time users click on one, the anonymous function will run.
2. Three variables are created:
i) `$img` will be used to create new `<img>` elements that will hold the larger images when they load.
ii) `src` (a function-level variable) holds the path to the new image (it was in the `href` attribute of the link).
iii) `request` (a global variable) holds the same path.
3. The link is prevented from loading the image.
4. The `active` class is removed from *all* the thumbs and is added to the thumb that was clicked on.
5. If the image is in the `cache` object and it has finished loading, the script calls `crossfade()`.
6. If the image has not yet loaded, the script creates a new `<img>` element.
7. It is added to the `cache`. `isLoading` is set to `true`.
8. At this point, the image has not loaded yet (only an empty `<img>` element was created). When the image loads, the `load` event triggers a function (which needs to be written *before* the image loads).
9. First, the function hides the image that just loaded.
10. It then removes the `is-loading` class from the frame and adds the new image to the frame.
11. In the `cache` object, `isLoading` is set to `false` (as it will have loaded when this function runs).
12. An if statement checks if the image that just loaded is the one the user last requested. To see how this is done, look back at step 2 again:
- The `src` variable holds the path to the image that just loaded. It has function-level scope.
- The `request` variable is updated each time the user clicks on an image. It has global scope.
So, if the user has clicked on an image since this one, the `request` and `src` variables will not be the same and nothing should be done. If they do match, then: `crossfade()` is called to show the image.
13. Having set all of this in place, it is time to load the image. The `is-loading` class is added to the frame.
14. Finally, by adding a value to the `src` attribute on the image, the image will start to load. Its alt text is retrieved from the `title` attribute on the link.
15. The last line of the script simulates the user clicking on the first thumbnail. This will load the first image into the viewer when the script first runs.

```javascript
① $(document).on('click', '.thumb', function(e){   // When a thumb is clicked on
     var $img;                                       // Create local variable called $img
② ⎰ var src = this.href;                             // Store path to image
   ⎱ request = src;                                  // Store path again in request

③   e.preventDefault();                              // Stop default link behavior

④ ⎰ $thumbs.removeClass('active');                   // Remove active from all thumbs
   ⎱ $(this).addClass('active');                     // Add active to clicked thumb

     if (cache.hasOwnProperty(src)) {                // If cache contains this image
⑤ ⎰   if (cache[src].isLoading === false) {          // And if isLoading is false
   ⎱     crossfade(cache[src].$img);                 // Call crossfade() function
       }
     } else {                                        // Otherwise it is not in cache
⑥     $img = $('<img/>');                            // Store empty <img/> element in $img
       cache[src] = {                                // Store this image in cache
⑦ ⎰     $img: $img,                                  // Add the path to the image
   ⎱     isLoading: true                             // Set isLoading property to true
       };

       // Next few lines will run when image has loaded but are prepared first
⑧     $img.on('load', function() {                   // When image has loaded
⑨       $img.hide();                                 // Hide it
         // Remove is-loading class from frame & append new image to it
⑩       $frame.removeClass('is-loading').append($img);
⑪       cache[src].isLoading = false;                // Update isLoading in cache
         // If still most recently requested image then
⑫ ⎰       if (request === src) {
   ⎱         crossfade($img);                        // Call crossfade() function
           }                                         // Solves asynchronous loading issue
       });

⑬     $frame.addClass('is-loading');                 // Add is-loading class to frame

⑭ ⎰   $img.attr({                                    // Set attributes on <img> element
   ⎱     'src': src,                                 // Add src attribute to load image
         'alt': this.title || ''                     // Add title if one was given in link
       });

     }

});

// Last line runs once (when rest of script has loaded) to show the first image
⑮ $('.thumb').eq(0).click();                         // Simulate click on first thumbnail
```

RESPONSIVE SLIDER

A slider positions a series of items next to each other, but only shows one at a time. The images then slide from one to the next.

This slider loads several panels, but only shows one at a time. It also provides buttons that allow users to navigate between each of the slides and a timer to move them automatically after a set interval.

In the HTML, the entire slider is contained within a `<div>` element whose `class` attribute has value of `slider-viewer`. In turn, the slider needs two further `<div>` elements:

- A container for the slides. Its `class` attribute has a value of `slide-group`. Inside this container, each individual slide is in another `<div>` element.
- A container for the buttons. Its `class` attribute has a value of `slide-buttons`. The buttons are added by the script.

If the HTML contains markup for more than one slider, the script will automatically transform all of them into separate sliders.

Other slider scripts include Unslider, Anything Slider, Nivo Slider, and WOW Slider. Sliders are also included in jQuery UI and Bootstrap.

When the page first loads, the CSS hides all of the slides, which takes them out of normal flow. The CSS then sets the display property of the first slide block to make it visible.

The script then goes through each slide and:
- Assigns an index number to that slide
- Adds a button for it under the slide group

For example, if there are four slides, when the page first loads, the first slide will be shown by default, and four buttons will be added underneath it.

The index numbers allow the script to identify each individual slide. To keep track of which slide is currently being shown, the script uses a variable called currentIndex (holding the index number of the current slide). When the page loads, this is 0, so it shows the first slide. It also needs to know which slide it is moving to, which is stored in a variable called newSlide.

When it comes to moving between the slides (and creating the sliding effect), if the index number of the new slide is *higher* than the index number of the current slide, then the new slide is placed to the *right* of the group. As the visible slide is animated to the left, the new slide automatically starts to come into view, taking its place.

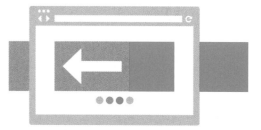

If the index number of the new slide is *lower* than the current index, then the new slide is placed to the *left* of the current slide, and as it is animated to the right, the new slide starts to come into view.

After the animation, the hidden slides are placed behind the one that is currently active.

USING THE SLIDER

As long as you include the script within your page, any HTML that uses the structure shown here will get transformed into a slider.

There could be several sliders on the page and each one will be transformed using the same script that you see on the next double-page spread.

```html
<div class="slide-viewer">
  <div class="slide-group">
    <div class="slide slide-1"><!-- slide content --></div>
    <div class="slide slide-2"><!-- slide content --></div>
    <div class="slide slide-3"><!-- slide content --></div>
    <div class="slide slide-4"><!-- slide content --></div>
  </div>
</div>
<div class="slide-buttons"></div>
```

The width of the slide-viewer is not fixed, so it works in a responsive design. But a height does need to be specified because the slides have an absolute position (this removes them from the document flow and without it they could only be 1px tall).

Each slide is shown at the same width and height as the viewer. If the content of a slide is larger than the viewer, the overflow property on the slide-viewer hides the parts of the slides that extend beyond the frame. If it is smaller it is positioned to the top-left.

c11/css/slider.css

CSS

```css
slide-viewer {
  position: relative;
  overflow: hidden;
  height: 300px;}

.slide-group {
  width: 100%;
  height: 100%;
  position: relative;}

.slide {
  width: 100%;
  height: 100%;
  display: none;
  position: absolute;}

.slide:first-child {
  display: block;}
```

SLIDER SCRIPT OVERVIEW

A jQuery selector finds the sliders within the HTML markup.
An anonymous function then runs for each one to create the slider.
There are four key parts to the function.

1: SETUP

Each slider needs some variables, they are in function-level scope so they:

- Can have different values for each slider
- Do not conflict with variables outside of the script

2: CHANGING SLIDE: `move()`

`move()` is used to move from one slide to another, and to update the buttons that indicate which slide is currently being shown. It is called when the user clicks on a button, and by the `advance()` function.

3: A TIMER TO SHOW THE NEXT SLIDE AFTER 4 SECONDS: `advance()`

A timer will call `move()` after 4 seconds.
To create a timer, JavaScript's `window` object has a `setTimeout()` method. It executes a function after a number of milliseconds. The timer is often assigned to a variable, and it uses the following syntax:

```
var timeout = setTimeout(function, delay);
```

- *timeout* is a variable name that will be used to identify the timer.
- *function* can be a named function or an anonymous function.
- *delay* is the number of milliseconds before the function should run.

To stop the timer, call `clearTimeout()`. It takes one parameter: the variable used to identify the timer:
```
clearTimeout(timeout);
```

4: PROCESSING EACH OF THE SLIDES THAT APPEAR WITHIN A SLIDER

The code loops through each of the slides to:

- Create the slider
- Add a button for each slide with an event handler that calls the `move()` function when users clicks it

SLIDER SCRIPT

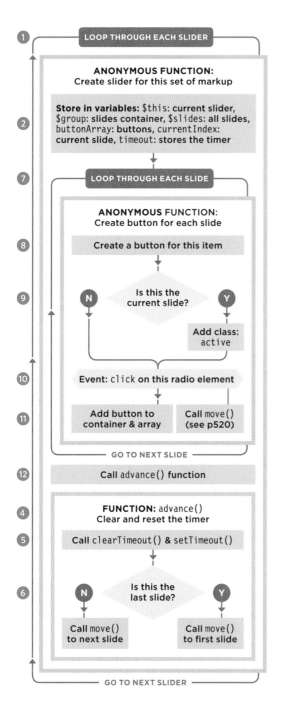

1. There may be several sliders on a page, so the script starts by looking for every element whose `class` attribute has a value of `slider`. For each one, an anonymous function is run to process that slider.

2. Variables are created to hold:

i) The current slider

ii) The element that wraps around the slides

iii) All of the slides in this slider

iv) An array of buttons (one for each slide)

v) The current slide

vi) The timer

3. The `move()` function appears next; see p520.

Please note: This is not shown in the flowchart.

4. The `advance()` function creates the timer.

5. It starts by clearing the current timer. A new timer is set and when the time has elapsed it will run an anonymous function.

6. An `if` statement checks whether or not the current slide is the last one.

If it is not the last slide then it calls `move()` with a parameter that tells it to go to the next slide.

Otherwise it tells `move()` to go to the first slide.

7. Each slide is processed by an anonymous function.

8. A `<button>` element is created for each slide.

9. If the index number of that slide is the same as the number held in the `currentIndex` variable, then a class of `active` is added to that button.

10. An event handler is added to each button. When clicked it calls the `move()` function. The slide's index number indicates which slide to move to.

11. The buttons are then added to the button container, and to the array of buttons.

This array is used by the `move()` function to indicate which slide is currently being shown.

12. `advance()` is called to start the timer.

```
① $('.slider').each(function(){                // For every slider
    var $this    = $(this);                    // Get the current slider
    var $group   = $this.find('.slide-group'); // Get the slide-group (container)
    var $slides = $this.find('.slide');        // jQuery object to hold all slides
② var buttonArray   = [];                      // Create array to hold nav buttons
    var currentIndex = 0;                       // Index number of current slide
    var timeout;                                // Used to store the timer

③   // move() - The function to move the slides goes here (see next page)

④   function advance() {                        // Sets a timer between slides
      clearTimeout(timeout);                    // Clear timer stored in timeout
⑤    // Start timer to run an anonymous function every 4 seconds
      timeout = setTimeout(function(){          //
        if (currentIndex < ($slides.length - 1)) {  // If not the last slide
          move(currentIndex + 1);               // Move to next slide
⑥      } else {                                // Otherwise
          move(0);                              // Move to the first slide
        }
      }, 4000);                                 // Milliseconds timer will wait
    }

⑦   $.each($slides, function(index){
      // Create a button element for the button
⑧    var $button = $('<button type="button" class="slide-btn">&bull;</button>');
      if (index === currentIndex) {    // If index is the current item
⑨      $button.addClass('active');     // Add the active class
      }
⑩    $button.on('click', function(){  // Create event handler for the button
        move(index);                   // It calls the move() function
⑪    }).appendTo('.slide-buttons');   // Add to the buttons holder
      buttonArray.push($button);       // Add it to the button array
    });

⑫   advance();                 // Script is set up - call advance() to start timer

  });
```

PROBLEM: GETTING THE RIGHT GAP BETWEEN SLIDES USING A TIMER

Each slide should show for four seconds (before the timer moves it on to the next slide). But if the user clicks a button after two seconds, then the new slide might not show for four seconds because the timer is already counting down.

SOLUTION: RESET THE TIMER WHENEVER A BUTTON IS CLICKED

The advance() function clears the timer before setting it off again. Every time the user clicks on a button the move() function (shown on the next two pages) it calls advance() to ensure the new slide is shown for four seconds.

SLIDER MOVE() FUNCTION

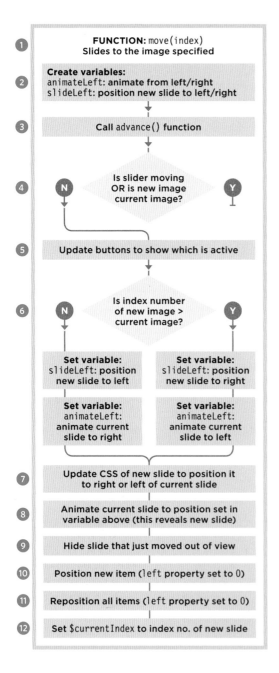

FUNCTION: move(index)
Slides to the image specified

Create variables:
animateLeft: animate from left/right
slideLeft: position new slide to left/right

Call advance() function

Is slider moving
OR is new image
current image?

N   **Y**

Update buttons to show which is active

Is index number
of new image >
current image?

N   **Y**

Set variable:
slideLeft: position
new slide to left

Set variable:
slideLeft: position
new slide to right

Set variable:
animateLeft:
animate current
slide to right

Set variable:
animateLeft:
animate current
slide to left

Update CSS of new slide to position it
to right or left of current slide

Animate current slide to position set in
variable above (this reveals new slide)

Hide slide that just moved out of view

Position new item (left property set to 0)

Reposition all items (left property set to 0)

Set $currentIndex to index no. of new slide

1. The move() function will create the animated sliding movement between two slides. When it is called, it needs to be told which slide to move to.

2. Two variables are created that are used to control whether the slider is moving to the left or right.

3. advance() is called to reset the timer.

4. The script checks if the slider is currently animating or if the user selected the current slide. In either case, nothing should be done, and the return statement stops the rest of the code from running.

5. References to each of the buttons were stored in an array in step 11 of the script on the previous page. The array is used to update which button is active.

6. If the new item has a higher index number, then the slider will need to move from right to left. If the item has a lower index number, the slider will need to move from left to right. These variable values are set first and are then used in step 7.

slideLeft positions the new slide in relation to the current slide. (100% sits the new slide to the right of it and -100% sits the new slide to the left of it.)

animateLeft indicates whether the current slide should move to the left or the right, letting the new slide take its place. (-100% moves the current slide to the left, 100% moves the current slide to the right.)

7. The new slide is positioned to the right or the left of the current slide using the value in the slideLeft variable and its display property is set to block so that it becomes visible. That new slide is identified using newIndex, which was passed into the function.

8. The current slide is then moved to the left or right using the value stored in the animateLeft variable. That slide is selected using the currentIndex variable, which was defined at the start of the script.

```
      // Setup of the script shown on the previous page

①    function move(newIndex) {          // Creates the slide from old to new one
②      var animateLeft, slideLeft;       // Declare variables

③      advance();                        // When slide moves, call advance() again

        // If current slide is showing or a slide is animating, then do nothing
        if ($group.is(':animated') || currentIndex === newIndex) {
④         return;
        }

⑤      buttonArray[currentIndex].removeClass('active'); // Remove class from item
        buttonArray[newIndex].addClass('active');        // Add class to new item

        if (newIndex > currentIndex) {   // If new item > current
          slideLeft = '100%';            // Sit the new slide to the right
          animateLeft = '-100%';         // Animate the current group to the left
⑥      } else {                         // Otherwise
          slideLeft = '-100%';           // Sit the new slide to the left
          animateLeft = '100%';          // Animate the current group to the right
        }
        // Position new slide to left (if less) or right (if more) of current
⑦      $slides.eq(newIndex).css( {left: slideLeft, display: 'block'} );
⑧      $group.animate( {left: animateLeft} , function() {   // Animate slides and
⑨        $slides.eq(currentIndex).css( {display: 'none'} ); // Hide previous slide
⑩        $slides.eq(newIndex).css( {left: 0} ); // Set position of the new item
⑪        $group.css( {left: 0} );               // Set position of group of slides
⑫        currentIndex = newIndex;               // Set currentIndex to new image
        });
      }

      // Handling the slides shown on p519
```

Once the slide has finished animating, an anonymous function performs housekeeping tasks:

9. The slide that was the currentIndex is hidden.

10. The position of the left-hand side of the new slide is set to 0 (left-aligning it).

11. The position of all of the other slides is set so the left-hand side is 0 (left-aligning them).

12. At this point, the new slide will be visible, and the transition is complete, so it is time to update the currentIndex variable to hold the index number of the slide that has just been shown. This is easily done by giving it the value that was stored in the newIndex variable.

Now that this function has been defined, as you saw on the p519, the code creates a timer and goes through each slide adding a button and an event handler for it. (Steps 4-12 on the page p519.)

CREATING A JQUERY PLUGIN

jQuery plugins allow you to add new methods to jQuery without customizing the library itself.

jQuery plugins have benefits over plain scripts:
- You can perform the same task on any elements that match jQuery's flexible selector syntax
- Once the plugin has done its job, you can chain other methods after it (on the same selection)
- They facilitate re-use of code (either within one project or across multiple projects)
- They are commonly shared within the JavaScript and jQuery community
- Namespace collisions (problems when two scripts use the same variable name) are prevented by placing the script is placed in an IIFE (immediately invoked function expression, which you met on p97)

You can turn any function into a plugin if it:
- Manipulates a jQuery selection
- Can return a jQuery selection

The basic concept is that you:
- Pass it a set of DOM elements in a jQuery selection
- Manipulate the DOM elements using the jQuery plugin code
- Return the jQuery object so that other functions can be chained off it

This final example shows you how to create a jQuery plugin. It takes the accordion example you saw at the start of the chapter and turns it into a plugin.

The earlier version applied to all matching markup on the page; the plugin version requires that users call the `accordion()` method on a jQuery selection.

Here a jQuery selection is made collecting elements with a class of `menu`. The `.accordion()` method is called; once that has run, `.fadeIn()` is called.

$('.menu').accordion(500).fadeIn();

1. A jQuery selection is made containing any elements which have the class of `menu`.

2. The `.accordion()` method is called on those elements. It has one parameter; the speed of animation (in milliseconds).

3. The `.fadeIn()` method is applied to the same selection of elements once `.accordion()` has done its job.

BASIC PLUGIN STRUCTURE

1) ADDING A METHOD TO JQUERY

jQuery has an object called `.fn` which helps you extend the functionality of jQuery.

Plugins are written as methods that are added to the `.fn` object.

Parameters that can be passed to the function are placed inside the parentheses on the first line:

```
$.fn.accordion = function(speed) {
  // Plugin will go here
}
```

2) RETURNING THE JQUERY SELECTION TO CHAIN METHODS

jQuery works by collecting a set of elements and storing them in a **jQuery** object. The jQuery object's methods can be used to alter the selected elements.

Because jQuery lets you chain multiple methods to the same selection, once the plugin has done its job it should return the selection for the next method.

The selection is returned using:
1. The **return** keyword (sends a value back from a function)
2. `this` (refers to the selection that was passed in)

```
$.fn.accordion = function(speed) {
  // Plugin will go here
  return this;
}
```

3) PROTECTING THE NAMESPACE

jQuery is not the only JavaScript library to use $ as a shorthand, so the plugin code lives in an IIFE, which creates function-level scope for the code in the plugin.

On the first line below, the IIFE has one named parameter: **$**. On the last line, you can see that the **jQuery** selection is passed into the function.

Inside the plugin, **$** acts like a variable name. It references the **jQuery** object containing the set of elements that the plugin is supposed to be working with.

```
(function($){
  $.fn.accordion = function(speed) {
    // Plugin code will go here
  }
})(jQuery);
```

If you want to pass in more values, it is typically done using a single parameter called `options`.

When the function is called, the `options` parameter contains an object literal.

The object can contain a set of key/value pairs for the different options.

THE ACCORDION PLUGIN

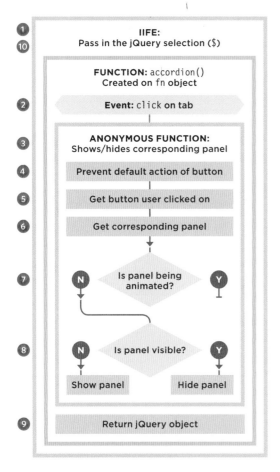

(1)
(10)
IIFE:
Pass in the jQuery selection ($)

FUNCTION: accordion()
Created on fn object

(2) Event: click on tab

(3) ANONYMOUS FUNCTION:
Shows/hides corresponding panel

(4) Prevent default action of button

(5) Get button user clicked on

(6) Get corresponding panel

(7) **N** Is panel being animated? **Y**

(8) **N** Is panel visible? **Y**

Show panel   Hide panel

(9) Return jQuery object

To use the plugin, you create a jQuery selection that contains any <ul> elements that hold an accordion. In the example on the right, the accordion is in a <ul> element that has a class name of menu (but you could use any name you wish). You then call the .accordion() method on that selection, like so:

```
$('.menu').accordion(500);
```

This code could be placed in the HTML document (as shown on the right-hand page), but it would be better placed in a separate JavaScript file that runs when the page loads (to keep the JavaScript separate from the HTML).

You can see the full code for the accordion plugin on the right. The parts in orange are identical to the accordion script at the start of the chapter.

1. The plugin is wrapped in an IIFE to create function-level scope. On the first line, the function is given one named parameter: $ (which means you can use the $ shortcut for jQuery in the function).
10. On the last line of code, the jQuery object is passed into the function (using its full name jQuery rather than its shortcut $). This jQuery object contains the selection of elements that the plugin is working with. Together, points 1 and 10 mean that in the IIFE, $ refers to the jQuery object and it will not be affected if other scripts use $ as a shorthand, too.

2. Inside the IIFE, the new .accordion() method is created by extending the fn object. It takes the one parameter of speed.

3. The this keyword refers to the jQuery selection that was passed into the plugin. It is used to create an event handler that will listen for when the user clicks on an element with a class attribute whose value is accordion-control. When the user does, the anonymous function runs to animate the corresponding panel into or out of view.

4. The default action of the link is prevented.
5. In the anonymous function, $(this) refers to a jQuery object containing the element that the user clicked upon.
6. 7. 8. The only difference between this anonymous function and the one used in the example at the start of the chapter is that the .slideToggle() method takes a parameter of speed to indicate how fast the panel should be shown or hidden. (It is specified when the .accordion() method is called.)

9. When the anonymous function has done its work, the jQuery object containing the selected elements is returned from the function, allowing the same set of elements to be passed to another jQuery method.

```
①   (function($){                                   // Use $ as variable name
②     $.fn.accordion = function(speed) {            // Return the jQuery selection
③       this.on('click', '.accordion-control', function(e){
④           e.preventDefault();
⑤           $(this)
⑥               .next('.accordion-panel')
⑦               .not(':animated')
⑧               .slideToggle(speed);
      });
⑨     return this;                                   // Return the jQuery selection
      }
⑩   })(jQuery);                                      // Pass in jQuery object
```

Note how the filename for the jQuery plugin starts with `jquery.` to indicate that this script relies upon jQuery.

After the accordion plugin script has been included, the `accordion()` method can be used on any jQuery selection.

Below you can see the HTML for the accordion. This time it includes both the jQuery script and the jQuery accordion script.

```html
<ul class="menu">
  <li>
    <a href="#" class="accordion-control"><h3>Classics</h3></a>
    <div class="accordion-panel">If you like your flavors traditional...</div>
  </li>
  <li>
    <a href="#" class="accordion-control"><h3>The Flower Series</h3></a>
    <div class="accordion-panel">Take your tastebuds for a gentle...</div>
  </li>
  <li>
    <a href="#" class='accordion-control'><h3>Salt o' the Sea</h3></a>
    <div class="accordion-panel">Ahoy! If you long for a taste of...</div>
  </li>
</ul>
<script src="js/jquery.js"></script>
<script src="js/jquery.accordion.js"></script>
<script>
  $('.menu').accordion(500);
</script>
```

SUMMARY
CONTENT PANELS

▶ Content panels offer ways to show more content within a limited area.

▶ Popular types of content panels include accordions, tabs, photo viewers, modal windows, and sliders.

▶ As with all website code, it is advisable to separate content (HTML), presentation (CSS), and behavior (JavaScript) into different files.

▶ You can create objects to represent the functionality you want (as with the modal window).

▶ You can turn functions into jQuery plugins that allow you to re-use code and share it with others.

▶ Immediately invoked function expressions (IIFEs) are used to contain scope and prevent naming collisions.

12

FILTERING,
SEARCHING
& SORTING

If your pages contain a lot of data, there are tree techniques that you can use to help your users to find the content they are looking for.

FILTERING

Filtering lets you reduce a set of values, by selecting the ones that meet stated criteria.

SEARCH

Search lets you show the items that match one or more words the user specifies.

SORTING

Sorting lets you reorder a set of items on the page based on criteria (for example, alphabetically).

Before you get to see how to deal with filtering, searching, and sorting, it is important to consider how you are going to store the data that you are working with. In this chapter many of the examples will use arrays to hold data stored in objects using literal notation.

JAVASCRIPT ARRAY METHODS

An array is a kind of object. All arrays have the methods listed below; their property names are index numbers. You will often see arrays used to store complex data (including other objects).

Each item in an array is sometimes called an **element**. It does not mean that the array holds HTML elements; element is just the name given to the pieces of information in the array. *Note some methods only work in IE9+.

ADDING ITEMS	push()	Adds one or more items to end of array and returns number of items in it
	unshift()	Adds one or more items to start of array and returns new length of it
REMOVING ITEMS	pop()	Removes last element from array (and returns the element)
	shift()	Removes first element from array (and returns the element)
ITERATING	forEach()	Executes a function once for each element in array*
	some()	Checks if some elements in array pass a test specified by a function*
	every()	Checks if all elements in array pass a test specified by a function*
COMBINING	concat()	Creates new array containing this array and other arrays/values
FILTERING	filter()	Creates new array with elements that pass a test specified by a function*
REORDERING	sort()	Reorders items in array using a function (called a compare function)
	reverse()	Reverses order of items in array
MODIFYING	map()	Calls a function on each element in array & creates new array with results

JQUERY METHODS FOR FILTERING & SORTING

jQuery collections are array-like objects representing DOM elements.
They have similar methods to an array for modifying the elements.
You can use other jQuery methods on the selection once they have run.

In addition to the jQuery methods shown below, you may see animation methods chained after filtering and sorting methods to create animated transitions as the user makes a selection.

ADDING OR COMBINING ITEMS	`.add()`	Adds elements to a set of matched elements
REMOVING ITEMS	`.not()`	Removes elements from a set of matched elements
ITERATING	`.each()`	Applies same function to each element in matched set
FILTERING	`.filter()`	Reduces number of elements in matched set to those that either match a selector or pass a test specified by a function
CONVERTING	`.toArray()`	Converts a jQuery collection to an array of DOM elements, enabling the use of the array methods shown on the left-hand page

SUPPORTING OLDER BROWSERS

Older browsers do not support the latest methods of the `Array` object. But a script called the ECMAScript 5 Shim can reproduce these methods. ECMAScript is the standard that modern JavaScript is based upon.

A BRIEF HISTORY OF JAVASCRIPT

1996	Jan	
	Feb	
	Mar	····· Netscape Navigator 2 contains the
	Apr	first version of JavaScript written
	May	by Brendan Eich
	Jun	
	Jul	
	Aug	····· Microsoft created a compatible
	Sep	scripting language called JScript
	Oct	
	Nov	····· Netscape gave JavaScript to the
	Dec	ECMA standards body so that its
		development could be standardized

1997	Jan	
	Feb	
	Mar	
	Apr	
	May	
	Jun	····· ECMAScript 1 was released
	Jul	
	Aug	
	Sep	
	Nov	
	Dec	

2014	May	····· Time of writing: ECMAScript 6 is close to being finalized

ECMAScript is the official name for the standardized version of JavaScript, although most people still call it JavaScript unless they are discussing new features.

ECMA International is a standards body that looks after the language, just like the W3C looks after HTML and CSS. And, browser manufacturers often add features beyond the ECMA specs (just as they do with HTML & CSS).

In the same way that the latest features from the HTML and CSS specifications are only supported in the most recent browsers, so the latest features of ECMAScript are only found in recent browsers. This will not affect much of what you have learned in this book (and jQuery helps iron out issues with backwards compatibility), but it is worth noting for the techniques you meet in this chapter.

The following methods of the `Array` object were all introduced in ECMAScript version 5, and they are not supported by Internet Explorer 8 (or older): `forEach()`, `some()`, `every()`, `filter()`, `map()`.

For these methods to work in older browsers you include the ECMAScript 5 Shim, a script that reproduces their functionality for legacy browsers: `https://github.com/es-shims/es5-shim`

ARRAYS VS. OBJECTS CHOOSING THE BEST DATA STRUCTURE

In order to represent complex data you might need several objects. Groups of objects can be stored in arrays or as properties of other objects. When deciding which approach to use, consider how you will use the data.

OBJECTS IN AN ARRAY

When the order of the objects is important, they should be stored in an array because each item in an array is given an index number. (Key-value pairs in objects are not ordered.) But note that the index number can change if objects are added/removed. Arrays also have properties and methods that help when working with a sequence of items, e.g.,

- The sort() method reorders items in an array.
- The length property counts the number of items.

```
var people = [
  {name: 'Casey', rate: 70, active: true},
  {name: 'Camille', rate: 80, active: true},
  {name: 'Gordon', rate: 75, active: false},
  {name: 'Nigel', rate: 120, active: true}
]
```

To retrieve data from an array of objects, you can use the index number for the object:
```
// This retrieves Camille's name and rate
person[1].name;
person[1].rate;
```

To add/remove objects in an array you use array methods.

To iterate over the items in an array you can use forEach().

OBJECTS AS PROPERTIES

When you want to access objects using their name, they work well as properties of another object (because you would not need to iterate through all objects to find that object as you would in an array).

But note that each property must have a unique name. For example, you could not have two properties both called Casey or Camille within the same object in the following code.

```
var people = {
  Casey = {rate: 70, active: true},
  Camille = {rate: 80, active: true},
  Gordon = {rate: 75, active: false},
  Nigel = {rate: 120, active: true}
}
```

To retrieve data from an object stored as a property of another object, you can the object's name:
```
// This retrieves Casey's rate
people.Casey.rate;
```

To add/remove objects to an object you can use the delete keyword or set it to a blank string.

To iterate over child objects you can use Object.keys.

FILTERING

Filtering lets you reduce a set of values.
It allows you to create a subset of data that meets certain criteria.

To look at filtering, we will start with data about freelancers and their hourly rate. Each person is represented by an object literal (in curly braces). The group of objects is held in an array:

```
var people = [
  {
    name: 'Casey',
    rate: 60
  },
  {
    name: 'Camille',
    rate: 80
  },
  {
    name: 'Gordon',
    rate: 75
  },
  {
    name: 'Nigel',
    rate: 120
  }
];
```

The data will be filtered before it is displayed. To do this we will loop through the objects that represent each person. If their rate is more than $65 and less than $90, they are put in a new array called results.

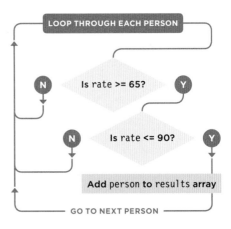

NAME	HOURLY RATE ($)
Camille	80
Gordon	75

DISPLAYING THE ARRAY

On the next two pages, you will see two different approaches to filtering the data in the `people` array, both of which involve using methods of the `Array` object: `.forEach()` and `.filter()`.

Both methods will be used to go through the data in the `people` array, find the ones who charge between $65 and $90 per hour and then add those people to a new array called `results`.

Once the new `results` array has been created, a `for` loop will go through it adding the people to an HTML table (the result is shown on the left-hand page).

Below, you can see the code that displays the data about the people who end up in the `results` array:
1. The entire example runs when the DOM is ready.
2. The data about people and their rates is included in the page (this data is shown on left-hand page).
3. A function will filter the data in the `people` array and create a new array called `results` (next page).
4. A `<tbody>` element is created.
5. A `for` loop goes through the array and uses jQuery to create a new table row for each person and their hourly rate.
6. The new content is added to the page after the table heading.

JAVASCRIPT   c12/js/filter-foreach.js and c12/js/filter-filter.js

```
①  $(function() {
②    // DATA ABOUT PEOPLE GOES HERE (shown on left-hand page)

③    // FILTERING CODE (see p537) GOES HERE - CREATES A NEW ARRAY CALLED results

     // LOOP THROUGH NEW ARRAY AND ADD MATCHING PEOPLE TO THE RESULTS TABLE
④    var $tableBody = $('<tbody></tbody>');                // New content jQuery
     for (var i = 0; i < results.length; i++) {            // Loop through matches
       var person = results[i];                            // Store current person
       var $row = $('<tr></tr>');                          // Create a row for them
⑤     $row.append($('<td></td>').text(person.name));      // Add their name
       $row.append($('<td></td>').text(person.rate));      // Add their rate
       $tableBody.append( $row );                          // Add row to new content
     }

     // Add the new content after the body of the page
⑥    $('thead').after($tableBody);                         // Add tbody after thead
   });
```

USING ARRAY METHODS TO FILTER DATA

The array object has two methods that are very useful for filtering data.
Here you can see both used to filter the same set of data.
As they filter the data, the items that pass a test are added to a new array.

The two examples on the right both start with an array of objects (shown on p534) and use a filter to create a new array containing a subset of those objects. The code then loops through the new array to show the results (as you saw on the previous page).

- The first example uses the forEach() method.
- The second example uses the filter() method.

Note how **person** is used as a parameter name and acts as a variable inside the functions:

- In the forEach() example it is used as a parameter of the anonymous function.
- In the filter() example it is used as a parameter of the priceRange() function.

It corresponds to the current object from the **people** array and is used to access that object's properties.

forEach()

The forEach() method loops through the array and applies the same function to every item in it. forEach() is very flexible because the function can perform any kind of processing with the items in an array (not just filtering as shown in this example). The anonymous function acts as a filter because it checks if a person's rates are within a specified range and, if so, adds them to a new array.

1. A new array is created to hold matching results.
2. The **people** array uses the forEach() method to run the same anonymous function on each object (that represents a person) in the **people** array.
3. If they match the criteria, they are added to the **results** array using the push() method.

filter()

The filter() method also applies the same function to each item in the array, but that function only returns **true** or **false**. If it returns **true**, the filter() method adds that item to a new array.

The syntax is slightly simpler than forEach(), but is only meant to be used to filter data.

1. A function called priceRange() is declared; it will return **true** if the person's wages are within the specified range.
2. A new array is created to hold matching results.
3. The filter() method applies the priceRange() function to each item in the array. If priceRange() returns **true**, that item is added to the **results** array.

STATIC FILTERING OF DATA

JAVASCRIPT   c12/js/filter-foreach.js

```
$(function() {
  // DATA ABOUT PEOPLE GOES HERE (See p534)

  // CHECKS EACH PERSON AND ADDS THOSE IN RANGE TO ARRAY
① var results = [];                                // Array for people in range
② people.forEach(function(person) {                // For each person
    if (person.rate >= 65 && person.rate <= 90) {  // Is rate in range
③     results.push(person);                        // If yes add to array
    }
  });

  // LOOP THROUGH RESULTS ARRAY & ADD MATCHING PEOPLE TO RESULTS TABLE (p535)
});
```

JAVASCRIPT   c12/js/filter-filter.js

```
$(function() {
  // DATA ABOUT PEOPLE GOES HERE (shown on p534)

  // THE FUNCTION ACTS AS A FILTER
① function priceRange(person) {                              // Declare priceRange()
    return (person.rate >= 65) && (person.rate <= 90); // In range returns true
  };
  // FILTER THE PEOPLE ARRAY & ADD MATCHES TO THE RESULTS ARRAY
② var results = [];                              // Array for matching people
③ results = people.filter(priceRange);           // filter() calls priceRange()

  // LOOP THROUGH RESULTS ARRAY & ADD MATCHING PEOPLE TO RESULTS TABLE (p535)
});
```

The code that you saw on the p535 to show the table results could live in the `.forEach()` method, but it is separated out here to illustrate the different approaches to filtering and how they can create new arrays.

DYNAMIC FILTERING

If you let users filter the contents of a page, you can build all of the HTML content, and then show and hide the relevant parts as the user interacts with the filters.

Imagine that you were going to provide the user with a slider so that they could update the price that they were prepared to pay per hour. That slider would automatically update the contents of the table based upon the price range the user had specified.

If you built a new table every time the user interacts with the slider (like the previous two examples that showed filtering), it would involve creating and deleting a lot of elements. Too much of this type of DOM manipulation can slow down your scripts.

A far more efficient solution would be to:

1. Create a table row for *every* person.

2. Show the rows for the people that are within the specified range, and hide the rows that are outside the specified bounds.

Below, the range slider used is a jQuery plugin called noUiSlider (written by Léon Gerson).
`http://refreshless.com/nouislider/`

Before you see the code for this example, take a moment to think about how to approach this script... Here are the tasks that the script needs to perform:

i) It needs to go through each object in the array and create a row for that person.

ii) Once the rows have been created, they need to be added to the table.

iii) Each row needs to be shown / hidden depending on whether that person is within the price range shown on the slider. (This task happens each time the slider is updated.)

In order to decide which rows to show / hide, the code needs to cross-reference between:

- The `person` object in the `people` array (to check how much that person charges)
- The row that corresponds to that person in the table (which needs to be made visible or hidden)

To build this cross-reference we can create a new array called **rows**. It will hold a series of objects with two properties:

- `person`: a reference to the object for this person in the `people` array
- `$element`: a jQuery collection containing the corresponding row in the table

In the code, we create a function to represent each of the tasks identified on the left. The new cross-reference array will be created in the first function:

`makeRows()` will create a row in the table for each person *and* add the new object into the **rows** array

`appendRows()` loops through the **rows** array and adds each of the rows to the table

`update()` will determine which rows are shown or hidden based on data taken from the slider

In addition, we will add a fourth function: `init()` This function contains all of the information that needs to run when the page first loads (including creating the slider using the plugin).

`init` is short for **initialize**; you will often see programmers using this name for functions or scripts that run when the page first loads.

Before looking at the script in detail, the next two pages are going to explain a little more about the **rows** array and how it creates the cross-reference between the objects and the rows that represent each person.

STORING REFERENCES TO OBJECTS & DOM NODES

The **rows** array contains objects with two properties, which associate:
1: References to the objects that represent people in the **people** array
2: References to the row for those people in the table (jQuery collections)

You have seen examples in this book where variables were used to store a reference to a DOM node or jQuery selection (rather than making the same selection twice). This is known as **caching**.

This example takes that idea further: as the code loops through each object in the **people** array creating a row in the table for that person, it also creates a new object for that person and adds it to an array called **rows**. Its purpose is to create an association between:

- The object for that person in the source data
- The row for that person in the table

When deciding which rows to show, the code can then loop through this new array checking the person's rate. If they are affordable, it can show the row. If not, it can hide the row.

This takes less resources than recreating the contents of the table when the user changes the rate they are willing to pay.

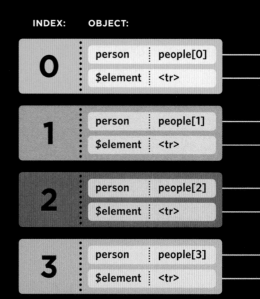

ROWS ARRAY

On the right, you can see the **Array** object's **push()** method creates a new entry in the **rows** array. The entry is an object literal, and it stores the **person** object and the row being created for it in the table.

```
rows.push({
    person: this,          // person object
    $element: $row         // jQuery collection
});
```

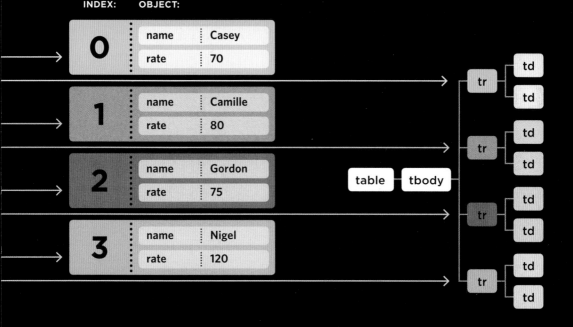

The **people** array already holds information about each person and the rates that they charge, so the object in the **rows** array only needs to point to the original object for that person (it does not copy it).

A jQuery object was used to create each row of the table. The objects in the **rows** array store a reference to each individual row of the table. There is no need to select or create the row again.

DYNAMIC FILTERING

1. Place the script in an IIFE (not shown in flowchart). The IIFE starts with the `people` array.

2. Next, four global variables are created as they are used throughout the script:

`rows` holds the cross-referencing array .

`$min` holds the input to show the minimum rate.

`$max` holds the input to show the maximum rate.

`$table` holds the table for the results.

3. `makeRows()` loops through each person in the `people` array calling an anonymous function for each object in the array. Note how **person** is used as a parameter name. This means that within the function, **person** refers to the current object in the array.

4. For each person, a new jQuery object called **$row** is created containing a **<tr>** element.

5. The person's name and rate are added in **<td>**s.

6. A new object with two properties is added to the `rows` array: **person** stores a reference to their object, **$element** stores a reference to their **<tr>** element.

7. `appendRows()` creates a new jQuery object called `$tbody` containing a **<tbody>** element.

8. It then loops through all of the objects in the **rows** array and adds their **<tr>** element to **$tbody**.

9. The new **$tbody** selection is added to the **<table>**.

10. `update()` goes through each of the objects in the **rows** array and checks if the rate that the person charges is more than the minimum and less than the maximum rate shown on the slider.

11. If it is, jQuery's `show()` method shows the row.

12. If not, jQuery's `hide()` method hides the row.

13. `init()` starts by creating the slide control.

14. Every time the slider is changed, the `update()` function is called again.

15. Once the slider has been set up, the `makeRows()`, `appendRows()`, `update()` functions are called.

16. The `init()` function is called (which will in turn call the other code).

② **Create variables:**
rows: an array linking people with rows
$min & $max: minimum and maximum rate inputs
$table: stores the table that holds the results

③ **FUNCTION: makeRows()**
Creates table rows & populates the rows array

LOOP THROUGH OBJECTS IN **people** ARRAY

ANONYMOUS FUNCTION

④
⑤ Create $row holds <tr> element
Add <td>s holding name & rate

⑥ Add new object to rows array
Add references to person & $row

GO TO NEXT OBJECT IN people ARRAY

FUNCTION: appendRows() adds rows to <tbody>

⑦ Create <tbody> to hold <tr> elements

LOOP THROUGH OBJECTS IN rows ARRAY

⑧ Add $row to $tbody element

GO TO NEXT OBJECT IN rows ARRAY

⑨ Add <tbody> to <table>

⑩ **FUNCTION: update()** updates table contents

LOOP THROUGH OBJECTS IN rows ARRAY

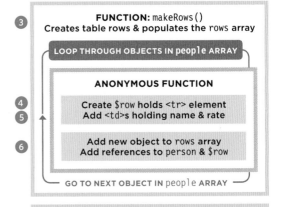

Is rate >= min & rate <= max?

⑫ N → Hide row

⑪ Y → Show row

GO TO NEXT OBJECT IN rows ARRAY

⑬ **FUNCTION: init()** sets up the script

⑭
⑮ Set up slider
Call makeRows(), appendRows(), update()

⑯ Call init() when the DOM has loaded

FILTERING AN ARRAY

```
(1) (function(){ // PEOPLE ARRAY (see p534) GOES HERE BEFORE THE REST OF THE CODE
      var rows = [],                      // rows array
(2)       $min = $('#value-min'),         // Minimum text input
          $max = $('#value-max'),         // Maximum text input
          $table = $('#rates');           // The table that shows results
(3)   function makeRows() {               // Create table rows and the array
(4)     people.forEach(function(person) { // For each person object in people
          var $row = $('<tr></tr>');      // Create a row for them
(5)       $row.append( $('<td></td>').text(person.name) ); // Add their name
          $row.append( $('<td></td>').text(person.rate) ); // Add their rate
          rows.push({ // Add object to cross-references between people and rows
(6)         person: person,               // Reference to the person object
            $element: $row                // Reference to row as jQuery selection
          });
        });
      }
(7)   function appendRows() {             // Adds rows to the table
        var $tbody = $('<tbody></tbody>'); // Create <tbody> element
        rows.forEach(function(row) {      // For each object in the rows array
(8)       $tbody.append(row.$element);    // Add the HTML for the row
        });
(9)     $table.append($tbody);            // Add the rows to the table
      }
(10)  function update(min, max) {         // Update the table content
        rows.forEach(function(row) {      // For each row in the rows array
(11)      if (row.person.rate >= min && row.person.rate <= max) { // If in range
            row.$element.show();          // Show the row
(12)      } else {                        // Otherwise
            row.$element.hide();          // Hide the row
          }
        });
      }
(13)  function init() {                   // Tasks when script first runs
        $('#slider').noUiSlider({         // Set up the slide control
          range: [0, 150], start: [65, 90], handles: 2, margin: 20, connect: true,
          serialization: { to: [$min,$max], resolution: 1 }
(14)    }).change(function() { update($min.val(), $max.val()); });
        makeRows();                       // Create table rows and rows array
(15)    appendRows();                     // Add the rows to the table
        update($min.val(), $max.val());   // Update table to show matches
      }
(16)  $(init);                            // Call init() when DOM is ready
    }());
```

FILTERED IMAGE GALLERY

In this example, a gallery of images are tagged.
Users click on filters to show matching images.

IMAGES ARE TAGGED

In this example, a series of
photos are tagged. The tags are
stored in an HTML attribute
called `data-tags` on each of the
`<img>` elements. HTML5 allows
you to store any data with an
element using an attribute that
starts with the word `data-`. The
tags are comma-separated.
(See right-hand page)

TAGGED OBJECT

The script creates an object
called `tagged`. The script then
goes through each of the images
looking at its tags. Each tag
is added as a property of the
`tagged` object. The value of that
property is an array holding a
reference to each `<img>` element
that uses that tag.
(See p546–p547)

FILTER BUTTONS

By looping through each of the
keys on the `tagged` object, the
buttons can automatically be
generated. The tag counts come
from the `length` of the array.
Each button is given an event
handler. When clicked, it filters
the images and only shows those
with the tag the user selected.
(See p548–p549)

TAGGED IMAGES

```html
<body>
  <header>
    <h1>CreativeFolk</h1>
  </header>
  <div id="buttons"></div>
  <div id="gallery">
    <img src="img/p1.jpg" data-tags="Animators, Illustrators" alt="Rabbit" />
    <img src="img/p2.jpg" data-tags="Photographers, Filmmakers" alt="Sea" />
    <img src="img/p3.jpg" data-tags="Photographers, Filmmakers" alt="Deer" />
    <img src="img/p4.jpg" data-tags="Designers" alt="New York Street Map" />
    <img src="img/p5.jpg" data-tags="Filmmakers" alt="Trumpet Player" />
    <img src="img/p6.jpg" data-tags="Designers, Animators" alt="Logo Ident" />
    <img src="img/p7.jpg" data-tags="Photographers" alt="Bicycle Japan" />
    <img src="img/p8.jpg" data-tags="Designers" alt="Aqua Logo" />
    <img src="img/p9.jpg" data-tags="Animators, Illustrators" alt="Ghost" />
  </div>
  <script src="js/jquery.js"></script>
  <script src="js/filter-tags.js"></script>
</body>
```

On the right, you can see the **tagged** object for the HTML sample used in this example. For each new tag in the images' **data-tags** attribute, a property is created on the **tagged** object. Here it has five properties: **animators**, **designers**, **filmmakers**, **illustrators**, and **photographers**. The value is an array of images that use that tag.

```
tagged = {
  animators: [p1.jpg, p6.jpg, p9.jpg],
  designers: [p4.jpg, p6.jpg, p8.jpg]
  filmmakers: [p2.jpg, p3.jpg, p5.jpg]
  illustrators: [p1.jpg, p9.jpg]
  photographers: [p2.jpg, p3.jpg, p8.jpg]
}
```

PROCESSING THE TAGS

Here you can see how the script is set up. It loops through the images and the `tagged` object is given a new property for each tag. The value of each property is an array holding the images with that tag.

1. Place the script in an IIFE (not shown in flowchart).
2. The `$imgs` variable holds a jQuery selection containing the images.
3. The `$buttons` variable holds a jQuery selection holding the container for the buttons.
4. The `tagged` object is created.
5. Loop through each of the images stored in `$imgs` using jQuery's `.each()` method. For each one, run the same anonymous function:
6. Store the current image in a variable called `img`.
7. Store the tags from the current image in a variable called `tags`. (The tags are found in the image's `data-tags` attribute.)
8. If the `tags` variable for this image has a value:
9. Use the `String` object's `split()` method to create an array of tags (splitting them at the comma). Chaining the `.forEach()` method off the `split()` method lets you run an anonymous function for each of the elements in the array (in this case, each of the tags on the current image). For each tag:
10. Check if the tag is already a property of the `tagged` object.
11. If not, add it as a new property whose value is an empty array.
12. Then get the property of the `tagged` object that matches this tag and add the image to the array that is stored as the value of that property.

Then move onto the next tag (go back to step 10). When all of the tags for that image have been processed, move to the next image (step 5).

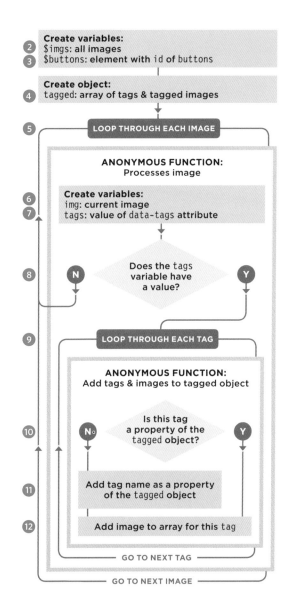

THE TAGGED OBJECT

JAVASCRIPT   c12/js/filter-tags.js

```javascript
① (function() {

②   var $imgs = $('#gallery img');              // Store all images
③   var $buttons = $('#buttons');               // Store buttons element
④   var tagged = {};                            // Create tagged object

⑤   $imgs.each(function() {                      // Loop through images and
⑥     var img = this;                           // Store img in variable
⑦     var tags = $(this).data('tags');          // Get this element's tags

⑧     if (tags) {                               // If the element had tags
⑨       tags.split(',').forEach(function(tagName) { // Split at comma and
⑩         if (tagged[tagName] == null) {        // If object doesn't have tag
⑪           tagged[tagName] = [];               // Add empty array to object
           }
⑫         tagged[tagName].push(img);            // Add the image to the array
       });
     }
   });

   // Buttons, event handlers, and filters go here (see p549)

}());
```

FILTERING THE GALLERY

The filter buttons are created and added by the script. When a button is clicked, it triggers an anonymous function, which will hide and show the appropriate images for that tag.

1. The script lives in an IIFE (not shown in flowchart).
2. Create the button to show all images. The second parameter is an object literal that sets its properties:
3. The text on the button is set to say 'Show All'.
4. A value of `active` is added to the `class` attribute.
5. When the user clicks on the button, an anonymous function runs. When that happens:
6. This button is stored in a jQuery object and is given a `class` of `active`.
7. Its siblings are selected, and the `class` of `active` is removed from them.
8. The `.show()` method is called on all images.
9. The button is then appended to the button container using the `.appendTo()` method. This is chained off the jQuery object that was just created.
10. Next, the other filter buttons are created. jQuery's `$.each()` method is used to loop through each property (or each tag) in the `tagged` object. The same anonymous function runs for each tag:
11. A button is created for the tag using the same technique you saw for the 'Show All' button.
12. The text for the button is set to the tag name, followed by the length of the array (which is the number of images that have that tag).
13. The `click` event on that button triggers an anonymous function:
14. This button is given a `class` of `active`.
15. `active` is removed from all of its siblings.
16. Then all of the images are hidden.
17. The jQuery `.filter()` method is used to select the images that have the specified tag. It does a similar job to the `Array` object's `.filter()` method, but it returns a jQuery collection. It can also work with an object or an element array (as shown here).
18. The `.show()` method is used to show the images returned by the `.filter()` method.
19. The new button is added to the other filter buttons using the `.appendTo()` method.

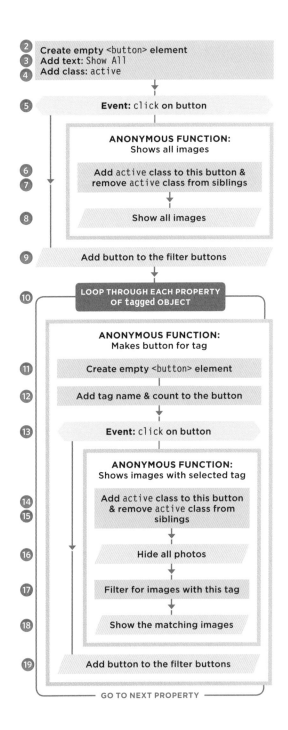

THE FILTER BUTTONS

```
(1)  (function() {

        // Create variables (see p547)
        // Create tagged object (see p547)

(2)    $('<button/>', {                              // Create empty button
(3)       text: 'Show All',                          // Add text 'show all'
(4)       class: 'active',                           // Make it active
(5)       click: function() {                        // Add onclick handler to it
(6)         $(this)                                  // Get the clicked on button
             .addClass('active')                     // Add the class of active
(7)          .siblings()                             // Get its siblings
             .removeClass('active');                 // Remove active from them
(8)        $imgs.show();                             // Show all images
         }
(9)    }).appendTo($buttons);                        // Add to buttons

(10)   $.each(tagged, function(tagName){             // For each tag name
(11)     $('<button/>', {                            // Create empty button
(12)       text: tagName + ' (' + tagged[tagName].length + ')', // Add tag name
(13)       click: function() {                       // Add click handler
(14)         $(this)                                 // The button clicked on
             .addClass('active')                     // Make clicked item active
(15)          .siblings()                            // Get its siblings
             .removeClass('active');                 // Remove active from them
(16)        $imgs                                    // With all of the images
             .hide()                                 // Hide them
(17)         .filter(tagged[tagName])                // Find ones with this tag
(18)         .show();                                // Show just those images
         }
(19)   }).appendTo($buttons);                        // Add to the buttons
       });
     }());
```

SEARCH

Search is like filtering but you show only results that match a search term.
In this example, you will see a technique known as livesearch.
The `alt` text for the image is used for the search instead of tags.

SEARCH LOOKS IN ALT TEXT OF IMAGES

This example will use the same set of photos that you saw in the last example, but will implement a livesearch feature. As you type, the images are narrowed down to match the search criteria.

The search looks at the `alt` text on each image and shows only `<img>` elements whose `alt` text contains the search term.

IT USES INDEXOF() TO FIND A MATCH

The `indexOf()` method of the `String` object is used to check for the search term. If it is not found, `indexOf()` returns `-1`. Since `indexOf()` is case-sensitive, it is important to convert all text (both the `alt` text and the search term) to lowercase (which is done using the `String` object's `toLowerCase()` function).

SEARCH A CUSTOM CACHE OBJECT

We do not want to do the case conversion for each image every time the search terms change, so an object called `cache` is created to store the text along with the image that uses that text.

When the user enters something into the search box, this object is checked rather than looking through each of the images.

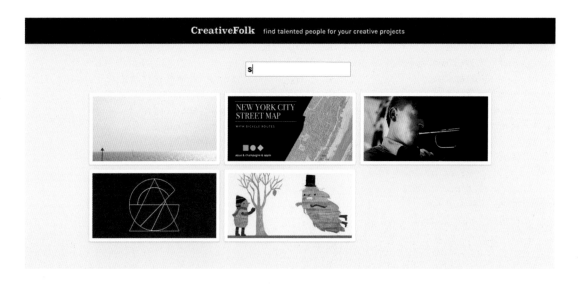

SEARCHABLE IMAGES

```html
<body>
  <header>
    <h1>CreativeFolk</h1>
  </header>
  <div id="search">
    <input type="text" placeholder="filter by search" id="filter-search" />
  </div>
  <div id="gallery">
    <img src="img/p1.jpg" data-tags="Animators, Illustrators" alt="Rabbit" />
    <img src="img/p2.jpg" data-tags="Photographers, Filmmakers" alt="Sea" />
    <img src="img/p3.jpg" data-tags="Photographers, Filmmakers" alt="Deer" />
    <img src="img/p4.jpg" data-tags="Designers" alt="New York Street Map" />
    <img src="img/p5.jpg" data-tags="Filmmakers" alt="Trumpet Player" />
    <img src="img/p6.jpg" data-tags="Designers, Animators" alt="Logo Ident" />
    <img src="img/p7.jpg" data-tags="Photographers" alt="Bicycle Japan" />
    <img src="img/p8.jpg" data-tags="Designers" alt="Aqua Logo" />
    <img src="img/p9.jpg" data-tags="Animators, Illustrators" alt="Ghost" />
  </div>
  <script src="js/jquery.js"></script>
  <script src="js/filter-search.js"></script>
</body>
```

For each of the images, the cache array is given a new object. The array for the HTML above would look like the one shown on the right (except where it says img, it stores a reference to the corresponding <img> element).

When the user types in the search box, the code will look in the text property of each object, and if it finds a match, it will show the corresponding image.

```
cache = [
  {element: img, text: 'rabbit'},
  {element: img, text: 'sea'},
  {element: img, text: 'deer'},
  {element: img, text: 'new york street map'},
  {element: img, text: 'trumpet player'},
  {element: img, text: 'logo ident'},
  {element: img, text: 'bicycle japan'},
  {element: img, text: 'aqua logo'},
  {element: img, text: 'ghost'}
]
```

SEARCH TEXT

This script can be divided into two key parts:

SETTING UP THE CACHE OBJECT

1. Place the script in an IIFE (not shown in flowchart).
2. The `$imgs` variable holds a jQuery selection containing the images.
3. `$search` holds search input.
4. The `cache` array is created.
5. Loop through each image in `$imgs` using `.each()`, and run an anonymous function on each one:
6. Use `push()` to add an object to the `cache` array representing that image.
7. The object's `element` property holds a reference to the `<img>` element.
8. Its `text` property holds the `alt` text. Note that two methods process the text:
`.trim()` removes spaces from the start and end.
`.toLowerCase()` converts it all to lowercase.

FILTERING IMAGES WHEN USER TYPES IN SEARCH BOX

9. Declare a function called `filter()`.
10. Store the search text in a variable called `query`. Use `.trim()` and `.toLowerCase()` to clean the text.
11. Loop through each object in the `cache` array and call the same anonymous function on each:
12. A variable called `index` is created and set to 0.
13. If `query` has a value:
14. Use `indexOf()` to check if the search term is in the `text` property of this object.
The result is stored in the `index` variable. If found, it will be a positive number. If not, it will be -1.
15. If the value of `index` is `-1`, set the `display` property of the image to `none`. Otherwise, set `display` to a blank string (showing the image). Move onto the next image (step 11).
16. Check if the browser supports the `input` event. (It works well in modern browsers, but is not supported in IE8 or earlier.)
17. If so, when it fires on the search box, call the `filter()` function.
18. Otherwise, use the `input` event to trigger it.

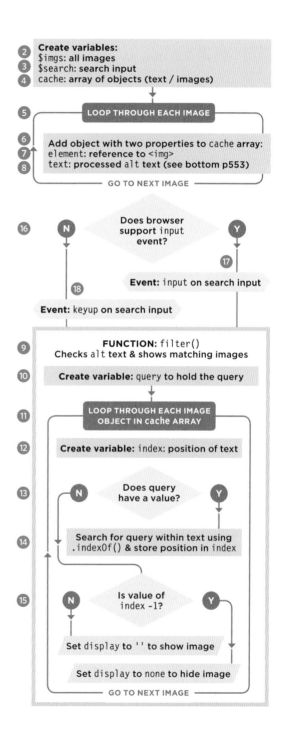

LIVESEARCH

```
(1)  (function() {                                  // Lives in an IIFE
(2)    var $imgs = $('#gallery img');               // Get the images
(3)    var $search = $('#filter-search');           // Get the input element
(4)    var cache = [];                              // Create an array called cache

(5)    $imgs.each(function() {                       // For each image
(6)      cache.push({                               // Add an object to the cache array
(7)        element: this,                           // This image
(8)        text: this.alt.trim().toLowerCase()      // Its alt text (lowercase trimmed)
       });
     });

(9)    function filter() {                          // Declare filter() function
(10)     var query = this.value.trim().toLowerCase();  // Get the query

(11)     cache.forEach(function(img) {              // For each entry in cache pass image
(12)       var index = 0;                           // Set index to 0
(13)       if (query) {                             // If there is some query text
(14)         index = img.text.indexOf(query);       // Find if query text is in there
         }

(15)       img.element.style.display = index === -1 ? 'none' : '';  // Show / hide
       });
     }

(16)     if ('oninput' in $search[0]) {             // If browser supports input event
(17)       $search.on('input', filter);             // Use input event to call filter()
       } else {                                     // Otherwise
(18)       $search.on('keyup', filter);             // Use keyup event to call filter()
       }
   }());
```

The alt text of every image and the text that the user enters into the search input are cleaned using two jQuery methods. Both are used on the same selection and are chained after each other.

METHOD	USE
trim()	Removes whitespace from start or end of string
toLowerCase()	Converts string to lowercase letters because indexOf() is case-sensitive

SORTING

Sorting involves taking a set of values and reordering them. Computers often need detailed instructions about in order to sort data. In this section, you meet the `Array` object's `sort()` method.

When you sort an array using the `sort()` method, you change the order of the items it holds.

Remember that the elements in an array have an index number, so sorting can be compared to changing the index numbers of the items in the array.

By default, the `sort()` method orders items **lexicographically**. It is the same order dictionaries use, and it can lead to interesting results (see the numbers below).

To sort items in a different way, you can write a compare function (see right-hand page).

Lexicographic order is as follows:
1. Look at the first letter, and order words by the first letter.
2. If two words share the same first letter, order those words by the second letter.
3. If two words share the same first two letters, order those words by the third letter, etc.

SORTING STRINGS

Take a look at the array on the right, which contains names. When the `sort()` method is used upon the array, it changes the order of the names.

```
var names = ['Alice', 'Ann', 'Andrew', 'Abe'];
names.sort();
```

The array is now ordered as follows:
```
['Abe', 'Alice', 'Andrew', 'Ann'];
```

SORTING NUMBERS

By default, numbers are also sorted lexicographically, and you can get some unexpected results. To get around this you would need to create a compare function (see next page).

```
var prices = [1, 2, 125, 19, 14, 156];
prices.sort();
```

The array is now ordered as follows:
```
[1, 125, 14, 156, 19, 2]
```

CHANGING ORDER USING COMPARE FUNCTIONS

If you want to change the order of the sort, you write a compare function.
It compares two values at a time and returns a number.
The number it returns is then used to rearrange the items in the array.

The sort() method only ever compares two values at a time (you will see these referred to as *a* and *b*), and it determines whether value *a* should appear before or after value *b*.

Because only two values are compared at a time, the sort() method may need to compare each value in the array with several other values in the array (see diagram on the next page).

sort() can have an anonymous or a named function as a parameter. This function is called a **compare function** and it lets you create rules to determine whether value *a* should come before or after value *b*.

COMPARE FUNCTIONS MUST RETURN NUMBERS

A compare function should return a number. That number indicates which of the two items should come first.

The sort() method will determine which values it needs to compare to ensure the array is ordered correctly.

You just write the compare function so that it returns a number that reflects the order in which you want items to appear.

<0

Indicates that it should show *a* before *b*

0

Indicates that the items should remain in the same order

>0

Indicates that it should show *b* before *a*

To see the order in which the values are being compared, you can add the console.log() method to the compare function. For example: console.log(a + ' - ' + b + ' = ' + (b - a));

HOW SORTING WORKS

Here an array holds 5 numbers that will be sorted in ascending order.
You can see how two values (**a** and **b**) are compared against each other.
The compare function has rules to decide which of the two goes first.

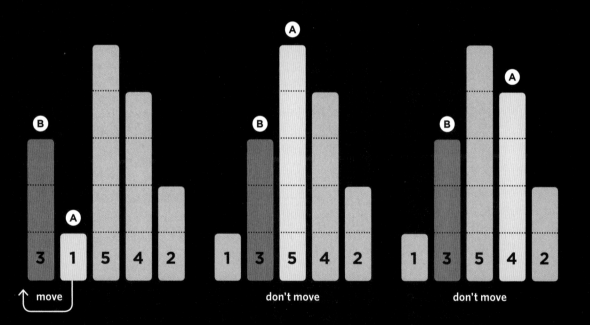

a should go *before* b

$$1 - 3 = -2$$
$$a - b = < 0$$

a should go *after* b

$$5 - 3 = 2$$
$$a - b = > 0$$

a should go *after* b

$$4 - 3 = 1$$
$$a - b = > 0$$

It is up to the browser to decide which order to sort items in .
This illustrates the order used by Safari. Other browsers sort items in a different order.

```
var prices = [3, 1, 5, 4, 2];    // Numbers stored in an array
prices.sort(function(a, b) {     // Two values are compared
  return a - b;                  // Decides which goes first
});
```

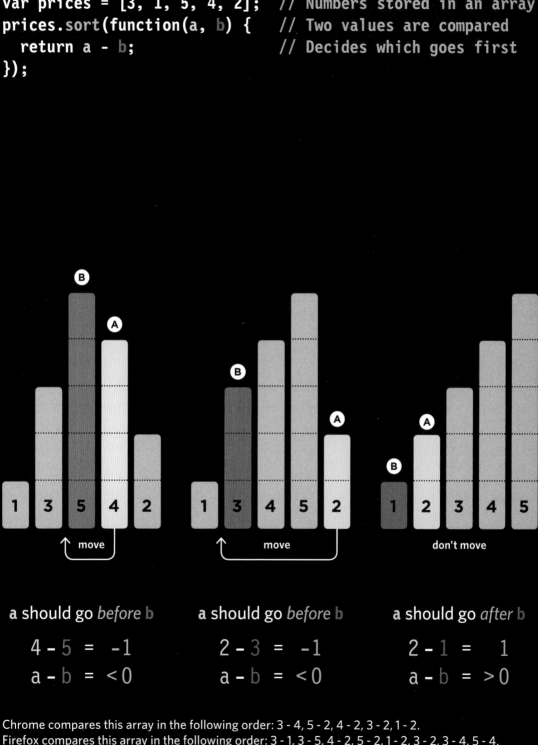

a should go *before* **b**

$$4 - 5 = -1$$

$$a - b = < 0$$

a should go *before* **b**

$$2 - 3 = -1$$

$$a - b = < 0$$

a should go *after* **b**

$$2 - 1 = 1$$

$$a - b = > 0$$

Chrome compares this array in the following order: 3 - 4, 5 - 2, 4 - 2, 3 - 2, 1 - 2.
Firefox compares this array in the following order: 3 - 1, 3 - 5, 4 - 2, 5 - 2, 1 - 2, 3 - 2, 3 - 4, 5 - 4.

SORTING NUMBERS

Here are some examples of compare functions that can be used as a parameter of the sort() method.

ASCENDING NUMERICAL ORDER

To sort numbers in an ascending order, you subtract the value of the second number *b* from the first number *a*. In the table on the right, you can see examples of how two values from the array are compared.

```
var prices = [1, 2, 125, 2, 19, 14];
prices.sort(function(a, b) {
  return a - b;
});
```

a	OPERATOR	b	RESULT	ORDER
1	-	2	-1	*a* comes before *b*
2	-	2	0	leave in same order
2	-	1	1	*b* comes before *a*

DESCENDING NUMERICAL ORDER

To order numbers in a descending order, you subtract the value of the first number *a* from the second number *b*.

```
var prices = [1, 2, 125, 2, 19, 14];
prices.sort(function(a, b) {
  return b - a;
});
```

b	OPERATOR	a	RESULT	ORDER
2	-	1	1	*b* comes before *a*
2	-	2	0	leave in same order
1	-	2	-1	*a* comes before *b*

RANDOM ORDER

This will randomly return a value between -1 and 1 creating a random order for the items.

```
var prices = [1, 2, 125, 2, 19, 14];
prices.sort(function() {
  return 0.5 - Math.random();
});
```

SORTING DATES

Dates need to be converted into a `Date` object so that they can then be compared using < and > operators.

```
var holidays = [
  '2014-12-25',
  '2014-01-01',
  '2014-07-04',
  '2014-11-28'
];

holidays.sort(function(a, b){
    var dateA = new Date(a);
    var dateB = new Date(b);

    return dateA - dateB
});
```

The array is now ordered as follows:

```
holidays = [
  '2014-01-01',
  '2014-07-04',
  '2014-11-28',
  '2014-12-25'
]
```

DATES IN ASCENDING ORDER

If the dates are held as strings, as they are in the array shown on the left, the compare function needs to create a `Date` object from the string so that the two dates can be compared.

Once they have been converted into a `Date` object, JavaScript stores the date as the number of milliseconds since the 1st January 1970.

With the date stored as a number, two dates can be compared in the same way that numbers are compared on the left-hand page.

SORTING A TABLE

In this example, the contents of a table can be reordered.
Each row of the table is stored in an array.
The array is then sorted when the user clicks on a header.

SORT BY HEADER

When users click on a heading, it triggers an anonymous function to sort the contents of the array (which contains the table rows). The rows are sorted in ascending order using data in that column.

Clicking the same header again will show the same column sorted in descending order.

DATA TYPES

Each column can contain one of the following types of data:

- Strings
- Time durations (mins/secs)
- Dates

If you look at the `<th>` elements, the type of data used is specified in an attribute called `data-sort`.

COMPARE FUNCTIONS

Each type of data needs a different compare function. The compare functions will be stored as three methods of an object called `compare`, which you create on p563:

- `name()` sorts strings
- `duration()` sorts mins/secs
- `date()` sorts dates

CreativeFolk	find talented people for your creative projects

My Videos

Camille Berger
♀ Paris, France

GENRE	▲ TITLE	DURATION	DATE
Film	Animals	6:40	2005-12-21
Film	The Deer	6:24	2014-02-28
Animation	The Ghost	11:40	2012-04-10
Animation	Wagons	21:40	2007-04-12
Animation	Wildfood	3:47	2014-07-16

HTML TABLE STRUCTURE

1. The `<table>` element needs to carry a `class` attribute whose value contains `sortable`.

2. Table headers have an attribute called `data-sort`. It reflects the type data in that column.

The value of the `data-sort` attribute corresponds with the methods of the `compare` object.

HTML

c12/sort-table.html

```
<body>
  <table class="sortable">
    <thead>
      <tr>
        <th data-sort="name">Genre</th>
        <th data-sort="name">Title</th>
        <th data-sort="duration">Duration</th>
        <th data-sort="date">Date</th>
      </tr>
    </thead>
    <tbody>
      <tr>
        <td>Animation</td>
        <td>Wildfood</td>
        <td>3:47</td>
        <td>2014-07-16</td>
      </tr>
      <tr>
        <td>Film</td>
        <td>The Deer</td>
        <td>6:24</td>
        <td>2012-02-28</td>
      </tr>
      <tr>
        <td>Animation</td>
        <td>The Ghost</td>
        <td>11:40</td>
        <td>2013-04-10</td>
      </tr>...
    </tbody>
  </table>
  <script src="js/jquery.js"></script>
  <script src="js/sort-table.js"></script>
</body>
```

COMPARE FUNCTIONS

1. Declare the `compare` object. It has three methods used to sort names, time durations, and dates.

THE `name()` METHOD

2. Add a method called `name()`. Like all compare functions, it should take two parameters: a and b.
3. Use a regular expression to remove the word 'the' from the beginning of both of the arguments that have been passed into the function (for more on this technique, see the bottom of the right-hand page).
4. If the value of a is lower than that of b:
5. Return -1 (indicating that a should come before b).
6. Otherwise, if a is greater than b, return 1. Or, if they are the same, return 0. (See bottom of page.)

THE `duration()` METHOD

7. Add a method called `duration()`. Like all compare functions, it should take two parameters: a and b.
8. Duration is stored in minutes and seconds: `mm:ss`. The `String` object's `split()` method splits the string at the colon, and creates an array with minutes and seconds as separate entries.
9. To get the total duration in seconds, `Number()` converts the strings in the arrays to numbers. The minutes are multiplied by 60 and added to the number of seconds.
10. The value of a - b is returned.

THE `date()` METHOD

11. Add a method called `date()`. Like all compare functions, it should take two parameters: a and b.
12. Create a new `Date` object to represent each of the arguments passed into the method.
13. Return the value of a minus b.

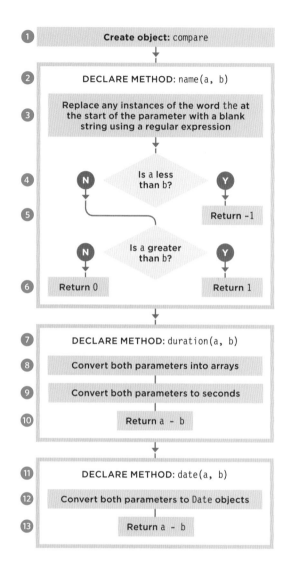

```
return a > b ? 1 : 0
```

A shorthand for a conditional operator is the **ternary operator**. It evaluates a condition and returns one of two values. The condition is shown to the left of the question mark.

The two options are shown to the right separated by a colon. If the condition returns a truthy value, the first value is returned. If the value is falsy, the value after the colon is returned.

THE COMPARE OBJECT

```
①  var compare = {                              // Declare compare object
②    name: function(a, b) {                     // Add a method called name
③      a = a.replace(/^the /i, '');             // Remove The from start of parameter
       b = b.replace(/^the /i, '');             // Remove The from start of parameter

④      if (a < b) {                             // If value a is less than value b
⑤        return -1;                             // Return -1
       } else {                                 // Otherwise
⑥        return a > b ? 1 : 0;                  // If a is greater than b return 1 OR
       }                                        // if they are the same return 0
     },
⑦    duration: function(a, b) {                 // Add a method called duration
⑧      a = a.split(':');                        // Split the time at the colon
       b = b.split(':');                        // Split the time at the colon

⑨      a = Number(a[0]) * 60 + Number(a[1]);    // Convert the time to seconds
       b = Number(b[0]) * 60 + Number(b[1]);    // Convert the time to seconds

⑩      return a - b;                            // Return a minus b
     },
⑪    date: function(a, b) {                     // Add a method called date
⑫      a = new Date(a);                         // New Date object to hold the date
       b = new Date(b);                         // New Date object to hold the date

⑬      return a - b;                            // Return a minus b
     }
   };
```

a.replace(/^the /i, '');

The `replace()` method is used to remove any instances of *The* from the start of a string. `replace()` works on any string and it takes one argument: a regular expression (see p612). It is helpful when *The* is not always used in a name, e.g., for band names or film titles. The regular expression is the first parameter of `replace()` method.

- The string you are looking for is shown between the forward slash characters.
- The caret ^ indicates that *the* must be at the start of the string.
- The **space** after *the* indicates there must be a space after it.
- The i indicates that the test is case insensitive.

When a match for the regular expression is found, the second parameter specifies what should take its place. In this case it is an empty string.

SORTING COLUMNS

1. For each element that has a `class` attribute with a value of `sortable`, run the anonymous function.

2. Store the current `<table>` in `$table`.

3. Store the table body in `$tbody`.

4. Store the `<th>` elements in `$controls`.

5. Put each row in `$tbody` into an array called `rows`.

6. Add an event handler for when users click on a header. It should call an anonymous function.

7. `$header` stores that element in a jQuery object.

8. Store the value of that heading's `data-sort` attribute in an variable called `order`.

9. Declare a variable called `column`.

10. In the header the user clicked upon, if the `class` attribute has a value of `ascending` or `descending`, then it is already sorted by this column.

11. Toggle the value of that `class` attribute (so that it shows the other value `ascending`/`descending`).

12. Reverse the rows (stored in the `rows` array) using the `reverse()` method of the array.

13. Otherwise, if the row the user clicked on was not selected, add a `class` of `ascending` to the header.

14. Remove the class of `ascending` or `descending` from all other `<th>` elements on this table.

15. If the `compare` object has a method that matches the value of the `data-type` attribute for this column:

16. Get the column number using the `index()` method (it returns the index number of the element within a jQuery matched set). That value is stored in the `column` variable.

17. The `sort()` method is applied to the array of rows and will compare two rows at a time. As it compares these values:

18. The values a and b are stored in variables:
`.find()` gets the `<td>` elements for that row.
`.eq()` looks for the cell in the row whose index number matches the `column` variable.
`.text()` gets the text from that cell.

19. The `compare` object is used to compare a and b. It will use the method specified in the `type` variable (which was collected from the `data-sort` attribute in step 6).

20. Append the rows (stored in the `rows` array) to the table body.

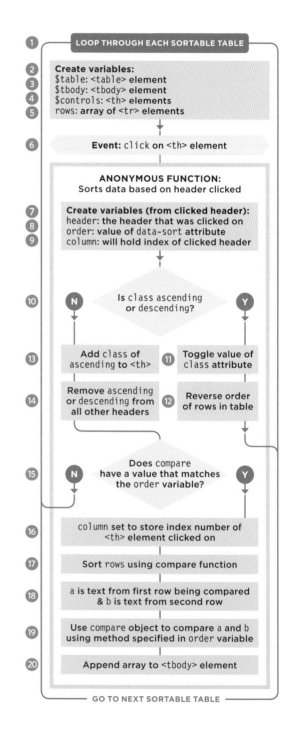

SORTABLE TABLE SCRIPT

JAVASCRIPT   c12/js/sort-table.js

```javascript
① $('.sortable').each(function() {
②   var $table = $(this);                    // This sortable table
③   var $tbody = $table.find('tbody');        // Store table body
④   var $controls = $table.find('th');        // Store table headers
⑤   var rows = $tbody.find('tr').toArray();   // Store array containing rows

⑥   $controls.on('click', function() {        // When user clicks on a header
⑦     var $header = $(this);                  // Get the header
⑧     var order = $header.data('sort');       // Get value of data-sort attribute
⑨     var column;                             // Declare variable called column

     // If selected item has ascending or descending class, reverse contents
⑩     if ($header.is('.ascending') || $header.is('.descending')) {
⑪       $header.toggleClass('ascending descending');  // Toggle to other class
⑫       $tbody.append(rows.reverse());                // Reverse the array
     } else {                                // Otherwise perform a sort
⑬       $header.addClass('ascending');               // Add class to header
       // Remove asc or desc from all other headers
⑭       $header.siblings().removeClass('ascending descending');
⑮       if (compare.hasOwnProperty(order)) {  // If compare object has method
⑯         column = $controls.index(this);      // Search for column's index no

⑰         rows.sort(function(a, b) {           // Call sort() on rows array
⑱           a = $(a).find('td').eq(column).text();// Get text of column in row a
            b = $(b).find('td').eq(column).text();// Get text of column in row b
⑲           return compare[order](a, b);        // Call compare method
         });

⑳         $tbody.append(rows);
       }
     }
   });
 });
```

SUMMARY
FILTERING, SEARCHING & SORTING

▸ Arrays are commonly used to store a set of objects.

▸ Arrays have helpful methods that allow you to add, remove, filter, and sort the items they contain.

▸ Filtering lets you remove items and only show a subset of them based on selected criteria.

▸ Filters often rely on custom functions to check whether items match your criteria.

▸ Search lets you filter based upon data the user enters.

▸ Sorting allows you to reorder the items in an array.

▸ If you want to control the order in which items are sorted, you can use a compare function.

▸ To support older browsers, you can use a shim script.

13

FORM ENHANCEMENT & VALIDATION

Forms allow you to collect information from visitors, and JavaScript can help you get the right information from them.

Since JavaScript was created, it has been used to enhance and validate forms. Enhancements make forms easier to use. Validation checks whether the user has provided the right information before submitting the form (if not, it provides feedback to the user). This chapter is divided into the following three sections:

FORM ENHANCEMENT

This section features many examples of form enhancement. Each one introduces the different properties and methods you can use when working with form elements.

HTML5 FORM ELEMENTS

HTML5 contains validation features that do not use JavaScript. This section addresses ways in which you can offer validation to old and new browsers in a consistent way.

FORM VALIDATION

The final, and longest, example in the book shows a script that validates (and enhances) the registration form that you can see on the right-hand page. It has over 250 lines of code.

The first section of this chapter also drops jQuery in favor of plain JavaScript, because you should not always rely upon jQuery (especially for scripts that use little of its functionality).

HELPER FUNCTIONS

The first section of this chapter uses plain JavaScript, no jQuery.
We will create our own JavaScript file to handle cross-browser issues,
it will contain one helper function to create events.

Forms use a lot of event handlers and (as you saw in Chapter 6) IE5-8 used a different event model than other browsers. You can use jQuery to deal with cross-browser event handling. But, if you do not want to include the entire jQuery script just to handle events in older version of IE, then you need to write your own fallback code to handle the events.

Instead of writing the same fallback code every time you need an event handler, you can write the fallback code once in a **helper function**, and then call that function every time you need to add an event handler to a page.

On the right-hand page you can see a function called addEvent(). It lives in a file called utilities.js. Once that file has been included in the HTML page, any scripts included *after* it will be able to use this function to create cross-browser event handler:

addEvent(*el, event, callback*);
      (i)   (ii)   (iii)

The function takes three parameters:
i) *el* is a DOM node representing the element that the event will be added to or removed from.
ii) *event* is the type of event being listened for.
iii) *callback* is the function that is to be run when the event is triggered on that element.

The utilities.js file on the website also has a method to remove events.

If you look inside the addEvent() method on the right-hand page, a conditional statement checks whether the browser supports addEventListener(). If it does, a standard event listener will be added. If not, then the IE fallback will be created.

The fallback addresses three points:
- It uses IE's the attachEvent() method.
- In IE5-8, the **event** object is not automatically passed into the event-handling function (and is not available via the this keyword) see p264. Instead it is available on the window object. So the code must pass the **event** object into the event handler as a parameter.
- When you pass parameters to an event-handling function, the call must be wrapped in an anonymous function see p256.

To achieve this, the fallback adds two methods to the element the event handler will be placed upon (see steps 5 and 6 on the right-hand page). It then uses IE's attachEvent() method to add the event handler code to the element.

The functions demonstrate two new techniques:
- **Adding new methods to DOM nodes:**
  You can add methods to DOM nodes because they are just objects (that represent elements).
- **Creating method names using a variable:**
  Square brackets can be used to set a property/method, their content is evaluated into a string.

UTILITIES FILE

Here, you can see the `addEvent()` function that will be used to create all of the event handlers in this chapter. It lives in a file called `utilities.js`.

These reusable functions are often referred to as **helper functions**. As you write more JavaScript, you are increasingly likely to create this type of function.

c13/js/utilities.js

```
   // Helper function to add an event listener
1  function addEvent(el, event, callback) {
2    if ('addEventListener' in el) {               // If addEventListener works
3      el.addEventListener(event, callback, false);// Use it
4    } else {                                        // Otherwise
5      el['e' + event + callback] = callback;       // Make callback a method of el
6      el[event + callback] = function() {           // Add second method
         el['e' + event + callback](window.event);  // Use it to call prev func
       };
7      el.attachEvent('on' + event, el[event + callback]); // Use attachEvent()
     }              // to call the second function, which then calls the first one
   }
```

1. The `addEvent()` function is declared with three parameters: element, event type, callback function.
2. A conditional statement checks if the element supports the `addEventListener()` method.
3. If it does, then `addEventListener()` is used.
4. If not, the fallback code will run instead.

The fallback must add two methods to the element the event handler will be placed upon. It then uses Internet Explorer's `attachEvent()` method to call them when the event occurs on that element.

5. The first method added to the element is the code that should run when the event occurs on this element (it was the third parameter of the function).
6. The second method calls the method from the previous step. It is needed in order to pass the **event** object to the function in step 5.
7. The `attachEvent()` method is used to listen for the specified event, on the specified element. When the event fires, it calls the method that it added in step 6, which in turn calls the method in step 5 using the correct reference to the **event** object.

In steps 5 and 6, square bracket notation is used to add a method name to an element:

$$el['e' + event + callback]$$
   (i)   (ii)

i) The DOM node is stored in `el`. The square brackets add the method name to that node. That method name must be unique to that element, so it is created using three pieces of information.

ii) The method names are made up of:
- The letter e (used for the first method in step 5 but not used in step 6)
- The event type (e.g., `click`, `blur`, `mouseover`)
- The code from the callback function

In the code on the right-hand page, the value of this method is the callback function. (This could lead to a long method name, but it serves the purpose.) This function is based on one by John Resig, who created jQuery (`http://ejohn.org/projects/flexible-javascript-events/`).

THE FORM ELEMENT

DOM nodes for form controls have different properties, methods, and events than some of the other elements you have met so far.
Here are some you should note for the `<form>` element.

PROPERTY	DESCRIPTION
action	The URL the form is submitted to
method	If it is to be sent via GET or POST
name	Rarely used, more common to select a form by the value of its id attribute
elements	A collection of the elements in the form that users can interact with. They can be accessed via index numbers or the values of their name attributes.

METHOD	DESCRIPTION
submit()	This has the same effect as clicking the submit button on a form
reset()	Resets the form to the initial values it had when the page loaded

EVENT	DESCRIPTION
submit	Fires when the form is submitted
reset	Fires when the form is reset

The DOM methods you saw in Chapter 5, such as `getElementById()`, `getElementsByTagName()`, and `querySelector()`, are the most popular techniques for accessing both the `<form>` element and the form controls within any form. However, the **document** object also has something called the **forms collection**. The forms collection holds a reference to each of the `<form>` elements that appear on a page.

Each item in a collection is given an index number (a number starting at 0, like an array). This would access the second form using its index number:
`document.forms[1];`

You can also access a form using the value of its name attribute. The following would select a form whose name attribute has a value of `login`:
`document.forms.login`

Each `<form>` element in the page also has an **elements collection**. It holds all of the form controls within that form. Each item in the `elements` collection can also be accessed by index number or by the value of its name attribute.

The following would access the *second* form on the page and then select the *first* form control within it:
`document.forms[1].elements[0];`

The following would access the *second* form on the page, then select the element whose name attribute had a value of **password** from that form:
`document.forms[1].elements.password;`

Note: index numbers in a collection of elements can change if the markup of a page is altered. So, use of index numbers ties a script to the HTML markup (– it does not achieve a separation of concerns).

FORM CONTROLS

Each type of form control uses a different combination of the properties, methods, and events shown below. Note that the methods can be used to simulate how a user would interact with the form controls.

PROPERTY	DESCRIPTION
value	In a text input, it is the text the user entered; otherwise, it is the value of the value attribute
type	When a form control has been created using the <input> element, this defines the type of the form element (e.g., text, password, radio, checkbox)
name	Gets or sets the value of the name attribute
defaultValue	The initial value of a text box or text area when the page is rendered
form	The form that the control belongs to
disabled	Disables the <form> element
checked	Indicates which checkbox or radio buttons have been checked. This property is a Boolean; in JavaScript it will have a value of true if checked
defaultChecked	Whether the checkbox or radio button was checked or not when the page loaded (Boolean)
selected	Indicates that an item from a select box has been selected (Boolean – true if selected)

METHOD	DESCRIPTION
focus()	Gives an element focus
blur()	Removes focus from an element
select()	Selects and highlights text content of an element, (e.g., text inputs, text areas, and passwords)
click()	Triggers a click event upon buttons, checkboxes, and file upload. Also triggers a submit event on a submit button, and the reset event on a reset button

EVENT	DESCRIPTION
blur	When the user leaves a field
focus	When the user enters a field
click	When the user clicks on an element
change	When the value of an element changes
input	When the value of an <input> or <textarea> element changes
keydown, keyup, keypress	When the user interacts with a keyboard

SUBMITTING FORMS

In this example, a basic login form lets users enter a username and password. When the user submits the form, a welcome message will replace the form. On the right-hand page you can see both the HTML and the JavaScript for this example.

In the HTML page, the `utilities.js` file you saw on p571 is included before the `submit-event.js` script because its `addEvent()` function is used to create the event handlers for this example. `utilities.js` is included for all examples in this section.

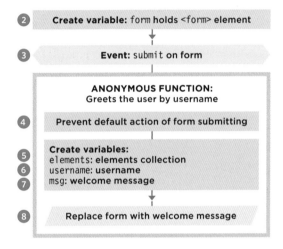

1. Place the script in an Immediately Invoked Function Expression (IIFE see p97). (This is not shown in the flowchart.)

2. A variable called **form** is created and it is set to hold the `<form>` element. It is used in the event listener in the next line of code.

3. An event listener triggers an anonymous function when the form is submitted. Note how this is set using the `addEvent()` function that was created in the `utilities.js` file that you saw on p571.

4. To prevent the form being sent (and to allow this example to show a message to the user) the `preventDefault()` method is used on the form.

5. The collection of elements in this form is stored in a variable called `elements`.

6. To get the username, first select the username input from the `elements` collection using the value of its `name` attribute. Then, to get the text the user entered, the `value` property of that element is used.

7. A welcome message is created and stored in a variable called `msg`; this message will incorporate the username that the visitor entered.

8. The message replaces the form within the HTML.

The event listener waits for the `submit` event on the form (rather than a `click` on the submit button) because the form can be submitted in other ways than clicking on the submit button. For example, the user might press the Enter key.

THE SUBMIT EVENT & GETTING FORM VALUES

                c13/submit-event.html

```html
<form id="login" action="/login" method="post">...
  <div class="two-thirds column" id="main">
    <fieldset>
      <legend>Login</legend>
      <label for="username">Username:</label>
      <input type="text" id="username" name="username" />
      <label for="pwd">Password:</label>
      <input type="password" id="pwd" name="pwd" />
      <input type="submit" value="Login" />
    </fieldset>
  </div> <!-- .two-thirds -->
</form> ...
<script src="js/utilities.js"></script>
<script src="js/submit-event.js"></script>
```

            c13/js/submit-event.js

```javascript
(function(){
  var form = document.getElementById('login');        // Get form element

  addEvent(form, 'submit', function(e) {              // When user submits form
    e.preventDefault();                                // Stop it being sent
    var elements = this.elements;                      // Get all form elements
    var username = elements.username.value;            // Select username entered
    var msg      = 'Welcome ' + username;              // Create welcome message
    document.getElementById('main').textContent = msg; // Write welcome message
  });
}());
```

When selecting a DOM node, if you are likely to use it again, it should be cached. On the right, you can see a variation of the above code, where the username and the main element have both been stored in variables outside of the event listener. If the user had to resubmit the form, the browser would not have to make the same selections again.

```javascript
var form = document.getElementById('login');
var elements = form.elements;
var elUsername = elements.username;
var elMain = document.getElementById('main');
addEvent(form, 'submit', function(e) {
  e.preventDefault();
  var msg = 'Welcome ' + elUsername.value;
  elMain.textContent = msg;
});
```

CHANGING TYPE OF INPUT

This example adds a checkbox under the password input. If the user checks that box, their password will become visible. It works by using JavaScript to change the **type** property of the input from **password** to **text**. (The **type** property in the DOM corresponds to **type** attribute in the HTML.)

Changing the **type** property causes an error in IE8 (and earlier), so this code is placed in a **try...** **catch** statement. If the browser detects an error, the script continues to run the second code block.

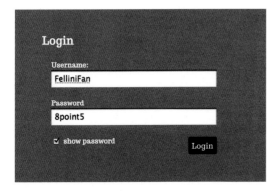

1. Place the script in an IIFE (not shown in flowchart).
2. Put password input and checkbox in variables.
3. An event listener triggers an anonymous function when the show password checkbox is changed.
4. The target of the event (the checkbox) is stored in a variable called target. As you saw in Chapter 6, **e.target** will retrieve this for most browsers. **e.srcElement** is only used for old versions of IE.
5. A **try... catch** statement checks if an error is caused when the **type** attribute is updated.
6. If the checkbox is selected:
7. The value of the password input's **type** attribute is set to **text**.
8. Otherwise, it is set to **password**.
9. If trying to change the type causes an error, the **catch** clause runs another code block instead.
10. It shows a message to tell the user.

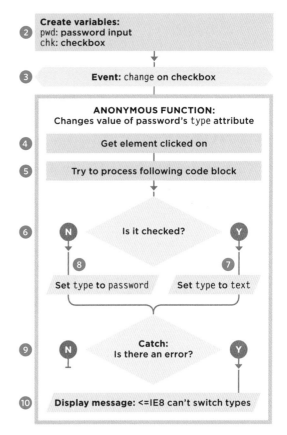

As you saw in Chapter 10, an error can stop a script from running. If you know something may cause an error for some browsers, placing that code in a **try... catch** statement lets the interpreter continue with an alternative set of code.

SHOWING A PASSWORD

```html
<fieldset>
  <legend>Login</legend>
  <label for="username">Username:</label>
  <input type="text" id="username" name="username" />
  <label for="pwd">Password:</label>
  <input type="password" id="pwd" name="pwd" />
  <input type="checkbox" id="showPwd">
  <label for="showPwd">show password</label>
  <input type="submit" value="Login" />
</fieldset> ...
<script src="js/utilities.js"></script>
<script src="js/input-type.js"></script>
```

```javascript
① (function(){

②   var pwd = document.getElementById('pwd');       // Get password input
     var chk = document.getElementById('showPwd');   // Get checkbox

③   addEvent(chk, 'change', function(e) {           // When user clicks on checkbox
④     var target = e.target || e.srcElement;        // Get that element
⑤     try {                                         // Try the following code block
⑥       if (target.checked) {                       // If the checkbox is checked
⑦         pwd.type = 'text';                        // Set pwd type to text
         } else {                                    // Otherwise
⑧         pwd.type = 'password';                    // Set pwd type to password
         }
⑨     } catch(error) {                              // If this causes an error
⑩       alert('This browser cannot switch type');   // Say 'cannot switch type'
       }
     });

   }());
```

SUBMIT BUTTONS

This script disables the submit button when:

- The script first loads. The `change` event then checks when the password changes and enables submit if the password is given a value.
- The form has been submitted (to prevent the form being sent multiple times).

The button is disabled using the `disabled` property. It corresponds with the HTML `disabled` attribute, and can be used to disable any form elements that a user can interact with. A value of `true` disables the button; `false` lets the user click on it.

1. Place the script in an IIFE (not shown in flowchart).
2. Store the form, password input, and submit button in variables.
3. The `submitted` variable is known as a **flag**; it remembers if the form has been submitted yet.
4. The submit button is disabled at the start of the script (rather than in the HTML) so that the form can still be used if a visitor has JavaScript disabled.
5. An event listener waits for the `input` event on the password input; it triggers an anonymous function.
6. Store the target of the event in `target`.
7. If the password input has a value, the submit button is enabled, and (8) its style updated.
9. A second event listener checks for when the user submits the form (and runs an anonymous function).
10. If the submit button is disabled, or the form has been submitted, the subsequent code block is run.
11. The default action of the form (submitting) is prevented, and `return` leaves the function.
12. If step 11 did not run, the form is submitted, the submit button disabled, the `submitted` variable updated with a value of `true`, and its `class` updated.

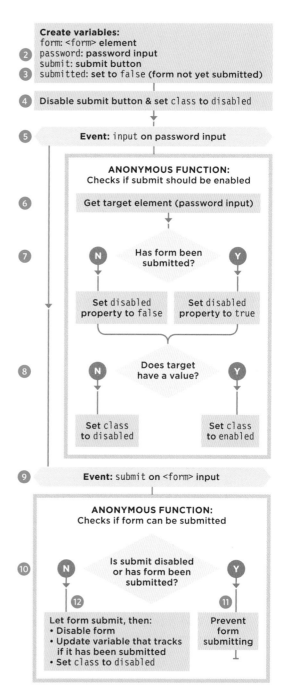

DISABLE SUBMIT BUTTON

```html
<label for="pwd">New password:</label>
<input type="password" id="pwd" />
<input type="submit" id="submit" value="submit" />
```

```javascript
(function(){
  var form     = document.getElementById('newPwd');  // The form
  var password = document.getElementById('pwd');      // Password input
  var submit   = document.getElementById('submit');   // Submit button

  var submitted = false;                              // Has form been submitted?

  submit.disabled = true;                             // Disable submit button
  submit.className = 'disabled';                      // Style submit button

  // On input: Check whether or not to enable the submit button
  addEvent(password, 'input', function(e) {           // On input of password
    var target = e.target || e.srcElement;            // Target of event
    submit.disabled = submitted || !target.value;     // Set disabled property
    // If form has been submitted or pwd has no value set CSS to disabled
    submit.className = (!target.value || submitted ) ? 'disabled' : 'enabled';
  });

  // On submit: Disable the form so it cannot be submitted again
  addEvent(form, 'submit', function(e) {              // On submit
    if (submit.disabled || submitted) {               // If disabled OR sent
      e.preventDefault();                             // Stop form submission
      return;                                         // Stop processing function
    }                                                 // Otherwise continue...
    submit.disabled = true;                           // Disable submit button
    submitted = true;                                 // Update submitted var
    submit.className = 'disabled';                    // Update style

    // Demo purposes only: What would have been sent & show submit is disabled
    e.preventDefault();                               // Stop form submitting
    alert('Password is ' + password.value);           // Show the text
  });
}());
```

CHECKBOXES

This example asks users about their interests. It has an option to select or deselect all of the checkboxes. It has two event handlers:

- The first fires when the **all** checkbox is selected; it loops through the options, updating them.
- The second fires when the **options** change; if one is deselected, the *all* option must be deselected.

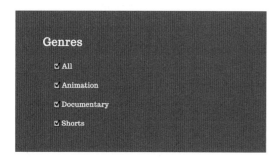

You can use the change event to detect when the value of a checkbox, radio button, or select box changes. Here, it is used to tell when the user selects / deselects a checkbox. The checkboxes can be updated using the checked property, which corresponds with HTML's checked attribute.

1. Place the script in an IIFE (not shown in flowchart).
2. The form, all of the form elements, the options, and the *all* checkbox are stored in variables.
3. The updateAll() function is declared.
4. A loop runs through each of the options.
5. For each one, the checked property is set to the same value as the checked property on the *all* option.
6. An event listener waits for the user to click on the *all* checkbox, which fires a change event and calls the updateAll() function.
7. The clearAllOption() function is defined.
8. It gets the target of the option the user clicked on.
9. If that option is deselected, then the *all* option is also deselected (as they are no longer all selected).
10. A loop runs through the options, adding an event listener. When the change event happens on any of them, clearAllOption() is called.

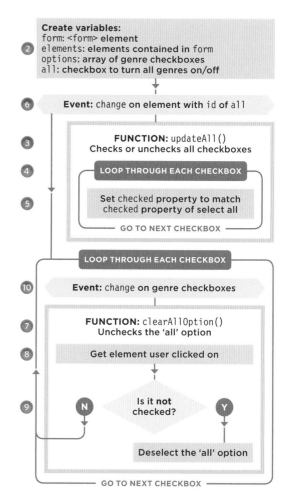

SELECT ALL CHECKBOXES

HTML   c13/all-checkboxes.html

```html
<label><input type="checkbox" value="all" id="all">All</label>
<label><input type="checkbox" name="genre" value="animation">Animation</label>
<label><input type="checkbox" name="genre" value="docs">Documentary</label>
<label><input type="checkbox" name="genre" value="shorts">Shorts</label>
```

JAVASCRIPT   c13/js/all-checkboxes.js

```javascript
①  (function(){
②    var form     = document.getElementById('interests'); // Get form
      var elements = form.elements;                        // All elements in form
      var options  = elements.genre;                       // Array: genre checkboxes
      var all      = document.getElementById('all');       // The 'all' checkbox

③    function updateAll() {
④      for (var i = 0; i < options.length; i++) {          // Loop through checkboxes
⑤        options[i].checked = all.checked;                 // Update checked property
        }
      }
⑥    addEvent(all, 'change', updateAll);                   // Add event listener

⑦    function clearAllOption(e) {
⑧      var target = e.target || e.srcElement;              // Get target of event
        if (!target.checked) {                             // If not checked
⑨          all.checked = false;                            // Uncheck 'All' checkbox
        }
      }
⑩    for (var i = 0; i < options.length; i++) {            // Loop through checkboxes
        addEvent(options[i], 'change', clearAllOption);    // Add event listener
      }

    }());
```

RADIO BUTTONS

This example lets users say how they heard about a website. Every time the user selects a radio button, the code checks if the user selected the option that says *other*, and one of two things happens:

- If *other* is selected, a text input is shown so they can add further detail.
- If the first two options are selected, the text box is hidden and its value is emptied.

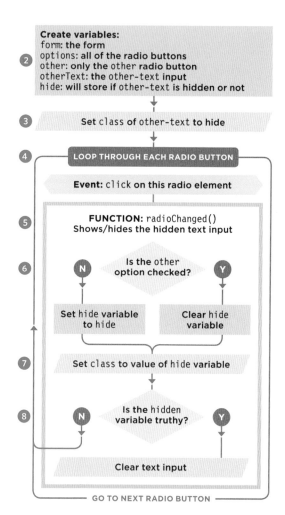

1. Place the script in an IIFE (not shown in flowchart).
2. The code starts out by setting up variables to hold the form, all radio buttons, the radio button for the *other* option, and the text input.
3. The text input is hidden. This uses JavaScript to update the `class` attribute so that the form still works if the user has JavaScript disabled.
4. Using a `for` loop, an event listener is added to each of the radio buttons. When one of them is clicked, the `radioChanged()` function is called.
5. The `radioChanged()` function is declared.
6. If `other` is checked, the value of the `hide` variable is set to be a blank string, otherwise it is set to `hide`.
7. The `hide` variable is, in turn, used to set the value of the `class` attribute on the text input. If it is blank, the other option is shown; if it has a value of `hide`, the text input is hidden.
8. If the `hide` attribute has a value of `hide`, then the contents of the text input are emptied (so that the text input is blank if it is shown).

RADIO BUTTONS

```html
<form id="how-heard" action="/heard" method="post">
  ...
  <input type="radio" name="heard" value="search" id="search" />
  <label for="search">Search engine</label><br>

  <input type="radio" name="heard" value="print" id="print" />
  <label for="print">Newspaper or magazine</label><br>

  <input type="radio" name="heard" value="other" id="other" />
  <label for="other">Other</label><br>
  <input type="text" name="other-input" id="other-text" />

  <input id="submit" type="submit" value="submit" />
  ...
</form>
```

```javascript
(1)  (function(){
       var form, options, other, otherText, hide;         // Declare variables
       form       = document.getElementById('how-heard');  // Get the form
(2)    options    = form.elements.heard;                    // Get the radio buttons
       other      = document.getElementById('other');       // Other radio button
       otherText  = document.getElementById('other-text');  // Other text input
(3)    otherText.className = 'hide';                         // Hide other text input

(4)    for (var i = [0]; i < options.length; i++) {          // Loop through radios
         addEvent(options[i], 'click', radioChanged);       // Add event listener
       }

(5)    function radioChanged() {
(6)      hide = other.checked ? '' : 'hide';                // Is other checked?
(7)      otherText.className = hide;                         // Text input visibility
         if (hide) {                                         // If text input hidden
(8)        otherText.value = '';                             // Empty its contents
         }
       }
     }());
```

SELECT BOXES

The `<select>` element is more complex than the other form controls.
Its DOM node has a number of extra properties and methods.
Its `<option>` elements contain the values a user can select.

This example features two select boxes. When the user selects an option from the first select box, the contents of the second select box are updated with corresponding options.

In the first select box, users can choose to rent a camera or a projector. When they make their choice, a list of options are shown in the second select box. Because this example is a bit more complex than the ones you have seen so far in this chapter, the HTML and screen shots are shown to the right, and the JavaScript file is discussed on p586-p587.

When the user selects an option from the drop-down list, the **change** event fires. This event is often used to trigger scripts when the user changes the value of a select box.

The `<select>` element also has some extra properties and methods that are specific to it; these are shown in the tables below.

If you want to work with the individual options the user can select from, a collection of `<option>` elements is available.

PROPERTY	DESCRIPTION
options	A collection of all the `<option>` elements
selectedIndex	Index number of the option that is currently option
length	Number of options
multiple	Allows users to select multiple options from the select box (Rarely used because the user-experience is not very good)
selectedOptions	A collection of all the selected `<option>` elements

METHOD	DESCRIPTION
add(*option*, *before*)	Adds an item to the list: The first parameter is the new option; the second is the element it should go before If no value is given, the item will be added to the end of the options
remove(*index*)	Removes an item from the list: Has only one parameter – the index number of the option to be removed

SELECT BOXES

HTML   c13/populate-selectbox.html

```
<label for="equipmentType">type</label>
<select id="equipmentType" name="equipmentType">
  <option value="choose">Please choose a type</option>
  <option value="cameras">camera</option>
  <option value="projectors">projector</option>
</select><br>

<label for="model">model</label>
<select id="model" name="model">
  <option>Please choose a type first</option>
</select>

<input id="submit" type="submit" value="submit" />
```

RESULT

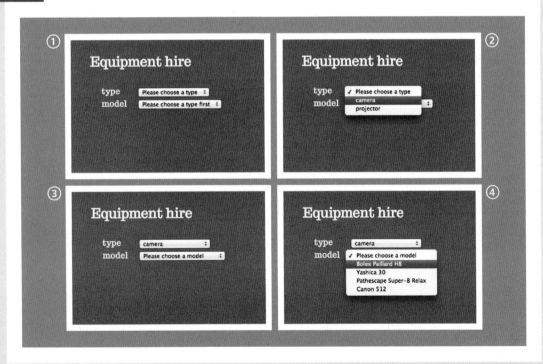

SELECT BOXES

1. Place the script in an IIFE (not shown in flowchart).

2. Variables hold the two select boxes.

3. Two objects are created; each one holds options used to populate the second select box (one has types of cameras, the other has types of projectors).

4. When the user changes the first select box, an event listener triggers an anonymous function.

5. The anonymous function checks if the first select box has a value of choose.

6. If so, the second select box is updated with just one option, which tells the user to select a type.

7. No further processing is needed, and the return keyword exits the anonymous function (until the user changes the first select box again).

8. If a type of equipment has been selected, the anonymous function continues to run, and a models variable is created. It will store one of the objects defined in step 3 (cameras or projectors). This correct object is retrieved using the getModels() function declared at the end of the script (9+10). The function takes one parameter this.value, which corresponds to the value from the option that was selected in first select box.

9. Inside the getModels() function, an if statement checks if the value passed in was cameras; if so, it returns the cameras object.

10. If not, it continues to run, checking to see if the value was projectors, and if so, it returns the projectors object.

11. A variable called options is created. It will hold all the <option> elements for the second select box. When this variable is created the first <option> is added to it; it tells users to choose a model.

12. A for loop goes through the contents of the object that was placed in the models variable in step (8-10). Inside the loop, key refers to the individual items in the object.

13. Another <option> element is created for every item in the object. Its value attribute uses the property name from the object. The content that sits between the <option> tags is that property's value.

14. The options are then added to the second select box using the innerHTML property.

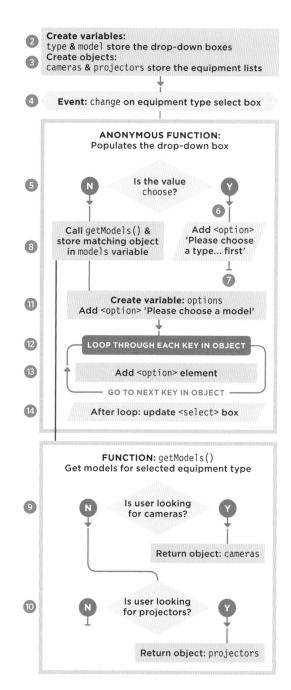

SELECT BOXES

```
① (function(){
②    var type  = document.getElementById('equipmentType');// Type select box
      var model = document.getElementById('model');        // Model select box
      var cameras = {                                      // Object stores cameras
        bolex: 'Bolex Paillard H8',
        yashica: 'Yashica 30',
        pathescape: 'Pathescape Super-8 Relax',
        canon: 'Canon 512'
      };
③    var projectors = {                                   // Store projectors
        kodak: 'Kodak Instamatic M55',
        bolex: 'Bolex Sound 715',
        eumig: 'Eumig Mark S',
        sankyo: 'Sankyo Dualux'
      };

      // WHEN THE USER CHANGES THE TYPE SELECT BOX
④    addEvent(type, 'change', function() {
⑤      if (this.value === 'choose') {                     // No selection made
⑥        model.innerHTML = '<option>Please choose a type first</option>';
⑦        return;                                          // No need to proceed further
        }
⑧      var models = getModels(this.value);                // Select the right object

        // LOOP THROUGH THE OPTIONS IN THE OBJECT TO CREATE OPTIONS
⑪      var options = '<option>Please choose a model</option>';
⑫      for (var key in models) {                          // Loop through models
⑬        options += '<option value="' + key + '">' + models[key] + '</option>';
        } // If an option could contain a quote, key should be escaped
⑭      model.innerHTML = options;                         // Update select box
      });

      function getModels(equipmentType) {
⑨      if (equipmentType === 'cameras') {                 // If type is cameras
          return cameras;                                // Return cameras object
⑩      } else if (equipmentType === 'projectors') {      // If type is projectors
          return projectors;                             // Return projectors object
        }
      }
    }());
```

TEXTAREA

In this example, users can enter a biography of up to 140 characters. When the cursor is in the textarea, a `<span>` element will be shown with a count of how many characters the user has remaining. When the textarea loses focus, this message is hidden.

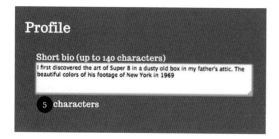

Profile

Short bio (up to 140 characters)

I first discovered the art of Super 8 in a dusty old box in my father's attic. The beautiful colors of his footage of New York in 1969

5 characters

1. Place the script in an IIFE (not shown in flowchart).
2. The script sets up two variables to hold:
a reference to the `<textarea>` element and
a reference to the `<span>` that holds the message.
3. Two event listeners monitor the `<textarea>`.
The first checks for when the element gains focus;
the second checks for a `input` event. Both events
trigger a function called `updateCounter()` **(6-11)**
The `input` event does not work in IE8, but you can
use `keyup` to support older browsers.
4. A third event listener triggers an anonymous
function when the user leaves the `<textarea>`.
5. If the number of characters is less than or equal
to 140 characters, the length of the bio is okay, and
it hides the message (because it is not needed when
the user is not interacting with the element).
6. The `updateCounter()` function is declared.
7. It gets a reference to the element that called it.
8. A variable called `count` holds the number of
characters left to use (it does this by subtracting the
number of characters used from 140).
9. `if... else` statements are used to set the CSS
class for the element that holds the message (these
can also show the message if it was hidden).
10. A variable called `charMsg` is created to store the
message that will be shown to the user.
11. The message is added to the page.

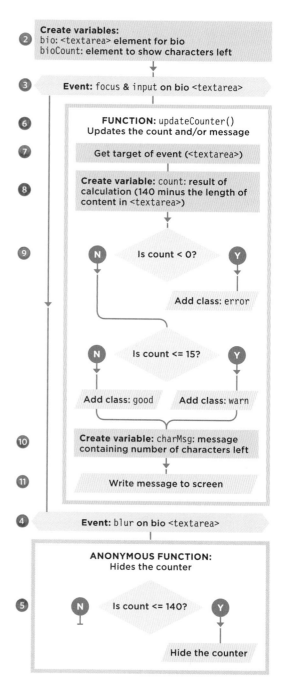

CHARACTER COUNTER

HTML

```html
    <label for="bio">Short Bio (up to 140 characters)</label>
    <textarea name="bio" id="bio" rows="5" cols="30"></textarea>
    <span id="bio-count" class="hide"></span>
...
<script src="js/utilities.js"></script>
<script src="js/textarea-counter.js"></script>
```

JAVASCRIPT

```javascript
① (function () {
②   var bio      = document.getElementById('bio');       // <textarea> element
     var bioCount = document.getElementById('bio-count');  // Character count el

③   addEvent(bio, 'focus', updateCounter);      // Call updateCounter() on focus
     addEvent(bio, 'input', updateCounter);      // Call updateCounter() on input

④   addEvent(bio, 'blur', function () {          // On leaving the element
       if (bio.value.length <= 140) {            // If bio is not too long
⑤        bioCount.className = 'hide';            // Hide the counter
       }
     });

⑥   function updateCounter(e) {
⑦     var target = e.target || e.srcElement;     // Get the target of the event
⑧     var count  = 140 - target.value.length;    // How many characters are left
       if (count < 0) {                          // If less than 0 chars free
         bioCount.className = 'error';           // Add class of error
       } else if (count <= 15) {                 // If less than 15 chars free
⑨        bioCount.className = 'warn';            // Add class of warn
       } else {                                  // Otherwise
         bioCount.className = 'good';            // Add class of good
       }
⑩     var charMsg = '<b>' + count + '</b>' + ' characters'; // Message to display
⑪     bioCount.innerHTML = charMsg;              // Update the counter element
     }

   }());
```

HTML5 ELEMENTS & ATTRIBUTES

HTML5 adds form elements and attributes to perform tasks that had previously been performed by JavaScript. However, their appearance can vary a lot between different browsers (especially their error messages).

SEARCH

```
<input type="search"
  placeholder="Search..."
  autofocus>
```

SAFARI

| sheepdog | ⊗ |

FIREFOX

| sheepdog |

CHROME

| sheepdog |

Safari rounds the corners of its search inputs to match the user interface of the operating system. When you enter text, Safari shows a cross icon which, when clicked or tapped, allows the user to clear the text from the field. Other browsers show an input like any other text input.

EMAIL, URL, PHONE

```
<input type="email">
<input type="url">
<input type="telephone">
```

SAFARI

| hello@javascriptbook.com |

FIREFOX

| hello@javascriptbook.com |

CHROME

| hello@javascriptbook. |

Email, URL, and phone inputs all look like text input fields, but the browser performs checks on the data entered into these inputs to see if it is in the right format to be an email address, URL, or phone number, then shows a message if it is not.

NUMBER

```
<input type="number"
  min="0"
  max="10"
  step="2"
  value="6">
```

SAFARI

| 6 ⇕ |

FIREFOX

| 6 |

CHROME

| 6 |

Number inputs sometimes add arrows to increase or decrease the number specified (also known as **spinboxes**). You can specify a minimum and a maximum value, a step (or increment), and an initial value. The browser checks that the user entered a number, and shows a message if a number was not entered.

ATTRIBUTE	DESCRIPTION
autofocus	Gives focus to this element when the page is loaded
placeholder	Content of this attribute is shown in the `<input>` element as a hint (see p594)
required	Checks that the field has a value – could be text entered or an option selected (see p606)
min	Minimum permitted number
max	Maximum permitted number
step	Intervals by which numbers should increase or decrease
value	Default value for a number when the control first loads on the page
autocomplete	On by default: shows list of past entries (disable for credit card numbers / sensitive data)
pattern	Lets you to specify a regular expression to validate a value (see p612)
novalidate	Used on the `<form>` element to disable the HTML5 built-in form validation (see p604)

RANGE

```
<input type="range"
  min="0"
  max="10"
  step="2"
  value="6">
```

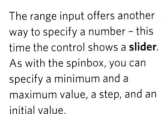

The range input offers another way to specify a number – this time the control shows a **slider**. As with the spinbox, you can specify a minimum and a maximum value, a step, and an initial value.

COLOR PICKER

```
<input type="color">
```

At the time of writing, Chrome and Opera are the only browsers to implement a color input. It allows users to specify a color. When they click on the control, the browser will usually show the operating system's default color picker (except for Linux, which offers a more basic palette). It inserts a hex color value based on the user's selection.

DATE

```
<input type="date"> (below)
<input type="month">
<input type="week">
<input type="time">
<input type="datetime">
```

There are several different date inputs available. At the time of writing, Chrome was the only browser to have implemented a date picker.

SUPPORT & STYLING

HTML5 form elements are not supported in all browsers and, when they are, the inputs and error messages can look very different.

DESKTOP BROWSERS

At the time of writing, many developers were still using JavaScript instead of these new HTML5 features because:

- Older browsers do not support the new input types (they just show a text box in their place).
- Different browsers present the elements and their error messages in very different ways (and designers often want to give users a consistent experience across browsers).

Below, you can see how the error messages look very different in two of the main browsers.

MOBILE

On mobile devices the situation is very different, as most modern mobile browsers:

- Support the main HTML5 elements
- Show a keyboard that's adapted to the type: `email` brings up a keyboard with the @ sign `number` type brings up a number keyboard
- Give helpful versions of the date picker

Therefore, in mobile browsers, the new HTML5 types and elements make forms more accessible and usable for your visitors.

ERROR MESSAGE FOR AN EMAIL INPUT IN CHROME:

DATE INPUT IN IOS:

CURRENT APPROACHES

Until more visitors' browsers support these new features, and do so in a consistent way, developers will think carefully about how they use them.

POLYFILLS

A polyfill is a script that provides functionality you may expect a browser to support by default. For example, because older browsers do not support the new HTML5 elements, polyfills can be used to implement a similar experience / functionality in those older browsers. Typically this is achieved using JavaScript or a jQuery plugin.

Polyfills often come with CSS files that are used to style the functionality the script adds.

You can find a list of polyfills for various features here:
`http://html5please.com`

There is an example of how to use a polyfill on p594, where you see how to get the HTML5 `placeholder` attribute to show up in older browsers.

FEATURE DETECTION

Feature detection means checking whether a browser supports a feature or not. You can then decide what to do if a feature is, or is not, supported. On p415 you learned about a script called `modernizr.js`, which tests for browser features.

Commonly, if a feature is not supported, a polyfill script will be loaded to emulate that feature. To save loading the polyfill script into browsers that do not need it, Modernizr includes a **conditional loader**; it will only load a script if the test indicates that the script is needed.

Another popular conditional loader is `Require.js` (available from `http://requirejs.org`), but it is a bit more complex when you are first starting out because it offers many other features.

CONSISTENCY

Many designers and developers want to control the appearance of form controls and error messages to give a consistent experience across all browsers. (Consistency in error messages is considered important because different styles of error messages can confuse users.)

Therefore, the long example used at the end of this chapter will disable HTML5 validation and try to use JavaScript validation as its first choice. (HTML5 validation is only shown if the user does not have JavaScript enabled; it is used as a fallback in modern browsers.)

In that example, you also see jQuery UI used to ensure that the date picker is consistent across all devices, with as little code as possible.

PLACEHOLDER FALLBACK

The HTML5 `placeholder` attribute lets you put words in text inputs (to replace labels or to add hints about what to enter). When the input gains focus and the user starts typing, the text disappears. But it only works in modern browsers, so this script ensures that the user sees placeholder text in older browsers too. It is a basic example of a polyfill.

1. Place the script in an IIFE (not shown in flowchart).
2. Check if the browser supports the HTML5 `placeholder` attribute. If it does, there is no need for the fallback. Use `return` to exit the function.
3. Find out how many forms are on the page using the `length` property of the `forms` collection.
4. Loop through each <form> element on the page and call `showPlaceholder()` for each one, passing it the collection of elements in that form.
5. The `showPlaceholder()` function is declared.
6. A `for` loop runs through elements in the collection.
7. An `if` statement checks each element to see if the element has a `placeholder` attribute with a value.
8. If there is no `placeholder` attribute, `continue` tells it to go on to the next element. Otherwise, it:
9. Changes the text color to gray, and sets the value of the element to be the placeholder text.
10. An event listener triggers an anonymous function when the element gains `focus`.
11. If the current value of the element matches the placeholder text, the value is cleared (and color changed to black).
12. An event listener triggers an anonymous function when the element loses focus.
13. If the input is empty, the placeholder text is added back in (and its color changed to gray).

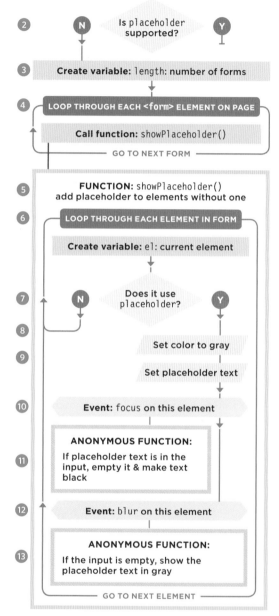

PLACEHOLDER POLYFILL

JAVASCRIPT   c13/js/placeholder-polyfill.js

```
①  (function () {                                        // Place code in an IIFE
       // Test: Create an input element, and see if the placeholder is supported
②     if ('placeholder' in document.createElement('input')) {
          return;
       }

③     var length = document.forms.length;               // Get number of forms
       for (var i = 0, l = length; i < l; i++ ) {        // Loop through each one
④        showPlaceholder(document.forms[i].elements);    // Call showPlaceholder()
       }

⑤     function showPlaceholder(elements) {               // Declare function
⑥        for (var i = 0, l = elements.length; i < l; i++) { // For each element
             var el = elements[i];                       // Store that element
⑦           if (!el.placeholder) {                       // If no placeholder set
⑧              continue;                                 // Go to next element
             }                                           // Otherwise
⑨           el.style.color = '#666666';                  // Set text to gray
             el.value = el.placeholder;                  // Add placeholder text

⑩           addEvent(el, 'focus', function () {          // If it gains focus
                if (this.value === this.placeholder) {   // If value=placeholder
⑪                 this.value = '';                       // Empty text input
                   this.style.color = '#000000';         // Make text black
                }
             });

⑫           addEvent(el, 'blur', function () {           // On blur event
                if (this.value === '') {                 // If the input is empty
⑬                 this.value = this.placeholder;         // Make value placeholder
                   this.style.color = '#666666';         // Make text gray
                }
             });
                                                         // End of for loop
          }                                              // End showPlaceholder()
       }
    }());
```

There are a few differences from the HTML5's placeholder attribute: e.g., if the user deletes their text, the placeholder only returns when the user leaves the input (not immediately – as with some browsers). It will not submit text that has the same value as the placeholder. Placeholder values may be saved by autocomplete.

POLYFILL USING MODERNIZR & YEPNOPE

You met Modernizr in Chapter 9, here you can see it used with a conditional loader so that it only loads a fallback script if one is needed.

Modernizr lets you test whether or not a browser and device support certain features; this is known as feature detection. You can then take different courses of action depending on whether or not the features were supported. For example, if an older browser does not support a feature, you might decide to use a polyfill.

Modernizr is sometimes included in the <head> of an HTML page when it needs to perform checks before the page has loaded (for example, some HTML5 / CSS3 polyfills must be loaded before the page).

Rather than loading a polyfill script for everyone who visits your site (even if they do not need to use it), you can use something called a **conditional loader**, which will let you load different files depending on whether a condition returns true or false. Modernizr is commonly used with a conditional loader called YepNope.js, so polyfills are only loaded if needed.

Once you have included the YepNope script in your page, you can call the yepnope() function. It uses object literal syntax to indicate a condition to test, and then what files to load depending on whether the condition returned true or false.

MODERNIZR ON ITS OWN

Each feature you test using Modernizr becomes a property of the Modernizr object. If the feature is supported, the property contains true; if not, it contains false. You then use the properties of the Modernizr object in a conditional statement as shown below. Here, if Modernizr's cssanimations property does not return true the code in the curly braces runs.

```
if (!Modernizr.cssanimations) {
  // CSS animations are not supported
  // Use jQuery animation instead
}
```

MODERNIZR + YEPNOPE

YepNope is passed an object literal, which usually contains a minimum of three properties:
- test is the a condition being checked. Here Modernizr is used to check if cssanimations are supported.
- yep is the file to load if the condition returns true.
- nope is the file to load if the condition returns false (here it loads two files using array syntax).

```
yepnope({
  test: Modernizr.cssanimations,
  yep: 'css/animations.css',
  nope: ['js/jquery.js', 'js/animate.js']
});
```

CONDITIONAL LOADING OF A POLYFILL

c13/number-polyfill.html

```html
<head>
  ...
  <script src="js/modernizr.js"></script>
  <script src="js/yepnope.js"></script>
  <script src="js/number-polyfill-eg.js"></script>
</head>
<body>
  <label for="age">Enter your age:</label>
  <input type="number" id="age" />
</body>
```

JAVASCRIPT c13/js/number-polyfill-eg.js

```javascript
yepnope({
  test: Modernizr.inputtypes.number,
  nope: ['js/numPolyfill.js', 'css/number.css'],
  complete: function() {
    console.log('YepNope + Modernizr are done');
  }
});
```

RESULT

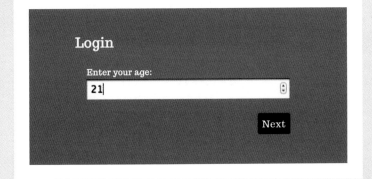

This example tests if the browser supports the `<input>` element using a **type** attribute with a value of **number**. Both Modernizr and YepNope are included in the `<head>` of the page so that the fallback is shown correctly.

The **yepnope()** function takes an object literal as a parameter. It's properties include:

- **test**: the feature you are checking for. In this case it is checking Modernizr to see if the number input is supported.
- **yep**: not used in this example can load files if the feature *is* supported.
- **nope**: what to do if feature *is not* supported (you can load multiple files in an array).
- **complete**: can run a function when the checks are complete, and any necessary files have loaded. Here it adds a message to the console to demonstrate how it works.

Note that Modernizr stores the value of the `<input>` element's type attribute, in a child object called **inputtypes**. E.g., to check if the HTML5 date selector is supported, you use: `Modernizr.inputtypes.date` (not `Modernizr.date`).

FORM VALIDATION

The final section of this chapter uses one big script to discuss the topic of form validation. It helps users give you responses in the format you need. (The example also has some form enhancements, too.)

Validation is the process of checking whether a value meets certain rules (for example, that a password has a minimum number of characters). It lets you tell users if there is a problem with the values they entered so that they can correct the form before they resubmit it. This has three key advantages:

- You are more likely to get the information you need in a format you can use.
- It is faster to check values in the browser than it is to send data to the server to be checked.
- It saves resources on the server.

In this section you see how to check the values a user enters into a form. These checks happen when the form is submitted. To do this users could press submit or use the Enter on the keyboard, so the validation process will be triggered by the `submit` event (not the `click` event of a submit button).

We will look at validation using one long example. You can see the form below, and the HTML is shown on the right. It uses HTML5 form controls, but the validation is going to be done using JavaScript to make sure that the experience is consistent across all browsers (even if they do support HTML5).

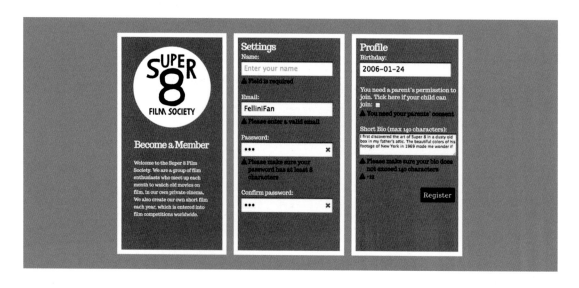

FORM HTML

This example uses HTML5 markup, but validation is performed using JavaScript (not HTML5 validation).

Due to limited space, the code below only shows the form inputs (not the markup for the columns).

HTML   c13/validation.html

```html
<form method="post" action="/register">
  <!-- Column 1 -->
  <div class="name">
    <label for="name" class="required">Name:</label>
    <input type="text" placeholder="Enter your name" name="name" id="name"
           required title="Please enter your name">
  </div>
  <div class="email">
    <label for="email" class="required">Email:</label>
    <input type="email" placeholder="you@example.com" name="email" id="email"
           required>
  </div>
  <div class="password">
    <label for="password" class="required">Password:</label>
    <input type="password" name="password" id="password" required>
  </div>
  <div class="password">
    <label for="conf-password" class="required">Confirm password:</label>
    <input type="password" name="conf-password" id="conf-password" required>
  </div>
  <!-- Column 2 -->
  <div class="birthday">
    <label for="birthday" class="required">Birthday:</label>
    <input type="date" name="birthday" id="birthday" placeholder="yyyy-mm-dd"
           required>
    <div id="consent-container" class="hide">
      <label for="parents-consent"> You need a parent's permission to join.
        Tick here if your child can join:</label>
      <input type="checkbox" name="parents-consent" id="parents-consent">
    </div>
  </div>
  <div class="bio">
    <label for="bio">Short Bio (max 140 characters):</label>
    <textarea name="bio" id="bio" rows="5" cols="30"></textarea>
    <span id="bio-count" class="hide">140</span>
  </div>
  <div class="submit"><input type="submit"></div>
</form>
```

VALIDATION OVERVIEW

This example has over 250 lines of code and will take 22 pages to explain. The script starts by looping through each element on the page performing two generic checks on every form control.

GENERIC CHECKS

First, the code loops through every element in the form and performs two types of **generic** checks. They are generic checks because they would work on any element, and would work with any form.

1. Does the element have the `required` attribute? If so, does it have a value?
2. Does the value match with the `type` attribute? E.g., Does an `email` input hold an email address?

CHECKING EACH ELEMENT

To work through each element in the form, the script makes use the form's `elements` collection (which holds a reference to each form control). The collection is stored in a variable called `elements`. In this example, the `elements` collection will hold the following form controls. The right-hand column tells you which elements are required to have a value:

INDEX	ELEMENT	REQUIRED
0	elements.name	Yes
1	elements.email	Yes
2	elements.password	Yes
3	elements.conf-password	Yes
4	elements.birthday	Yes
5	elements.parents-consent	If under 13
6	elements.bio	No

Some developers proactively cache form elements in variables in case validation fails. This is a good idea, but to keep this (already very long) example simpler, the nodes for the form elements are not cached.

If you have not already done so, it would be helpful to download the code for this example from the website, javascriptbook.com, and have it ready when you are reading through the following pages.

Once the generic checks have been performed, the script then makes some checks that apply to individual elements on the form. Some of these checks apply only to this specific form.

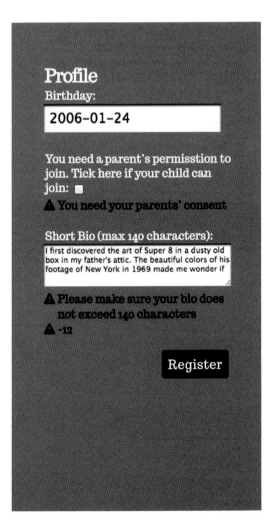

CUSTOM VALIDATION TASKS

Next the code performs checks that correspond with specific elements in the form (not *all* elements):

- Do the passwords match?
- Is the bio in the textarea under 140 characters?
- If the user is less than 13 years old, is the parental consent checkbox selected?

These checks are specific to this form and only apply to selected elements in the form (not all of them).

TRACKING VALID ELEMENTS

To keep track of errors, an object called `valid` is created. As the code loops through each element performing the generic checks, a property is added to the `valid` object for each element:

- The property name is the value of its `id` attribute.
- The value is a Boolean. Whenever an error is found on an element, this value is set to `false`.

PROPERTIES OF THE VALID OBJECT

```
valid.name
```
```
valid.email
```
```
valid.password
```
```
valid.conf-password
```
```
valid.birthday
```
```
valid.parents-consent
```
```
valid.bio
```

DEALING WITH ERRORS

If there are errors, the script needs to prevent the form being submitted and tell the user what they need to do in order to correct their answers.

As the script checks each element, if an error is found, two things happen:
- The corresponding property of the `valid` object is updated to indicate the content is not valid.
- A function called `setErrorMessage()` is called. This function uses jQuery's `.data()` method, which allows you to store data *with* the element. So the error message is stored in memory along with the form element that has the problem.

After each element has been checked, then error messages can be shown using `showErrorMessage()`. It retrieves the error message and puts it in a `<span>` element, which is added after the form control.

Each time the user tries to submit the form, if an error was *not* found on an element it is important to remove any error messages from that element. Consider the following scenario:
a) A user filled out a form with more than one error.
b) This triggered multiple error messages.
c) The user fixes one problem, so its corresponding message must be removed, while error message(s) for problems that have not been fixed must remain visible.

Therefore, when each of the elements is looped through, either an error message is set, or the error message is removed.

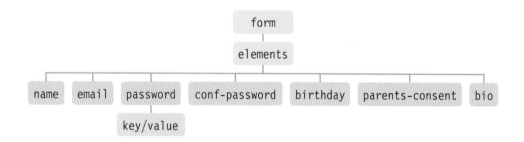

Above you can see a representation of the form and its `elements` collection. There was a problem with the email input, so the `.data()` method has stored a key/value pair with that element.

This is how the `setErrorMessage()` function will store the error messages to show to the user. If the error is fixed, then the error value is cleared (and the element with the error message removed).

SUBMITTING THE FORM

Before sending the form, the script checks whether there were any errors.
If there were, the script stops the file from being submitted.

In order to check whether any errors were found, a variable called isFormValid is created and is given a value of true. The script then loops through each property of the valid object, and if there was an error (if *any* property of that object has a value of false), then there is an error in the form and the isFormValid variable is also set to false.

So, isFormValid is being used as a **flag** (you can think of it being like a master switch) if an error is found, it is turned off. At the end of the script, if isFormValid is false then an error must have been found and the form should not be submitted (using the preventDefault() method).

It is important to check and process all of the elements before deciding whether to submit the form so that you can show all of the relevant error messages in one go.

If every value has been checked, the user can be shown all of the things they have to amend before re-submitting the form.

If the form only showed the first error it came across, and stopped, the user would only see one error each time they submitted the form. This could soon become frustrating for the user if they were to keep trying to submit the form and see new errors.

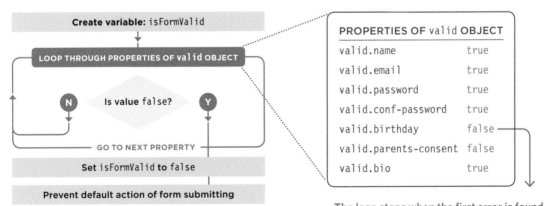

Create variable: isFormValid

LOOP THROUGH PROPERTIES OF valid OBJECT

N   **Is value false?**   Y

GO TO NEXT PROPERTY

Set isFormValid **to** false

Prevent default action of form submitting

PROPERTIES OF valid OBJECT

valid.name	true
valid.email	true
valid.password	true
valid.conf-password	true
valid.birthday	false
valid.parents-consent	false
valid.bio	true

The loop stops when the first error is found.
(Note that error messages are already visible.)

CODE OVERVIEW

On the right is an outline of the validation code, split into four sections. On line 3, an anonymous function is called when the form is submitted. It orchestrates the validation, in turn calling other functions (not all of which are shown on the right-hand page, see further pages for more).

A: SET UP THE SCRIPT

1. The code lives inside an IIFE (creating function-level scope).

2. This script uses JavaScript validation to ensure that error messages look the same on all browsers, so HTML5 validation is turned off by setting the noValidate property of the form to true.

3. When the user submits the form, an anonymous function is run (this contains the validation code).

4. elements holds a collection of all form elements.

5. valid is the object that keeps track of whether or not each form control is valid. Each form control is added as a property of the valid object.

6. isValid is a flag that is re-used to check whether individual elements are valid.

7. isFormValid is a flag that is used as a master switch to check whether the *entire* form is valid.

B: PERFORM GENERIC CHECKS

8. The code loops through each form control.

9. It performs two generic checks on each one:

i) Is the element required? If so, does it have a value? Uses validateRequired(). See p606.

ii) Does the value correspond with the type of data it should hold? Uses validateTypes(). See p610.

If either of these functions does not return true, then isValid is set to false.

10. An if...else statement checks if that element passed the tests (by checking if isValid is false).

11. If the control is not valid, showErrorMessage() shows an error message to the user. See p609.

12. If it is valid, removeErrorMessage() removes any errors associated with that element.

13. The value of the element's id attribute is added as a property valid object; its value is whether or not the element was valid.

C: PERFORM CUSTOM VALIDATION

14. After the code has looped through every element on the form, the custom validation can occur. There are three types of custom validation occurring (each one uses its own function):

i) Is the bio too long? See p615.

ii) Do passwords match?

iii) Is user old enough to join on own? If not, is the parental approval checkbox selected? See p617.

15. If an element fails one of the custom validation checks, showErrorMessage() will be called, and the corresponding property in the valid object will be set to false.

16. If the element passes the check, removeErrorMessage() is called for that element.

D: DID THE FORM PASS VALIDATION?

The valid object now has a property for each element, and the value of that property states whether or not the element was valid or not.

17. The code loops through each property in the valid object.

18. An if statement checks to see if the element was *not* valid.

19. If it was not valid, set isFormValid to false and stop the loop.

20. Otherwise, isFormValid is set to true.

21. Finally, having looped through the valid object, if isFormValid is not true, the preventDefault() method prevents the form being submitted. Otherwise, it is sent.

```
     // SET UP THE SCRIPT
(1)  (function () {
(2)    document.forms.register.noValidate = true; // Disable HTML5 validation
(3)    $('form').on('submit', function(e) {        // When form is submitted
(4)      var elements = this.elements;             // Collection of form controls
(5)      var valid = {};                           // Custom valid object
(6)      var isValid;                              // isValid: checks form controls
(7)      var isFormValid;                          // isFormValid: checks entire form

       // PERFORM GENERIC CHECKS (calls functions outside the event handler)
(8)      for (var i = 0, l = (elements.length - 1); i < l; i++) {
         // Next line calls validateRequired() see p606 & validateTypes() p610
(9)        isValid = validateRequired(elements[i]) && validateTypes(elements[i]);
(10)       if (!isValid) {                         // If it does not pass these two tests
(11)         showErrorMessage(elements[i]);        // Show error messages (see p608)
           } else {                               // Otherwise
(12)         removeErrorMessage(elements[i]);     // Remove error messages
           }                                      // End if statement
(13)       valid[elements[i].id] = isValid;       // Add element to the valid object
         }                                        // End for loop

       // PERFORM CUSTOM VALIDATION (just 1 of 3 functions - see p614-p617)
(14)     if (!validateBio()) {                    // Call validateBio(), if not valid
(15)       showErrorMessage(document.getElementById('bio'));   // Show error
           valid.bio = false;                     // Update valid object-not valid
         } else {                                 // Otherwise
(16)       removeErrorMessage(document.getElementById('bio')); // Remove error
         } // two more functions follow here (see p614-p617)

       // DID IT PASS / CAN IT SUBMIT THE FORM?
       // Loop through valid object, if there are errors set isFormValid to false
(17)     for (var field in valid) {               // Check properties of the valid object
(18)       if (!valid[field]) {                   // If it is not valid
           isFormValid = false;                   // Set isFormValid variable to false
(19)         break;                               // Stop the for loop, error was found
           }                                      // Otherwise
(20)       isFormValid = true;                    // The form is valid and OK to submit
         }
       // If the form did not validate, prevent it being submitted
       if (!isFormValid) {                        // If isFormValid is not true
(21)     e.preventDefault();                      // Prevent the form being submitted
       }
     });                                          // End event handler
     ...                                          // Functions called above are here
   }());                                          // End of IIFE
```

REQUIRED FORM ELEMENTS

The HTML5 `required` attribute indicates a field must have a value. Our `validateRequired()` function will first check for the attribute. If present, it then checks whether or not it has a value.

`validateRequired()` is called for each element individually (see step 9, p605). Its one parameter is the element it is checking.

In turn, it calls upon three other named functions.
i) `isRequired()` checks for the `required` attribute.

ii) `isEmpty()` can check if the element has a value.
iii) `setErrorMessage()` sets error messages if there are problems.

```
     function validateRequired(el) {
 (1)    if (isRequired(el)) {                            // Is this element required
 (2)      var valid = !isEmpty(el);                      // Is value not empty (true/false)
 (3)      if (!valid) {                                  // If valid variable holds false
 (4)        setErrorMessage(el, 'Field is required');    // Set the error message
          }
 (5)      return valid;                                  // Return valid variable (true/false)
        }
 (6)    return true;                                     // If not required, all is okay
      }
```

A: DOES IT HAVE A REQUIRED ATTRIBUTE?

1. An `if` statement uses a function called `isRequired()` to check whether the element carries the `required` attribute. You can see the `isRequired()` function on the right-hand page. If the attribute is present, the subsequent code block is run.

6. If not, the code skips to step 6 to say this element is OK.

B: IF SO, DOES IT HAVE A VALUE?

If the field is required, the next step is to check whether or not it has a value. This is done using a function called `isEmpty()`, also shown on the right-hand page.

2. The result from `isEmpty()` is stored in a variable called `valid`. If it is *not* empty, the `valid` variable will hold a value of **true**. If it is empty, it holds **false**.

C: SHOULD AN ERROR MESSAGE BE SET?

3. An `if` statement checks if the `valid` variable is *not* **true**.

4. If it is not true, an error message is set using the `setErrorMessage()` function, which you meet on p608.

5. The `valid` variable is returned on the next line, and that is where this function ends.

`validateRequired()` uses two functions to perform checks:
1: `isRequired()` checks whether the element has a `required` attribute.
2: `isEmpty()` checks whether the element has a value.

isRequired()

The `isRequired()` function takes an element as a parameter and checks if the `required` attribute is present on that element. It returns a Boolean.

There are two types of check: The first, in blue, is for browsers that support the HTML5 `required` attribute. The one in orange is for older browsers.

To check if the `required` attribute is present, the `typeof` operator is used. It checks what datatype the browser thinks the `required` attribute is.

```
function isRequired(el) {
  return ((typeof el.required === 'boolean') && el.required) ||
    (typeof el.required === 'string');
}
```

MODERN BROWSERS

Modern browsers know the `required` property is a Boolean, so the first part of this check tells us if it is a modern browser. The second part checks if it is present on this element.
If the attribute is present, it will evaluate to `true`. If not, it returns `undefined`, which is considered a falsy value.

OLDER BROWSERS

Browsers that do not know HTML5 can still tell whether or not an HTML5 attribute is present on an element. In those browsers, if the `required` attribute is present, it gets treated as a string, so the condition would evaluate to `true`. If not, the type would be `undefined`, which is falsy.

WHAT IS VALIDATED

It is important to note that the `required` attribute only indicates that *a* value is required. It doesn't stipulate how long the value should be, nor does it perform any other kind of validation. Specific checks, such as these, would have to be added in the `validateTypes()` function or the script's custom validation section.

isEmpty()

The `isEmpty()` function (below) takes an element as a parameter and checks to see if it has a value. As with `isRequired()`, two checks are used to handle both new and older browsers.

ALL BROWSERS

The first check looks to see if the element does *not* have a value. If it has a value, the function should return `false`. If it is empty, it will return `true`.

OLDER BROWSERS

If older browsers use a polyfill for placeholder text, the value would be the same as the placeholder, so it is considered empty if those values match.

```
function isEmpty(el) {
  return !el.value || el.value === el.placeholder;
}
```

CREATING ERROR MESSAGES

The validation code processes elements one by one;
any error messages are stored using jQuery's `.data()` method.

HOW ERRORS ARE SET

Throughout the validation code, whenever an error is found, you will see calls to a function called `setErrorMessage()`, which takes two parameters:
i) `el`: the element that the error message is for
ii) `message`: the text the error message will display

For example, the following would add the message 'Field is required' to the element that is stored in the `el` variable:

`setErrorMessage(el, 'Field is required');`

HOW DATA IS STORED WITH NODES

Each error message is going to be stored with the element node that it relates to using the jQuery `.data()` method. When you have elements in a jQuery matched set, the `.data()` method allows you to store information in key/value pairs for each individual element.

The `.data()` method has two parameters:
i) The key, which is always going to be `errorMessage`
ii) The value, which is the text that the error message will display

setErrorMessage()

```
① function setErrorMessage(el, message) {
②   $(el).data('errorMessage', message);              // Store error message with element
  }
```

DISPLAYING ERROR MESSAGES

After each element has been checked, if one or more were not valid, showErrorMessage() will display the error messages on the page.

HOW ERRORS ARE DISPLAYED

If an error message needs to be shown, first a <span> element will be added to the page directly after the form field with the error.

Next, the message is added into the <span> element. To get the text for the error message, the same jQuery .data() method that set the message is used again. This time, it only takes one parameter: the key (which is always errorMessage).

This all happens within the function called showErrorMessage() which is shown below.

1. $el holds a jQuery selection containing the element that the error message relates to.
2. $errorContainer looks for any existing errors on this element by checking if it has any sibling elements that have a class of error.
3. If the element does not have an error message associated with it, the code in the curly braces runs.
4. $errorContainer is set to hold a <span> element. Then .insertAfter() adds the <span> element into the page after the element causing the error.
5. The content of the <span> element is populated with the error message for that element, which is retrieved using the .data() method of the element.

showErrorMessage()

```
function showErrorMessage(el) {
  var $el = $(el);                                      // Find element with the error
  var $errorContainer = $el.siblings('.error');         // Does it have errors already

  if (!$errorContainer.length) {                        // If no errors found
    // Create a <span> to hold the error and add it after the element with the error
    $errorContainer = $('<span class="error"></span>').insertAfter($el);
  }
  $errorContainer.text($(el).data('errorMessage'));     // Add error message
}
```

VALIDATING DIFFERENT TYPES OF INPUT

HTML5's new types of input come with built-in validation. This example uses HTML5 inputs, but validates them with JavaScript to ensure that the experience is consistent across all browsers.

The `validateTypes()` function is going to perform the validation just like modern browsers do with HTML5 elements, but it will do it for all browsers. It needs to:

- Check what type of data the form element should hold
- Ensure the contents of the element matches that type

1. The first line in the function checks if the element has a value. If the user has not entered any information, you cannot validate the type of data. Furthermore, it is not the *wrong* type of data. So, if there is *no* value, the function returns `true` (and the rest of the function does not need to run).

2. If there is a value, a variable called `type` is created to hold the value of the `type` attribute. First, the code checks to see if jQuery stored info about the type using its `.data()` method (see why on p618). If not, it gets the value of the `type` attribute.

```
function validateTypes(el) {
  if (!el.value) return true;                             // If element has no value, return true
                                                          // Otherwise get the value from .data()
  var type = $(el).data('type') || el.getAttribute('type'); // or get the type of input
  if (typeof validateType[type] === 'function') {         // Is type a method of validate object?
    return validateType[type](el);                        // If yes, check if the value validates
  } else {                                                // If not
    return true;                                          // Return true as it cannot be tested
  }
}
```

The `getAttribute()` method is used rather than the DOM property for `type` because all browsers can return the value of the `type` attribute, whereas browsers that don't recognize a new HTML5 DOM property types would just return **text**.

3. This function uses an object called `validateType` (shown on the next page) to check the content of the element. The `if` statement checks if the `validateType` object has a method whose name matches the value of the `type` attribute.

If it has a method name that matches the type of form control:
4. The element is passed to the object; it returns **true** or **false**.
5. If there is no matching method, the object is not able to validate the form control and no error message should be set.

CREATING AN OBJECT TO VALIDATE DATA TYPES

The `validateType` object (outlined below) has three methods:

```
var validateType = {
  email: function(el) {
  // Check email address
  },
  number: function(el) {
  // Check it is a number
  },
  date: function(el) {
  // Check date format
  }
}
```

The code inside each method is virtually identical. You can see the format of the `email()` method below. Each method validates the data using something called a **regular expression**. The regular expression is the only thing that changes in each method to test the different data types.

Regular expressions allow you to **check for patterns** in strings, and here they are used with a method called `test()`.

You can learn more about regular expressions and their syntax on the next two pages. For now, you just need to know that they are used to check the data contains a specific pattern of characters.

Storing these checks as methods of an object makes it easy to access each of the the different checks when it comes time to validate the different types of input in a form.

```
/[^@]+@[^@]+/.test(el.value);
```

i) The regular expression is `[^@]+@[^@]+` (it is between the / and / characters). It states a pattern of characters that are found in a typical email address.

ii) The `test()` method takes one parameter (a string), and checks whether the regular expression can be found within the string. It returns a Boolean.

iii) In this example, the `test()` method is passed the value of the element you want to check. Below you can see the method to test email addresses.

```
email: function (el) {                                      // Create email method
  var valid = /[^@]+@[^@]+/.test(el.value);                 // Store result of test in valid
  if (!valid) {                                             // If the value of valid is not true
    setErrorMessage(el, 'Please enter a valid email');      // Set error message
  }
  return valid;                                             // Return the valid variable
},
```

1. A variable called `valid` holds the result of the test using the regular expression.

2. If the string does not contain a match for the regular expression,
3. an error message is set.

4. The function returns the value of the `valid` variable (which is `true` or `false`).

REGULAR EXPRESSIONS

Regular expressions search for characters that form a pattern. They can also replace those characters with new ones.

Regular expressions do not just search for matching letters; they can check for sequences of upper/lowercase characters, numbers, punctuation, and other symbols.

The idea is similar to the functionality of find and replace features in text editors, but it makes it possible to create far more complicated searches for combinations of characters.

Below you can see the building blocks of regular expressions. On the right-hand page, you can see some examples of how they are combined to create powerful pattern-matching tools.

.

any single character (except newline)

[ ]

single character contained within brackets

[^]

single character not contained within brackets

^

the starting position in any line

$

the ending position in any line

( )

sub expressions (sometimes called a block or capturing group)

*

preceding element zero or more times

\n

nth marked subexpression (n is digit 1-9)

{m,n}

preceding element at least m, but no more than n, times

\d

digit

\D

non-digit character

\s

whitespace character

\S

anything but whitespace

\w

alphanumeric character (A-Z, a-z, 0-9)

\W

non-alphanumeric character (except _)

COMMON REGULAR EXPRESSIONS

Here are a selection of regular expressions you can use in your code. Some of these are more powerful than those adopted by browsers.

At the time of writing, some of the validation rules applied by the major browsers were not very strong. Some of the regular expressions shown below are more stringent.

But regular expressions are not perfect. There are still strings that would not be valid data, but would pass these tests below.

Also, bear in mind that there are many different ways to express the same thing using regular expressions. So you may see a very different regular expression that does something similar.

```
/^\d+$/
```
number

```
^[ \s]+
```
whitespace at start of line

```
/[^@]+@[^@]+/
```
email

```
/^#[a-fA-F0-9]{6}$/
```
hex color value

```
!"#$%&\'()*+,-./@:;<=>[\\]^_`{|}~
```
hex color value

```
/^(\d{2}\/\d{2}\/\d{4})|(\d{4}-\d{2}-\d{2})$/
```
date yy-mm-dd

CUSTOM VALIDATION

The final part of the script performs three checks that apply to individual form elements; each check lives in a named function.

On the next pages, you will see these three functions. Each is called in the same manner as the `validateBio()` function shown below. (The full code that calls them is available from the website, along with the code for all examples from the book.)

FUNCTION	PURPOSE
`validateBio()`	Check bio is 140 characters or less
`validatePassword()`	Check password is at least 8 characters
`validateParentsConsent()`	If user is under 13, test if parental consent box is checked

Each of these functions will return a value of **true** or **false**.

```
①if (!validateBio()) {                                      // Call validateBio(), if not valid
②  showErrorMessage(document.getElementById('bio'));        // Show error message
    valid.bio = false;                                       // Update valid object - not valid
  } else {                                                   // Otherwise remove error message
③  removeErrorMessage(document.getElementById('bio'));
  }
```

1. The function is called as a condition in an `if... else` statement. This was shown in steps 14-16 on p605.

2. If the function returns `false`, an error message is shown and the corresponding property of the `valid` object is set to `false`.

3. If the function returns `true`, the error message is removed from the corresponding element.

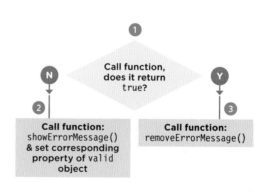

BIO & PASSWORD VALIDATION

The `validateBio()` function:
1. Stores the form element containing the user's biography in a variable called `bio`.

2. If the length of the bio is less than or equal to 140 characters, the `valid` variable is set to `true` (otherwise, it is set to `false`).
3. If `valid` is not `true`, then...

4. The `setErrorMessage()` function is called (see p608).
5. The `valid` attribute is returned to the calling code, which will show or hide the error.

(see p608)

JAVASCRIPT   c13/js/validation.js

```javascript
  function validateBio() {
①   var bio   = document.getElementById('bio');  // Store ref to bio text area
②   var valid = bio.value.length <= 140;          // Is bio <= 140 characters?
③   if (!valid) {                                 // If not, set an error message
④     setErrorMessage(bio, 'Your bio should not exceed 140 characters');
    }
⑤   return valid;                                 // Return Boolean value
  }
```

The `validatePassword()` function starts by:
1. Storing the element containing the password in a variable called `password`.

2. If the length of the value in the password input is greater than or equal to 8, `valid` is set to `true` (otherwise, it is set to `false`).
3. If `valid` is not `true`, then...

4. The `setErrorMessage()` function is called.
5. The `valid` attribute is returned to the calling code, which will show or hide the error.

JAVASCRIPT   c13/js/validation.js

```javascript
  function validatePassword() {
①   var password = document.getElementById('password');// Store ref to element
②   var valid    = password.value.length >= 8;          // Is its value >= 8 chars
③   if (!valid) {                                       // If not, set error msg
④     setErrorMessage(password, 'Password must be at least 8 characters');
    }
⑤   return valid;                                       // Return true / false
  }
```

CODE DEPENDENCIES & REUSE

In any project, avoid writing two sets of code that perform the same task. You can also try to reuse code across projects (for example, using utility scripts or jQuery plugins). If you do, note any dependencies in your code.

DEPENDENCIES

Sometimes one script will require another script to be included in the page in order to work. When you write a script that relies on another script, the *other* script is known as a dependency.

For example, if you are writing a script that uses jQuery, then your script depends upon jQuery being included in the page in order to work; otherwise, you would not be able to use its selectors or methods.

It is a good idea to note dependencies in a comment at the top of the script so that they are clear to others. The final custom function in this example depends on another script that checks the user's age.

CODE REUSE VS. DUPLICATION

When you have two sets of code that do the same job, it is referred to as code duplication. This is usually considered bad practice.

The opposite is code reuse where the same lines of code are used in more than one part of a script (functions are a good example of code reuse).

You may hear programmers refer to this as the **DRY principle**: don't repeat yourself. "Every piece of knowledge must have a single, unambiguous, authoritative representation within a system." It was formulated by Andrew Hunt and Dave Thomas in a book called *The Pragmatic Programmer* (Addison-Wesley, 1999).

To encourage reuse, programmers sometimes create a set of smaller scripts (instead of one big script). Therefore, code reuse can lead to more code dependencies. You have already seen an example of this with the helper functions for event handling. You are about to see another example...

VALIDATING PARENTAL CONSENT

When the validation script was introduced, it was noted that the form would use a couple of scripts to enhance the page. You start to see those scripts on the next page, but one of them needs to be noted now because it hides the parental consent checkbox when the page loads.

That parental consent checkbox is only shown again if the user indicates that they are 13 years old or younger.

The validation code to check whether the parent has given their consent will only run if that checkbox is showing.

So the code to check whether the parent has given consent depends upon (reuses) the same code that checked if the checkbox should be shown. This works well as long as the other script (to show/hide the checkbox) is included in the page before the validation script.

The `validateParentsConsent()` function is called in the same way as the other two custom validation checks (see p614). Inside the function:
1. It stores the checkbox for parental consent and its containing element in variables.
2. Sets a `valid` variable to `true`.

3. An `if` statement checks whether the container for the checkbox is *not* hidden. It does this by fetching the value of its `class` attribute and using the `indexOf()` function (which you saw on p128) to check if it contains a value of `hide`. If the value is *not* found, then `indexOf()` will return -1.

4. If it is not hidden, the user is under 13. So, if the checkbox is selected, the `valid` variable is set to the `true`, and if it was not selected, it will be set to `false`.
5. If it is not valid, an error message is added to the element.
6. The function returns the value of the `valid` variable to indicate whether the consent was given.

```
JAVASCRIPT                                                    c13/js/validation.js

     function validateParentsConsent() {
       var parentsConsent   = document.getElementById('parents-consent');
 ①     var consentContainer = document.getElementById('consent-container');
 ②     var valid = true;                           // Variable: valid set to true
 ③     if (consentContainer.className.indexOf('hide') === -1) { // If checkbox shown
         valid = parentsConsent.checked;           // Update valid: is it checked/not
 ④       if (!valid) {                             // If not, set the error message
 ⑤         setErrorMessage(parentsConsent, 'You need your parents\' consent');
         }
       }
 ⑥     return valid;                               // Return whether valid or not
     }
```

HIDE PARENTAL CONSENT

As you saw on the previous page, the subscription form uses two extra scripts to enhance the user experience. Here is the first; it does two things:

- Uses the jQuery UI date picker to show a consistent date picker across browsers
- Checks whether the parental consent checkbox should be shown when the user leaves the date input (it does this if they are under 13)

1. Place the script in an IIFE (not shown in flowchart).
2. Three jQuery selections store the input where users enter their birthday, the consent checkbox, and the container for the consent checkbox.
3. The jQuery selection for the date of birth input is converted from a date input to a text input so that it does not conflict with HTML5 date picker functionality (done using the jQuery `.prop()` method to alter the value of its `type` attribute). The selection uses `.data()` to note that it is a date input and jQuery UI's `.datepicker()` method to create the jQuery UI date picker.
4. When the user leaves the date input, the `checkDate()` function is called.
5. The `checkDate()` function is declared.
6. A variable called `dob` is created to hold the date the user selected. The date is converted into an array of three values (month, day, and year) using the `split()` method of the `String` object.
7. `toggleParentsConsent()` is called. It has one parameter: the date of birth. It is passed into the function as a `Date` object.
8. `toggleParentsConsent()` is declared.
9. Inside the function, it checks the date is a number. If not, `return` indicates the function should stop.
10. The current time is obtained by creating a new `Date` object (the current time is the default value of a new `Date` object). It is stored in a variable called `now`.
11. To find the user's age, the date of birth is subtracted from the current date. For simplicity, leap years are ignored. If that is less than 13 years:
12. Show the container for the parental consent.
13. Otherwise, the container of the consent box is hidden, and the checkbox is unchecked.

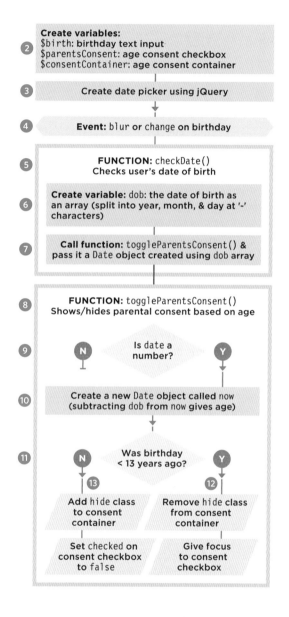

Create variables:
$birth: birthday text input
$parentsConsent: age consent checkbox
$consentContainer: age consent container

③ Create date picker using jQuery

④ **Event:** blur or change on birthday

⑤ **FUNCTION:** checkDate()
Checks user's date of birth

⑥ **Create variable:** dob: the date of birth as an array (split into year, month, & day at '-' characters)

⑦ **Call function:** toggleParentsConsent() & pass it a Date object created using dob array

⑧ **FUNCTION:** toggleParentsConsent()
Shows/hides parental consent based on age

⑨ N — Is date a number? — Y

⑩ Create a new Date object called now (subtracting dob from now gives age)

⑪ N — Was birthday < 13 years ago? — Y

⑬ Add hide class to consent container

⑫ Remove hide class from consent container

Set checked on consent checkbox to false

Give focus to consent checkbox

AGE CONFIRMATION

```
① (function() {
② var $birth           = $('#birthday');              // D-O-B input
   var $parentsConsent  = $('#parents-consent');       // Consent checkbox
   var $consentContainer = $('#consent-container');    // Checkbox container
   // Create the date picker using jQuery UI
③ $birth.prop('type', 'text').data('type', 'date').datepicker({
     dateFormat: 'yy-mm-dd'                            // Set date format
   });
④ $birth.on('blur change', checkDate);                // D-O-B loses focus
⑤ function checkDate() {                               // Declare checkDate()
⑥   var dob = this.value.split('-');                   // Array from date
     // Pass toggleParentsConsent() the date of birth as a date object
⑦   toggleParentsConsent(new Date(dob[0], dob[1] - 1, dob[2]));
   }
⑧ function toggleParentsConsent(date) {                // Declare function
⑨   if (isNaN(date)) return;                           // Stop if date invalid
⑩   var now = new Date();                              // New date obj: today
     // If difference (now minus date of birth, is less than 13 years
     // show parents consent checkbox (does not account for leap years)
     // To get 13 yrs ms * secs * mins * hrs * days * years
⑪   if ((now - date) < (1000 * 60 * 60 * 24 * 365 * 13)) {
⑫     $consentContainer.removeClass('hide');           // Remove hide class
       $parentsConsent.focus();                        // Give it focus
     } else {                                          // Otherwise
⑬     $consentContainer.addClass('hide');              // Add hide to class
       $parentsConsent.prop('checked', false);         // Set checked to false
     }
   }
 }());
```

When creating a date picker using jQuery UI, you can specify the format in which you want the date to be written. On the right you can see several options for the format of the date and what this would look like if the date were the 20th December 1995. In particular note that y gives you two digits for the year, and yy gives you four digits for the year.

FORMAT	RESULT
mm/dd/yy	12/20/1995
yy-mm-dd	1995-12-20
d m, y	20 Dec, 95
mm d, yy	December 20, 1995
DD, d mm, yy	Saturday, 20 December, 1995

PASSWORD FEEDBACK

The second script designed to enhance the form provides feedback to the users as they leave either of the password inputs. It changes the value of the `class` attribute for the password inputs, offering feedback to show whether or not the password is long enough and whether or not the value of the password and its confirmation box match.

1. Place the script in an IIFE (not shown in flowchart).
2. Variables store references to the password input and the password confirmation input.
3. `setErrorHighlighter()` function is declared.
4. It retrieves the target of the event that called it.
5. An `if` statement checks the value of that element. If it is less than 8 characters, that element's `class` attribute is given a value of `fail`. Otherwise, it is given a value of `pass`.
6. `removeErrorHighlighter()` is declared.
7. It retrieves the target of the event that called it.
8. If the value of the `class` attribute is `fail`, then the value of the `class` attribute is set to a blank string (clearing the error).
9. `passwordsMatch()` is declared (it is only called by the password confirm box).
10. It retrieves the target of the event that called it.
11. If the value of that element is the same as the first password input, its `class` attribute is given a value of `pass`; otherwise, it is given a value of `fail`.
12. Event listeners are set up:

ELEMENT	EVENT	METHOD
password	focus	removeErrorHighlighter()
password	blur	setErrorHighlighter()
conf-password	focus	removeErrorHighlighter()
conf-password	blur	passwordsMatch()

This demonstrates how scripts often group all of the functions and the event handlers together.

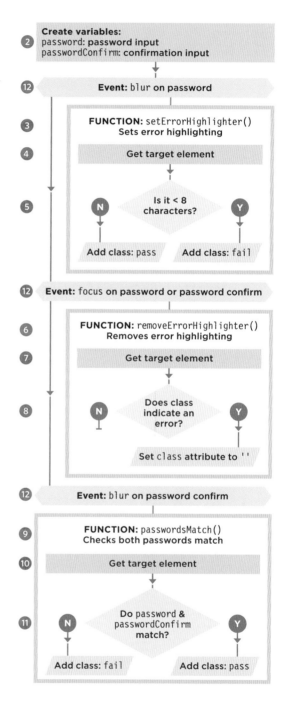

PASSWORD SCRIPT

```
①  (function () {
②   var password = document.getElementById('password');   // Store password inputs
    var passwordConfirm = document.getElementById('conf-password');
③   function setErrorHighlighter(e) {
④     var target = e.target || e.srcElement;              // Get target element
       if (target.value.length < 8) {                      // If its length is < 8
         target.className = 'fail';                        // Set class to fail
⑤     } else {                                            // Otherwise
         target.className = 'pass';                        // Set class to pass
       }
     }
⑥   function removeErrorHighlighter(e) {
⑦     var target = e.target || e.srcElement;              // Get target element
       if (target.className === 'fail') {                  // If class is fail
⑧       target.className = '';                            // Clear class
       }
     }
⑨   function passwordsMatch(e) {
⑩     var target = e.target || e.srcElement;              // Get target element
       // If value matches pwd and it is longer than 8 characters
       if ((password.value === target.value) && target.value.length >= 8){
         target.className = 'pass';                        // Set class to pass
⑪     } else {                                            // Otherwise
         target.className = 'fail';                        // Set class to fail
       }
     }
     addEvent(password, 'focus', removeErrorHighlighter);
     addEvent(password, 'blur', setErrorHighlighter);
⑫   addEvent(passwordConfirm, 'focus', removeErrorHighlighter);
     addEvent(passwordConfirm, 'blur', passwordsMatch);
   }());
```

SUMMARY
FORM ENHANCEMENT & VALIDATION

▸ Form enhancements make your form easier to use.

▸ Validation lets you give users feedback before the form data is sent to the server.

▸ HTML5 introduced new form controls which feature validation (but they only work in modern or mobile browsers).

▸ HTML5 inputs and their validation messages look different in various browsers.

▸ You can use JavaScript to offer the same functionality as the new HTML5 elements in all browsers (and control how they appear in all browsers).

▸ Libraries like jQuery UI help create forms that look the same across different browsers.

▸ Regular expressions help you find patterns of characters in a string.

INDEX

SYMBOLS

A

C

D

G